RELIGION AND US EMPIRE

NORTH AMERICAN RELIGIONS

Series Editors: Tracy Fessenden (Arizona State University), Laura Levitt (Temple University), and David Harrington Watt (Haverford College).

Since its inception, the North American Religions book series has steadily disseminated gracefully written, pathbreaking explorations of religion in North America. Books in the series move among the discourses of ethnographic, textual, and historical analysis and across a range of topics, including sound, story, food, nature, healing, crime, and pilgrimage. In so doing they bring religion into view as a style and form of belonging, a set of tools for living with and in relations of power, a mode of cultural production and reproduction, and a vast repertory of the imagination. Whatever their focus, books in the series remain attentive to the shifting and contingent ways in which religious phenomena are named, organized, and contested. They bring fluency in the best of contemporary theoretical and historical scholarship to bear on the study of religion in North America. The series focuses primarily, but not exclusively, on religion in the United States in the twentieth and twenty-first centuries.

Books in the series

Ava Chamberlain, *The Notorious Elizabeth Tuttle: Marriage, Murder, and Madness in the Family of Jonathan Edwards*

Terry Rey and Alex Stepick, *Crossing the Water and Keeping the Faith: Haitian Religion in Miami*

Isaac Weiner, *Religion Out Loud: Religious Sound, Public Space, and American Pluralism*

Hillary Kaell, *Walking Where Jesus Walked: American Christians and Holy Land Pilgrimage*

Brett Hendrickson, *Border Medicine: A Transcultural History of Mexican American Curanderismo*

Jodi Eichler-Levine, *Suffer the Little Children: Uses of the Past in Jewish and African American Children's Literature*

Annie Blazer, *Playing for God: Evangelical Women and the Unintended Consequences of Sports Ministry*

Elizabeth Pérez, *Religion in the Kitchen: Cooking, Talking, and the Making of Black Atlantic Traditions*

Kerry Mitchell, *Spirituality and the State: Managing Nature and Experience in America's National Parks*

Finbarr Curtis, *The Production of American Religious Freedom*

M. Cooper Harriss, *Ralph Ellison's Invisible Theology*

Ari Y. Kelman, *Shout to the Lord: Making Worship Music in Evangelical America*

Joshua Dubler and Isaac Weiner, *Religion, Law, USA*

Shari Rabin, *Jews on the Frontier: Religion and Mobility in Nineteenth Century America*

Elizabeth Fenton, *Old Canaan in a New World: Native Americans and the Lost Tribes of Israel*

Alyssa Maldonado-Estrada, *Lifeblood of the Parish: Masculinity and Catholic Devotion in Williamsburg, Brooklyn*

Caleb Iyer Elfenbein, *Fear in Our Hearts: What Islamophobia Tells Us about America*

Rachel B. Gross, *Beyond the Synagogue: Jewish Nostalgia as Religious Practice*

Jenna Supp-Montgomerie, *When the Medium was the Mission: The Religious Origins of Network Culture*

Philippa Koch, *The Course of God's Providence: Religion, Health, and the Body in Early America*

Jennifer Scheper Hughes, *The Church of the Dead: The Epidemic of 1576 and the Birth of Christianity in the Americas*

Tisa Wenger and Sylvester A. Johnson, *Religion and US Empire: Critical New Histories*

Religion and US Empire

Critical New Histories

Edited by
Tisa Wenger *and* Sylvester A. Johnson

NEW YORK UNIVERSITY PRESS
New York

NEW YORK UNIVERSITY PRESS
New York
www.nyupress.org

© 2022 by New York University
All rights reserved

References to Internet websites (URLs) were accurate at the time of writing. Neither the author nor New York University Press is responsible for URLs that may have expired or changed since the manuscript was prepared.

Library of Congress Cataloging-in-Publication Data
Names: Wenger, Tisa Joy, 1969– editor. | Johnson, Sylvester A., 1972– editor.
Title: Religion and US empire : critical new histories / edited by Tisa Wenger and Sylvester A. Johnson.
Description: New York : New York University Press, 2022. | Series: North American religions | Includes bibliographical references and index.
Identifiers: LCCN 2021044599 | ISBN 9781479810345 (hardback) | ISBN 9781479810390 (paperback) | ISBN 9781479810376 (ebook) | ISBN 9781479810352 (ebook other)
Subjects: LCSH: United States—Religion. | Imperialism. | Religion and politics—United States.
Classification: LCC BL2525 .R46255 2022 | DDC 322/.10973—dc23/eng/20211112
LC record available at https://lccn.loc.gov/2021044599

New York University Press books are printed on acid-free paper, and their binding materials are chosen for strength and durability. We strive to use environmentally responsible suppliers and materials to the greatest extent possible in publishing our books.

Manufactured in the United States of America

10 9 8 7 6 5 4 3 2 1

Also available as an ebook

CONTENTS

Introduction   1
Tisa Wenger and Sylvester A. Johnson

PART I. FORMATIONS: SLAVERY, SETTLERS, AND
SALVATION   17

1. Rebellion and Religion: Slavery and Empire in
   Early America   19
   Katharine Gerbner

2. Making Religion in Michilimackinac: Settler Secularism
   and US Empire   41
   Tisa Wenger

3. A Colony Called Freedom: Religion, Empire, and Black
   Christian Settlers   63
   Sylvester A. Johnson

PART II. BIOPOLITICS: IMPERIAL CLASSIFICATIONS,
SENTIMENTAL REFORM, AND INDIGENOUS TACTICS
OF SURVIVAL   83

4. Religion on the Brink: Settler-Colonial Knowledge
   Production in the US Census   85
   Sarah Dees

5. Imperial Intersections: Social Surveys, Sentimental
   Biopolitics, and Religion at Hull House   103
   Cara Lea Burnidge

6. "They Call It Ghost Dance . . . But It's Feather Dance":
   Indigenous Histories in the Study of Religion and
   US Empire   124
   Jennifer Graber

PART III. ENTANGLEMENTS: GLOBAL NETWORKS, CHRISTIAN
MISSIONS, AND THE RACIAL PROJECTS OF US EMPIRE   149

7. "The Same Blood as We in America": Industrial Schooling
   and American Empire   151
   Karine Walther

8. Black Spiritual Protest in Global Imperial Contexts,
   1893–1920   179
   Heather D. Curtis

9. An Evangelical Occupation: The Racial and Imperial Politics
   of US Protestant Missions in the Dominican Republic   203
   Christina C. Davidson

PART IV. DIALECTICS: WASTELANDING, WEAPONRY,
AND CAPITALIST EXCLUSIONS   229

10. The Trouble of an Indian Diocese: Catholic Priests
    and Sexual Abuse in Colonized Places   231
    Kathleen Holscher

11. Fire from Heaven: Napalm, the Drone, and Evangelical
    Territoriality in the Age of Empire   253
    Jonathan Ebel

12. American Islam, Settler Colonialism, and Democratic
    Empires in the Work of Robert D. Crane   275
    Zareena A. Grewal and Brennan McDaniel

13. Decolonization™   298
    Lucia Hulsether

Acknowledgments   321
Bibliography   323
About the Editors   349
About the Contributors   351
Index   355

Introduction

TISA WENGER AND SYLVESTER A. JOHNSON

The United States has always been an empire, and this empire is inextricably intertwined with American religion.¹ Our accounts of US empire are therefore incomplete without attending to the potentials and problematics of religion, and we cannot understand the religious history of the United States and the territories it has controlled without accounting for its imperial frame. It is hardly novel to suggest that Christianity facilitated and enabled both European empire building in the Americas and, after the United States won its independence, the westward expansions of what Thomas Jefferson called an "empire of liberty."² This relationship was less overt but still very much in place during the US colonization of new territories across the Pacific and the Caribbean, such as Hawaii, the Philippines, Guam, the Marshall Islands, and Puerto Rico. Few Christian missionaries (Protestant or Catholic) were direct or intentional agents of the US Empire, but most collaborated with US colonial agents and celebrated US imperialism as a triumph for both Christianity and civilization.³

The historical intersections between religion and US empire, however, are far more complex than a simple story of collusion and common interests would allow. Many Indigenous people responded to missions by reframing the message and the power of Christianity to sustain their own communities in the face of empire.⁴ Christianity, moreover, must not control our accounts of American religion. When Native Americans and other colonized peoples claimed the status of religion on behalf of their own non-Christian practices and traditions, they used the category to assert their equality under US law and to push back against US imperial rule.⁵ In all of these ways and more, US imperialism indelibly molded American religious traditions and American ideas about the scope and role of religion. Over the course of thirteen chapters, this book shows how the cultural logics and material structures of US imperialism molded American religion—by which we mean American conceptualizations of *religion* as well as the social formations that we call *religions*—and reveals the multifaceted roles of American religions in structuring, enabling, surviving, and resisting US empire.[6]

Defined in the broadest terms, an empire is a geopolitical system in which one powerful polity controls a large landscape of differentiated and subordinated others. Empires have structured human political and economic relations for thousands of years, and despite persistent claims that the United States is *not* an empire or is a different *kind* of empire, it can readily be identified as such. Over many years, scholars have identified several concepts that are relevant to understanding what empires are and how they function. Although every empire throughout history has been unique, a cluster of themes has emerged from comparative imperial studies. These include colonies, extraction, settlers, and the relationship of metropole to periphery. To build an empire is to exert control over populations and territories previously outside the metropole's orbit of power. The conquered or dominated territory becomes a colony by virtue of this political relationship. Colonies routinely become dependent on the conquering entity and lose their self-determining ability. In the age of nation-states (since the 1700s), empires have frequently structured this colonial relationship with the semblance of sovereignty for the colony. For instance, until Cuba broke free of US colonialism in 1957, it was under the control of the United States despite having its own Cuban flag, Cuban currency, and Cuban political leaders. It had a constitution, but one written by the United States Congress. Its leaders were determined by the United States and prioritized US interests over those of Cubans.[7]

Empires have historically been motivated by material interests, including the extraction of natural resources and labor from colonies. Thus, the past and present of empire is intimately intertwined with the history and afterlives of slavery. Imperial extraction of such resources inherently benefits the empire at significant cost to the colony. As demonstrated across the chapters of this volume, there are always beneficiaries of this exploitative relationship with colonial populations. Europeans successfully enslaved Africans because African merchants who were not enslaved were their willing and prosperous business partners.

Of special interest is the case of settler colonialism, which occurs when a population from the empire-state inhabits the colonized territory and attempts to replace its Indigenous population, with historically devastating consequences. Examples of settler colonialism abound, chief among them the United States. Other examples are Canada, South Africa, and Australia. Because settlers have desired the very land beneath the feet of an Indigenous population, this form of colonialism has frequently led to mass killings—wars of extermination and policies of genocide or ethnic cleansing. This book demonstrates multiple instances of such conflicts, while also surfacing examples of alliances, however fraught, between Indigenous and settler populations.[8]

Finally, it is worth addressing what a number of scholars have termed the "salt-water fallacy"—the belief that real empires must have overseas colonies and that the lack of such has meant the United States is not an actual empire but can only be considered so, at best, metaphorically—e.g., a hegemon but not quite an empire. The British colonization of India, by contrast, frequently functions as the exemplum of overseas empire—England as metropole and South Asia as periphery. This fallacy can obscure the role of various intermediaries, from local elites to corporate entities, who have often exercised considerable power. The colonial relationship, moreover, is not constituted through physical distance over an ocean or sea. It emerges instead through a differential of power, not geography. One important lesson to be drawn from British colonialism in India is the role of private capital and private corporations. The governing polity that colonized India, starting in the 1600s, was actually the English East India Company, not the British monarchy. This joint-stock company was just one of many that operated during the 1600s and 1700s to administer colonial rule. Not until the 1850s did the British crown officially become the governing polity over India.[9]

The United States itself emerged through private corporations becoming vehicles of imperial power. The Virginia Company and the Plymouth Company were responsible for colonizing North America. The Royal African Company, chartered by the British crown, established its headquarters in West Africa and colonized the region to profiteer from the African slave trade. The Dutch East India Company was easily the most powerful of these company-states, as it operated its own military, minted its own currency, and consolidated many functions of today's nation-states before existing territorial states were doing so.[10]

Most importantly, what is commonly imagined as a simple geography of the United States is actually a more complex combination of Indigenous nations forced onto reservations within North America in ultimate proximity to the United States. The borders between the United States and its neighboring nation-states (Canada and Mexico) crossed over many Native American nations, which exceed and transgress these geopolitical lines. And there is no physical distance separating Native nations from the United States—no seas or oceans or other vast geographical barriers. As will become evident throughout this volume, the US reservation system has indelibly shaped the political realities of US imperialism, both because of the proximity of settlers and Indigenous nations and because Indigenous lands and nations were the first targets of US imperial expansion.

This history of attempts to reckon with the United States as an empire is itself instructive. The most deliberate and astute studies of US colonialism first emerged in Indigenous studies, Latinx studies, and Black studies. Opposition to US control of Puerto Rico, for instance, generated significant analysis of the United States as a colonial power in the 1960s and 1970s. The same is true for studies of US relations to sovereign Native American nations. Decades later, scholars working in the discipline of history, particularly in diplomatic history and international relations, began to produce important studies of American empire. Of special import has been the work of Chalmers Johnson and Andrew Bacevich, who have focused on the United States military as a crucial nexus for the production and exercise of US empire. Johnson, in particular, argued that United States military bases—at one point numbering approximately one thousand—have functioned as settler colonies, exerting violent power to impose American political fiat throughout the globe. As early as 1970, the historian of American religion Martin Marty examined the United States as a "righteous empire" (his use of "empire" was literal, not metaphorical) that emerged through the intersection of race, religion, and politics. Almost forty years would pass, however, before a critical mass of religion scholars began to study American empire. In just the past decade, however, the scholarship on US power over putatively sovereign entities has more commonly acknowledged American empire, notwithstanding that many scholars have continually insisted that identifying the United States as a colonial power violates principles of American exceptionalism and misconstrues its putative beneficence.[11]

How might we understand the situation and the role of religion in the global history of empires? It is crucial first of all to separate the histories of the cultural formations we know today as religions from the singular concept of *religion*. Many of the traditions that have come to be known as world religions bear the stamp of the imperial systems in which they originated. Zoroastrianism and Judaism in the ancient Persian Empire, Christianity under ancient Roman and Byzantine empires, and Islam within the context of the Mughal and Ottoman empires are just a few examples. All of these were closely identified with the peoples who practiced them and, in one way or another, all were intertwined with local and imperial systems of power. Christianity and Islam both distinguished themselves as being particularly focused on evangelism or expansion: on incorporating new peoples into their folds. In the process they became increasingly diverse, multifarious, and contested traditions. They also became rivals—in what we now know as the medieval societies of the Mediterranean and beyond—both for control of what they both viewed as the Holy Land and as agents of competing empires.

The modern concept of *religion* as a distinct and more or less universal sphere of human activity, comparable across societies and traditions, did not take shape until the eighteenth century in Europe, even as the Spanish, Portuguese, French, and British empires were jockeying for land and for the profits of the transatlantic slave trade. Despite their ongoing conflicts, the people of these competing empires were coming to understand themselves under the collective category of *Europeans*. They claimed that their Christianity marked an inherent civilizational superiority over the "heathen" and a divinely ordained right to possess the lands they "discovered," even though these lands were already occupied, and even though Christianity had originated and flourished far beyond the (sub)continent that was coming to be known as Europe. The ideas of a universal category of *religion* and of multiple, comparable *religions* did not challenge this sense of civilizational superiority, but rather developed as part of broader Enlightenment attempts to catalogue and systematize knowledge of all kinds. For European Christian leaders and Enlightenment thinkers alike, these efforts demonstrated that Christianity was indeed the one true religion—or, alternatively, the most advanced and elevated religion—and further illustrated their own intellectual superiority. These scientific pursuits, including the new scientific study of religion, also mapped the world in ways that facilitated colonial control.[12]

Consider the full title of Thomas Broughton's 1742 text:

> *An Historical Dictionary of all religions, from the creation of the world to this present time. Containing, I. A Display of all the Pagan Systems of Theology, their Origin, their Superstitious Customs, Ceremonies, and Doctrines. II. The Jewish, Christian, and Mohammedan Institutions, with the Ecclesiastical Laws, and History respecting each Denomination. III. The Rise and Progress of the various Sects, Heresies, and Opinions, which have sprung up in different Ages and Countries; with an Account of the Founders and Propagators thereof. IV. A Survey of the several Objects of Adoration; Deities and Idols. Of Persons dedicated to the Sacred Function; Priests and Religious Orders. Times, and Places of Divine Worship; Fasts, Festivals, Temples, Churches, and Mosques. V. Of Sacred Books and Writings, the Vestments of Religious Orders, and a Description of all the Utensils employed in Divine Offices. VI. The Changes and Alterations, which Religion has undergone both in ancient and modern Times, Compiled from the best authorities, by Thomas Broughton, A.M., Rector of Stibington in Huntingtonshire.*

Like his more skeptical Enlightenment contemporaries (e.g., David Hume), Broughton aimed at an all-encompassing history of a singular Religion. This Anglican clergyman hastened to assure his readers that "True Religion must ever be the same and invariable," and therefore there could be "but ONE TRUE RELIGION," by which he meant Protestant Christianity, shorn of its "Romish" corruptions, and yet at the same time he identified a much broader category of "*Religion*, in the utmost latitude of the word . . . including every thing likewise *falsely so called*," which he judged it necessary (and endlessly fascinating) to catalogue. Hannah Adams, in one of the first books of comparative religions in the new United States, sought to liberalize Broughton's model but maintained his assumption of Christian superiority. As David Chidester has shown in the case of South Africa, and Sarah Dees's chapter in this book demonstrates for the United States, later European and Anglo-American colonial authorities would find immense utility in the project of describing and ranking religious differences, which they did in ever greater detail.[13]

At the same time, the creation of this more expansive category of *religion* opened the door for colonized and minoritized peoples to claim the status that it could provide. The ceremonies and traditions practiced by these peoples, of course, long predated this way of conceptualizing them. Native Americans, enslaved Africans, and others who would be colonized by the United States had their own ways of calling on other-than-human powers, of healing individual and collective ills, of maintaining or restoring the balance of the world. These ways of being and knowing would continue to serve as sources of strength and as ways to envision the world otherwise, as Jennifer Graber illustrates in this book. At the same time, colonized peoples necessarily and pragmatically refigured and reconfigured Indigenous practices and traditions to be legible as *religions*. Many of them also embraced and adapted Christianity as a new source of individual and collective power, one that could be more acceptable and more legible to colonial authorities as religion. For enslaved people, colonial officials sometimes found this affiliation too threatening to allow. It offered the promise of a spiritual and legal equality that led authorities across the early colonial Atlantic to restrict its practice and, in the process, as Katharine Gerbner's chapter explains, their notions of what counted as legitimate religion. Over the next two centuries, as other chapters in this volume show, many of those colonized by the United States would find liberating messages in Christianity even as they fit themselves into colonial molds for what counted as *religion*.

This book leverages insights from the study of religion to interpret American empire. Why is this important? First, religious institutions have been integral to structuring and administering colonial power. Christian missionaries constitute a major example of this, as they have frequently functioned in tandem with military campaigns and commercial networks to engage with Indigenous populations, rationalize imperial conquest, and establish schools, work camps, and publishing houses. Second, whether through Native American traditions or through Islam, Christianity, Judaism, or African-derived religions in the Americas, religion has frequently been a site for contesting or, at times, subverting colonial power. And third, religion has for centuries functioned as a chief means of organizing alliances and boundaries of imperial identities. The very notion of Christendom and the centuries-long legacy of Islamicate polities demonstrate the ease with which the traditions we know as religions have exceeded popular notions of the category. Post-Enlightenment liberal thinkers construed "religion" as primarily private, a matter of internal conscience and belief, and at least ideally separate from the realms of politics, economics, and statecraft. But this separation was never realized in practice, as religious traditions served both imperial and anti-imperial ends. Indeed, the very notion of religion as (ideally) privatized belief became a way to rank civilizations and to condemn those who upset the social-imperial order as not authentically religious—as superstitious, barbaric, or fanatical rather than as true or good religion—and so not deserving the protections granted to religion under the US Constitution. A rigorous account of religion is therefore essential to a full understanding of empires; this is as true for the United States as for any other empire, and maybe even truer.

We identify four thematic areas that have helped to crystallize scholarly attention to the study of religion and US empire. Of major importance is Indigenous studies. Scholars of Indigenous nations in North America have long appreciated that studying race, religion, and culture demands recognizing that the United States has administered rule over tribal nations through an elaborate reservation system by breaching treaties (instruments of diplomacy between sovereign entities), controlling governing powers of Indigenous nations, seizing Indigenous lands and forcibly displacing Indigenous people, and exerting a range of tactics from militarism to diplomacy to expand the territorial possessions and sovereign power of the United States at the expense of Indigenous sovereignty. It is no news flash that the United States has exercised colonial power over sovereign peoples—their lands and their polities—by denying or destroying their sovereignty. The field of Indigenous studies has helped scholars across disciplines see America's creation, expansion, and dominance as imperial operations that provided a training ground, as well as key cultural and legal foundations, for subsequent expansions of the US Empire across the globe.[14]

The history of American religion, all of it, unfolded on these imperial grounds. Indigenous studies helps in diagnosing the imperial Christianity that inaugurated and still fosters the Doctrine of Discovery, which sits at the foundations of US sovereignty and US property law.[15] Even more important, this field directs our attention to the actions and experiences of Indigenous people and Indigenous nations. Religion was not a native category for the precontact Indigenous languages and societies of North America (or, for that matter, in most of the languages and cultures around the world). Thus Indigenous studies quite rightly does not center the study of religion, prioritizing instead Indigenous struggles for cultural and political sovereignty and for Indigenous lands. Scholars in this field also prioritize Indigenous ontologies and epistemologies, so as to decenter the models of scholarship (including religious studies) that have actively fostered US imperialism, and so to decolonize the academy and its presumptive norms. If *religion* is an imperial frame, then it may not always be appropriate for Indigenous studies. That said, Indigenous communities have necessarily had to adapt themselves to colonial conditions and colonial ways of knowing. For Native Americans in the United States, especially, that has included the category of religion. Scholars who bridge the fields of religious studies and Indigenous studies, then, seek to center Indigenous categories and ways of knowing, while also unpacking and appreciating the ways in which Indigenous people have strategically deployed the category of religion and the new formations that have emerged under its sway.[16]

Critical ethnic studies—broadly conceived to encompass such disciplines as Black studies, race and ethnicity studies, and gender and sexuality studies—has been especially integral to advancing our understanding of empire by attending to intersectional forces of race, slavery, carceral systems, and gender. Of special importance is the provenance of these disciplines. They emerged as one outcome of transnational protests against white-supremacist, imperial, patriarchal, and heteronormative standards for what counted as knowledge in academic institutions. Black studies, for instance, was established during a time of anticolonial movements throughout Africa and the Caribbean and concurrent with a transnational Black Power movement. By foregrounding the inclusion and intellectual leadership of historically dominated peoples in the study of political power, racial injustice, and colonialism, critical ethnic studies has enabled significant advances in understanding how imperial power has been put to work in tandem with slavery, incarceration, sexual regulation, and economic inequality.[17]

It is instructive to consider the epistemic struggles that have shaped this disciplinary history. W. E. B. Du Bois, a pioneer of Africana studies, led the effort to study slavery and apartheid systems as highly destructive institutions operating in tandem with colonialism. He did so at a time when the overwhelming majority of White scholars defended slavery as a beneficent institution and based their methods on racist theories of cultural deprivation, Black criminality, and so forth. Other scholars in these disciplines—Angela Davis is exemplary—have established more exacting approaches to discerning how integral carceral systems are to global and transnational institutions of inequality. Other areas such as sexual labor and exploitation have become sites of productive research as well, further illuminating the complex ways in which empire and religion have indelibly shaped histories of power.[18]

Postcolonial studies has produced a vast body of scholarship intersecting with studies of religion and theology, race, gender, sexuality, and transnationalism. Among the many things that might be said about postcolonialism is the epistemic shift it produced, departing from colonial biases that dehumanized colonized populations and beginning instead with the human dignity and worth of colonized peoples. One need only revisit Aimé Césaire's *Discourse on Colonialism* to appreciate the difference made by this epistemic shift. Postcolonial studies dispensed with defending vaunted heroes of Western empires and instead sought to document the human cost of empire and to humanize the millions of people who suffered loss of lands, life, sovereignty, and identity because of colonialism. This intellectual mission made possible an astounding range of scholarship that has clarified the devastation and complexity that imperial systems have wrought. By attending to the many ways colonized people have navigated multiple statuses and identities (liminality and so-called hybridity) or have participated in colonial enterprises when expedient, postcolonial studies has also offered a more sophisticated window into the legacy of imperial systems.[19]

Finally, critical secularism studies clarifies how religion is produced, managed, and deployed within—and often as an agent of—US empire. Secularism, as the philosopher Akeel Bilgrami has explained, is not the absence of religion or necessarily in opposition to religion but a political doctrine, "*a stance to be taken about religion*," specifically that the state ought to maintain equal distance from and remain neutral towards all religious identities and positions. Secularism emerged out of the particular histories and trajectories of European societies, starting with the Peace of Westphalia (1648) when newly forming nation-states began to separate religious from political authority and so to delineate a separate sphere for *religion*. (Indeed, this emerging secularism made possible the later conceptualizations of religion that we have described above. In a related series of events, it was these emerging nation-states that had already begun to mobilize as empires.) Political secularism is possible only against the backdrop of what Saba Mahmood has called "secularity," the cultural and social formations that make this distinction between *religion* and other cultural domains conceivable. While secularism has never been only a European phenomenon, European models of secularism moved with European imperialism and indelibly shaped the diverse histories of secularism around the world.[20]

Following Mahmood, Talal Asad, and other anthropologists and critical theorists of secularism, we understand secularism as the set of cultural and political systems that demarcate and govern religion—or, in other words, the systematic ordering of knowledge and power that *puts religion in its place*. By disestablishing religion and guaranteeing its free exercise, the US Constitution did not solve the problem of religion or eliminate religious conflict but rather changed its contours. It set up new and ongoing controversies over what counted as religion, how far its sphere of authority should go, and where its boundaries with the "political" and other domains now identified as "secular" should lie. Secularism emerges in this field of study as a governing mechanism of modern imperialism—and, more recently, of the modern security state—one of the ways in which Europe and the United States have marked themselves off as *modern* and defined their racialized colonial subjects, in contrast, as primitive and in need of an allegedly benevolent colonial rule. To develop this critique is not to yearn for a return to "theocracy" or any other mode of Christian/religious domination, but rather to diagnose newer and ongoing systems of knowledge and power. As Tracy Fessenden pointed out fifteen years ago, secularism promised freedom for all but has nevertheless reinscribed hierarchies of race and religion in which whiteness and Christianity are very often still located at the top, assumed to be most rational and most free.[21]

In short, when we identify the United States as an empire, born in the crucible of imperial conflicts and acting imperially from the start, then we cannot adequately narrate the history of American religion—or of American secularism—without taking imperialism into account. And as soon as we begin to see the many ways in which the social formations we call religions have worked to sustain, survive, and resist the US Empire, then it becomes clear that our histories of this empire must also attend to religion and its study.

Structure of the Book

The thirteen chapters collected in this book offer discrete entry points into the intertwined histories of religion and US empire. Woven together in this volume, these chapters reveal the contours of a much larger story that is still ongoing today. In the broadest terms, this book contends that American forms of religion and empire have developed in tandem, inextricably shaping and reshaping each other over the course of US history. This empire and its configurations of religion have also exceeded the boundaries of the United States and its territorial possessions. Because it became so globally powerful, and because imperialism always transgresses (or seeks to transgress) other sovereignties, the religious formations of US imperialism have also impacted places that are not part of the United States or formally marked as US colonies.

This book is organized into four parts. The first, "Formations," shows how the constitutional and cultural frameworks for American religion developed to serve an increasingly expansive US empire. The three chapters in part 2, "Biopolitics," suggest that the most visible forms of mid- to late-nineteenth-century religion supported biopolitical projects of colonial management and control, even as subaltern religious forms fostered new possibilities for resistance. The chapters in part 3, "Entanglements," explore the transnational networks of missions and reform that reshaped both American religion and the increasingly global US empire of the early twentieth century. And finally, part 4, "Dialectics," argues that the dynamics of contemporary American religion were forged by its dual roles as cheerleader for and critic of US imperial power from the Second World War up to the present.

Part 1, "Formations," begins in chapter 1 with the rebellions led by enslaved peoples of the eighteenth-century Caribbean and the Americas. Katharine Gerbner shows how slaveholders systematically excluded Black practices from the category of "religion" and deemed them "rebellious" instead. Gerbner concludes that slavery and imperialism indelibly shaped early American conceptualizations of religion. Chapter 2 shifts our attention to the distinctive site of Michilimackinac, Michigan. With careful attention to Indigenous Anishinaabe peoples, to Protestant and Catholic missionaries and settlers, and to a group of dissident Mormons on nearby Beaver Island, Tisa Wenger asks how settler colonialism configured American religious traditions along with the category of "religion" at the contested northern borders of early-nineteenth-century US rule. In chapter 3, Sylvester Johnson charts the emergence of what was arguably the first overseas settler colony of the United States—Liberia. Johnson interprets the anti-Indigenous politics of this Black Christian colony called "freedom" in relation to the Anglo-American missionaries who targeted Indigenous Americans under US territorial expansion.

Part 2, "Biopolitics," begins with chapter 4, by Sarah Dees, who shifts the paradigm for understanding the intersection of empire and population studies by focusing on the role of the US census in producing knowledge about Native Americans—including representations of Indigenous religions—that historically facilitated settler-colonial rule. In chapter 5, Cara Burnidge reinterprets the history of social gospel reformers by foregrounding their role as "amateur imperialists." Despite viewing themselves as beneficent actors, these reformers nevertheless proved effective purveyors of surveillance and cultural chauvinism. In chapter 6, Jennifer Graber attends to Indigenous Kiowa conceptions of the Feather Dance—the Kiowa name for what US authorities called the Ghost Dance—in order to demonstrate the need for scholars to attend not only to imperial frames, or structures of knowledge, but also to Indigenous frames. The result is to decolonize the study of Native visionary movements by critically scrutinizing the linkage of Indigenous sovereignty, competing epistemologies, and US empire.

Part 3, "Entanglements," opens with chapter 7, by Karine Walther, who examines the global Christian networks behind industrial schools for colonized youths. Walther identifies the web of vectors that connected industrial education in Hawaii, the Philippines, and the continental United States. In chapter 8, Heather Curtis focuses on African American reformers Ida B. Wells and Georgia Patton, whose racial-justice leadership leveraged biblical theology and collective activism for social transformation. The legacies of Wells and Patton were shaped by the entanglements of the United States' acquisition of overseas territories following the Spanish American War, the ongoing emigration of African Americans from the South to the West and to Liberia, and the emergence of Black anticolonial religious movements in the early twentieth century. Chapter 9, by Christina Davidson, shows how White American missionaries in the Spanish Caribbean employed colonial governance to produce a racialized vision of the Dominican Republic that held lasting consequences for Haitians, Dominicans, and US missionary agents.

Finally, part 4, "Dialectics," illuminates the contradictions and ongoing power relations of religion and US empire in the late twentieth and early twenty-first centuries. In chapter 10, Kathleen Holscher examines the problem of sexual abuse at the hands of Catholic priests in the largely Native American diocese of Gallup, demonstrating the intimate consequence of US empire for Indigenous women and youths. Holscher shows how Catholic doctrine—the sin of scandal, on one hand, and *cura animarum*, or the priest's unique capability and responsibility for soul care, on the other—propelled the bodies of "problem" clerics, and shaped trajectories by which they traveled from east to west, from settlement to reservation, from White Catholic parishes to Native and Latinx communities. Chapter 11, by Jonathan Ebel, interprets the relationship of evangelicals to American empire through the lens of military weaponry, specifically napalm and the drone. Spanning the Vietnam War and the Global War on Terror, Ebel demonstrates how American faiths have been interwoven with the material culture and the science and the industry of war. Next, in chapter 12, coauthors Zareena Grewal and Brennan McDaniel use the work of self-proclaimed Cherokee Muslim Robert Crane as a lens into the fraught politics of American Muslim counterpublics. Grewal and McDaniel conclude that Crane's elaboration of an Islamic Cherokee history not only serves as an effort to make Islam American (by literally indigenizing it) but also participates in a liberal narrative of belonging that actively obscures the ongoing erasure of Indigenous sovereignty in the United States.

Chapter 13, by Lucia Hulsether, concludes part 4 and this book by examining how capitalism and humanitarianism intersect under the sign of empire. Just in case any of our readers might be tempted to tuck these histories safely into the past, this chapter challenges all of us (especially scholars of religion and US empire) to interrogate our own desires to conjure narratives of "resistance," silver linings, or tidy resolutions for our accounts—especially when the US Empire has so predictably folded such hopes into the logics of its own expansion. This chapter makes it clear that the racializing and commodifying logics of US imperialism diagnosed in this book are very much alive. The social formations we call "religions" continue to take shape, to enable and sustain, and sometimes to offer visions of a world otherwise, within this imperial frame.

NOTES

1 We are grateful to Lucia Hulsether for her incisive advice on this introduction.
2 Guyatt, *Providence and the Invention of the United States*; Haselby, *The Origins of American Religious Nationalism*; Saler, *The Settlers' Empire*.
3 Arista, *The Kingdom and the Republic*; Conroy-Krutz, *Christian Imperialism*; Harris, *God's Arbiters*; Martinez, *Catholic Borderlands*; McCullough, *The Cross of War*; Moran, *The Imperial Church*; Osorio, *Dismembering Lāhui*; Matthew Smith, "Settler Colonialism and U.S. Home Missions"; Tinker, *Missionary Conquest*; Tyrrell, *Reforming the World*.
4 The literature on this topic is vast. Among many others, see Graber, *The Gods of Indian Country*; Lewis, *Creating Christian Indians*; Martin and Nichols, eds., *Native Americans, Christianity, and the Reshaping of the American Religious Landscape*; McNally, *Ojibwe Singers*; Tarango, *Choosing the Jesus Way*; Wheeler, *To Live upon Hope*.
5 Beliso-De Jesús, *Electric Santeria*; Ramsey, *The Spirits and the Law*; Wenger, *Religious Freedom*; Wenger, *We Have a Religion*.
6 This book intervenes in the robust scholarship on the cultures of US imperialism (e.g., Kaplan and Pease, eds., *Cultures of United States Imperialism*; Goldstein, ed., *Formations of United States Colonialism*) by insisting on a more expansive and sophisticated account of religion. At the same time, we call on scholars of religion to take imperialism more seriously as the context in which American religious history unfolds. This reckoning has begun in the work of many of this volume's contributors, among others (e.g., Moran, *The Imperial Church*), but has not yet permeated the field.
7 Benjamin, *Encyclopedia of Western Colonialism since 1450*; Immerman, *Empire for Liberty*; Gregerson and Juster, eds., *Empires of God*; Chidester, *Empire of Religion*; S. A. Johnson, *African American Religions, 1500–2000*; Horne, *The Apocalypse of Settler Colonialism*; Immerwahr, *How to Hide an Empire*.
8 J. Byrd, *The Transit of Empire*; Kauanui, "A Structure, Not an Event"; Moreton-Robinson, *The White Possessive*; Morgensen, "The Biopolitics of Settler Colonialism"; Whyte, "Indigeneity and U.S. Settler Colonialism"; and Wolfe, "Settler Colonialism and the Elimination of the Native."
9 Hechter, *Internal Colonialism*; Hardt and Negri, *Empire*; Blauner, "Internal Colonialism and Ghetto Revolt."
10 Stern, *The Company-State*; Arrighi, *The Long Twentieth Century*.

11 Marty, *Righteous Empire*; Porter, *Empire and Superempire*; Immerman, *Empire for Liberty*; Grandin, *Empire's Workshop*.
12 Balagangahara, *"The Heathen in His Blindness"*; Chidester, *Empire of Religion*; Harrison, *"Religion" and the Religions in the English Enlightenment*; King, *Orientalism and Religion*; Mandair, *Religion and the Specter of the West*; Masuzawa, *The Invention of World Religions*.
13 Thomas Broughton, *An Historical Dictionary of All Religions* (London: Printed for C. Davis and T. Harris, 1742), i–iii; Hannah Adams, *A View of Religions, in Two Parts* (Boston: Printed by John West Folsom, 1791); Chidester, *Savage Systems*.
14 Among many others, see Banner, *How the Indians Lost Their Land*; Barker, ed., *Sovereignty Matters*; Go, *Patterns of Empire*; Greer, *Property and Dispossession*; Kauanui, *Hawai'ian Blood*; Saunt, *Unworthy Republic*; A. Simpson, *Mohawk Interruptus*; L. Simpson, *As We Have Always Done*.
15 R. Miller, *Native America, Discovered and Conquered*; R. Miller, *Discovering Indigenous Lands*; Newcomb, *Pagans in the Promised Land*; Wenger, "Sovereignty."
16 Barnes and Talamantez, eds., *Teaching Religion and Healing*; Denison, *Ute Land Religion in the American West*; Graber, *The Gods of Indian Country*; Hale, *Fugitive Religion*; McNally, *Defend the Sacred*; Pesantubbee, *Choctaw Women in a Chaotic World*; Schermerhorn, *Walking to Magdalena*; L. Smith, *Decolonizing Methodologies*; Wenger, *We Have a Religion*.
17 Biondi, *The Black Revolution on Campus*; Ferguson, *The Reorder of Things*; Williams, Squire, and Tuitt, *Plantation Politics and Campus Rebellions*.
18 Morris, *The Scholar Denied*; Hernandez, *City of Inmates*; Perdue, *Slavery and the Evolution of Cherokee Society, 1540–1866*; Perdue, *"Mixed Blood" Indians*; A. Davis, *Abolition Democracy*.
19 Césaire, *Discourse on Colonialism*; Said, *Orientalism*; Bhabha, *The Location of Culture*; Guha and Spivak, eds., *Selected Subaltern Studies*; Mbembé, *On the Postcolony*.
20 Bilgrami, *Secularism, Identity, and Enchantment*, 4; Mahmood, *Religious Difference in a Secular Age*; Dressler and Mandair, eds., *Secularism and Religion-Making*; Jakobsen and Pellegrini, eds., *Secularisms*; Cady and Hurd, eds., *Comparative Secularisms in a Global Age*.
21 Asad, *Formations of the Secular*; Agrama, *Questioning Secularism*; Wenger, *Religious Freedom*; Coviello, *Make Yourselves Gods*; Fessenden, *Culture and Redemption*.

PART I

Formations

Slavery, Settlers, and Salvation

The United States was formed in the midst of clashing European empires. White settler colonies, rooted in Christian identity and institutions of religious authority, were prizes for competing European empires, particularly France, Britain, and Spain. These settler colonies countered (and sometimes formed temporary alliances with) Indigenous polities that were fighting to preserve their lands and their sovereignty. When the new republic rebelled against the authority of the vast British Empire, it was at the same time establishing its own imperial status. And as these competing empires fought for control of territories such as the Great Lakes region, settler and missionary forms of Christianity interfaced with Indigenous and African religious traditions in many different ways. Christianity marked the imperial status of White settlers, legitimated their membership in the political community of the United States, and (through the Doctrine of Discovery) validated imperial claims to the land. In an expanding system of racial slavery, moreover, Africans and Indigenous Americans were racialized as "heathens" and relegated to highly vulnerable positions.

The British Caribbean, integral to the political and economic life of the early United States, intensified this demographic situation as a condition of empire. Jamaica transitioned from an Indigenous majority to a Black majority, following violent wars of extermination by European militarists and the forced displacement of abducted Africans into Jamaica as an enslaved labor force. During the 1700s, White Jamaican slaveholders were killing up to 20 percent of newly arrived Blacks within months by working them to death.[1] Jamaica was particularly shaped by numerous Black freedom wars and rebellions against such a murderous system of slavery. As African-derived and Christianized religions among Blacks were regularly implicated in rebellions and freedom wars, White slaveholders allied with political elites to repress and even criminalize various formations of Black religion. Weaponizing religion as a means of racial and colonial control, thus, became a regular feature of American empire.

From the 1700s to the early 1800s, the population of Whites in the United States grew from 3.1 million in 1790 to almost 20 million by 1850. Due to the overwhelming force of racial slavery, the African-descended population grew from about 760,000 to approximately 3.6 million in the same period. Despite being marginalized politically, Blacks were a significant population. Along the outskirts of the imperial republic and in many regions such as Mississippi, Florida, and Georgia, Indigenous Americans and Africans easily rivaled or outnumbered the White population. Native Americans—Choctaw, Chickasaw, and more—were the majority population in Mississippi until the US military violently forced them out of the state in the 1830s. At that point, Blacks became the majority and would remain so for another century. Not until the 1940s did White Mississippians constitute a majority of the state's population. Creating free Black settlements through Black settler colonies in the Caribbean and in Africa—Liberia is perhaps the best-known instance—was an ongoing effort that promised an opportunity for free and enslaved Blacks to seek refuge from a White republic that opposed multiracial democracy while placating Whites who viewed Black freedom as a fundamental threat to the United States. It also became a central means for Black Christian missionary religion to emerge on a transnational scale. African American religion as we know it emerged within and often in opposition to this imperial frame.

Set on this broad historical stage, the three chapters in this section show how the imperial contests of the eighteenth and early nineteenth centuries (re)formed American religion. Rather than offering an exhaustive history, these chapters dig deeply into particular cases that open up much larger worlds. How did enslaved people, as well as slaveholders and imperial authorities, change what counted as "religion" in early America? How did US westward expansions and the rise of settler governance impact the definition and practices of both Indigenous and White settler religions? How did the imperial systems of settler colonialism also shape the history of African American religion?

NOTE

1 Burnard, *Jamaica in the Age of Revolution*, 92–93.

1

Rebellion and Religion

Slavery and Empire in Early America

KATHARINE GERBNER

In 1669, the political philosopher John Locke was in the process of reading and revising a bold document that would create a frame of government for a new American colony.[1] The document, the Fundamental Constitutions of Carolina, provided guiding principles for English settlers as they created a new colony in North America.[2] As Locke and his coauthors developed their vision, they debated several topics, including the relationship between religion, slavery, and empire. The evidence of their debates lives on in their annotated manuscripts.[3] How could slave ownership, they asked, be reconciled with religious diversity and imperial authority? Could enslaved people become Christian without undermining property rights? And if they did, which church could they attend?[4]

These questions—about the relationship between religion and empire, and the relationship between "religion" and the "church"—were not the exclusive purview of political theorists like John Locke and his fellow imperialists. As enslaved Africans were forcibly settled in the English colonies and, later, the new United States, they made their own choices about religion, slavery, and empire that fundamentally transformed imperial policy and the concept of "religion."

This chapter repositions slave rebellion in the British Empire and the early United States as a formative influence on changing ideas about religion and empire. It argues that rebellions should be interpreted alongside written documents like the Fundamental Constitutions in order to understand the intellectual, religious, and political history of the United States.[5] Rebellions transformed religion and empire in at least two ways. First, while slave rebellion is usually understood simply as a rejection of slavery, this chapter argues that rebellion was also imperial warfare.⁶ Enslaved and free rebels participated in, and capitalized on, imperial rivalries through rebellion. The strategic choices of enslaved and free rebels changed the trajectory of imperial policy in both Great Britain and the United States.

Second, ideas about religion evolved in conjunction with imperial politics and slave rebellion. The very boundaries of "religion" were in flux as enslavers sought to control the enslaved population. Whites lived in perpetual fear of rebellion, and when uprisings did occur, White people responded not only with terrorizing violence but also through legal innovations and restrictions on religion. These efforts changed the parameters of both "religion" and "the church."

The formation of the category of "religion" has received extensive scholarly attention in the past decades. Scholars like Talal Asad, Jonathan Z. Smith, and others have shown how the modern category of religion grew, in part, out of the dynamics of European imperialism.⁷ Yet despite the prolonged emphasis on empire as formative for the meaning of religion, most scholarship on the category of religion does not consider the role that enslaved men and women played in this history. This is the case because Europeans and White Americans intentionally sought to *exclude* Africana religious practices from the category of religion.

As a result, it is essential to examine the formation of religion as a category alongside the intentional efforts to exclude certain religious practices from the modern category of "religion." In order to see how this happened, this chapter breaks the construct of modern religion into constituent parts: into ideas about time, space, assemblies of people, and communal bonds. Doing so provides new insight into the way slave rebellion influenced emerging ideas about "religion." Specifically, it reveals how imperialists and enslavers wrote laws that intentionally excluded Black religious practices—including congregating, oath making, and drum beating—from the category of religion through a dual process of criminalization and delegitimization. I focus on the execution and aftermath of three insurrections: the Stono Rebellion (1739), Tacky's Revolt (1760), and the Denmark Vesey conspiracy (1822). Each rebellion demonstrates a different aspect of the evolving relationship among slavery, imperial governance, and religion.

The Stono Rebellion of 1739, which began on a Sunday morning while many White colonists were at church, revealed how the rhythm of the Christian calendar could be a threat to colonial governance. It also showed how enslaved men and women used their knowledge of imperial and religious rivalries—in this case, the tension between British Protestant South Carolina and Spanish Catholic Florida—to challenge British religious and political authority. Tacky's Revolt, which convulsed the British colony of Jamaica in 1760, was the largest uprising in the eighteenth-century British Atlantic World. It was also the clearest example of how rebellion could lead to the criminalization of Africana religions. In the wake of the rebellion, White Jamaican lawmakers criminalized obeah, an African-inspired religio-medical practice. The final section moves to Vesey's conspiracy, a thwarted rebellion planned for the summer of 1822 in Charleston, South Carolina. The Vesey affair shows how even when enslaved and free Blacks became Protestants, the incorporation of separate Black churches challenged White authority and fell afoul of many of the laws that were passed in the wake of previous insurrections. It also speaks to the continued influence of Caribbean slavery on the formation of religion in the early republic.

Examining these three rebellions together allows us to recognize the ways in which Black practices were systematically excluded from the emerging category of "religion" and deemed as "rebellious." This approach also brings to light the numerous strategies that Africans and their descendants used to respond to this epistemological warfare. It shows that we cannot understand religion, or the meaning of a "church," without recognizing the way that slavery, and the rebellion of enslaved people, fundamentally shifted the category of religion.

The Stono Rebellion and the Religious Politics of Time and Space

September 9, 1739, was a Sunday. While not all White colonists made their way to church, the day was still regarded as a day of rest. For the enslaved men and women living in the colony, Sunday was the only day they were granted a reprieve from labor. Despite this, few people of color were permitted into the churches of the colonists. Instead, enslaved men and women used Sundays to harvest their own food and to commune with each other.

On this particular Sunday, a group of recently arrived men from West Central Africa—probably the Kingdom of Kongo—assembled to enact a plan of their own.[8] After lengthy planning and deliberation, they rose up against their enslavers and marched to the local armory at Stonehow. There, they killed two men and "took a pretty many small Arms and Powder." After acquiring arms and ammunition, they "turned back and marched Southward" on the road towards Georgia. On the way, they spared the tavern owner, Mr. Wallace, "for he was a good Man," but killed others who had not warranted a similar reputation.[9]

As the Africans marched south, White witnesses reported that they called out "Liberty" and wore their "Colours displayed" with "two Drums beating."[10] Nearly all the accounts of the rebellion note that the rebels were headed to Spanish Florida, where they were promised freedom. The king of Spain had recently issued a proclamation promising "Protection and Freedom to All Negroes Slaves that would resort thither."[11] According to one report, a recent group of escaped slaves from Carolina had successfully reached St. Augustine after traveling through Georgia. There, they were "received . . . with great honours" and "one of them had a Commission given to him, and a Coat faced with Velvet."[12]

The rebels, some of whom probably spoke Portuguese and professed the Catholic religion, were aware of the promise of freedom in Catholic Florida. For months, English settlers had been concerned about the existence of Spanish spies in Carolina who, they feared, were spreading the word about the Catholic colony among the enslaved population. One account of the insurrection noted that "several Spaniards" had been "for some time past strolling about Carolina" upon "Diverse Pretences." Two Spanish travelers who refused to explain their presence had been "taken up and committed to Jayl in Georgia."[13] William Bull, who wrote to the commissioners for trade and plantation less than a month after the rebellion, explicitly linked the African rebels with a broader pattern of desertion. Since the king's proclamation, he wrote, "several parties have deserted and are there openly received and protected." The rebellion of September 9, he wrote, was one of "many attempts" to escape to the Spanish colony.[14]

The Stono rebels never made it to Florida. After they marched about ten miles, the colonial militia caught up with the rebels. Many were killed on the spot, while others fled. Some went into hiding. Those who were found were executed. Still, the rebels' sense of geography—with their knowledge that Spanish Florida offered both Catholicism and freedom—is a reminder that the political and religious map of the colonial Carolinas was deeply intertwined with transatlantic imperial and religious rivalries. Furthermore, the rebels, many of whom spoke Portuguese and had either converted to, or been introduced to, Catholicism in Africa, were part of what Vincent Brown has recently called a "cartography of insurrection" in the Atlantic World.[15]

The timing of the revolt—on a Sunday—should give us pause as well. It certainly gave White colonists pause at the time. The Salzburgers, a group of German Pietists in Georgia, bemoaned the fact that the rebellion had "begun on the day of the Lord."[16] Less observant White Christians noticed as well. In fact, slaveholders throughout the colonial period were hyperaware of implications of the Christian calendar, and particularly the Sabbath, for slavery. Even before the Stono Revolt, White colonists in South Carolina had noted time and again that Sunday church services posed a security threat. In the 1712 Act for the Better Ordering and Governing of Negroes and Slaves, lawmakers specified that "no master, mistress, overseer, or other person whatsoever ... shall give their negroes and other slaves leave, on Sundays, holidays, or any other time, to go out of their plantations."[17] Lawmakers sought to protect against the danger of the Christian Sabbath by requiring "all and every" constable in Charlestown "on every Sunday and the holidays at Christmas, Easter and Whitsuntide" to "go through all or any of the streets, and also, round about Charlestown" to look for "any meeting or concourse of any such negroes or slaves." They further noted that "great numbers of slaves which do not dwell in Charlestown, on Sundays and holidays resort thither, to drink, quarrel, fight, curse, and swear, and profane the Sabbath."[18] Later acts reiterated the clause on Sundays and holidays.

Fears about the Sabbath and other Christian holidays also led to a debate about Saturday afternoons. As early as the mid-seventeenth century, some Protestant missionaries suggested that Saturday afternoons should be free from work, so that enslaved people could attend worship services on Sundays. Predictably, many slave owners fought back against this proposition. Some did so because they wanted to exploit their labor a full six days per week. But others also had misgivings about the proposition of allowing enslaved people to come to church or become Christians.[19]

Why was the Stono rebellion planned for Sunday, September 9? Most scholars who have considered this question have presumed that it was because Sundays provided the only reprieve from work, but the historian Mark M. Smith has theorized that the rebels chose this particular Sunday because it was preceded by Saturday, September 8: the day of Nativity of the Virgin Mary, and an important holy day for Catholics. In Smith's words, it was a day associated with a "protecting, and empowering Kongolese religious icon."[20] While Smith's argument is speculative, it is important to consider the conflicting—and sometimes overlapping—concepts of sacred time that existed in early America. African Catholic notions of sacred time, including Kongolese Catholicism, were being enacted and called upon for the practice of rebellion.

Integrating African Catholic ideas about religious time broadens our understanding of slave rebellion and religion. The Stono Revolt, like other rebellions, was not simply a conflict between masters and slaves; it should also be understood as a transatlantic imperial and religious conflict. As John Thornton has argued, many of the Stono rebels had probably participated in imperial wars in West Central Africa, and they brought both military strategies and religious ideas to bear on their choices and decisions in South Carolina.[21]

In the wake of Stono, lawmakers passed a new slave code intended to prevent future insurrections. Several aspects of this slave code are striking. Most notably, the law sought to limit the autonomy of enslaved people by banning their assembly, and it specified that seven enslaved men traveling together—without a White person—would be forbidden.[22] It also sought to delegitimize and criminalize Africana religions without referring specifically to "religion." Clause 22 of the 1740 code reads, "And whatsoever master, owner or overseer shall permit or suffer his or their Negro or other slave or slaves, at any time hereafter, to beat drums, blow horns, or use any other loud instruments or whosoever shall suffer and countenance any public meeting or feastings of strange Negroes or slaves in their plantations, shall forfeit ten pounds, current money, for every such offence, upon conviction or proof as aforesaid." Here, "religion" is never specifically mentioned; instead, the legal wording targets a series of actions (beating drums, blowing horns, loud instruments) as well as specific types of groupings (public meetings and feasts), all of which could be considered aspects of religious practice, as being illegal, especially on Sundays and the Saturday evenings that preceded them. While the clauses were meant to prevent insurrection, they had important consequences for the practice of religion, since they implied that Black religious gatherings were not only suspicious, but criminal.

The 1740 act was not the first to make these types of restrictions. Regulations about assemblies and congregations are ubiquitous within slave codes once one begins to look for them. In fact, nearly every slave code in the British Atlantic World had a clause aimed at policing practices associated with religion without calling those practices "religious." Virginia's slave code of 1680 notes that the "frequent meetings of considerable numbers of Negro slaves under pretense of feasts and burials is judged of dangerous consequence." One scholar has argued that the 1680 act's prohibition of slave meetings "under pretense of feast and burials" can be viewed as the first colonial restriction on African American religious assembly, although earlier ones do the same, without necessarily specifying burials.[23]

There was an imperial governance strategy underlying the 1740 slave code and other laws intended to restrict assemblies of the enslaved. While their stated aim was to prevent insurrection, the reality was far broader. They sought to undercut the creation of religious and political authority among the enslaved without using the words "religion" or "politics." Even as Whites aimed to restrict Black religious practices, however, Africans and their descendants continued to recognize, and capitalize on, imperial and religious rivalries. As they did so, they challenged European ideas about "religion" and drew upon unseen networks spanning British North America, the Caribbean, and Africa.

Tacky's Revolt and the Criminalization of Africana Religions

If the Stono Revolt shows how enslaved rebels could capitalize on the Christian calendar and imperial religious rivalries to undermine the colonial state, Tacky's Revolt (1760) revealed how rebellion and imperial governance led to the criminalization of Africana religious practices. Tacky's Revolt, which was the largest slave rebellion in the eighteenth-century British Atlantic World, was led, in part, by obeah practitioners who used sacred oaths to bind rebels together and protect themselves from English bullets. In response, the colonial government criminalized obeah and defined it as a "wicked Art." It was the first time that an African-derived practice was specifically named in British colonial law.

Understanding obeah is, itself, a lesson in the deeply problematic archive of slavery, religion, and empire.[24] There are only a handful of written sources that exist about obeah before its criminalization in 1760, and the sources that do survive are all written by Europeans. The earliest references, which were written by an English army officer named Thomas Walduck and date to 1710 and 1712, refer to obeah as a form of witchcraft. In 1729, an Anglican minister in Barbados defined "Oby Negroes" as "conjurers" while other references suggest that obeah practitioners were "physicians or conjurers."[25] The slippage between the concepts of witchcraft and medicine is representative of a broader inability to fit "obeah" into European categories such as "religion," "medicine," and "superstition."

On Jamaica, the Moravian missionary Zacharias George Caries, who was a native German speaker and unfamiliar with English customs on the island, provided a slightly different description of obeah, noting that the term meant a "Seer, or one who is able to see things in the future."[26] He added that his enslaved congregants used the term to refer to him, suggesting that obeah was a crucial category for Afro-Caribbean interpretation of European religion and healing practices.[27] Caries's letter about obeah, which was written in 1755, aligns with Dianne Stewart's argument that obeah should be understood as "an institution entailing much more than expert knowledge of botanic therapeutic properties."[28] It was also a source of political power that was used in order to bind individuals together.

In 1760, obeah women and men were instrumental in launching an island-wide rebellion, which became the largest uprising in the eighteenth-century British Atlantic World. According to colonial records of the time, obeah men and women prepared rebels for battle through sacred oaths and rituals. Like the Stono rebels, the leaders of Tacky's Revolt also capitalized on interimperial conflict as they planned their rebellion. In 1760, the British were in the midst of what became known as the Seven Years War. Enslaved rebels recognized that the imperial war between England, Spain, and France meant that there were fewer troops stationed on Jamaica. Furthermore, those who were present were focused primarily on foreign attack, rather than an uprising of the enslaved.[29]

The rebellion itself began in Saint Mary's parish on Easter, when an enslaved man named Tacky led a raid on Fort Haldane.[30] A second, more successful rebellion began the following month on Whitsuntide under the leadership of a man named Wager, or Apongo.[31] The rebellion thus had several phases, and, as Vincent Brown has argued, it was far more complex than simply a fight between masters and slaves. It was also part of an archipelago of warfare that spread across the Atlantic and drew upon African political and religious strategies.[32]

After the rebellion, White lawmakers contemplated how best to respond to the uprising. Many of their strategies built on existing legal precedents. They rewarded informants, committed to building new barracks, and forbade assemblies or gatherings among the enslaved.[33] They also reiterated the need for extra vigilance on Sundays and Christian holidays. But Jamaican lawmakers also developed new innovations. Most significantly, the Act to Remedy the Evils Arising from Irregular Assemblies of Slaves extended and transformed previous efforts to control life among the enslaved.

As with earlier acts, lawmakers specified a variety of instruments as being disruptive and dangerous. Unlike previous laws, however, the 1760 act named obeah as a capital offense, punishable by execution or transportation. The specific language of the act is significant. It reads,

> And in order to prevent the many Mischiefs that may hereafter arise from the wicked Art of Negroes going under the appellation of Obeah Men and Women, pretending to have Communication with the Devil and other evil spirits, whereby the weak and superstitious are deluded into a Belief of their having full Power to exempt them whilst under their Protection from any Evils . . . any Negro or other Slave who shall pretend to any Supernatural Power, and be detected in making use of any Blood, Feathers, Parrots Beaks, Dogs Teeth, Alligators Teeth, Broken Bottles, Grave Dirt, Rum, Egg-shells or any other Materials relative to the Practice of Obeah or Witchcraft in order to delude and impose on the Minds of others shall

upon Conviction thereof before two Magistrates and three Freeholders suffer death or Transportation any thing in this Act or any other Law to the contrary notwithstanding.

In criminalizing obeah, lawmakers drew on English conceptions of witchcraft while also seeking to distance the practice of obeah from witchcraft.[34] Significantly, the 1760 act also shows how material objects were central to the way that lawmakers defined and policed African religious and political practice. In fact, it is essential to stress that colonial authorities utilized a terminology in their lawbooks that limited most descriptions of African religious practice to a *description of objects*—in this case, "Blood, Feathers, Parrots Beaks, Dogs Teeth, Alligators Teeth, Broken Bottles, Grave Dirt, Rum, Egg-shells or any other Materials relative to the Practice of Obeah or Witchcraft."[35]

The criminalization of obeah is the clearest example of how African-derived authority was targeted by colonial and imperial lawmakers in an effort to regulate slavery. As people of African descent drew on African-inspired practices of power and authority, White colonials sought to suppress those practices. They did so through two distinct processes: criminalization and delegitimization. Criminalization is easier to trace, while delegitimization was a more opaque process that occurred as White colonials policed the boundaries of "religion" and the "church." By refusing to recognize Africana religious practices as "religion," White authorities sought to diminish their power. While this process was never complete, it did have long-term consequences for the meaning and practice of obeah, which remains a criminal practice in some Caribbean nations.

Denmark Vesey and the Incorporation of Black Churches

Unlike the Stono Rebellion and Tacky's Revolt, the Denmark Vesey uprising never occurred. Historians have debated whether Vesey, a free Black carpenter, actually organized a rebellion or whether he was targeted by paranoid Whites.[36] Either way, the Vesey conspiracy sheds light on continuing efforts to contain and govern Black religion in the antebellum United States. Placing the Vesey conspiracy in conversation with two colonial rebellions—Stono and Tacky's Revolt—shows how lawmakers and politicians in the United States expanded upon colonial and Caribbean precedents in their efforts to govern and control the religious lives of enslaved and free people of color.

The Vesey conspiracy occurred in 1822—well into the antebellum period of the United States. It was nearly a century after the Stono Rebellion, and the political geography of South Carolina had changed drastically in the interim. In 1752, Georgia became a colony—in part, to stem the flow of runaway slaves from the Carolinas to Spanish Florida, the likely destination of the Stono rebels. When the American Revolution in 1776 broke formal ties with the British Empire, Florida remained part of the Spanish Empire. The Louisiana Purchase of 1803 demonstrated that the new United States embraced an imperial identity as White settlers expanded both westward and southward into Indian country, but it was not until 1822—the same year as the Vesey conspiracy—that Florida became a territory of the United States.

The expansionist regime of the United States in the nineteenth century has led many historians to focus on the continental dimensions of American empire in the first half of the nineteenth century, but more recent scholarship has shown that the Caribbean remained crucial to the development of the early United States. American merchants maintained close ties with Caribbean colonies like Jamaica and Barbados. The Haitian Revolution, meanwhile, led to a mass exodus of Whites and enslaved people from the French Caribbean colony, many of whom migrated to the United States. The free Black republic haunted White Americans, as they feared that their own human property would follow in the footsteps of Black revolutionaries like Louverture and Dessalines. The specter of Haiti would resurface again in the Vesey conspiracy, which allegedly culminated with a plan to escape from South Carolina to the independent Black republic.

Denmark Vesey's own life demonstrates the continuing influence of the Caribbean on the continental United States. Vesey, who may have been born in West Africa, spent his early years in the Danish West Indies (now the US Virgin Islands), where he was introduced to a variety of transatlantic religious movements.[37] The Moravian church, which was headquartered in Germany with major settlements in North Carolina and Pennsylvania, dominated religious life on the island, and half of the Black population belonged to one of the Moravian churches on the island. As a result, the young Vesey was either a member of or at least well-acquainted with the church and its practice of promoting Black leadership.[38]

Vesey was sold off the island in 1781, when he was fourteen, but he maintained ties with the Caribbean and visited Saint Domingue in the years before the Haitian revolution.[39] He became a member of the African Church in Charleston sometime between 1817 and the early 1820s. Before then, he probably attended several different Protestant churches before joining the newly formed Second Presbyterian Church, where he became a communicant in 1817.[40] Vesey may also have frequented one of the Methodists churches, which served as feeders to the African Church. Either way, Vesey's religious history mirrored the expansion of evangelical worship practices in the early republic, as individuals experimented with different denominations and created new religious communities.

Vesey's life also provides a window into the expansion and transformation of Black Protestantism. As the number of Black Christians grew, the long history of racism within White Protestant churches became increasingly apparent. For over a century, Whites in the British colonies and in early America had demonstrated a deep distrust of Black religiosity—regardless of whether it was Christian or non-Christian. The Stono Rebellion, with its concerns over Afro-Catholicism and Spanish Florida, demonstrated one aspect of this suspicion, while Tacky's Revolt and the criminalization of obeah exhibited a different manifestation of a similar anxiety.

Black Protestantism was no exception to this general rule. As early as the mid-seventeenth century, English colonists claimed that conversion to Protestantism would make enslaved people rebellious and desirous of freedom. Their antagonism was directed not only at Black converts but also towards White missionaries who preached to enslaved and free Blacks.[41] Despite White resistance, enslaved and free Blacks advocated for their right to become baptized members of Protestant churches. Moravians, who offered leadership positions to people of color, and Methodists, who modeled many aspects of their missionary efforts after the Moravians, proved especially popular among enslaved and free Blacks in early America and the Caribbean.[42] Yet even as Black Christians became integral to Protestant churches, they continued to battle White racism and hostility.

It was in response to racism that Richard Allen, a former slave who became an ordained Black Methodist, decided to found the separate African Methodist Episcopal (AME) Church in Philadelphia in 1816.[43] The following year, thousands of enslaved and free Blacks walked out of the Methodist churches in Charleston. Like other Black Christians, they protested prejudicial treatment and discrimination.[44]

The creation of an African Methodist Church in Charleston enraged many White Charlestonians. Their efforts to persecute Black Christians drew on previous efforts to control Black religion, including the legislation passed in the wake of the Stono Rebellion. When Black Methodists met for worship, they ran afoul of laws prohibiting assemblies of the enslaved. In 1818, 140 enslaved and free Blacks were arrested during a worship service of the African Church on Sunday, June 7.[45] In newspaper accounts of the arrest, Whites noted that the meeting of the African Church was "unlawful," and specified that "by sundry Acts of the Legislature, it is positively forbidden that Slaves, or Free People of Colour should assemble 'for the purpose of mental instruction,' unless a majority of the assembly be composed of white people." The law referenced had "been in force since the year 1800," and it drew directly on the 1740 slave code, passed after the Stono Rebellion.[46]

Despite persecution, leaders of the African Church boldly submitted a petition to the South Carolina House of Representatives to request an exception to the law prohibiting Black assemblies. Noting that they had recently "erected a house of worship, at Hampstead, on Charleston-Neck, at the corner of Hanover and Reed Street," they requested permission to keep the "doors of the said build" open from "the rising of the sun, until the going down of the same." To counter White anxieties, they invited "all white ministers of the Gospel of every denomination" to "officiate in the said Church, whenever disposed so to do," and they offered "separate seats" for any White citizens who desired to attend a service.[47] The petition was signed by twenty-six free Blacks as well as thirty-two Whites, including several prominent White ministers in Charleston.[48]

The same year, more than 140 Whites—most of them slaveholding planters—submitted a competing petition to the House, stating that "schools or assemblages of negroes slaves to be taught reading and writing" were an "evil [of] the greatest magnitude." They blamed White missionaries, who they claimed had been paid by abolitionists "for the avowed purpose of educating our Negroes." Again, legal precedent played a central role in their argument. They pointed to "an Act of the Legislature" that forbade Blacks from "being taught to write" and argued that it needed to be updated to include a prohibition on reading as well.[49]

The antiliteracy act was another reference to the 1740 slave code. In addition to criminalizing Black assemblies, the 1740 act was the first in the British colonies to forbid enslaved people from learning how to write.[50] Whites recognized that literacy could be used for subversive purposes, such as writing transportation passes or communicating across distances. But this was not the only cause for concern. Learning to read the Bible was often the first "step" towards Protestant baptism, and literacy education was closely connected to Protestant conversion. But as Black Christians developed their own interpretations of biblical verses, they challenged White proslavery theology. This issue of interpretation had long been controversial, even among White missionaries eager to promote conversion.[51]

Biblical interpretation became a key axis of debate during the Vesey trials. In 1822, Vesey was accused of planning a rebellion to kill Whites, liberate slaves, and escape to the Black republic of Haiti. While there are no surviving records written by Vesey himself, all extant archival sources from the trials agree that biblical interpretation played a central role in Vesey's planning and conception of rebellion.[52] During the trial, several witnesses reported that Vesey referred frequently to the Exodus story, in which the Israelites escaped from Egyptian slavery. Rolla Bennett, an associate of Vesey who was also hanged on July 2, 1822, claimed that Vesey "was the first to rise up and speak, and he read to us from the Bible, how the *Children of Israel were delivered out of Egypt from bondage*."[53] Vesey's references to Exodus had a long history within Black Protestant thought. Absalom Jones, the first Black priest in the Episcopal Church, had cited Exodus 3:7-8 in his 1808 speech celebrating the end of the slave trade, and enslaved Black Christians had long noted the similarity between their experience of bondage and that of the Israelites in Egypt.[54]

Yet Exodus was not Vesey's only scriptural touchstone. A newspaper article written by Benjamin Elliot in September 1822 suggests that Vesey viewed the White residents of Charleston as "antitypes for Canaanites . . . whom God instructs the Israelites to slaughter so as to settle in their land as an inheritance."[55] As Jeremy Schipper has suggested, a close reading of the trial records suggests that Vesey believed not only that slavery went against divine law but also that "a successful, divinely endorsed liberation through bloodshed was inevitable."[56]

While Vesey's interpretation provided an important intellectual foundation for the conspiracy, several scholars have shown how non-Christian African religious practices were also called upon to develop pan-African solidarity for the revolt. As Walter Rucker has argued, "Gullah Jack" Pritchard was an important leader of the rebellion who drew upon his experiences as a doctor and "conjurer" in both Angola and the United States.[57] Like the obeah practitioners in Tacky's Revolt, Gullah Jack utilized African religious and political strategies to create solidarity among enslaved and free Blacks.

In their response to the Vesey conspiracy, magistrates again relied on the 1740 Act for the Better Ordering and Governing of Negroes to guide their legal innovations. As Douglas Egerton and Robert Paquette have argued, the 1740 act "remained the foundation of slave law in South Carolina until the end of the Civil War."[58] Vesey was tried and hanged with five others on July 2, 1822. Eventually, thirty-five enslaved and free Blacks were executed, and thirty-two were banished.

Whites also targeted the African Church in Charleston. Even though church leaders were not accused of participation, the church was burned to the ground. The destruction of the African Church signaled the persistent challenge of Black religion to White authority, even when the Black religion was Protestantism. The use of the anti-assembly laws to police Afro-Protestant practice further showed how legal tactics intended to subvert rebellion were utilized to persecute Black Christian institutions. Even as the African Church in South Carolina was destroyed, however, Black-led congregations spread quickly throughout early America. As Sally Gordon has argued, the efforts of Black Protestants to incorporate their own churches demonstrates an important and long-lasting religious and legal strategy intended to shelter Black churches from White aggression.[59]

Conclusion

In 1978, the scholar Albert Raboteau famously described Black religion under slavery as the "invisible institution."[60] Yet even as some Black religious practices were suppressed by White authorities to the point of "invisibility," they continued to exert a formative influence on emerging ideas about religion, freedom, and empire. Their influence is often difficult to recognize in colonial and early American archives because Whites worked tirelessly to exclude Black practices from the category of "religion" and to denigrate them as "superstitious" or "criminal." Still, their imprint is discernible if we use different methods to examine archival materials.

When we break the construct of "religion" into parts—into notions of sacred time, sacred space, communal bonds, and assembled people—we can recognize the strategies that White colonists used to deconstruct and delegitimize African diasporic religions—including Black Christianity. We can also recognize the strategies that Africans and their descendants used to respond to this epistemological warfare. Thinking through the construction of religion as a process happening *in tandem* and *in response* to slavery also invites us to think more generally about how the category of religion was being defined in response to slave rebellion.

In order to understand this dialogic process, it is helpful to ponder the following questions. First, how many people do you need to start a religion? And second, how many people do you need to start a rebellion? The answer to both questions varies, but according to English colonial law, it hovers around *seven*. Here, we can return to the 1669 Fundamental Constitutions of Carolina, coauthored by John Locke. The Constitutions granted that "any Seven or more persona agreeing in any religion" could "constitute a church or profession" of their own.[61] Yet as we know from the 1740 slave code, passed after the Stono Rebellion, seven is also the number of enslaved people who were forbidden from gathering together. It is telling that the same number is the tipping point in moving from "gathering" to either a "church" or a "rebellion."

Not every definition of a "gathered church" or a potential rebellion used the number seven as its tipping point, but the correlation is still revealing: it is a reminder that a gathering of people—an assembly—can easily slip between the perception of religion and the perception of rebellion based on *who is gathered*. If religion is defined by the gathering of seven people who are "of the same religion," as the Carolina Constitution defines it, then Black religion is literally a crime.

This underlying correlation helps to explain why the word "religion" was rarely used in conjunction with African practices during the colonial period and early republic. Rather than using the language of religion, lawmakers focused on material objects and actions such as drumming and dancing that they then criminalized. This tactic was intentional—an attempt to delegitimize African diasporic religious and intellectual history by materializing and deconstructing it. Moreover, the suspicion of Black congregations on holy days shows how the politics of sacred time were part of a larger strategy of excluding Black practices from the sphere of the legitimately "religious." Resurrecting this history of Black religion from the colonial archives that undermined them is essential for any accurate accounting of either religion or empire.

NOTES

1 I am grateful to Tisa Wenger and Sylvester Johnson, and to the other authors in this volume, for their excellent comments and suggestions on this chapter. I would also like to thank Shari Rabin for her helpful feedback on an earlier draft. Participants in the "Space and Time in Early America" conference, organized by Seth Perry at Princeton University, offered helpful suggestions on what became part 1. Finally, I am grateful to Paul Schneider-Krumpus for his help analyzing and interpreting primary and secondary sources from the Denmark Vesey conspiracy.

2 On Locke's involvement in the creation of the Fundamental Constitutions, as well as the influence of Carolina on his later political philosophy, see Armitage, "John Locke, Carolina, and the 'Two Treatises of Government'"; Farr, "Locke, Natural Law, and New World Slavery"; and Hinshelwood, "The Carolinian Context of John Locke's Theory of Slavery." On the significance of Locke's thinking about slavery, see Brewer, "Slavery, Sovereignty, and 'Inheritable Blood.'"

3 As they discussed and revised the Fundamental Constitutions, either Locke or one of his coauthors added the words "power and" to a sentence declaring that "every Freeman of Carolina shall have absolute power and Authority over his Negro slaves of what opinion or Religion soever." The manuscript was found in the papers of Locke's patron, Lord Shaftesbury. David Armitage has claimed that Locke himself added the terms "power and" to the phrase providing freemen "absolute power" over "Negro slaves," although James Farr has suggested that the ampersand in the annotation "does not appear to be Locke's." Regardless, both agree that Locke was closely connected with the Fundamental Constitutions, and its references to slavery and religion. Armitage, "John Locke, Carolina, and the 'Two Treatises of Government,'" 609; Farr, "Locke, Natural Law, and New World Slavery," 518 n.26.

4 For example, the Fundamental Constitutions specified that enslaved people could be "of what church any of them shall think best." This provision, which appeared

to provide religious freedom to the enslaved, was modified by the specification that "no slave shall hereby be exempted from that civil dominion his master has over him." Farr, "Locke, Natural Law, and New World Slavery," 499. On the Fundamental Constitutions and the history of "religious freedom," see Lippy, "Chastized by Scorpions"; Wenger, *Religious Freedom*.

5 For the scope of this chapter, there are two distinct, but interconnected, empires under examination. First, there is the British Empire, which expanded into the eastern seaboard of North America and into the Caribbean in the seventeenth and eighteenth centuries. Second, there is the US Empire. While some scholars have suggested that the early US republic should not be considered an empire, this chapter builds on scholarship that argues that it was, in fact, an imperial power from its inception. See S. A. Johnson, *African American Religions, 1500–2000*, 160; and S. A. Johnson, "Religion, Race, and American Empire."

The early US republic can be considered an empire in two distinct ways. First, White Americans continued to expand westward, transgressing established borders between their new nation and those of Indigenous nations. Second, the new United States expanded the practice of slavery. As several scholars have argued, slavery should be understood as a system of governance and dominance, rather than a "peculiar" or separate institution. It was a form of "internal colonialism" that sought to control the movement and behavior of an entire population of inhabitants who were granted little to no legal rights or protections. Bryant, *Rivers of Gold, Lives of Bondage*; S. A. Johnson, *African American Religions, 1500–2000*; Brown, *Tacky's Revolt*.

6 On this point, see especially Brown, *Tacky's Revolt*.

7 Asad, *Genealogies of Religion*; J. Z. Smith, "Religion, Religions, Religious."

8 Historical records call the rebels "Angolans," but the historian John Thornton has argued that they were more likely from the neighboring Kingdom of Kongo, rather than the Portuguese colony of Angola. Thornton, "African Dimensions of the Stono Rebellion." For important narratives and interpretations of the Stono Rebellion, see especially Wood, *Black Majority*; Thornton, "African Dimensions of the Stono Rebellion"; M. M. Smith, "Remembering Mary, Shaping Revolt"; M. M. Smith, *Stono*.

9 Allen D. Candler, William L. Northern, and Lucian L. Knight, eds., *Colonial Records of the State of Georgia: Original Papers, Correspondence, Trustees, General Oglethorpe, and Others*. Vol. 22, part 2 (Atlanta: Byrd, 1913), 232–34.

10 Candler, Northern, and Knight, eds., *Colonial Records of the State of Georgia*, 234.

11 Candler, Northern, and Knight, eds., *Colonial Records of the State of Georgia*, 232.

12 Candler, Northern, and Knight, eds., *Colonial Records of the State of Georgia*, 232–33.

13 Candler, Northern, and Knight, eds., *Colonial Records of the State of Georgia*, 232–33.

14 William Bull, "William Bull to Commissioners for Trade and Plantations. Charleston," October 5, 1739, in *The Calendar of State Papers, Colonial: North America and the West Indies, 1574–1739*, vol. 45 (Abingdon, Oxfordshire: Taylor & Francis), 195–96. On the fate of ex-slaves who successfully escaped from South Carolina to Florida, see Landers, "Gracia Real de Santa Teresa de Mose."
15 Brown, *Tacky's Revolt*.
16 Entry for Friday, the 28th of September [1739], Samuel Urlsperger, *Detailed Reports on the Salzburger Emigrants Who Settled in America*, trans. George Fenwick Jones and Renate Wilson, vol. 6 (Athens: University of Georgia Press, 1981), 226.
17 David J. McCord and Thomas Cooper, eds., *The Statutes at Large of South Carolina*, vol. 7 (Columbia, SC: Johnston, 1840), 352, http://hdl.handle.net.
18 McCord and Cooper, eds., *The Statutes at Large of South Carolina*, 7:354.
19 The ambivalence around slave conversion permeates the Statutes of South Carolina. The 1690 Act for the Better Ordering of Slaves specified that "no slave shall be free by becoming a Christian," thereby addressing a widespread fear at the time. The 1712 act, however, included a clause that suggested that "negroes" or "slaves" could never become "Christian" or "white." The full text forbade "any negro or slave whatsoever" from "offer[ing] any violence to any christian or white person." By juxtaposing "negro and slave" with "christian or white," South Carolina lawmakers reiterated a longstanding assumption among European Protestants that enslavement could be justified only for non-Christians. This assumption was in the process of changing, but its presence in the 1712 act suggests the continued fear of slave conversion among White Protestant slave owners.
20 M. M. Smith, "Remembering Mary, Shaping Revolt," 528.
21 Thornton, "African Dimensions of the Stono Rebellion."
22 The specification of enslaved men was, in part, a response to the perception that the Stono Rebellion was led and dominated by men. But it also reflected a general perception among white authorities that men were more rebellious and bellicose than enslaved women. While many historians have shared this assumption, recent scholarship has shown how enslaved women were core participants not only in acts of "resistance" but also in armed rebellion. See Brown, *Tacky's Revolt*, 151.
23 May, "Holy Rebellion."
24 Wisecup, "Knowing Obeah"; Paton, *The Cultural Politics of Obeah*; Paton, "Obeah Acts."
25 Handler and Bilby, "On the Early Use and Origin of the Term 'Obeah' in Barbados and the Anglophone Caribbean"; Handler and Bilby, *Enacting Power*.
26 "Gemein Nachrichten, Vol. 5," 1755. Unitätsarchiv der Evangelischen Brüder-Unität, Herrnhut, Germany, GN 1755 5 A.44 (I–XL), 743–47. Translation by K. Gerbner.
27 On Caries and his use of obeah, see Gerbner, "'They Call Me Obea.'"
28 Stewart, *Three Eyes for the Journey*, 43.
29 Brown, *Tacky's Revolt*; Bollettino, "Slavery, War, and Britain's Atlantic Empire"; Rugemer, *Slave Law and the Politics of Resistance in the Early Atlantic World*.

30 For a narrative of Tacky's Revolt, see Brown, *Tacky's Revolt*, chaps. 4–5; Rugemer, *Slave Law and the Politics of Resistance in the Early Atlantic World*, chap. 4.
31 While "Tacky's Revolt" is the standard name for the rebellion, it is misleading. "Tacky" refers to one of the rebel leaders in the first stage of the revolt, which occurred in St. Mary's parish in April of 1760. But by using Tacky's name, this designation collapses a much more complex and complicated series of events. Vincent Brown argues that "Tacky's Revolt" was actually just "one episode in a much larger Coromantee war." Brown, *Tacky's Revolt*, 131.
32 Brown, *Tacky's Revolt*.
33 While there were many similarities between the 1740 slave code in South Carolina and the 1760 act in Jamaica, Edward Rugemer has argued that there were important differences as well. Most notably, South Carolina lawmakers sought to "domesticate" slavery by preventing more slave imports while Jamaican Whites aimed to further militarize their slave society by building barracks. Rugemer, *Slave Law and the Politics of Resistance in the Early Atlantic World*, 169.
34 Paton, *The Cultural Politics of Obeah*, 40. The association between Africana religions and "witchcraft" had a long history and can be traced to fifteenth-century Portuguese commentators and the concept of *feitiçaria*. See Pietz, "The Problem of the Fetish, I"; Pietz, "The Problem of the Fetish, II"; S. A. Johnson, *African American Religions, 1500–2000*, chap. 2.
35 An Act to Remedy the Evils arising from Irregular Assemblies of Slaves, Jamaica 1760, in CO 139/21, The National Archives, UK, https://obeahhistories.org.
36 Michael Johnson has argued that Denmark Vesey was not planning a rebellion but was instead a victim of a court that "colluded with a handful of intimidated witnesses to collect testimony about an insurrection that, in fact, was not about to happen." M. P. Johnson, "Denmark Vesey and His Co-Conspirators," 916. Several historians responded to Johnson's argument in a forum in the *William & Mary Quarterly*. Douglas Egerton, the author of a book about Vesey that was the subject of Johnson's critique, argued that Johnson's depiction of Vesey as a "passive 'fall guy'" in the conspiracy is unwarranted, and that Johnson is overly suspicious of even the "simplest data." Egerton, "Forgetting Denmark Vesey," 143–52. See also Paquette, "Jacobins of the Lowcountry," 185–92. Egerton and Paquette reiterated their argument about the reality of the conspiracy in Egerton and Paquette, eds., "Introduction," in *The Denmark Vesey Affair*, xix–xxvi. At this point, most—but not all—historians believe that the conspiracy was real.
37 There is no record of Denmark Vesey's birth. For a discussion of the possibilities, see Egerton and Paquette, eds., "Part 1: Preconditions," in *The Denmark Vesey Affair*, 2 n.3. For a narrative account of Denmark Vesey's early life, see Egerton, *He Shall Go Out Free*, chap. 1.
38 Catron, "Evangelical Networks in the Greater Caribbean and the Origins of the Black Church," 77–114.
39 For documents related to Denmark Vesey's early life, see Egerton and Paquette, "Part 1: Preconditions."

40 John Catron has suggested that Vesey may have attended William Hammet's Primitive Methodist Church before it closed in 1803. Catron, "Evangelical Networks in the Greater Caribbean and the Origins of the Black Church." Vesey joined Second Presbyterian in 1811, soon after it was founded, and Michael Johnson has suggested that he probably attended First Presbyterian before then, since First Presbyterian was the "parent church" for Second Presbyterian. The fact that Vesey was received as a communicant in a Presbyterian church means he was interviewed by church leaders to confirm the "authenticity" of his faith as well as his theological knowledge. See M. P. Johnson, "Telemaque's Pilgrimage?"
41 Gerbner, *Christian Slavery*; Frey and Wood, *Come Shouting to Zion*.
42 Sensbach, *Rebecca's Revival*; Frey and Wood, *Come Shouting to Zion*.
43 Mills, "Allen, Richard (1760–1831)."
44 For the precipitating events for this separation, see Melton, *A Will to Choose*, 158; Egerton, *He Shall Go Out Free*, 110.
45 Five of them, including one bishop and four ministers, were given the choice of a month's imprisonment or departure from South Carolina. Eight others were sentences to either ten lashes or a fine of five dollars. *Southern Patriot, and Commercial Advertiser* (Charleston, SC), June 8, 1818, reprinted in Egerton and Paquette, *The Denmark Vesey Affair*, 26.
46 *Southern Patriot, and Commercial Advertiser* (Charleston, SC), June 10, 1818, reprinted in Egerton and Paquette, *The Denmark Vesey Affair*, 26–27.
47 Petition no. 1893, n.d. [ca. 1820], series S165015, Petitions to the General Assembly, SCDAH, reprinted in Egerton and Paquette, *The Denmark Vesey Affair*, 32–34.
48 Egerton and Paquette, *The Denmark Vesey Affair*, 34 n.1.
49 Petition of the Inhabitants of Charleston, October 16, 1820, Petitions to the General Assembly, no. 143, series S165015, SCDAH, reprinted in Egerton and Paquette, *The Denmark Vesey Affair*, 55–58.
50 "Act for the Better Ordering," clause XLV.
51 Francis Le Jau, one of the earliest and more vociferous proponents of slave conversion, became increasingly wary of black biblical interpretation during his years as a missionary in South Carolina. See Gerbner, *Christian Slavery*, chaps. 6–8.
52 Schipper, "'Misconstruction of the Sacred Page,'" 24.
53 "Examination of Rolla belonging to Thomas Bennett," Senate Transcript, June 25, 1822, reprinted in Douglas R. Egerton and Robert L. Paquette, eds., "Part 3: Trials—The Official Report and the Senate Transcript," in *The Denmark Vesey Affair*, 294–95. See also Schipper, "'Misconstruction of the Sacred Page,'" 27.
54 Schipper, "'Misconstruction of the Sacred Page,'" 28.
55 Schipper, "'Misconstruction of the Sacred Page,'" 35.
56 Schipper, "'On Such Texts Comment Is Unnecessary,'" 1036, 1032–49.
57 Rucker, "Conjure, Magic, and Power."

58 Douglas R. Egerton and Robert L. Paquette, eds., "Part 2: Proceedings," in *The Denmark Vesey Affair*, 110.
59 Gordon, "The African Supplement."
60 Raboteau, *Slave Religion*.
61 Fundamental Constitutions of Carolina, 1669, clause 97, https://avalon.law.yale.edu. See also Wenger, *Religious Freedom*, introduction.

2

Making Religion in Michilimackinac

Settler Secularism and US Empire

TISA WENGER

Mackinac Island, once known as Michilimackinac, sits at the western edge of Lake Huron near the northern tip of Michigan's lower peninsula. The island today is a tourist destination, popular for its beautiful scenery, historic fort, and delicious fudge. Until the mid-nineteenth century, though, it was a strategic point of contact between Indigenous nations and the competing empires of France, Great Britain, and the United States. The Anishinaabe peoples of the region—Odawa (Ottawa), Ojibwe (Chippewa), and Potawatomi—knew Michilimackinac as a place of origins, geographically and cosmologically central to their worlds. As long as waterways served as the major transportation routes across the continent, this island was an essential meeting and trading post for Indigenous peoples, métis traders who claimed both French and Native heritages, and, eventually, white American settlers from the east as well. Nineteenth-century travelers regularly mentioned voyages to and from Michilimackinac and commented on its fur trade, its missions, and the military troops stationed there. Territorial governors worried about its defense. Up through the 1840s, when roads and railways displaced the interior waterways and settler rule really took hold, this island was a pivotal site on the northern borderlands of an expanding US empire.[1]

I have found Michilimackinac a useful vantage point for seeing how imperialism shaped American religion.[2] Throughout the Great Lakes region, the United States built on earlier French and British models of extractive colonialism. These older empires had prioritized the fur trade and did not attempt to significantly change Indigenous ways of life. All three imperial systems employed the Doctrine of Discovery, which asserted a right to sovereignty over "discovered" lands on the basis of

Christianity and a purportedly superior civilization. But the settler-colonial model implemented by the United States required the almost total dispossession of Indigenous peoples. Thomas Jefferson famously called the United States an "empire of liberty," and its new constitution promised liberty and equality to all, including the free exercise of religion. In practice, however, religion in the new United States took shape in service to settler-colonial ends.

In conversation with critical secularism studies, this chapter tracks the religious histories of Michilimackinac to suggest that the cultural and legal norms of settler colonialism structured both American secularism and American religion. Following Talal Asad, scholars have defined secularism not as the absence of religion, or in opposition to it, but rather as the systematic ordering of knowledge and power that *puts religion in its place.* Secularism emerges in this scholarship as a governing mechanism of modern empire building, one of the ways in which Europe and the United States marked themselves off as modern and defined their racialized colonial subjects, in contrast, as primitive and requiring an allegedly benevolent colonial rule.[3] Secularism not only distinguishes between the religious and the not-religious (or secular) but also inserts a third category—call it superstition, "bad belief," or fanaticism—that defines the limits of good religion.[4] While promising freedom for all, US secularism developed in collaboration with Christianity to provide a doubled rationale for white settler rule. Christianity became the paradigmatic good religion because it promised to save and redeem good citizens for an ordered and orderly society. Protestant-Catholic competition helped forge this model for good religion. The racialized category of fanaticism, in contrast, threatened the body politic, the settled hierarchies of the settler society. Those who could not fit secularism's mold for good religion also could not be granted secularism's vaunted freedoms. Labeled as superstitious, deluded, or fanatical—not truly religious at all—such groups required discipline and perhaps even the violent hand of the state to keep them under control. "Settler secularism" is the best name I have found for this assemblage of knowledge and power.

Settler secularism exerted a regulatory force that channeled but could never entirely contain Indigenous and other nonconforming religious traditions. The cultural and legal value granted to religion in the United States created powerful incentives for colonized and minority peoples to define their communal identities as *religious* and to voice their appeals in its name.⁵ As they struggled to hold on to their lands, and settler authorities condemned their traditions as "savage" or "heathen," Anishinaabe peoples around Michilimackinac also claimed the privileged status of religion. Some did so as Christians and others on behalf of Indigenous traditions, such as the Midewiwin, that they had not previously conceptualized in this way. Even though Indigenous traditions never quite fit settler secularism's mold for good religion, these efforts helped the Anishinaabek hold on to a bit of land and maintain their identity as a people. But they were not the only people in northern Michigan to be labeled as fanatical. The dissident Mormon leader James Jesse Strang, who settled in the 1840s with his followers on Beaver Island in Lake Michigan, tried and mostly failed to secure the status of the good (civilized and civilizing) settler religion. With Michilimackinac as our point of departure, then, this chapter tracks the definition and delineation of good religion under settler-secular rule. I make no claims to special significance for this island. Every place has its story, and a similar tale could arguably be spun from any of them. But Michilimackinac helps us see how the category of religion—along with the bewildering variety of traditions it describes—took shape in and through the anxieties and imperatives of empire.

Good Religion under Settler Rule

In the summer of 1820, Governor Lewis Cass of Michigan led a scientific expedition to map the lands and mineral resources of the vast territory he claimed to govern. Henry Rowe Schoolcraft, geologist for the expedition, began his account of six days in Michilimackinac with a history of "interesting events" that had occurred in and around this island. Schoolcraft was very clear about what it lacked. "There appears in the present society of 'Mackinac the want of a preacher, a school-master, an attorney, and a physician," he wrote, "while of merchants there are always too many." It is clear from his account that the fur trade and the ways of life it sustained were flourishing. "Since our arrival here there has been a great number of Indians of the Chippeway and Ottaway tribes, encamped near the town," he wrote. He was surprised to see a bustle of activity: "Vessels have been constantly entering or leaving the harbor, giving the town an appearance of bustle and business, which was not expected." But this hub of culture and commerce was not the sort of "civilization" that he wanted to see. Michilimackinac had not yet been subordinated to the settler-secular systems of science, law, and religion that would authorize and implement US rule.[6]

In the Great Lakes, emerging US ideologies of good religion built on a French model in which Catholicism had been the sole imperial religion. Long before any Europeans arrived, Michilimackinac was a place for trade and diplomacy among the region's Huron and Anishinaabe nations. In the late seventeenth century, the Jesuit Jacques Marquette built a mission nearby on Michigan's Lower Peninsula. Across the *pays d'en haut*, the Canadian back country, an Indigenous and métis world of fur traders and voyageurs coalesced around a scattered network of forts, missions, and trading posts. Outside these settlements, the church held little sway. Imperial authorities had almost no knowledge of the region's wider geography and no authority over its Indigenous people. This was a colonial system organized for trade, not settlement, and the *pays d'en haut* was ruled by what one historian has called "an infinity" of Native nations.[7] Not much changed with the ascendancy of the British in 1763 or, at first, when the United States claimed the region in the 1780s. Throughout these years, the people of Michilimackinac continued to identify "religion" with a distinctly Catholic imperial order. A group of French-speaking voyageurs, assembled on the island in the summer of 1786, petitioned the Bishop of Quebec "to send them a wise director to guide them in the way of salvation . . . [T]he lustre of religion," they explained, "must be preserved in the midst of savage tribes." These voyageurs hoped to reassert the joint hold of the Catholic Church and the British empire. The singular "religion" marked their sense of superiority as imperial subjects over the people they called "savage."[8]

Anishinaabe forces in alliance with the British occupied Michilimackinac in the War of 1812 and held it until the war's end in 1815. When the United States (re)gained control, its agents forged new distinctions between (good) religion, which served the state, and delusion or superstition, which did not. William Puthuff, the first US Indian agent in Michilimackinac, warned Governor Cass in 1816 that British officials were using Indigenous "prophets, juglars, and persons professing to have supernatural powers" to manipulate "that deluded People" for nefarious ends. Assuming the skeptical posture of an enlightened modern, Puthuff derided the credulity of a people susceptible to false "prophets" or "juglars." The figure of the Indian prophet featured heavily in white settler anxieties, racializing Indigenous resistance as a product of heathenism.[9] To Puthuff, Indians were irrational "savages" without the capacity to plan for themselves. Their delusions could too easily be manipulated by an imperial foe. Cass warned that the "Shawnese Prophet," Tenskwatawa, was planning a "great Council" with the British at Malden, Ontario, to revive the resistance that his brother Tecumseh had previously led. White settlers in Michigan were "surrounded by a people in the rudest state of barbarism," the governor concluded, "brave, ferocious, and vindictive, restrained by no moral or legal considerations from the intemperate gratification of their passions." Indians in his view were irrational, prone to delusion and manipulation. They lacked reason, law, and good religion. In other words, they were racially incapable of being pliable secular subjects of the settler state.[10]

Cass and Puthuff were not the only ones determined to transform this Indigenous world. In 1820, Congregationalist clergyman and geographer Jedidiah Morse also visited Michilimackinac. Morse traveled under the auspices of the Northern Missionary Society, later renamed the American Board of Commissioners for Foreign Missions (ABCFM). President James Monroe also commissioned the expedition to ascertain "for the use of the government, the actual state of the Indian tribes in our country." Morse called on the United States and Canada to bury their differences in order to "raise the long neglected native tribes, whom the Providence of God has placed under our care . . . from their present state of ignorance and wretchedness" to "all the blessings of civilization and of our holy religion." He construed religion—by which he meant Protestant Christianity—as a gift from God, delivered by a benevolent nation to those it conquered. Neglecting the region's long history of Catholic missions, he praised the newly appointed US Indian agent, George Boyd, and other local Protestants who had pledged funds to support "a minister and schoolmaster" for the island. "Probably there is no situation of more importance to the government of the United States, in promoting the civilization of the Indians, than Mackinaw," he wrote.[11] Both Catholics and Protestants would shape their rhetoric and their institutions to attract converts and curry favor from the US government. The new contours of religion in territorial Michigan—Protestant, Catholic, and Indigenous—developed within this settler-colonial frame.

Catholic leaders hastened to rebuild their church within the new order. Michilimackinac had had no resident priest since 1769. There were devout Catholics, to be sure, such as the Odawa laywoman Magdeleine LaFramboise, who ran a thriving fur trading business and taught the catechism to children on the side.[12] But Detroit's Father Gabriel Richard worried that the island's church was falling into disrepute and disrepair. "I have been informed lately that the summer before last, a dead dog was found on the altar where it had been put in mockery by a young Protestant named Maxwell," he wrote in 1803, "and that the priest's house which is joined to the church was a public brothel." In his eyes, Protestants, dissemblers, atheists, and outlaws all threatened the good order that only Catholicism could provide.[13] Over the next few decades, the indefatigable Richard brought the first printing press to Michigan, worked with Catholic laywomen to build a system of schools in and around Detroit, and became a trustee for the new University of Michigan. Richard was also elected in 1823 as territorial delegate to Congress, where he proposed legislation to fund the first road from Detroit to Chicago. Through such dedicated efforts, the Catholic Church repositioned itself as a good religion for settler-colonial rule.[14]

Protestants soon followed. At Morse's recommendation, the ABCFM sent William and Amanda Ferry in 1823 to establish the first long-term Protestant mission on the island. The Ferrys built Mackinaw Mission School with help from the Civilization Fund, appropriated by Congress to educate Indigenous children. Unlike most white settlers, the missionaries believed that Indians were precious in God's eyes and capable of being civilized. Yet their benevolence also solidified racial distinctions. "Can these dry bones live?" asked Jedidiah Stevens, who taught at Mackinac in the late 1820s. "Can these polluted, degraded, ignorant beings ever be civilized—washed, sanctified, made heirs of God, citizens of heaven?"[15] Despite the promise of spiritual equality under Christ, "heathen" and its cognates—"pagan," "savage," and "primitive," words with distinct but intersecting genealogies—were treated as racial characteristics that Indians could never quite escape. If true religion was a gift, Native people, racialized as superstitious heathens, were perpetually identified as inferiors to whom it must be given.[16]

The vehemence of William Ferry's preaching against "priestcraft" helped form a small Protestant community in Michilimackinac. Few of the new church members and "hopeful conversions" who attended Ferry's services, however, belonged to the region's long-established Indigenous and métis communities. Instead, they were mostly new arrivals, identified by visiting Baptist missionary Abel Bingham as "the principal men in the village," such as Robert Stuart, agent for John Jacob Astor's American Fur Company, and soldiers from the garrison.[17] Where priests like Richard could draw longtime residents back to the Catholic fold, Protestant missions attracted newer settlers, lapsed or nominal Protestants recently arrived from the east. Missionary attacks on Catholicism and appeals "to unite and possess the land," as the *American Home Missionary Society* put it, resonated with settlers and soldiers who could not understand why local people did not receive them with open arms. Such rhetoric gave them a sense of benevolent purpose and a national destiny that God himself had ordained.[18]

An 1831 debate between Ferry and a new priest in Michilimackinac exacerbated these confessional divides. Samuel Mazzuchelli, a Dominican recruited in Rome, had spent a year studying English in Cincinnati before Bishop Edward Fenwick sent him to Michilimackinac. There he boasted of easy victories over "the Calvinist." He complained to the bishop that Ferry "did not doubt to tell his congregants that Catholics do not scruple to get drunk, to break the Sabbath day, to swear &c." But Mazzuchelli conceded a grain of truth in these attacks. Some Canadians "had almost forgotten our holy religion" and were "living a bad life," he wrote, and he would likely need "to excommunicate one or two" so as to return the rest to the fold. Ferry had hit a nerve. Mazzuchelli wanted to prove that the island's métis Catholics were a civilized people who already belonged to "our holy religion." Multiplied across the United States, such competitions placed Catholics and Protestants in oppositional roles as competing settler options for the status of good religion.[19]

Meanwhile, new missionary initiatives were shifting towards the incoming settler tide. Foreign mission societies began moving their scant resources west with Indian removals and overseas to places that both donors and prospective missionaries found more exotic. Mackinaw Mission School closed soon after Michigan gained statehood in 1837; a colleague later reported that Ferry had moved into "the pursuits of secular business making money."²⁰ An ABCFM executive lamented that it was difficult to replace him, because "foreign fields" were "more attractive to candidates for the missionary work, than the small, scattered, emigrating bands of our Indians."²¹ Home missions, designed not for Indians but for "our own people" on the "frontiers," now occupied the field. This shift symbolically incorporated places once considered "foreign" into the domestic terrain of the United States.²² Writing to a long-time minister in the region, an ABCFM correspondent marveled, "The ministers of Michigan are now forming the character of many generations.... Look back to the period when you first entered the territory—what rapid and astonishing changes!" Left unsaid was the fact that these transformations—the new settlers, towns, and churches—all relied on the expulsion of Indigenous people. Indians were spectral figures in such reports, haunting the successes of "religion" in domesticating the land.²³

Protestants and Catholics had settled into a routine of rivalry for settler and Indigenous souls. However heated their disputes, these competing Christianities appeared to most white settlers as the only thinkable options. Even Schoolcraft, a dedicated Presbyterian, wrote that the only hope for the "Aboriginal race" lay in the various "school and mission efforts" that might be able to "civilize" them. As acting superintendent of Indian affairs for Michigan, he reported in 1840 that Indians were only just coming "under the exclusive operation of state laws" after recently losing most of their lands. He went on to review the missions in Michigan—Presbyterian, Methodist, Baptist, Episcopalian, and Catholic—and offered measured praise to all. He posited a logical progression from Christian missions to the material habits of "civilization" and "liberty" under the law. Two decades after he had lamented the absence of science, law, and religion from Michilimackinac, he now affirmed their definitive arrival.²⁴

Conceptualizing Anishinaabe Religion

Settler secularism operated to define and discipline—but never entirely to contain—Indigenous religion. Writing in 1887, Odawa historian Andrew Blackbird described how the "Catholic Religion was Introduced Among the Ottawas." The people of L'Arbre Croche had first become Catholics, he explained, not at the priests' initiative but through the efforts of an Odawa man, Andowish, who returned home in 1824 from years in Montreal to teach his people "the faith of the Catholic religion." At the recommendation of their "half-breed relatives" in Michilimackinac, the Reverend Stephen Badin soon paid them a visit. But it was Blackbird's uncle, Assiginac, who had once led Odawa fighters in the War of 1812 before moving to Drummond Island in Ontario, who regularly visited L'Arbre Croche "to act as missionary in the absence of the priest." The crucial point was that the people had chosen Catholicism for themselves. "This was the very way that the first religion was introduced among the Ottawas," Blackbird wrote, "although everybody supposes that some white people or missionary societies brought the Christian religion" to them. His repetition of the word "religion" suggests that, for Blackbird, this concept identified the Odawas as civilized—or even as human—in a way that settler power brokers might actually respect.[25]

Around the same time, some Ojibwe people began to join in Protestant revivals. Travelers to Sault Ste. Marie and Michilimackinac heard missionaries reading from biblical texts newly translated into Ojibwe.[26] Indigenous evangelists, however, were far more compelling. Abel Bingham's first interpreter at Sault Ste. Marie was an Irish-Ojibwe woman named Charlotte Johnston (Ogenebugoquay), who "followed my discourse with an address of her own," he reported, and composed Ojibwe-language hymns that the congregation sang with gusto. Charlotte and her successors were not just interpreters but evangelists shaping Ojibwe Christianity on their own terms.[27] The most successful Ojibwe evangelist, though, was Shawundais, or John Sunday, a Methodist from southern Ontario. The Ojibwe worshiped an "idol God," Shawundais wrote, but some of them were coming to hear his preaching and "got 'ligion." In his lexicon, "religion" meant Christianity, and it offered a new kind of spiritual power along with a degree of respect from the settler society that was so rapidly swallowing up Indigenous lands. "Pray for us here," he concluded, "may the Lord help the poor Indians here."[28] This Indigenous Methodism linked revivalist Christianity with the pan-Indian tones sounded by Tenskwatawa a generation earlier. Shawundais brought a similarly unifying message of empowerment. Evangelicalism became such a revitalizing force in these years that some have called it an "Ojibwe Renaissance." A new Indigenous religion was forming out of the traumas of dispossession. While claiming the power of settler

Christianity, Anishinaabe evangelists transcended settler-secular prescriptions for what good religion should be.²⁹

Christianity became a valuable tool for Anishinaabe people struggling to hold on to their land and sovereignty. In July 1829, the headmen of L'Arbre Croche opened a petition to US Indian agent George Boyd in Michilimackinac with gratitude for their new priest, Pierre Dejean, who planned to bring some "good women . . . to teach our children to read the word of the Great Spirit." Then they moved to the heart of their petition: "Father—The Chief men . . . have come to a determination to sell no lands whatever to the U. States. Father—Some of our red people are foolish and wish to part with their land, but we will not sell ours." By naming themselves as Catholics, these Odawas laid claim to the status of civilized people, fit to govern themselves and their own land. This message, however, did not translate well across the settler-colonial chain of command. Bishop Fenwick attached it to his own request to the secretary of war for a greater share of the Civilization Fund. He did not even mention land but highlighted the Odawa request for a Catholic school, positioning Catholicism as a good religion in the interests of US rule.³⁰

No amount of Christian commitment could prevent the loss of Anishinaabe lands, but the presence of Christian missions did help some Anishinaabe communities avoid removal. In the early 1830s, L'Arbre Croche sent two promising young men to study for the priesthood in Rome. Augustin Hamlin Jr. and William Macketebenessy were cousins who had learned English at the Mackinaw Mission School and then studied under a Catholic priest in Cincinnati. They arrived at the Urban College with high expectations, but within a year Macketebenessy became ill and tragically died.³¹ Hamlin returned home and never completed his studies for the priesthood. The next year he joined a delegation to Washington hoping to make "some arrangements with government" that would allow the Odawa to maintain "the quiet possession of our lands." Hoping once again to prove themselves "civilized," the delegation asked Congress to increase the Civilization Fund and entrust it to Bishop Frederick Résé of Detroit for their children.³² In the end, though, the assembled Anishinaabe negotiators had little choice but to sign a treaty ceding almost half of Michigan. As they negotiated it, the 1836 Treaty of Washington would have secured "large, permanent reservations," the right to "hunt, fish, and gather on the land," and funding for schools, missions, and other amenities. But in a sadly typical land grab, the US Senate rewrote the treaty to make the reservations temporary, available for sale to white settlers after only five years.[33] Hamlin then continued to use his education to fight removal. In 1839 he petitioned the governor to recognize the Odawa "as citizens" so that they could "buy this very place the Little Traverse Bay where we are at present, and where our missionary priest is stationed." This "once powerful nation" had become "strangers in their own land," he lamented, while the white men had taken "the heritage of their fathers." Now "ameliorated by the influences of Christianity," he wrote, the Odawa people sought only "the rights and privileges of American citizenship." Hamlin's papers at the Detroit Public Library include a well-worn notebook, its first entry dated 1835, with prayers and reflections in Latin, French, and Odawa. Catholicism provided him with spiritual sustenance and helped nurture Odawa tradition. It also facilitated Odawa claims to the status of a "civilized" people, worthy under settler law to buy back their own ancestral lands.[34]

Protestant affiliations had the same potential. Presbyterian missionary Peter Dougherty arrived in Michilimackinac in 1838 and decided to locate his mission at Grand Traverse Bay, south of L'Arbre Croche. It was a critical time, just two years after the Treaty of Washington. Ojibwe headman Ahgosa invited Dougherty to start a new school; two more bands moved nearby so that their children could attend. The trappings of settler governance soon followed. Schoolcraft organized an agency office and sent a surveyor to map out a reservation under the terms of the 1836 treaty. With the agent's support, this small reservation was exempted from the initial sale of treaty lands. But the Ojibwe knew all too well that they could not rely on official benevolence. Rumors circulated that their land would soon be placed on the market and, with the reservation set to expire, Ojibwe headmen organized to purchase tracts of land. Ahgosa managed to buy several forty-acre plots off the reservation for his band; Dougherty then moved his mission to join them. The Anishinaabek of L'Arbre Croche, Grand Traverse, and elsewhere in the state continued to petition for citizenship and a guarantee that they would not be forcibly removed to the west; some fled to Canada to avoid that fate. A new treaty in 1855 eliminated ongoing annuity payments, defined new reservations to be allotted in severalty (divided up into individual landholdings), and promised schools and technical aid from the government. But with the collusion of local land offices, non-Indian squatters and speculators began to claim preemption rights even where Anishinaabek held clear title. Nevertheless, these Anishinaabe bands had leveraged their affiliations with Catholic and Protestant missions to resist the pressure for removal and, however precariously, to remain.[35]

The Midewiwin, the "Grand Medicine Society" of the Ojibwe, also changed within this settler-colonial frame. The Midē were highly trained practitioners who enlisted the aid of other-than-human powers, the *manido*, to heal both individual and collective ills. By describing themselves as a medicine society rather than a religion, they had long avoided placing themselves in direct competition with imperial Catholicism. Still, the Midewiwin had early on incorporated some Catholic influences. The Midē used scrolls as sacred objects, much as priests used the Bible, and developed a hierarchy that resembled the Catholic system of priests and bishops.[36] The Protestant missionaries who arrived in the 1820s predictably denigrated all of this as superstitious "mummery," a mix of devil worship and priestly deception, not religion. In a report to his mission board in 1825, William Ferry described the baptism of a girl named Me-sai-ainse, who "was to have been received as a full priestess or conjuress—had gone thro' all the previous mummery & was on the ten days singing and finishing scene." But Me-sai-ainse had a different view. She told Ferry that she wanted to share her story so that "all those who are deeply interested in the welfare of the poor Indian" would send funds for their support. Me-sai-ainse, who had followed an uncle's dream to leave her Midē training and attend the Mackinaw Mission School, saw continuity with rather than a sharp break from her prior commitments. Perhaps the love of God could help her fulfill her uncle's dreams by turning her into a new kind of healer for her people through Christianity, rather than the Midewiwin.[37]

Against the backdrop of Protestant and Catholic missions, some Anishinaabe began to speak of the Midewiwin as a distinct religion and pushed the missionaries to do the same. Abel Bingham described an "Indian woman" who, with her husband and her brother, had "renounced her meta religion" to follow Shawundais into the Methodist Church. "Probably there are few tribes of Indians in our country who are so ready to listen to religious instruction as the Ojibways," Bingham opined, "or are so easily convinced of the folly of their superstitions." But then he described a conversation with the woman's father, "a great mata [Midē] (or medicine) man," who ably described "the principles" of the society. The Midē responded to Bingham's challenges with his own comparative reflections. "He believed theirs must be the devil's religion," the missionary claimed, "for all their young men carried poison with them to kill each other . . . but he saw nothing in this religion [Christianity] that was calculated to injure any person." We need to read Bingham's account with caution. He had a vested interest in exaggerating Ojibwe praise for Christianity. It is possible that the Midē considered the Midewiwin partly responsible for the overwhelming problems facing his people, or worried that its powers could not solve them. But he also spoke with characteristic Ojibwe politeness and no doubt did not tell the missionary what he really thought of Christianity. In the end, far from rejecting the Midewiwin, he convinced Bingham to grant it a modicum of respect as "the religion of the heathen Indians." The story offers an intriguing glimpse of an Ojibwe Midē and a Baptist missionary thinking together about the relative merits of their traditions. Their dialogue suggests that missionary engagement with Indigenous practitioners helped shape a comparative category of religion that could be expanded—at least in theory—to include Indigenous traditions.[38]

For some Ojibwe people, conceptualizing the Midewiwin as religion provided an Indigenous alternative to either Catholic or Protestant Christianity. One woman at Tikuamina refused to attend Bingham's services in the mid-1840s because, she told him, "several of her relatives had professed Christianity and died soon after, from which she inferred that it was a sin in them to forsake the religion of their ancestors and embrace Christianity." She positioned the "religion of [her] ancestors" as the correct choice for her people.[39] As Christopher Vecsey has explained, the Midewiwin in this period became a "tribal religion" that provided the Ojibwe with "national pride." Identifying the Midewiwin as *religion* thus facilitated the development of Ojibwe nationalism under settler-colonial rule.[40] Whatever settler authorities might say, then, the Anishinaabek found sustenance in a variety of traditions. They made their own decisions about which movements—Protestant or Catholic, Indigenous or missionary-led—would best meet their needs. Those who embraced Christianity leveraged this affiliation to foster their own survival as Indigenous peoples. The history of Anishinaabe religious traditions, Christianity included, cannot be separated from the settler-colonial systems that structured the conditions of their practice.

Disciplining the Saints

After Michigan gained statehood, US authorities began to shift from the territorial project of Indigenous dispossession towards the new disciplinary problems of a settled society. It turned out that Protestants and Catholics were not the only people around Michilimackinac to claim the status of good religion, and that Indigenous traditions were not alone in being named fanatical or degraded. In the early 1840s, alarm bells rang in nearby Illinois over the Latter-day Saints, or Mormons, who were gathering in their city-state of Nauvoo along the Mississippi. These Saints believed in an all-encompassing gospel that refused the disciplinary imperatives of the settler-secular state. Their prophet, Joseph Smith Jr., had called the faithful to "make [themselves] gods" and taught them to expect the miraculous.[41] Thousands had moved to Nauvoo after fleeing mob violence in Missouri, where the state governor had famously called for their "extermination."[42] As the Saints' drama unfolded, a dissident group of Mormons took refuge on Beaver Island, not far from Michilimackinac, and soon sparked a similar controversy there.

Mormon leaders tried in self-defense to identify themselves with settler-colonial ideals of patriotism and good religion. "Must we, because we believe in enjoying the constitutional privilege and right of worshipping Almighty God according to the dictates of our own consciences, be expelled from the institutions of our country; the rights of citizenship, and the graves of our friends and brethren?" Smith asked. "If so, fare well freedom, adieu to personal safety,—and let the red hot wrath of an offended God purify the nation of such sinks of corruption!"[43] Smith shifted here between the registers of settler secularism and radical prophecy, calling down the wrath of God on a nation that in its treatment of the Mormons was betraying its own ideals. To other white settlers, though, Mormons were simply fanatics. Many in Hancock County feared the rise of a city-state with its own militia. Rumors circulated that the Mormons "were sworn to obey [Smith] as God" and that the prophet exercised "an intolerable tyranny . . . which he was about to extend over the neighboring country."[44] In June 1844, the governor of Illinois ordered the arrest of Joseph Smith and others under charges of destroying an independent newspaper in Nauvoo. A mob swarmed the jail, killing Joseph and his brother Hyrum Smith. Tensions rose as the Saints grieved and a militia assembled outside Nauvoo. The determinedly anti-Mormon *Warsaw Signal* opined that whatever Mormons might say, the term "religion" did not apply to lies and "sacerdotal tyranny." Mormons simply could not be permitted to claim the protections of religion.[45]

By this time, a contingent of Mormons had settled in Voree, Wisconsin, just west of Lake Michigan. James Jesse Strang had moved from New York in the 1830s, worked as a surveyor after an Indian treaty in Wisconsin, and joined Smith's circle of confidants for a time in Nauvoo. Now in Voree, he produced a letter, purportedly from Smith, anointing Strang as his successor, "the shepherd and stone of Israel."[46] While most Mormons prepared to follow Brigham Young west in 1846, Strang called them to come instead to the "Stake of Voree." Enough Saints found his claims compelling, including several members of Smith's own family, that Young called him out as a "wicked liar" and sent deputies to refute them. Strang established a new hierarchy for the church in Voree, called for tithes to build a new temple, and created the Order of the Illuminati "for the defense of the Christian religion." Those who followed his commandments would "become perfect as God our father is perfect," Strang proclaimed. Like Smith, Strang refused to see religion as properly distinct from political authority. For true believers, this was an ecstatically embodied and all-consuming religion that upended settler-secular constructs of what religion should do and be.[47]

It was also a settler-colonial religion, built on the expulsion of Indigenous people. Mormons understood Native Americans to be the descendants of the Lamanites, who had destroyed the righteous Nephites in the Book of Mormon and now must be redeemed. These Saints were not the only white settlers to identify Indians with the Lost Tribes of Israel, but they went the furthest in placing them at the heart of salvation history. At the same time, they actively displaced the people they called Lamanites. Warning of persecution in Wisconsin, Strang urged his followers to "gather" to the Beaver Islands, where "thousands of acres of better land" were "waiting to be possessed 'without money and without price.'"[48] Strang called on Congress to designate "all the uninhabited . . . islands" in Lake Michigan for the Mormons, but he knew very well that these islands were not "uninhabited." Later characterizing the local Ojibwe Indians as prone to "barbarism," he claimed that the traders had turned them against him. But the Ojibwe did not need outsiders to tell them that Mormons posed a threat. The US government policies that made Indigenous lands so readily available for white settlement had already facilitated Mormon migrations to Missouri, Illinois, Wisconsin, and Utah. Now Strang seized Beaver Island as the heart of his own kingdom.[49]

As the county seat, Michilimackinac served as a regional center for the adjudication of good religion, and, for most authorities, Mormonism did not qualify. Strang's legal troubles began in December 1850, when a county sheriff sailed from Michilimackinac to investigate complaints from non-Mormon settlers on Beaver.[50] As in Missouri and Illinois, even though Strang had multiple wives and scandals erupted over sexual indiscretions in the community, the public controversy did not focus on polygamy. Instead, it centered around the prophet's imperious behavior. Strang demanded that all residents pay a tithe to support the church, and his deputies seized fishing boats and other property from those who refused. James Archer, once a devout Saint, broke with Strang and filed a lawsuit demanding that all the property he had donated be returned.[51] Then two church leaders were charged with killing James Bennett, an outspoken local critic. Their grand jury indictment demonstrates how settler rhetorics of good religion drove anti-Mormon sentiment. "Not having the fear of God before their eyes, but being moved and seduced by the instigation of the Devil," the grand jury concluded, these Mormons had shot Bennett "feloniously, willfully, and with malice aforethought." When they fled, Strang and several others were indicted for helping them evade arrest. But authorities hesitated and the case dragged on for five years.[52]

Strang positioned himself as a settler patriarch with full authority to govern Beaver Island. The Mormons soon had enough votes to swing local elections and gained considerable influence in the county and state governments. Despite the ongoing threat of prosecution, Strang served as township supervisor and in the state legislature from 1851 to 1855. He was a capable politician and found friends in Detroit who were willing to intervene on his behalf. A fellow legislator proposed in 1853 that he be named governor of Utah. Strang had "acquired a reputation," this colleague wrote, "of which almost any member of our present Legislative body might well be proud." No doubt Strang relished the thought of displacing Brigham Young to gain authority over the large body of Latter-day Saints. But President Franklin Pierce preferred to work with the existing leadership in Utah and renewed Young's gubernatorial appointment. For the time being, despite their unorthodoxies and their claims to prophetic authority, both Strang and Young found ways to work within the structures of settler governance. These were not options available to the Anishinaabek, even those with a formal education in English and Latin like Hamlin.[53]

Strang also envisioned himself as a settler scientist, working to collect and systematize knowledge in the interests of scientific progress and settler (Mormon) control. He kept meticulous journals on Beaver Island's weather patterns, barometric pressure, and the many species of fish in the waters of Lake Michigan. His book *Ancient and Modern Michilimackinac* (1854) deployed the field of natural history against his most intractable enemies. He spun a tale of progress and decline, featuring heroic Jesuits who had "civilized" local Indians and built a virtuous empire, only to see it fall first to the Ojibwe and then to misguided and ineffective agents of the United States. The "half breeds" who made up most of the island's current population were "dissipated" drunkards, he wrote, and "rapidly disappearing." The men of modern Michilimackinac, "clothed with iniquity as with a garment," had "built up and dwelt in a Colossus of wickedness, at the vastness of which human nature stands aghast." In contrast, Strang described his own Mormons as upstanding citizens, persecuted by those who resented interference in the whiskey trade. They, not the degraded denizens of Michilimackinac, stood for science, religion, and settler civilization.[54]

Even the king of Beaver Island, however, could not hold off his troubles forever. More petitions complaining of Mormon "depradations" kept arriving in Michilimackinac and Detroit. Disillusioned former Saints testified that Strang had ordered them to steal and plunder. Eventually the governor appealed for help to the US attorney general, who instructed his deputy in Michilimackinac to charge Strang with the federal offenses of obstructing mail, cutting timber on public lands, and counterfeiting US currency. Forty marines sailed to arrest him and several of his deputies. Officials took depositions from 120 witnesses, most of them Mormons speaking in Strang's defense. But in early July 1856, as an officer escorted the prophet to the *U.S.S. Michigan*, two ex-Mormons took aim and fired on their former leader. He died several days later in Voree.[55] When opponents torched the temple on Beaver Island, Strang's remaining followers retreated to Wisconsin. Sixteen years later, Wingfield Watson, still faithful, worried that their children were being "swallowed up by the ungodly around them" and falling "into the hands of the devil." Watson found his only hope in "a revelation given to James in '46," which, he believed, showed "that the Saints are to remain among their enemies till the wrath of God is poured out upon all nations without measure and then all that have been scattered shall be gathered."[56] Like the disappointed members of so many other apocalyptic movements, Watson shifted the realm of the miraculous safely into the past and the future. The Saints of the tamed present could reconfigure their practice to fit the mold for good religion. But without the prophetic fervor of the first generation—or the dynamic leadership that Brigham Young and his successors offered in Utah—the Strangites were already fading into obscurity.

With its Mormon drama concluded, Mackinac settled into a comfortable routine. Although the fort remained until 1895, the island's fortunes declined with the fur trade and the rise of the railroads. After the Civil War, a new US Indian agent on the island, Richard Smith, reflected with a brazen confidence in the justice of white supremacy and Indigenous dispossession, "Treaty after treaty has been made . . . to extinguish what was conceded to [the Indians], their rights of occupancy," he wrote, "until the possession of nearly all of its territory has passed from the inferior to the superior race." Fending off any qualms of conscience, he asserted that all this was "exactly right and as it should be." The will of God and the Doctrine of Discovery provided the ultimate rationale. "It cannot be that Almighty God ever intended that this great country, with its diversified soil and climate and other sources of subsistence and comfort, should be and always remain the mere hunting ground for savages," he claimed. "Nor is it presumption in us to say, that the present indications of his providence, in the rapid progress of civil, social, and religious liberty, not only in our own country but also in other parts of the world, all go to confirm this view of the subject." Smith grounded his exceptionalist view of American freedoms in the settler religion of Christianity. Divine providence had enabled the US conquest, producing American empire and American freedoms. Settler secularism thus framed Christianity as good religion for white-supremacist rule.[57]

Twentieth-century Mackinac and its churches remained as pillars of this system. By the turn of the century, Mackinac was a summertime destination for wealthy denizens of Chicago and Detroit. Most of the island became a state park, a public memorial to settler rule. Christianity enjoyed a taken-for-granted starring role. Commemorating the early French Jesuits, especially, became a way for white Americans to position themselves as heirs to these benevolent pioneers.[58] In 1909, US Supreme Court justice William Day visited Mackinac to help dedicate a statue of the Jesuit Jacques Marquette, located prominently at the harbor in front of the fort. "Hand in hand with the warriors and governors went the faithful servants of the Church," Day proclaimed, "sharing the privations of the forest, and everywhere planting the altar beside the banner of the Sovereign." The Jesuits evoked a grander age. "Thousands who come from 'towered cities and the busy marts of trade,'" the justice wrote, "shall learn as they look upon this statue new lessons of duty, of self-reliance, and that faith in high ideals" that Marquette embodied. Other memorialists renovated the Old Mission Church, built by Ferry in 1829, opening it to clergymen from any (Protestant) denomination. "The motive in this movement," a trustee explained, "has been to preserve the old sanctuary as an historic relic and memorial of early Christian work, and to hold it as a summer chapel for religious services when visiting strangers crowd the Island."[59] These feats of ecumenical memorialization heightened the prominence of Christianity in Mackinac's built environment.[60] They celebrated a very particular version of the island's past, featuring heroic white Christian settlers who had tamed the wilderness and bestowed the gift of Christianity on its Indigenous inhabitants. In short, they embodied and inscribed the good religion of settler-secular rule.

NOTES

1 McDonnell, *Masters of Empire*, 21–23.
2 On Michilimackinac as a site that reorients our histories of eighteenth-century North America, see McDonnell, "Recentering Michilimackinac," chapter 1 in *Masters of Empire*.
3 Asad, *Formations of the Secular*; Mandair, *Religion and the Specter of the West*; Kahn and Lloyd, eds., *Race and Secularism in America*.

4. Josephson-Storm, "The Superstition, Secularism, and Religion Trinary"; Coviello, *Make Yourselves Gods*.
5. Wenger, *Religious Freedom*.
6. Henry Rowe Schoolcraft, *Narrative Journal of Travels through the Northwestern Regions of the United States* (Albany, NY: E. & E. Hosford, 1821), 110–24.
7. Witgen, *An Infinity of Nations*.
8. Paré, *The Catholic Church in Detroit*, 204–5, 234–35.
9. Puthuff to Cass, May 14, 1816, Lewis Cass Papers, Burton Historical Collection, Detroit Public Library (hereafter DPL); Graber, "Beyond Prophecy."
10. Cass to Calhoun, May 27, 1819; Cass to Calhoun, November 21, 1819; both in Cass Papers, DPL. On Tecumseh and Tenskwatawa, see Calloway, *The Shawnees and the War for America*.
11. Jedidiah Morse, *A Report to the Secretary of War of the United States, on Indian Affairs, Comprising a Narrative of a Tour Performed in the Summer of 1820* (New-Haven, CT: Printed by S. Converse, 1822), 2; Morse to Boyd, July 26, 1821, George Boyd Papers, DPL.
12. Sleeper-Smith, "'[A]n Unpleasant Transaction on This Frontier.'"
13. Richard to Carroll, July 28, 1803, Gabriel Richard Papers, 1792–1832, Bentley Historical Library (hereafter BHL), University of Michigan, Ann Arbor.
14. Gabriel Richard, "My Journal in the House of Representatives," 1824–1825, Richard Papers, BHL; US Congress, "Proceedings in Congress in Relation to the Territory of Michigan," May 4, 1824, Early Church Records and Gabriel Richard Collection, 1735–1834, box 2, f.29, Archdiocese of Detroit Archives (hereafter ADA), St. Mary's Seminary, Detroit.
15. Jedidiah Dwight Stevens Diary, 1841, DPL.
16. Gin Lum, "The Historyless Heathen and the Stagnating Pagan"; Goetz, *The Baptism of Early Virginia*.
17. Abel Bingham to Lucius Bolles, March 16, 1829, Church History Documents Collection (hereafter CHDC), box 1, folder 2, Special Collections Research Center, University of Chicago Regenstein Library; Widder, *Battle for the Soul*, 74–89.
18. American Home Missionary Society, *First Annual Report* (New York: The Society, 1827), 54–55.
19. Mazzuchelli to Fenwick, March 13, 1831, Archdiocese of Cincinnati Collection, II-4-d, University of Notre Dame Archives Hesburgh Library, Notre Dame, Indiana (hereafter UNDA); Alderson and Alderson, *The Man Mazzuchelli, Pioneer Priest*.
20. Peter Dougherty, Excerpts from Diary, 1838, Henry Rowe Schoolcraft Papers, BHL.
21. Green to Schoolcraft, September 2, 1834, Henry Rowe Schoolcraft Papers, Reel 6, Library of Congress, Washington, DC (hereafter LOC).
22. M. J. Smith, "Settler Colonialism and U.S. Home Missions."
23. Hale to Ruggles, December 11, 1834, CHDC, box 3, f.2.
24. Henry R. Schoolcraft, *Annual Report of the Acting Superintendent of Indian Affairs for Michigan* (Detroit: Asahel S. Bagg, 1840), 3–6, 16.

25 Andrew J. Blackbird, *History of the Ottawa and Chippewa Indians of Michigan* (Ypsilanti, MI: Ypsilanti Job Printing House, 1887); McClurken, *Gah-Baeh-Jhagwah-Buk*, 5–6.
26 Bingham to Bolles, August 3, 1831, CHDC, box 1, f.2.
27 Baptist Board of Foreign Missions, "Indian Stations," *American Baptist Missionary Magazine* 9, no. 1 (January 1829): 32; Bingham to Bolles, October 20, 1828, CHDC, box 1, f.2. On the Johnston family, see Brazer, *Harps upon the Willows*. On hymn singing as a way to maintain Ojibwe tradition, see McNally, *Ojibwe Singers*.
28 Sunday to Schoolcraft, February 14, 1833, Schoolcraft Papers, Reel 6, LOC.
29 Stoehr, "Nativism's Bastard," 175–90; Penner, "The Ojibwe Renaissance."
30 Seagini (Rash Man) and other Ottawa Chiefs to Boyd, June 14, 1829, Archdiocese of Detroit Collection, III-2-g, UNDA; Fenwick to Cass, November 30, 1831, Bishop Frederick Résé Collection, box 1, f.9, ADA.
31 McClurken, *Gah-Baeh-Jhagwah-Buk*, 33.
32 Hamelin to Cass, December 5, 1835, Résé Collection, box 1, f.10, ADA.
33 Fletcher, *The Eagle Returns*, 17–28.
34 Hamelin and Mis-kwa-wak, "To the Honorable the Legislature of the State of Michigan," December 4, 1843, Augustin Hamelin Jr. Papers, DPL; "Ex Libris Augustin Hamelin," 1835–n.d., Hamelin Papers, DPL; McClurken, *Gah-Baeh-Jhagwah-Buk*, 76–77.
35 Tanner, "Mapping the Grand Traverse Indian Country," 44–91; Fletcher, *The Eagle Returns*, 28–51.
36 Vecsey, *Traditional Ojibwa Religion*, 174–90; Angel, *Preserving the Sacred*.
37 Widder, *Battle for the Soul*, 17, 158–64; Rubin, *Perishing Heathens*.
38 Bingham to Bolles, December 19, 1831, CHDC, box 1, f.2; Bingham to Bolles, January 25, 1835, CHDC, box 1, f.3.
39 Abel Bingham, Journal, July 1843–January 1844, CHDC, box 1, f.6.
40 Vecsey, *Traditional Ojibwa Religion*, 184.
41 Coviello, *Make Yourselves Gods*.
42 Kinney, *The Mormon War*.
43 Smith, Wells, Spencer, et al., "Memorial of Inhabitants of Nauvoo in Illinois," November 28, 1843, National Archives Material on the Persecutions of the Church in Missouri, f.6, L. Tom Perry Special Collections, Harold Lee Library, Brigham Young University, Provo, Utah (hereafter BYU).
44 "Message of the Governor of the State of Illinois," *Warsaw Signal* (Illinois), January 8, 1845, David J. Whitaker Collection of non-Mormon Nauvoo and Illinois Area Newspapers, BYU.
45 "California—The Mormons," *Warsaw Signal*, November 19, 1845, Whitaker Collection, BYU; "The Anti-Mormon Convention," *Alton Telegraph and Democratic Review*, October 11, 1845, Whitaker Collection, BYU; Park, *Kingdom of Nauvoo*.
46 Smith to Strang, June 18, 1844, James Jesse Strang Collection, box 1, f.4, Beinecke Rare Books and Manuscripts Library, Yale University, New Haven, Connecticut (hereafter Strang Collection). Strang's work as a surveyor is mentioned in

M. A. Strang and David Strang to James J. Strang, July 27, 1845, Strang Collection, box 2, f.125.

47 Brigham Young, "To the Branches of the Church in the Neighborhood of Ottawa, Illinois," January 24, 1846, Strang Collection, box 1, f.11; William Smith to Strang, March 17, 1846, Strang Collection, box 1, f.13.

48 Strang, "An Epistle from Brother James," August 18, 1847, printed in *Zion's Reveille*, August 26, 1847, Church of Jesus Christ Records, f.2, BYU.

49 Strang, "A Testimony to the Nation: Buffalo, New York," 1850, Strang Collection; Strang, *Ancient and Modern Michilimackinac* (St. James, MI: Cooper and Chidester, 1854), 5, 31, Strang Collection.

50 Warren Post, Diary, December 7, 1850, Warren Post Diaries, Vault MSS 245, BYU.

51 Deposition of Finley Page, Suit of Archer vs. Strang as trustee of the Order of Enoch at Voree [1851], Strang Collection, box 2, f.177; on forced tithes see County Court for the County of Michilimackinac, "People vs. the Mormons, Samuel O'Brien Bennett's Statement," May 23, 1855, Jacob M. Howard Collection of Documents and Letters Relating to the Strangites (hereafter Howard Collection), f.4, Beinecke Rare Book and Manuscript Library, Yale University, New Haven, Connecticut.

52 County Court for the County of Michilimackinac, "People vs. Hezekiah D. McCullough and William Chambers," August 30, 1851, Howard Collection, f.1.

53 George C. Bates, "'King' Strang: The Beaver Island Prophet's Trial in this City in 1851," July 10, 1877, box 2, f.53, Strang Collection; Goodrich to Stuart, March 7, 1853, box 1, f.59, Strang Collection.

54 Strang, *Ancient and Modern Michilimackinac*, 3, 11–16, 39, 42.

55 A. J. Newton and Isaac Blanchard, "Memorial to Governor Bingham," May 1856, f.6; "Memo of Statements made to me by Hezekiah McCullough," May 15, 1856, f.7; "Deposition of Christopher Scott," June 3, 1856, f.10; and "Strangite Material," f.1, all in the Howard Collection.

56 Watson to Nichols, May 25, 1872, Church of Jesus Christ Records, f.4, BYU.

57 US Office of Indian Affairs, *Annual Report to the Secretary of the Interior* (Washington, DC: Government Printing Office, 1867), 335; see also Wenger, *Religious Freedom*.

58 Moran, *The Imperial Church*.

59 Wood, *Historic Mackinac: The Historical, Picturesque, and Legendary Features of the Mackinac Country* (New York: Macmillan, 1918), 494, 499, 414.

60 See G. Johnson, "Varieties of Native Hawaiian Establishment"; and Promey, "Material Establishment and Public Display."

3

A Colony Called Freedom

Religion, Empire, and Black Christian Settlers

SYLVESTER A. JOHNSON

Introduction

> The Republic of Liberia arises from Cape Mesurado, the middle of the West African coast, like an angel of light from a cloud of darkness, with the trumpet of the everlasting Gospel in her right hand, and the glittering jewels of civilization in her left—the magnificent gift of America to Africa.[1]

The American Colonization Society propagandized this lurid claim of Liberia as the bright hope of a benighted Africa in 1863, during the very time the United States was at war over slavery. This assertion of African redemption was by no means exceptional. Rather, in drawing on the symbolic language of lightness and darkness, it characterized the way both Black and White Christians of the United States rationalized the creation of a settler colony in West Africa.

Beginning in the 1820s and continuing after the US Civil War of the 1860s, thousands of free Africans left the United States to forge a new life in West Africa by settling in Liberia. For decades, the United States military supported the making of this settler colony in West Africa in alliance with the American Colonization Society. The enterprise culminated in the settler nation of Liberia. This transoceanic manifestation of US empire occurred largely through the Christian missionary enterprise. The twin projects of civilizing and Christianizing the Indigenous peoples under Liberian state control generated prolific claims about darkness and light that evidenced both semiotic and material structures of religious and secular conquest.

This chapter demonstrates that Liberia was of central importance for Black Christian settler colonialism. It argues that Liberia was structured as a settler colony in reciprocal relation with the United States of America, a premier settler state. In consequence, Liberia became a means of spreading what advocates of the Liberian colony called the "light" of Christianity and Western freedom in the African continent. The chapter presents this case by focusing on intersecting dimensions of these two racial states—that of the United States opposing Indigenous American sovereignty and enslaving Blacks, and that of Liberia, created by undermining Indigenous Africans to establish an Americo-Liberian colony named for freedom (from the Latin *"libertas"*). At the center of this story are Black Christian settlers from the United States who, in cooperation with White US politicians and philanthropic supporters, created Liberia as a beacon of enlightened knowledge that promised to dispel backwardness, slavery, and symbolic darkness to create a Black self-governing state. The consequence of this colonial project, however, was a colonial state founded on violent tactics of rule. This chapter, thus, shows how Liberia's creation as a Black Christian state produced enduring conflicts that undermined the legitimacy of African Indigenous religion and Indigenous sovereignty to secure democratic freedom for Black Christian settlers and their descendants.

Liberia, Colonization, and Transoceanic Empire

If asked when the United began exercising overseas colonialism (i.e., beyond the colonial occupation and conquest of Indigenous American polities), many experts will immediately think of the War of 1898 that brought US occupation of Cuba, the Philippines, Guam, and other overseas territories. Predating this period, however, was the colonial settlement and conquest of the region of West Africa that became the Liberian state. For over two hundred years, African political elites of this region had established a thriving trade with various European polities, including the Portuguese, the Dutch, and the British. By the late 1700s, the British empire began backing a private company, the Sierra Leone Company, to establish a trading colony using the most vulnerable population of Blacks living in the English metropole. This colony of Sierra Leone became the first Black settler colony in West Africa. In ideological, political, and material terms, it paved the way for the subsequent Liberia colony.

The most important reason for Liberia's emergence was the continuing paradox of colonialism and White racism. Abducted Africans were forced into slavery in the United States in increasing numbers while being denied the ability to belong politically (the body politic). White slaveholders wanted more Blacks but strictly as enslaved laborers. This inevitably led to a small but growing population of free Blacks whom Whites resented for embodying the possibility of Black freedom and threatening the fundamental racial logic of slavery. To resolve this, the governments of Britain and the United States attempted to create Black settler colonies so that free Blacks could be removed from White nations—if they were not enslaved, by this logic, they had no rightful place in the United States. In the 1780s, following the American Revolutionary War, a White settler rebellion against the British empire, Africans enslaved in the United States who had fought on behalf of the British were removed to Nova Scotia. This was Britain's underwhelming attempt to fulfill its bargain with these Black loyalists. In the 1790s, Britain created the Sierra Leone colony for resettling indigent Blacks living in England, which inspired more imagination about the utility of Black settler colonies.

By 1817, the pro-slavery American Colonization Society (ACS) had convinced the US government to aid its efforts to resettle free Blacks from the United States to West Africa. This led to a surprising symbiosis between free Africans in the United States and the pro-slavery ACS. The relationship was complicated but highly generative, if counterintuitive. One can identify three major characteristics of that alliance. First, the resettlement project was intended to be a secular enterprise but was primarily executed through Black Christian missionary activism. Second, the ACS had too little funding but ample political influence and connections; thus, the ACS successfully lobbied for the US War Department to employ naval vessels to escort Black settlers to West Africa and to attack native Africans under the guise of repressing the transatlantic slave trade. For their part, Black Christians raised their own funds and organized with modest monetary assistance from the ACS. Third, although White ACS members intended for White men to govern the Liberia colony, it was actually controlled mostly by Blacks such as Lott

Carey—informally, then later through formal leadership. This became necessary because White colonial governors became sick or even died within a short time after arriving at the colony. These three patterns demonstrate that despite intentions of Liberia being a secular, White-controlled colony that benefited White Americans, it was executed largely through Black Christian missionary agency and quickly became governed by Black settlers themselves, who relied on US militarism to assist in conducting warfare against Indigenous Africans.[2]

Black Missionary Settlers

The Black Quaker Paul Cuffe (1759–1817) was an early champion of Black American settlement in West Africa. Cuffe became a successful merchant in New England and aspired to establish a transatlantic trade network with African business partners. The son of an Indigenous (Wampanoag) woman and an abducted and enslaved Ashanti father, Cuffe became convinced that commercialism would enable free Africans on both sides of the Atlantic to achieve self-determination and security from slavery. He sailed to Sierra Leone multiple times between 1810 and 1816. Although Cuffe himself never moved to West Africa, several Black families from New England sailed to Sierra Leone with Cuffe to relocate and contribute to help grow a thriving trade between the Black settler colony of Sierra Leone and the United States.[3]

Despite overtures from the ACS, Cuffe advised but ultimately refused to support the pro-slavery organization. In the years that followed, collaboration with the ACS came from Black Christian missionaries aspiring to convert Africans from their Indigenous religions. The first voyage of Black settlers under the auspices of the ACS, in fact, was led by the African Methodist Episcopal (AME) minister Daniel Coker (1780–1846). Coker had worked closely with the AME bishop Richard Allen to establish their independent Black denomination in 1816, around the same time the ACS emerged. Both Allen and Coker were fiercely committed to converting more of their race to Christianity. Allen would devote his leadership and services to the Blacks in the United States. Coker, by contrast, seized on the opportunity to partner with the ACS to achieve his missionary plans. In 1820, he boarded the *Elizabeth*, a US naval vessel, and joined the first group of African Americans to settle West Africa under the colonization program of the ACS. The group numbered close to ninety and included families and individuals determined to achieve a life of freedom away from the yoke of racism, violence, and precarity in the United States.[4]

Coker's enterprising voyage to West Africa to begin establishing the Liberia colony was riveting for Blacks back in the United States. Few were as inspired as Lott Cary (1780–1828), enslaved from birth in Virginia. Cary purchased his freedom and that of his family in his early thirties. He attended a school for free Blacks, where he became steeped in missionary theology and was especially inspired by reports from West Africa of Christian conversion. By 1815, Cary was a licensed Baptist preacher and had teamed up with another African American missionary, Colin Teague (1780–1839). That year, they cofounded their own Black missionary society, named the Richmond African Baptist Missionary Society, with the ambition of funding a missionary trip to West Africa.[5]

Cary and Teague viewed the ACS as an especially fortuitous development, as they perceived the benefits of a possible partnership to missionize West Africa. The Black missionary society successfully raised a tidy sum (fourteen thousand dollars in today's dollars) to support their missionary ambitions in West Africa, then appealed to the ACS for additional funding, to the colonization society's delight. By 1821, Cary and Teague embarked with thirty-one other Blacks from Virginia to West Africa to advance the establishment of Liberia. Cary gave a rousing speech the day they set sail, declaring that he would gladly risk death at sea and encounters with "savage men" or "savage wild beasts on the Coast of Africa" as the price for taking the light of the Christian gospel to "poor Africans."[6]

Once in Africa, Black Christian settlers found themselves at odds with Indigenous Africans on several fronts. The Methodist missionary Daniel Coker expressed disdain at seeing barely clothed "Cruemen"— Indigenous African day laborers who profited by facilitating the many tasks, such as transporting people and loading cargo, required for the functioning of international trade. Coker lamented that these native Africans "adhere to their superstition . . . of charms and witchcraft," ignorant of the Christian gospel. He called them "children of nature." "Darkness has covered this land, and gross darkness the minds of these people," he continued. In what became a resounding pattern among other Black Christian settlers, Coker proclaimed that native Africans were standing in need of the civilizing Christian mission that Black Americans promised to bring from the United States. This sentiment of reprehension at the cultures and religions that thrived among Indigenous Africans was repeatedly on display among Black Christian settlers and was consistently filtered through consciousness of Christian supremacy. It ensured that the Liberian settler colony was represented as both a campaign for Black American freedom and a selfless mission to redeem heathen Africa from spiritual decay.[7]

Settler Abolitionism

This religious contempt was also wed to an indignation against the slave trade that had taken command of West Africa. This thriving institution of slavery that the ACS committed to protecting had always been possible because African merchants supplied a steady stream—hundreds at a time—of men, women, and children who had been kidnapped from their homes, bound, and forced on an arduous trek to one of several coastal dungeons where they awaited transport across the seas to the Americas and the Caribbean. It was a lucrative system that, over the centuries, had become integral to the entire economy of West Africa's coastal city-states and kingdoms. The Black Christians who arrived in West Africa rarely openly condemned the White slaveholders controlling the ACS. By contrast, they consistently expressed shock and abolitionist zeal upon witnessing the extensive nature of the coastal trade. In what became a most bitter irony, abolishing slavery in West Africa (but not in the United States) unified at a symbolic level the disparate aims of Black Christian settlers, the White pro-slavery ACS managers, and the imperial United States government. More pointedly, this African abolitionism became the secular wedge of the spiritual mission that Black Christians wielded to advance the Liberian settler colony.[8]

Why would the United States, a slaveholding empire, participate in liberating enslaved peoples from Africa, many of whom would have become enslaved in the United States? Ironically, the United States and Britain, whose empires were built on slavery and racism, were suppressing human trafficking of enslaved peoples across the Atlantic as a matter of policy by the early 1800s. This did not interfere with the American empire's ability to support slavery, however, because White slaveholders in the United States held a near monopoly supplying people forced into slavery. This meant that the trafficking of Black people became more profitable for those Whites who specialized in "breeding" slaves for domestic human trafficking—that is, in forcing Black women to be impregnated by Black men (or by the White men who routinely raped Black women with impunity) so that their children could be abducted and sold away to any White man willing to offer the right price. By structuring and commercializing this sexual assault and abduction in tandem with suppression of the transatlantic slave trade, the state of Virginia eventually distinguished itself during the 1800s as the leading source for the human trafficking of Black men, women, and children.[9]

Opposing the transatlantic slave trade was initially an African affair that inspired Western activists. The West-Central African monarch Queen Nzinga implemented a ban on the human trafficking supplying Portuguese merchants in the 1600s. More consequential was the decades-long effort by African Muslims in the 1700s to end the African slave trade and create a different paradigm of political power that was not predicated on the system of chattel. It was this movement that sounded throughout the Atlantic world and compelled multiple iterations of abolitionism among Westerners. By 1820, the United States declared slave trading to be a capital offense; Britain followed suit in 1824 (with the single exception of Nathaniel Gordon, no Whites were ever sentenced to death). By virtue of possessing the world's largest naval fleet, Britain began selectively enforcing a ban against transatlantic human trafficking, seizing Iberian slave ships and liberating the women, children, and men who had been abducted and forced aboard.[10]

By the time Black emigration to Liberia was underway, British and US naval ships were patrolling West Africa's coast to intercept any ships carrying abductees forced into slavery. When these patrolling ships captured a slave ship, they apprehended the White operators and released the Africans by settling them in Liberia. So, Africans who had been abducted from their families hundreds of miles inland wound up joining the settler population of Liberia, despite being Indigenous. This meant they occupied a complicated status—not quite on par with that of Westernized Blacks but with privileges not available to Indigenous populations born in the local nations proximate to or within Liberia.

In the early years, as these US Blacks emigrated to the fledgling settler colony, the lands they claimed—territory that belonged to several Indigenous African nations—were renamed, often on the basis of the American regions from whence the settlers hailed. As individual states such as Maryland, Mississippi, and Kentucky created their own colonization-society chapters, they often named the resulting colonies in West Africa—Mississippi-in-Africa, Maryland-in-Africa, etc. Virginia, North Carolina, and Maryland were disproportionately represented, as these three states accounted for more than two-thirds of Liberia's Black settlers by the early 1840s. Portions of the Liberia colony were all shaped by their specific geographies as well as the social conditions of those who hailed from various regions of the United States. Starting in the 1830s, the Maryland colony was an independent republic, separate and distinct from the sovereign Republic of Liberia that formed in 1847. Not until 1857 did the Republic of Maryland become incorporated into the larger Republic of Liberia. Virginia, which was the birth home of Liberia's first president, Joseph Jenkins Roberts, wielded exceptional influence as the origin of the greatest number of Americo-Liberian settlers (40 percent by the 1840s). North Carolina was the provenance of 775 Black settlers by 1843; the first group arrived in 1825 aboard the naval brig *Hunter*. US Blacks from Mississippi, constituting 158 manumitted Africans from the upper region of Mississippi, settled what became the city of Greenville, Liberia. This city, like others throughout Liberia, was named in honor of a White slaveholder who was instrumental in advancing colonization efforts.[11]

Notwithstanding the outsized influence that Americo-Liberians wielded, Liberia's settler population was also constituted by a small class of recaptured/repatriated Indigenous Africans whom Americo-Liberians came to call "Congoes," in reference to the Kongo kingdom of West-Central Africa that first normalized trade relations with Europeans. Despite this ethnic designation, Liberia's Congoes were native to a variety of Indigenous nations from the continent's interior. They had been abducted through the violent and wanton raids that fed a global demand for human trafficking. In an unparalleled stretch of violent mayhem lasting hundreds of years, more than twelve million Black people were forced into the slave trade, marched to the coastal slave-trading "castles," and crowded onto the slave ships destined for the Americas (the Caribbean or South America, most frequently). The wars, forced marches of enslaved abductees, and escalating violence cost the lives of tens of millions over four centuries.[12]

Religion, US Empire, and Anti-Indigenous Wars

The creation of "Mississippi in Africa," the portion of Liberia settled by Africans from a Mississippi plantation, evidences the complicated connections between Christian missions and empire in North America and the development of the Liberia settler colony in West Africa. At the very time Black Christian missionaries from the United States were establishing the Liberia settler colony, White missionaries in the United States were aggressively forging inroads into the sovereign lands of American Indians in an effort to propagate Christianity and expand the Anglo-American empire's racial power. During the decades of Liberia's early history, from the 1810s to the 1850s, three developments became especially prominent: (1) the creation of the ABCFM, Anglo-America's most influential foreign missionary organization of the era; (2) the Anglo-American wars against Indigenous nations, which favored genocidal extermination tactics against Indians; and (3) the fateful alliance between missionary religion and the US Department of War, which funded Protestant missionary zeal to replace Indigenous religion with "Christian civilization." Through a rich entanglement of events, US foreign missionaries working in Indigenous American nations helped forge conditions that expanded plantation slavery.

The creation of the American Board of Commissioners for Foreign Missions (ABCFM) was uniquely pivotal to these developments. This foreign missionary organization began in 1810 with a focus on expanding Christianity into foreign lands near and far. Indicative of the movement's ambition was the early focus on missionizing South Asia. The ABCFM's founders were equally enthralled with the prospect of conquering what they perceived as the "heathens" of North America by targeting citizens of Indigenous nations—the Choctaw and Chickasaw ("Mississippi Indians"), Creek, Cherokee, and Seminole polities loomed large in the missionary imagination. As a practical matter, the relative proximity of American Indians to the United States meant that the overwhelming majority of missionaries to foreign lands targeted so-called Indian country—the Indigenous nations of North America. This was no accident; anti-Indian wars were the main and ongoing concern of the United States military. Even US wars against European states typically involved warring against American Indians.

The First Seminole War (1816–1819) erupted when US general Andrew Jackson invaded the Florida lands claimed by the Seminole Nation, the British, and Spain. The war's demise left Spain relinquishing its land claims, and Anglo-American settlers eagerly eyed Indigenous lands with ambitions of creating vast plantations. This settler fixation, as always, was complicated by the fact that the land was beneath the feet of Indigenous Americans, who had entered into formal treaty with the United States to protect their lands from encroachment by US citizens.

Cyrus Kingsbury, a Christian minister working with a Connecticut missionary group, rose to leadership in the ABCFM and soon leveraged the fallout of multiple anti-Indian wars to secure funding from the US Department of War. Traveling to Washington with his plan of Christian redemption for American Indian nations in the 1820s, Kingsbury met with warm reception from James Monroe's administration and secured an agreement from Secretary of War John C. Calhoun to support missionary efforts in the foreign lands of Indian country. Kingsbury and other missionaries proved pragmatic, if subversive, by emphasizing to Indians the role of Christianity as a racial civilization—a way of life rooted in the material structures of commerce and built environment that differentiated settler and Indigenous economies. Indigenous polities typically employed a blend of trading, hunting, and agriculture that harmonized with the mobility of entire communities. Indian towns were designed to make a relatively light footprint, as Indians often relocated on the basis of migrations of game population, seasonal patterns, and other factors. Anglo-American settlers, by contrast, razed the land to create permanent towns, enslaved Blacks, often by the hundreds, to run each of thousands of plantations that could cover hundreds of acres each, and continually farmed the same land tracts, depleting the soil's nutrients and generating incessant demands for "new" (Indigenous) lands with "virgin" soil. In the derisive terms of settler shorthand, Indians "wandered" while Christians "settled," and it was these contrasting economic patterns that generations of White supremacists used to claim that Indians were "uncivilized" and thus unfit for self-governance (sovereignty).¹³

Starting in the 1810s, the ABCFM lobbied the chief executives of Indigenous nations to emphasize that the US military was threatening to exterminate Indigenous peoples who could not prove themselves arbiters of Christian civilization. The danger was real and imminent, they underscored. How best to don the garb of "civilized" habitudes and preserve their lives? The ABCFM offered a plan: Indians should permit the ABCFM missionaries to set up plantations—factories of civilization—on Indigenous lands to train Indians in the arts of Christian industry and commerce. In material terms, Whites would use Indigenous monies to build infrastructure, and Indian youths and adults would agree to work the plantations without pay—all in exchange for a type of racial-civilizational internship. In these terms, the ABCFM presented their role as a beneficent one that could save the lives of Indians from ethnic cleansing to secure their possible future under the expanding influence of the Anglo-American empire. Faced with the decades of violent deaths and displacement at the hands of US military, the Choctaw, Chickasaw, and Cherokee nations agreed to fund these factories of civilization, eventually using the annuity funds the US government paid sovereign Indian nations in compensation for lands ceded to the United States.¹⁴

By the 1820s, the US secretary of war arranged to divert to the ABCFM annuities that indemnified Indians for lands ceded to the United States. The impact on the Mississippi Indians is indicative of broader patterns of American empire and religion. The ABCFM established a series of missionary "stations" throughout the lands of the Mississippi Indians. The first was the Elliot mission, built in 1818. Next was the Mayhew mission (1820), followed by the Monroe and Newell (1821) stations. At least two more stations were operating in the mid-1820s—the Tikshish (1825) mission, devoted to the Indian children of White men who had become citizens of Indian nations, and Caney Creek (1826), which served the Chickasaw nation.¹⁵

The executive chiefs of the Indian nations deliberated carefully to chart a prudent path that could defend their sovereign status in the face of multiple imperial states—British, Spanish, and Anglo-American empires. Following the War of 1812 and the First Seminole War, it was largely the United States that threatened the national independence of American Indians. Indigenous chief executives had successfully negotiated with the Anglo-American state in the 1700s and early 1800s to establish legally binding assurances that the Western empire would acknowledge boundaries and Indigenous sovereignty, but these successes were followed by betrayals and illegal breaches of treaty terms by the United States. White US officials in the presidential administration and in the War Department made no secret of their commitment to granting land to White settler families, a practice that was impossible without the continuing seizure of Indigenous lands. Individual White settlers at times attempted to acquire land from individual Indians, despite the fact that such was prohibited by Indian laws. The Choctaw national constitution, for instance, stipulated that Choctaw lands belonged to the nation, not individuals.[16]

ABCFM missionaries worked assiduously to fulfill what they described as a divine mandate to conquer the spiritual darkness of Indian country through Christian battle fought with the mighty sword of conversion. Their missionary stations targeted Indian youths, as missionaries aspired to mold a generation of Indigenous Christians who might persuade their parents to abandon what Whites derisively termed "savage" Indian ways and who could one day raise their own families in the style of White civilization. The stations—veritable labor camps based on the plantation model of production—trained Indians in study of the Christian Bible and employed English-only instruction to teach literacy—all while subjecting the bodies of Indigenous youths to the arduous physical labor that generated revenue that White missionaries controlled.[17]

The heightening aggression of the US Army against Indigenous polities resonated at a practical level with the aims of Christian missionaries focusing on the Mississippi Indians. Both missionaries and Anglo-American political elites wanted to transform the Indigenous economy away from hunting and occupying vast regions of land toward concentrating their towns onto smaller regions. This was to proceed in tandem with forcing Indians into dependence on the US economy; if successful, Indians would purchase goods instead of manufacturing their own and depend on Anglo-American consumers to market their agricultural products being cultivated on plantations modeled after those of small-scale White farmers.[18]

The experience at the Elliot mission in Mississippi is telling. The timeline for building the mission proved too ambitious, as families of the Choctaw nation arrived with ten children as the first "students" to enroll in April 1820. Rather than dampen the optimism of the youths and their parents, the Elliot station missionaries enrolled the children. The ABCFM also succeeded in persuading the Choctaw nation to devote twelve hundred dollars annually to sustain the mission and to provide eighty-five cows and calves. A subsequent visit in July 1820 by Chiefs Pukshanubee and Mushollatubee—they shared executive leadership of the Choctaw nation at the time—revealed the extensive infrastructure their annuities funds were financing: a carpenter's shop, a mill, a brick yard, and other small factories. By the fall of 1820, the missionary plantation boasted more than $12,000 ($225,000 in today's dollars) in capital assets. The primary source of labor, of course, was the children, whose "training" in the ways of Christian civilization was integral to the financial model of the plantation. The impact on Indigenous youths, not surprisingly, was traumatic and abusive. The Choctaw children housed at the Elliot mission had originally been promised a Christian education and the opportunity to lead their nation as pioneers of religious conversion and racial civilization. As events unfolded, however, they begged to be reunited with their parents and freed from unjust treatment under the regime of the missionary plantation.[19]

Mississippi in Africa

The Revolutionary War of White settlers against the British crown yielded decisive and massive changes in the racial politics of Mississippi. General Thomas Sumter, a celebrated hero of the White settler rebellion against Britain, leveraged the eager militancy of White settlers such as Isaac Ross of South Carolina, achieving a rather unlikely David-and-Goliath outcome. Ross became a captain in the revolutionary army and abetted the settler colonies' defeat against the massive British empire.

Once America's White settler population possessed its own sovereign imperial state, it devoted endless resources to insatiable territorial expansion, pushing the Spanish out of Mississippi and creating the Anglo-American-controlled Mississippi Territory in 1798. This was precisely the situation that Isaac Ross sought to exploit as he joined hundreds of other wealthy Whites seeking the upper hand by moving to the Mississippi Territory during its tumultuous shift of racial power and wealth. Ross understood clearly that the newly formed United States had a new monarch; the British King George had been replaced by "King Cotton," a staple of global commerce whose scale of monetization was on par with that of sugar and other elite commodities of global capitalism.[20]

Of course, cotton cultivation required massive plantations, and Ross was determined to become a key player in this new era of the nation's history. As an Anglo-American settler of considerable means following the westward trail of violence against Indigenous nations, Ross arrived just in time to benefit optimally from the open access to the rich Mississippi soil forced from the possession of the Mississippi Indians. He eventually acquired five thousand acres in what became Jefferson County and established Prospect Hill Plantation.

In 1817, Native Americans were the majority of Mississippi's population. The rabid thirst for the wealth that plantation economics generated drove an ever-expanding demand for more Blacks to be imported, and as an enslaved labor force. By 1840, Blacks were the majority—almost all of them enslaved. They numbered more than 196,000, exceeding the White population by 11 percent. When Andrew Jackson rose to the US presidency in the 1828 election, he promised and delivered more land to common Whites, offering continuing opportunities to seize and exploit Native American territory. But Jackson was not inventing a White planter democracy of slavery and racism; he was expanding what already existed. Under his administration, White militias forced all remaining citizens of Indigenous nations to leave Mississippi in 1838; only a small number of stateless Indians remained.[21]

It was into this violent crucible of settler colonialism and capital accumulation that thousands of Africans were subjected to racial slavery. Many white slaveholders managed small-scale operations, exploiting the lives and labor of a few people at a time. But Isaac Ross was no small planter. He gradually expanded his holdings to approximately five thousand acres—approaching an area of eight miles square. This required a massive labor force. To this end, he enslaved hundreds of Blacks to run Prospect Hill, providing the skills for agriculture, masonry, carpentry, and virtually every other aspect of economic production.

In his later years, however, Ross experienced an unexpected set of encounters, meeting a number of abolitionists in his travels and considering the prospect of Black freedom. To the great dismay of his family, Ross eventually decided to mandate through his will that his entire estate be sold, following the death of his daughter, Margaret Reed, and that the proceeds from the sale be used to provide passage to Liberia for those he enslaved; they were to be manumitted if they agreed to settle in Liberia or else be sold (without the breakup of immediate families) if they refused to leave the United States.[22]

In 1849, approximately 200 of the 225 people enslaved by Ross emigrated to Liberia. They were joined by another approximately 200 Blacks freed by other Ross family members. The group of formerly enslaved Black settlers from Prospect Hill, Mississippi, constituted the largest group of emigrants from Mississippi to travel to Liberia.[23]

Settlers versus "Others"

From 1820 to 1843 (the date of Liberia's first comprehensive census), Liberia's settler population grew from a small cadre of eight members to a full-fledged colony. By the early 1840s, more than 4,454 Blacks had left the United States to settle in Liberia. The severe death toll that occurred in the colony's early decades wreaked devastating losses—approximately 2,200 settlers died during that time span, most frequently of what was called "African fever." Disease outbreaks leveled the settler population to a mere 1,736 people by 1843. This number of living inhabitants included 599 people born in the colony to settler parents and an additional 46 children who were of Indigenous parentage and were adopted by settlers, so the loss of life under colonial rule was overbearing.[24]

The numbers of Americo-Liberian settlers are striking, notwithstanding high mortality rates. And yet, they do not tell the whole story. Indigenous Africans were far and away the overwhelming majority of Liberia's population. This is typically the case with settler colonialism, and the West African colony was no exception. By 1836, Liberia boasted a population of three thousand Americo-Liberian settlers. The capital city of Monrovia alone had five hundred houses—many built of stone—and ten church buildings. But in purely statistical terms, this was negligible in comparison to the two hundred thousand Indigenous Africans living in the towns that had come under the control of Liberia. By 1860, the number of Blacks who left the United States to settle in Liberia numbered ten thousand. Although impressive on its own terms, this was still a small fraction of the population native to the lands that Liberia controlled.[25] As a consequence, a system of minority rule resulted from the distinctions between settlers and the Indigenous. This distinction was often described as Christian versus "heathen" or "savage."

Perhaps more than any other population, those Africans who had been abducted, forced onto slave ships (bound for the Americas), and recaptured by naval vessels suppressing the transatlantic slave trade were caught beneath the conflicting hierarchies of the Liberian settler state. They were not citizens of the local Indigenous nations. Rather, at a formal level, they were citizens of the colony. It is clear, however, that Liberia's political community, by design, was rooted in Black American Christian identity—Americo-Liberians. So-called recaptives did not share kinship with the Americo-Liberians who identified so strongly with Christianity and the United States. Of further practical significance were the linguistic and cultural differences that existed between the groups. English was the sole official language of Liberia. More precisely, it was the language of Americo-Liberians and was for many years a foreign tongue on the lips of all other inhabitants of Liberia.[26]

All of these dynamics underscored the overwhelming reality that Liberia was a settler state. This certainly meant, among other things, that Americo-Liberian settlers made themselves the authentic members of the political community—the true, authentic essence of what it meant to be a Liberian people. All others were forced into a marginal status.

Constitutional provisions structured formal rights for Liberia's inhabitants and citizens. Liberia's earliest governing document, drafted in 1820, acknowledged that the United States government's authority over recaptured people would be unaffected. With this exception, the constitution of 1820 recognized the American Colonization Society itself as Liberia's rightful governing body. Of equal importance was its stipulation that "all persons born within the limits" of Liberia or having moved there to reside "shall be free, and entitled to all the rights and privileges of the free people of the United States." The 1839 constitution endowed a governor of a "Commonwealth of Liberia" and a colonial council with governing authority. Laws governing the treatment of those who had been recaptured, whether on land or at sea, were established by Liberia's governor and council. The ACS board of directors, nevertheless, retained ultimate control, as they held the power to revoke any legislation passed by the council. This second constitution, furthermore, repeated the absolute prohibition against slavery.

Such provisions, by focusing on Americo-Liberians, left intact the highly vulnerable status of recaptives and the ease of their exploitation. As early as 1827, Liberia's colonial government was forcing recaptives to serve Americo-Liberians on the basis of indenture—without freedom or agency—for up to three years before becoming eligible to earn wages, own land, and command other privileges that African American settlers enjoyed upon arriving. This indentured labor was rationalized by pointing out that the Americo-Liberian families who hosted recaptives were responsible for feeding and clothing them. So, it was essential to address the material cost of supporting them. This, of course, laid the groundwork for a system of domination and exploitation that seemed hardly distinguishable from the slavery that settlers denounced as an evil stain they had arrived to extinguish from the pagan land.[27]

Conclusion

The rise of Liberia as a Christian settler colony and, later, as a sovereign republic, embodied fundamental relations of empire and religion that resonated powerfully with the institutions of US empire. The colony predated other overseas imperial establishments by seventy years (i.e., those resulting from the Spanish American War). By means of Liberia, Black Christians from the United States forged their own freedom, characterized by liberties and privileges on a scale unparalleled in the United States. A focus on the turpitudes and conflicts that ensued should not blind anyone to the self-determination achieved through this concert of religion and empire.

In addition to this, the colony unleashed devastating consequences for the overwhelming majority of inhabitants in Liberia—Indigenous Africans who increasingly fell into the orbit of a constantly expanding settler state. Families and individuals liberated from slavery in Mississippi, Virginia, North Carolina, Maryland, and other regions of the United States seized their fortunes to pursue a new life in Liberia by the thousands during the nineteenth century. Their legacy is a forceful reminder of how religion and US empire were conjoined in both predictable and counterintuitive ways to yield complicated linkages between noble ideals of democratic freedom for Black Christian settlers and unrelenting violence and destruction for Liberia's Indigenous populations.

NOTES

1 "Our Duty to Africa," *African Repository* 36, no. 6 (June 1863): 175.
2 Tomek and Hetrick, eds., *New Directions in the Study of African American Recolonization*, 8–17; David, *The American Colonization Society*; Burin, *Slavery and the Peculiar Solution*; Power-Greene, *Against Wind and Tide*.
3 L. D. Thomas, *Paul Cuffe*; Cuffe, *Captain Paul Cuffe's Logs and Letters, 1808–1817*.
4 Coker, *Journal of Daniel Coker*.
5 Fitts, *The Lott Carey Legacy of African American Missions*; Fitts, *Lott Carey*.
6 Tyler-McGraw, *An African Republic*, 97; Miles Mark Fisher, "Lott Carey: The Colonizing Missionary," *Journal of Negro History* 7, no. 4 (October 1922): 387–88, 391.
7 Coker, *Journal of Daniel Coker*, 34–37.
8 Ciment, *Another America*; Beyan, *African American Settlements in West Africa*.
9 D. B. Davis, *Inhuman Bondage*; Ware, "Slavery in Islamic Africa, 1400–1800," 47–81.
10 D. B. Davis, *Inhuman Bondage*; Ware, "Slavery in Islamic Africa, 1400–1800," 47–81.
11 United States Government, *Tables Showing the Number of Emigrants Sent to the Colony of Liberia*, 302.
12 Davidson, *The African Slave Trade*, 98; Eltis, *The Rise of African Slavery in the Americas*.
13 Phillips, *Protestant America and the Pagan World*, 61–62; Graber, *The Gods of Indian Country*, 26.
14 "Choctaw Nation," box 3, folder 1, Natchez Trace Research Collection, University of Southern Mississippi Library, Hattiesburg, Mississippi (hereafter NTRC).
15 "Choctaw Nation"; Phillips, *Protestant America and the Pagan World*, 68–72.
16 "Origins (Choctaw Mission)," box 2, folder 26, NTRC.
17 "Improvements," box 3, folder 28, NTRC; "Mayhew," box 2, folder 24, NTRC.
18 "Improvements," box 3, folder 28, NTRC; "Mayhew," box 2, folder 24, NTRC.
19 "Elliot Mission," box 2, folder 23, NTRC.
20 Dattel, *Cotton and Race in the Making of America*; Huffman, *Mississippi in Africa*.
21 "Mississippi—Race and Hispanic Origin: 1800 to 1990," US Census Bureau, census.gov, accessed April 21, 2020.
22 Huffman, *Mississippi in Africa*, 5, 37, 55.
23 United States Government, *Tables Showing the Number of Emigrants Sent to the Colony of Liberia*, 376.

24 United States Government, *Tables Showing the Number of Emigrants Sent to the Colony of Liberia*, 376.
25 United States Government, *Tables Showing the Number of Emigrants Sent to the Colony of Liberia*, 376; Yarema, "The American Colonization Society," 44–48.
26 Fett, *Recaptured Africans*.
27 *African Repository and Colonial Journal* 3, no. 8 (October 1827): 249.

PART II

Biopolitics

*Imperial Classifications, Sentimental Reform,
and Indigenous Tactics of Survival*

The late 1800s and early 1900s witnessed significant new efforts to develop and structure expert knowledge about citizens, denizens, and enemies in the imperial republic. Studying religion was integral to the larger enterprise of collecting demographic data about the diverse peoples that the expanding US Empire aimed to rule. Over the course of the nineteenth century, coerced treaties and warfare with Native American nations had allowed the United States to expand westward across the continent—a process that only retrospectively came to seem inevitable—annexing lands that were quickly turned over to plantation slavery in the South and to incoming settlers in the North. Growing numbers of immigrants, coming primarily from Europe, were drawn by the promises of land and labor. Rates of immigration grew rapidly in the nineteenth century, peaking in 1907 with almost 1.3 million new residents. These numbers would plummet in the First World War, resurge in the early 1920s, and then fall again with the restrictive Immigration Act of 1924 and the Great Depression.[1]

Experts classified African Americans, Native Americans, and new immigrants all as racial populations, defining and ranking their racial identities in part through their relationship to Christianity, Indigenous religious traditions, or other symbolic norms of moral constitution. Leveraging political power in ways that supported access to the means of life and security for some and its deprivation for others—biopolitics—was part and parcel of producing knowledge in the Anglo-American empire. This was especially consequential for African Americans, who secured emancipation from slavery after the Civil War but not from racial terror or new biopolitical regimes of racial control. Imperial biopolitics also impacted Native Americans, as the US military establishment through the nineteenth century was chiefly concerned with opposing Indigenous struggles for sovereignty, forced removals, and extermination campaigns that targeted entire Native American communities.

Imperial expansion required new tools for imperial management and control. As part of a larger shift towards professional and scientific expertise, social science surveys were deployed to collect and document demographic information about those deemed "foreign" to the body politic. This trend indelibly shaped religious efforts to advance a "social gospel" that aimed to uplift what were often immigrant populations. Studying the cultural life of Indigenous Americans took on special importance, particularly as more White American experts began predicting that Indians would "disappear" in short order and needed to be documented to preserve knowledge of their religion and customs. However, understanding the intertwined histories of religion and US empire requires careful attention not only to this imperial frame—to imperial modes of conceptualizing and classifying the world—but also to the Indigenous practices and epistemologies that Jennifer Graber (chapter 6) names as an Indigenous frame. Visionary forms of Indigenous religion—as in the Kiowa Feather Dance, known to US authorities as the Ghost Dance—become complicated sites of Indigenous survivance as well as imperial hostility and vilification.

How did new forms of biopolitical surveillance and control, targeting immigrants and Indigenous people, enable the expanding power of US empire? How did Native Americans and other imperial subjects push back against these biopolitical regimes, and to what extent were they able to maintain alternative lifeways and epistemologies along the way?

NOTE

1 "Legal Immigration to the United States, 1820–Present," Migration Policy Institute, www.migrationpolicy.org, consulted June 28, 2021. These numbers would not return to their early-twentieth-century levels until 1990.

4

Religion on the Brink

Settler-Colonial Knowledge Production in the US Census

SARAH DEES

Settler colonialism entails an outside community's seizure of lands and resources from the original inhabitants of a territory.[1] But more than this, these outsiders, or settlers, seek to supplant and erase the lands' original inhabitants.[2] These twin processes of settler colonialism—physical and ideological erasure—have been ongoing in the United States.[3] Over the course of the nineteenth century, the borders of the United States continued to expand from the original colonies into Native territories further west.[4] From the 1803 Louisiana Purchase to expansions in the Northwest and Southwest via war and negotiation in the mid-nineteenth century, the United States executed land deals with Mexico and European imperial powers. In addition, the US federal government negotiated numerous agreements and treaties with Indigenous nations to gain access to Native lands.[5]

As these expansions occurred, the US federal government sought to manage Indigenous peoples via federal Indian policies.[6] Some methods included the creation of reservations for Native Americans, combined with the often-violent removal of Native peoples from their homelands to these separate areas. While arguably the most well-known of the Indian removals was the "Trail of Tears," in which thousands of Cherokees, Chickasaws, Choctaws, Creeks, and Seminoles were removed from their ancestral homelands in the Southwest to Indian Territory over the 1830s and '40s, additional removals occurred throughout the United States.[7] They included the 1838 Potawatomi "Trail of Death" in what is now the Midwest and the 1864 "Long Walk" of the Diné (Navajo) in the Southwest.[8] However, US removal and reservation strategies became less tenable over the course of the nineteenth century as non-Native settlers continued to push for additional Native lands.

US federal Indian policy thus shifted in tandem with a changing political relationship between Native peoples and the United States.[9] By the end of the nineteenth century, federal Indian policies transformed from efforts to separate Native peoples from settlers into efforts to incorporate Native Americans into mainstream US citizenry.[10] The Dawes Act of 1887 created a system that divided up communally held Indian reservations into individual plots and sold "excess" lands to non-Natives, further reducing Native landholdings. In addition, this act called for the assimilation of Native Americans into US society, pressuring them to adapt their cultures and societies to Euro-American norms. As Tisa Wenger and Jennifer Graber each document in their contributions to this volume, religion has played a role in the United States' interactions with Native nations, both as a mechanism and as a target of imperial control. The US government explicitly singled out Native American religions during the assimilation era in the late nineteenth and early twentieth centuries.[11]

Historian Patrick Wolfe has argued that "invasion is a structure not an event."[12] In this way, he emphasizes the processes and systems that establish and maintain settler rule over Indigenous peoples and lands rather than acts of conquest alone and in themselves. Ultimately, he argues that a key feature of the structure of settler colonialism is a "logic of elimination."[13] In this vein, this chapter describes the US government's creation of knowledge about Native Americans, emphasizing their supposed decline, as a constitutive feature of US empire. A key feature of settler colonialism is indeed the seizure of lands from its original inhabitants. But in addition to acts of physical violence such as Indian removals and the targeting of Native traditions, the structures of settler colonialism include ideological formations—the production of information, ideas, and narratives that support and justify violent actions.

This chapter describes the settler-colonial production of knowledge via European and US enumerations of Native Americans, including official US Census publications. I discuss two ways in which religion factored into these histories of enumeration. First, when seeking to determine how to classify Native peoples, as either "untaxed" and outside of the purview of the US Census Bureau or "taxed" and subject to inclusion in the census, enumerators considered Native peoples' "habits." Chroniclers of Native cultures in the nineteenth century sometimes used this term to refer to what we would now describe as religious traditions, but in census documents it functioned to describe a general state of social and cultural assimilation that probably would have included (while not being limited to) the adoption of Christianity. Second, I describe the striking inclusion of Native religions as evidence of decline in key assimilation-era Indian census materials. The inclusion of religion in Indian census records is noteworthy given the fact that religion does not factor significantly into other US Census publications.[14] These census materials presented Native religions negatively, in contrast to what Tisa Wenger describes in this volume as the "good religion" of the settlers. The collection—or creation—of statistical data about Native Americans served the purposes of settler colonialism through its purportedly objective documentation of the "decline" of Native Americans, a form of erasure that justified settler supplanting of Native lands.

Early Enumeration of Native Americans

While Native Americans were not consistently enumerated in the US Census until the late nineteenth century, Europeans and Euro-Americans collected and recorded data on Native inhabitants of what is today the United States long before the nation was founded. During the colonial era, European military officers, missionaries, traders, and surveyors gathered information about Native religions and cultures via surveys, observations, and interviews. Original data was often replicated in later reports. In the 1782 edition of his *Notes on the State of Virginia*, Thomas Jefferson drew on four different sources of data to produce his own catalogues of Native Americans living within and outside of the United States. His sources included figures from earlier British, French, and US military reports and traders. Jefferson's tables included Native nations' names and subcategories or groups, with estimated numbers from each original data source and information about where they were located. Comparisons of Jefferson's sources reveal numerical discrepancies. For example, each data source has a number for Shawnees: five hundred, four hundred, three hundred, and three hundred located near the Scioto and Muskingum Rivers in Ohio.[15]

In the mid-nineteenth century, the federal government funded data collection on Native Americans for the purposes of regulating Indian affairs. In November of 1846, Congress approved a request for additional funding for the newly created Office of Indian Affairs. Henry Rowe Schoolcraft (whose earlier career is discussed in Wenger's chapter) was appointed to collect data about Native Americans under this office. Schoolcraft's data included four major groups: Iroquois, Algonquin, Dakota, and Appalachian, corresponding to the Northeast, Great Lakes, and Southeast regions, as well as general categories for "tribes of the new states and territories south and west, now including Texas and Mexican acquisitions, East of the Rocky Mountains." A final category included "fragmentary tribes in the older states."[16] By 1850, part of the Indian Appropriation Act of 1846 required Indian agents "to take a census and to obtain such other statistical information of the several tribes of Indians among whom they respectively reside." They reported this information to the secretary of war.

Overall, at least sixteen historical estimates or reports of Native populations were produced beginning in 1789, from a 1789 estimate from the secretary of war to the general 1890 census. Of this list of sixteen sources, four were produced by the secretary of war (1789, 1825, 1829, and 1834), three by Indian Affairs officers (1822, 1836, and 1837), and five by the US Census Office (in 1850, 1860, 1870, 1880, and 1890). An additional four were produced by scholars, at least one of which (particularly Gilbert Imlay's) drew heavily on previous figures.[17] By tracing changes in the ways agents of the government have gathered data about Native Americans, we can see the political shift in the relationship of Native Americans to the US body politic, and the government's efforts to assimilate Native Americans into the folds of mainstream US citizenry. We can also see the way that religion functions and its role in assimilation practices. The so-called progress of Native Americans outlined in census materials was part of the "progress" of the settler-colonial assimilation project of the United States.

The History of Native Americans in the US Census

Native Americans have historically been one of the US Census's most undercounted groups.[18] In 2010, Native Americans living on reservations were undercounted by 4.88 percent.[19] These undercounts, especially among those living on reservations, have several causes. The lack of access to means of communication—due to rurality or lack of economic resources—makes it difficult for some families on more remote reservation communities to self-report. Additional challenges have included linguistic barriers and the fact that some segments of Native American populations move frequently. In addition, many Native Americans are wary of participating in the US Census.[20]

The US Census, in fact, was specifically designed *not* to count Native Americans. While government agents did attempt to enumerate Native peoples in the colonial era for strategic reasons, the US Census initially excluded Native Americans in its counts. The US Constitution called for the regular enumeration of the population in order to determine political representation and the distribution of taxes. However, there were racial and political distinctions determining who would be counted. Article 1, Section 2 of the Constitution states, "Representatives and direct Taxes shall be apportioned among the several States which may be included within this Union, according to their respective Numbers, which shall be determined by adding to the whole Number of free Persons, including those bound to Service for a Term of Years, and *excluding Indians not taxed*, three fifths of all other Persons" (emphasis added). As outlined in the Constitution, people of African descent who were enslaved were not counted as full citizens.[21] Native Americans who were "not taxed" were specifically excluded from the counts. This latter condition reflects the reality that Native Americans were considered to be sovereign political entities, akin to foreign nations, as mentioned in Article 1, Section 8 of the Constitution. As a result, Native Americans were not counted in the first several decennial enumerations.

Scholars have documented how racial and ethnic categories in the US Census have changed over the years.[22] But the categories of "American Indian" or "Native American" do not merely represent a particular racial or ethnic group. Rather, Native Americans have a unique and specific *political* identity as members of sovereign nations that were eventually incorporated into the United States as "domestic dependent nations."[23] As the United States continued to expand its territorial boundaries over the course of the nineteenth century, new questions arose about whether and how to include Native Americans in the US Census, and how to interpret the Constitution's designation of "Indians not taxed."

Ultimately, according to census enumerators the category of "Indian" was not limited to heritage, parentage, or even blood quantum—it was also tied to individuals' actions and activities. Most generally, it referred to Native Americans who were not citizens, who were living among their own communities, and who engaged in Native cultural forms. In the censuses of 1850, 1860, and 1870, some Native people of mixed heritage were counted on surveys. They were considered "Indian" if they lived on reservations, and "white" if they did not. Information on "taxed" and "nontaxed" Native Americans was collected during the 1880 census, but it was not published. Finally, in 1890, the Census Bureau collected and published this information.[24]

While some information on Native populations was included in the 1850 census, the 1860 census was the first to contain significant data regarding Native Americans. There was no category for "Indian" in the 1860 census, but enumerators were instructed to count "families of Indians who have renounced tribal rule, and who under state or territory laws exercise the rights of citizens."[25] This census contained information on "taxed Indians" living in each state or territory, including age and sex.[26] When determining whether or not to count an individual as a "taxed Indian," the enumerator was instructed to decide whether individuals had given up tribal rule and were participating in broader society. If that was the case, they were included in the census as citizens and listed as "Indian." California's records are especially detailed in this year, while other states include totals of "Civilized Indians by Age and Sex." In the 1860 census, approximately forty thousand Native people who were considered "assimilated"—who owned land individually—were counted.

When preparing the 1870 census, agents expressed confusion about the category "Indians not taxed" and struggled with how to determine what category to place people into, especially for those with mixed heritage. Anyone living on a reservation by this point was considered "not taxed." But for those with mixed heritage, enumerators faced a challenge. There were few possibilities for determining the category—either by father's or mother's heritage, or by "superior" blood. But beyond ancestry, the categories of "Indian" versus "non-Indian" were delineated in part by features of culture. Ultimately, enumerators were instructed to place individuals in racial categories according to the "habits, tastes, and associations" of the individual.²⁷ This census included data on Indians divided into two categories, those who were "sustaining tribal relations" and those who were "out of tribal relations."²⁸

The 1880 census did not include as much detailed information about the Native American population. This census in particular was interested in presenting the idea of the progress of America. Minimal data was included about "uncivilized Indians," and "civilized Indians" were lumped together with Japanese and Chinese under the category of "colored—other." The 1890 census was the first comprehensive report that considered Indians taxed and not taxed (discussed in more detail below). Censuses produced after 1890 included information on Native Americans. Beginning in 1900, each decennial census contained information on Native Americans as part of the regular tabulations.

Tracing over these different years of the census enumeration and its exclusion or inclusion of Native Americans, we can see that a shift slowly occurred in the way Native peoples were included. At the time of the founding of the United States, the government engaged with Native peoples as sovereign nations, separate from the US body politic and thus not under the purview of the federal government in the same way as its citizens were. Ultimately, changes in the US Census Bureau's policies and practices regarding the enumeration of Native Americans have mirrored the changing political relationship between Native nations and the US government. Over the course of the nineteenth century, as the country's political boundaries continued to expand into Native lands, Census Bureau officials eventually directed enumerators to count Native Americans who were living in Euro-American society. While official census records thus began to include some Native Americans in the mid-nineteenth century, the Census Bureau did not complete full reports of the Native population, both on and off reservations, until the late nineteenth century, when Native American censuses were conducted in 1890, 1910, and 1930.

Questions about classification persisted throughout these years as, with the lack of official parameters, enumerators had to figure out their means of classifying Native Americans. Importantly, habits and customs—including individuals' levels of assimilation—were at times used to classify difference. The categories of "taxed" versus "untaxed" eventually gave way to categories judging the level of Native peoples' assimilation. While census materials did not explicitly describe religion in discussions of the "habits" that they mention, conversion to Christianity was a key goal of US assimilation efforts. Explicit discussions of Native American religions were present in the 1890 Indian census.

Native American Religions in the 1890 Indian Census

Political scientist Benedict Anderson described the census—along with the map and the museum—as three institutions of power that "profoundly shaped the way in which the colonial state imagined its dominion—the nature of the human beings it ruled, the geography of its domain, and the legitimacy of its ancestry."[29] Census publications function as empirical documents offering statistics about the US population. Yet, while the US Census Bureau today aims for rigor and accuracy, census enumeration and other forms of government-sponsored population counting have historically reflected political realities and agendas. As data scientist Margaret Jobe argues, despite their air of scientific objectivity, "census publications are artifacts of changing social and political values rather than objective statements of reality."[30] Indeed, assimilation-era Indian census publications included an array of highly variable data sets produced during the colonial era, as well as subjective qualitative accounts of Native populations and lifeways.

The US government's 1890 census report on American Indians contained typical census data, including population statistics and mortality rates, but it also included a great deal of historical and narrative information on Native cultures. However, unlike general population reports common in previous censuses, the report included commentary about Native religions. The census report's narrative about Indigenous population decline presented a picture of "religion on the brink," Native American traditions as teetering precariously on the edge of extinction. An analysis of the 1890 census report brings into sharper view the prevalent Euro-American perspective that Native American cultures would inevitably die out. This shared feature of both the census reports and other government reports—the narration, and even the fantasy, of the extinction of Native American people—offered a purportedly objective narrative justification for assimilation policies that targeted Indigenous beliefs and practices at the individual and communal levels.

In 1890, as part of the eleventh census, government agents traveled throughout the United States to gather information about Native American communities. This 1890 undertaking was the largest and most comprehensive census of Native Americans yet attempted.[31] Fifty-seven government agents worked as enumerators, and together they visited 148 Native communities, on and off reservations, for the purposes of gathering data about each nation. An additional thirty-six special agents visited Indian agencies to verify the statistical data that the enumerators gathered.[32]

Some of the census enumerators were Native Americans. For example, most of the agents who worked among the so-called Five Civilized Tribes removed to Indian Territory, present-day Oklahoma, belonged to one of those nations—Choctaw, Cherokee, Creek, Chickasaw, or Seminole. The US government did make an effort to cooperate with leaders to facilitate the work of the enumerators; the census report specifically mentioned this process through which it worked with members of the local population in Indian Territory.[33] But the majority of the enumerators were non-Native, outsiders to the communities they counted.

Those who prepared the census presented it as authoritative, "closely and accurately taken under a special law."[34] The government published a short preliminary report, primarily containing population statistics, in 1891. This report contained a brief and a number of charts and graphs detailing the demographics of different nations throughout the United States. The charts were divided, in part, according to location. Officials gathered and presented data on the Five Civilized Tribes who lived in Indian Territory separately from Eastern Cherokee people who remained in North Carolina. The report presented this information separately from those of other Native nations in the West, which was also distinct from information presented about Six Nations people from the Eastern Woodlands.[35] The census distinguished between Native Americans living on and off reservations. To further account for those living on reservations, census data included divisions based on separate agencies within the different states that contained reservations. For example, the chart for the state of Washington was divided according to the state's five Indian agencies: the Colville, Neah Bay, Puyallup, Tulalip, and Yakima agencies. These numbers were further divided on the basis of subdivisions within nations themselves, in some instances categorized by a smaller permanent community, in the case of the Anishinaabe people living in different towns near the La Pointe agency in Wisconsin.

On some reservations in the Plains region, where people lived in traditional semipermanent villages, the census bulletin listed divisions based on smaller, self-regulated groups rather than towns. This was the case for enumerations of Lakota people, described in the documents by the name "Sioux," whom the report organized into different "bands." In each of these tables, columns accounted for numbers of men and women. Another column entitled "Ration Indians" denoted those individuals who received food and supplies from the government. On the far right of each of these charts was a column that indicated whether or not the total population of each group was increasing or decreasing, based on a comparison of current data with numbers collected previously, as early as one year prior. According to the 1891 census bulletin, enumerators had gathered information about births and deaths from "several sources, including the agents' and physicians' reports."[36]

In 1894, the Government Printing Office published a more complete report of the 1890 Indian census. This publication included many additional charts that contained much more detailed information about the nations that the census officials had visited. In addition to enumerating the Native American population, the document drew on scholarly accounts, previous census data, historical overviews, maps, and discussions about language. This supplemental, historical information comprised approximately 20 percent of the report. The remainder of the 683-page document detailed information gathered about each community. In addition to population statistics, it included profiles on leaders and important people, as well as maps and portraits. This report offered what was, at that time, the most comprehensive single account of American Indian populations.

Many of the Native American communities that the census officials visited did not participate willingly in the process. In the 1891 census bulletin, census superintendent Robert P. Porter noted that many of the agents had difficulty in obtaining statistics from the communities they visited: "Many of the enumerators engaged in the work met with serious and dangerous opposition, their portfolios being looked upon with suspicion." Many Native communities were indeed unwilling to participate, concerned about what the information was for and what the result of their participation might be. In some cases, Porter noted, "These officials narrowly escaped with their lives."[37] However, the author of the report presented it as a success: Porter suggested that "the results accomplished have been most satisfactory."[38] Despite the difficulties, the members of the Census Office stood by their reports.

As the census report noted, Native American communities were concerned about what the census would mean for them. Some communities met to discuss its potential impact on their communities and how they might respond.[39] In some cases, religious leaders urged members of their communities not to participate in the survey. As explained in the census report, "Some of the reservation Indians were very cautious in their reception of the enumerators. [The agents'] portfolios were suggestive of books, and many Indians, considering them books of new religious creeds, refused to answer the questions. Others advised resistance, claiming that this enrollment was a scheme to get their names, which would then be attached to an alleged treaty, and they would be robbed of their right to remain on their lands."[40] The authors of the census, while noting these concerns, failed to take them seriously and viewed them as an impediment to the data-gathering process.

Given the ways in which the census presented data about Indigenous populations, and the analysis that the government agents used when discussing the data, Native communities' fears and resistance were warranted. The US Census collected information about the Native American populations in a way that would aid the government's management of Native populations. Broadly, it presented a cynical picture of Native American communities. The census narrated the decline of Native American populations and presented Indigenous culture and society as unimportant and inconsequential. In addition, the report indicated that its purpose was to aid in the government's assimilation interests. For example, in a discussion of land in the 1894 report detailing the 1890 census, the author suggested that one of the primary purposes of gathering information about Native Americans was to determine how many occupied the land. "Preliminary to [a] survey of lands within the public domain the United States requires the extinction of the Indian title or Indian right of occupancy thereof."[41] The report then outlined the most effective ways of extinguishing Indian land title.

One key feature of the census's discussion of Native American communities was its portrayal of Native people as inherently different from Euro-Americans. The racial descriptions found in this census described Native Americans as without logic or rationality, physically strong, and inherently indisposed to work.[42] Discussions of Indigenous religion in the census also echoed this point. According to the census, Native beliefs and practices were not logical and did not feature in any way scientific modes of thinking. The report attested that Native people "have no mathematics in their methods, and many of these alleged singular and complex religious and other systems would not be known save for their development or invention by white men. It remained, in many instances, for white men to tell the Indian what his methods and systems were."[43] At the same time, the census report denied that Native Americans had spiritual systems, calling into question anthropological studies of the day:

> That the North American Indian had or has any well-defined religious views or beliefs as we understand them remains yet to be ascertained. The ideal Indian has a religion, but the real Indian has none. "God," a word he first heard from the Europeans, has to him in fact no special significance. It means anything around and above him. His mythology is crude and embraces the natural features around him: fire, water, the air, earth, the sun, moon, and stars, and all animated nature. The real Indian hangs to his mythology, which is ingenious for its elements but unsatisfactory as a theory, with desperate tenacity.[44]

In a historical overview of Native Americans published in the census report, the author described the innate, inborn differences between Native Americans and Euro-Americans in psychological and spiritual terms. "The North American Indian, a child of nature, seems to possess a peculiar logic, and it seems to have been born in him."[45] Many resources refer to Native Americans as lacking "logic," so this innate "logic" refers rather to a system of beliefs and orientations that, on the basis of outsider ideas about the absence of Indigenous science or religion, the author would probably have characterized as "illogical." The report asserted, "While the North American Indians, according to some authors, have a complete system of religion in forms most ingenious and mathematical in its sequences, these same Indians are incapable of inventing, constructing, or building anything that requires the mental power of combination."[46] The census presented this lack of both science and religion as a feature of Native American cultures and as an inborn, essential difference between Native and Euro-American people.

Scholars in Native American studies have described the "declension narrative" in which Euro-Americans have depicted the decline of Native peoples.[47] Woven throughout the census is the same narrative about decline. In a historical overview of Native American cultures, the 1890 census suggested that upon the arrival of Europeans, Native communities that came into contact with Euro-Americans were "self-sustaining and self-reliant, with tribal governments, many forms of worship, and many superstitions, with ample clothing of skin and furs, and food fairly well supplied."[48] Following along with the declension narrative, the author suggested that, from the period of contact with Europeans, Native communities steadily declined in all ways of life.

Beyond offering an argument in support of the declension model, the author actually went a step further, narrating the annihilation of all Native Americans. The author suggested that "he could see that his race was about to be covered with a cloud that would eventually engulf it. . . . With clenched teeth, and club or gun in his hand, he places his back to the rock and dies in resistance."[49] The Native American, according to the census, "welcomes death."[50] The author argued, "Even nature, the Indian's god, is silent as to him, and speaks not. Such has been his life, such the result, that if the entire remaining Indians were instantly and completely wiped from the face of the earth they would leave no monuments, no buildings, no written language save one, no literature, no inventions, nothing in the arts or sciences, and absolutely nothing for the benefit of mankind."[51] This narration of the inevitable decline of Native American culture served to authorize the US government's assimilation policies. What is so striking about this statement is its imagining of an American future without Native Americans. The author claimed that writers had created romantic notions of Native Americans that did them a disservice. The problem, the author argued, was that these romantic notions had made the mainstream public and politicians *too hopeful* about the possibility that Native Americans could adapt to Euro-American civilization.[52]

The author of the census was apparently familiar with research on Native traditions but did not seem to take seriously the idea that Native Americans could have religion. The author even went so far as to suggest that ethnologists came up with their own theories about Native religious systems and then cajoled Native people into agreeing with the ethnologist about the theory they invented. According to the census report, "Any ingenious ethnologist or investigator wedded to a theory, if he has a vivid imagination and a stock of money or food, can obtain ample proof of that theory from an Indian."[53] In some ways, then, the ideas present in the census differed from those of government anthropologists at the time, who actively sought to document Native religions and cultures and systematically used the term "religion" to describe Indigenous beliefs and practices. While many government researchers also supported assimilation policies and advanced racialized theories of cultural evolution, their theories of Native religion operated in a slightly different way, insofar as they eventually conceded that "religion" existed among Native cultures.[54] The 1890 census presented a starker perspective, equating a lack of religion with the lack of humanity—and the absence of Native futures.

Conclusion: Inclusion in the 2020 Census as an "Act of Rebellion"

This chapter has drawn on data and narratives from the US government's enumerations of Native Americans to argue that these censuses documented the purported decline of Native cultures. Despite the relative absence of data about religion in their usual versions of the US Census, information about religion was included in Native American censuses, generally depicting it as evidence of the need for assimilation. One can interpret the US Census, vis-à-vis Native American communities, as a system of settler-colonial knowledge production with the ultimate goal of managing Indigenous life—what theorist Michel Foucault would describe as a technology of state power or biopolitics and what anthropologist David Scott would further describe as a feature of colonial governmentality.[55]

The US Census—and interpretations of it—have changed over time. Foucault's influence has shaped social scientists' research on governments' collection of information about the citizens and occupants of their countries.⁵⁶ According to this "state-centered" interpretation, government censuses can be interpreted as tools used by the state for the purposes of government.⁵⁷ However, this is not the only way to interpret the US Census. Social scientists have argued that it has shifted over time from an explicitly imperial tool to a system in which social groups have exerted their own pressure on the process. Drawing on Jennifer Graber's framework (chapter 6), we can consider a shift in the US Census from one that leveraged and extended an "imperial frame" to one that Indigenous communities have themselves leveraged. Since the 1960s, many minoritized communities, including Native Americans, have increasingly pressed the US Census Bureau to make changes that enable people to better represent themselves.⁵⁸

Data collection for the 2020 United States Census faced unprecedented challenges. In March of 2020, when US residents were invited to self-report their household information via surveys, the nation was stricken by the COVID-19 pandemic and its ensuing economic instability. In the summer, natural disasters including fires and massive storms hit different regions of the country. The Black Lives Matter movement, advocating for the lives and well-being of Black Americans, reemerged on a national scale in response to repeated and widespread police violence against people of color. This natural and sociopolitical context in which the 2020 census occurred was thus especially disruptive to the count. In previous years, Black, Indigenous, Asian American, and Latinx households; families with low income; and people living in rural areas were less likely to respond to the Census Bureau's requests for information. The natural, social, economic, and public health crises of 2020 created even more barriers to census reporting among these communities, many of whom have historically been undercounted.⁵⁹ Census undercounts can harm these communities, who may, as a result, miss out on both economic resources and political representation.⁶⁰

In recent decades, Native American organizers throughout the United States have worked to educate their communities about the significance of being counted in the census.⁶¹ Today, statistical data from the census directly impacts the distribution of resources to Native American communities. For example, in response to the COVID-19 pandemic, the US Congress passed the Coronavirus Aid, Relief, and Economic Security (CARES) Act in April of 2020. One outcome of this act was the distribution of monetary resources to tribal governments. This aid was essential to Native nations, many of whom were acutely affected by COVID-19.[62] According to a May 2020 study jointly produced by the Harvard Project on American Indian Economic Development and the University of Arizona's Native Nations Institute, rather than using self-reported numbers from nations themselves, the US Department of Treasury developed a population distribution formula utilizing racial data derived from the Department of Housing and Urban Development and the US Census to allocate funds. These publicly available numbers were known to be inconsistent with actual tribal enrollment numbers. This resulted in the uneven distribution of funds, in some cases significantly over or under what each nation should have gotten on the basis of actual numbers of enrolled members.[63]

The national count for the 2020 US Census began in a small, isolated Alaskan village in January of that year. While most census activities were scheduled to begin months later, the director of the Census Bureau, Steven Dillingham, explained to the media that beginning the process earlier in Alaska would ensure a more accurate count. When the ice begins to thaw in the spring, travel to remote villages throughout Alaska is more difficult. In addition, many members leave the village to pursue seasonal work. However, despite the early start, the events of 2020 would introduce a host of additional challenges to getting an accurate count of American Indian, Native Alaskan, and Hawaiian citizens. When describing the challenges, Natalie Landreth, a senior attorney for the Native American Rights Fund who advocates for policies supporting Native Americans and Native Alaskans and Hawaiians, stressed the significance of the census. Landreth said, "I want to tell every American Indian and Alaska Native to be counted as an act of rebellion because this census is not designed to count you."[64] Indeed, as documented in census reports, in the past, the federal government did imagine that Native cultures would cease to exist. Despite historical exclusion, and even recent challenges, inclusion in the US Census can be an avenue for Native Americans to access resources and exercise their rights.

NOTES

1. Wolfe, "Settler Colonialism and the Elimination of the Native," 388.
2. Whyte, "Indigeneity and US Settler Colonialism."
3. J. Byrd, *Transit of Empire*; Deloria, *Playing Indian*; J. O'Brien, *Firsting and Lasting*; Morgensen, "The Biopolitics of Settler Colonialism."

4　For a discussion of US expansion over the course of the nineteenth century and its impact on Native American religions, see Graber, *The Gods of Indian Country*.
5　Deloria and DeMallie, *Documents of American Indian Diplomacy*.
6　Duthu, *American Indians and the Law*.
7　Perdue and Green, *The Cherokee Nation and the Trail of Tears*.
8　Bowes, *Land Too Good for Indians*; Denetdale, "Discontinuities, Remembrances, and Cultural Survival."
9　Dees, "Religion and U.S. Federal Indian Policy."
10　Holm, *The Great Confusion in Indian Affairs*.
11　McNally, *Defend the Sacred*; Wenger, *We Have a Religion*.
12　Wolfe, "Settler Colonialism and the Elimination of the Native," 388.
13　Wolfe, "Settler Colonialism and the Elimination of the Native," 387.
14　Good, "Questions on Religion in the United States Census."
15　US Census Bureau, *Report on Indians Taxed and Not Taxed in the United States (Except Alaska) at the Eleventh Census: 1890* (Washington, DC: Government Printing Office, 1894), 5.
16　US Census Bureau, *Report on Indians Taxed and Not Taxed*, 15.
17　These included Croghan, Bouquet, Hutchins, Dodge, Carver, and other writers. US Census Bureau, *Report on Indians Taxed and Not Taxed*, 1–45.
18　Lujan, "As Simple as One, Two, Three."
19　Jacob Wallace, "Census Hasn't Always Counted Native Americans," *Journal* (Cortez, CO), August 11, 2020, https://the-journal.com, accessed February 15, 2021.
20　Lujan, "American Indians and Alaska Natives Count," 328–29.
21　Hickman, "The Devil and the One Drop Rule."
22　Lee, "Racial Classifications in the US Census: 1890–1990."
23　Duthu, *American Indians and the Law*.
24　Lujan, "American Indians and Alaska Natives Count," 321.
25　Collins, "Native Americans in the Census, 1860–1890," 1.
26　Jobe, "Native Americans and the U.S. Census," 70.
27　Francis A. Walker, *A Compendium of the Ninth Census* (Washington, DC: Government Printing Office, 1872), 19.
28　Jobe, "Native Americans and the U.S. Census," 71.
29　Anderson, *Imagined Communities*, 163–64.
30　Jobe, "Native Americans and the U.S. Census," 67.
31　Collins, "Native Americans in the Census, 1860–1890," 1–5.
32　U.S. Census Bureau, "Statistics of Indians," Census Bulletin 25 (1891), 1.
33　U.S. Census Bureau, "Statistics of Indians," Census Bulletin 25 (1891), 3.
34　U.S. Census Bureau, "Statistics of Indians," Census Bulletin 25 (1891), 14.
35　U.S. Census Bureau, "Statistics of Indians," Census Bulletin 25 (1891), 5.
36　U.S. Census Bureau, "Statistics of Indians," Census Bulletin 25 (1891), 14.
37　U.S. Census Bureau, "Statistics of Indians," Census Bulletin 25 (1891), 1.
38　U.S. Census Bureau, "Statistics of Indians," Census Bulletin 25 (1891), 1
39　U.S. Census Bureau, "Statistics of Indians," Census Bulletin 25 (1891), 3.

40 U.S. Census Bureau, "Statistics of Indians," Census Bulletin 25 (1891), 3.
41 US Census Bureau, *Report on Indians Taxed and Not Taxed in 1890*, 89.
42 On the changing stereotypical representations of Native Americans, see Berkhofer, *White Man's Indian*.
43 Berkhofer, *White Man's Indian*, 55.
44 Berkhofer, *White Man's Indian*, 55.
45 Berkhofer, *White Man's Indian*, 56.
46 Berkhofer, *White Man's Indian*, 55.
47 O'Brien, *Firsting and Lasting*.
48 US Census Bureau, *Report on Indians Taxed and Not Taxed in 1890*, 49.
49 US Census Bureau, *Report on Indians Taxed and Not Taxed in 1890*, 57.
50 US Census Bureau, *Report on Indians Taxed and Not Taxed in 1890*, 50.
51 US Census Bureau, *Report on Indians Taxed and Not Taxed in 1890*, 57.
52 Hoxie, *Final Promise*.
53 Hoxie, *Final Promise*, 55.
54 Dees, "An Equation of Language and Spirit."
55 Foucault, *"Society Must Be Defended,"* 243. Scott, "Colonial Governmentality."
56 Kertzer and Arel, eds., *Census and Identity*.
57 Emigh, Riley, and Ahmed, *Changes in Censuses from Imperialist to Welfare States*, 4.
58 Emigh, Riley, and Ahmed, *Changes in Censuses from Imperialist to Welfare States*, 147–76.
59 Aggie Yellow Horse, "Shortened Census Will Hurt Communities of Color," *Conversation*, August 31, 2020, https://theconversation.com.
60 Akee, Ong, and Longbear, "US Census Response Rates on American Indian Reservations in the 2020 Census and in the 2010 Census."
61 Juaqlin Estus, "Census Count Is 'an Act of Rebellion,'" *Indian Country Today*, January 20, 2020.
62 Bambino et al., "The Disproportionate Impact of COVID-19 on Racial and Ethnic Minorities in the United States," 1–4.
63 Akee, Ong, and Longbear, "US Census Response Rates on American Indian Reservations."
64 Estus, "Census Count Is 'an Act of Rebellion.'"

5

Imperial Intersections

*Social Surveys, Sentimental Biopolitics,
and Religion at Hull House*

CARA LEA BURNIDGE

In 1883, Jane Addams made her first trip to Europe at the age of twenty-three. A leave of absence from coursework at Woman's Medical College of Philadelphia and a two-year exploration of Europe were her doctor's prescriptions for her physical, emotional, and mental ailments. Addams's trip across the Atlantic overwhelmed her senses. On one particular Saturday night, a city missionary guided Addams and other tourists through London's East End. Sitting comfortably atop an omnibus on Mile End Road, Addams watched as the city's poorest residents raised their hands to bid on rotten and day-old food from street vendors. As each person "won" their bit of nutrition, Addams sat horrified as vendors "scornfully flung" items at their patrons. Much to her dismay, one man "hastily devoured" his "unwashed and uncooked" cabbage. In addition to the inadequate sustenance, "ragged, tawdry clothing" and "pinched and sallow faces" alarmed Addams. Yet, the image that would haunt and drive her career was the "myriad of hands, empty, pathetic, nerveless, and workworn, showing white in the uncertain light of the street, and clutching forward for food which was already unfit to eat." Following this enlightening experience, as Addams toured other European cities, she felt "irresistibly drawn to the poorer quarters of each city," but none evoked the intense feelings she felt in East London. Rather than feel relief or comfort during the rest of her stay—a time prescribed to her for its potentially restorative benefits—Addams found herself "bewildered that the world should be going on as usual."[1] This profound experience of observing physical pain and suffering gave her a new purpose and direction in life. The experience helped her decide to take up residence among the poor in her own country to cure the nation's social ills through the settlement house movement. After gathering more information from "the Oxford men" who founded Toynbee Hall, the first English settlement house, Addams and Ellen Gates Starr moved into a house on Halstead Street in Chicago's Nineteenth Ward and opened the doors to America's most notable settlement house, Hull House.[2]

Addams's sympathy toward the poor served as the foundation of Hull House. These feelings motivated her to pack up her belongings and settle in a new city among people whose life experiences were different from her own. The disturbing and unsettling feelings she felt in London empowered her to disrupt social, cultural, religious, and political norms shaping her place in public life. These feelings and the politics informing them were not her own creation but a script she and many other white women shared through popular sentimental literature. Women and Gender Studies scholar Kyla Schuller calls these scripts and the lived experience of them the "biopolitics of feeling," a discourse and site of asymmetrical power found at the intersection of science and sentimentalism. She argues that sentimentalism served as a "foundational technology" informing and masking a "politics of life" in which "state and nonstate actors govern by fostering the health and vitality of some members of the nation, while designating others for dispossession and death."[3] This "conceptual apparatus" structured a biopolitics of feeling encouraging the use of emerging sciences for the "calculating and regulating" of bodies in dynamic relation to one another.[4] With these complex power structures at play, the feelings, politics, and science framing Hull House place it at a crossroads of religion and US empire at the end of the nineteenth century.

The cultural and political location of Hull House at the intersection of religion, social science research, and governance reflects the entanglement of progressive ideologies and sentimental biopolitics in sustaining US empire. This chapter draws attention to Hull House as a cultural, religious, and political site developing and advancing foundational technologies supporting US imperialism. The advocacy for progressive legislation and grassroots organizing occurring at Hull House contributed to the development of US empire at the turn of the nineteenth century even as vocal residents, at times, challenged and attempted to resist capitalism and settler colonialism. Rather than assume that an imperial frame casts historical figures into fixed, binary positions "for" or "against" empire, this chapter seeks to show how these historical actors contributed to US empire even when they professed otherwise.[5] Hull House, as a home to progressive feelings, politics, and emergent social sciences, charted new territory in the expansion of US empire, despite the various reform-minded religious and political positions of its residents. Not least of all, Hull House residents developed and popularized new surveillance techniques and discourses through the success of *Hull House Maps and Papers*, a book sharing the results of their investigation of the living and working conditions in "a congested district of Chicago."[6]

Imperial Intersections

By design, Hull House was established to be an "intellectual and social centre" for Chicago's Nineteenth Ward, an area comprised of immigrants residing in tenements as well as various shops, saloons, factories, and "the omnipresent midwife."[7] As founders and residents of Hull House, Addams and Starr lived in the house on Halstead Street as they coordinated and facilitated the events and activities hosted within it. Such an arrangement was a signature feature of settlement houses, which encouraged highly educated, middle- and elite-classed white "residents" to leave their lives of privilege to live alongside working-class and immigrant "neighbors" in order to foster mutually beneficial interactions in a spirit of cooperation and collaboration.[8] When Addams and Starr moved into the neighborhood, they imagined their settlement as providing a "common stimulus" to the new community they called home. This biopolitical foundation to settlements assumed that close proximity, intentional contact, and social exchange among distinct populations would stimulate new vitality in the neighborhood, disrupting and disproving a pattern of thinking they assumed to be commonly held: that middle-class white Americans and nonwhite, working-class immigrants were inherently different from one another. As Addams explained, "The mere foothold of a house, easily accessible, ample in space, hospitable and tolerant in spirit, situated in the midst of the large foreign colonies which so easily isolate themselves in American cities, would be in itself a serviceable thing for Chicago."[9] As a result, Hull House offered educational programming, social events, and entertainments aimed at minimizing the power of social difference in order to offer "higher civic and social life" so the "blessings which we associate with a life of refinement and cultivation can be made universal."[10] These efforts to nurture progressive intellectual and social development further fed the settlement sensibility that white residents catalyzed intellectual and spiritual evolutions among nonwhite residents and neighbors. As a settlement surrounded by "foreign colonies," Hull House existed variously in a sentimental progressive imagination as a utopia, a refuge, and an imperial intervention reorienting foreign islands around a new, domestic metropole.

Hull House residents occupied a unique location in US empire's civic milieu, enjoying opportunities and privileges that similar institutions could not. They operated in an ideological and structural borderland, working alongside private, philanthropic, or religious charity organizations, institutions of higher education, and formal government entities, yet they remained distinct among these peer institutions. Unlike other settlement houses in the United States, which often operated as "sociological laboratories" for college students, Hull House resisted formal association with a university.[11] Similarly, Hull House did not hold a formal denominational affiliation, departing from the model established through Toynbee Hall, the original settlement house in England. Without the donations of students and faculty that funded university settlements, and without the regular donations from members of a congregation that funded religiously affiliated settlements, Hull House functioned through Addams's own wealth and, later, private donations. Such an arrangement allowed Hull House to be built according to Addams's design, and she dreamed of a religiously plural home, a "cathedral to humanity."[12] Addams delighted in informing an Oxford House colleague of the absence of a shared worship service at Hull House because "there were among us Jews, Roman Catholics, English Churchmen, Dissenters, and a few agnostics, and . . . we had found unsatisfactory the diluted form of worship which we could carry on together." Rather than fear a "diversity of creed," she considered it "our task [in American settlements] to live in a neighborhood of many nationalities and faiths."[13] Though she felt "the pressure toward religious profession" and "propagandists of diverse social theories" attempted to claim her as their own,

Addams insisted upon "passive resistance" to ideological affiliations with any one partisan or sectarian group.[14] The lack of a religious affiliation separated Hull House from its settlement forebears and made it a model in converting new Americans to a nonsectarian and nonpartisan form of citizenship informing greater humanitarian progress.

Even though there is some interpretive overlap between settlement-worker experiences and those of missionaries, maintaining distance from church and missionary organizations was important to most settlement houses in the United States. In "Religion in the Settlement," Dean George Hodges explained what seemed obvious: "The settlement is not a church."[15] The two institutions had distinct purposes, roles, and scopes of work in society. Whereas missionaries, churches, and other Christian organizations sought conversions or conducted charitable work in direct relation to their religious commitments and affiliations, most settlements did not have this same sense of evangelical or denominational mission. This did not mean that religion was absent from settlements. Religion could be found in and around the settlements in a number of ways. First, and most popular among scholars of this era, religion entered the settlement movement through the personal ideologies of its prominent members.[16] Second, and sometimes related to the first, settlement workers often articulated a personal and institutional mission invested in welcoming and engaging the "whole" of humanity. Addams embraced this idea through Edward Caird's *Evolution of Religion*, which asserts an ultimate "unity of mankind" that is "not merely a dogma, but an almost instinctive presupposition of all civilised men" supported through the science of evolution.[17] Caird explained, "We know now, in a way in which it was never known before, that humanity is a genus which has no proper species; i.e., that the divisions between men are as nothing in comparison with the fundamental fact of self-consciousness which unites them all to each other." This "modern" understanding of humanity evolved from a more "ancient" view "built on the principle of natural kinship, and therefore on a principle which carried with it tribal or national exclusiveness, even where it did not set up further barriers between the members of the society by immovable divisions of family from family, rank from rank, and caste from caste."[18] This religious, metaphysical, and scientific commitment to the idea of an ultimate unity of humanity encouraged a resistance to social distinctions, viewing them as mere "accidental differences" holding "comparative unimportance." Actions focusing on the "common" identity or shared purpose of humanity transcended ostensibly superficial markers of individual identity (like class, national origin, and race), which, in this view, served as barriers to improved community life.

Addams found comfort in this way of thinking, helping her navigate "the labyrinth of differing ethical teachings and religious creeds which the many immigrant colonies of our neighborhood presented." It is this focus on a "higher" calling and purpose that led to the third way many settlement workers imagined religion intersecting with their work: settlements as institutions distinct from churches but as ultimately fulfilling the purpose of religion. In this way, it was the actions of the settlement workers that Hodges and Addams understood to align with religious ideals and fulfill the purpose of religion, especially Christianity. "Its faith is made evident by its works," Hodges claimed.[19] Rather than thinking of "religion" as "institutionalism," "denominationalism," "barriers or badges," Hodges equated religion with "the spirit and life of Jesus Christ" as evidenced in "ministration to the fatherless and the widows in their affiliation, and as a keeping of the conscience unspotted in the world." Since settlements were "doing good" and tried to care for "those who are down," Hodges determined the settlement to be religious and "the house in which its workers live is the house of God."[20] By eschewing specific denominational affiliations and religious creeds yet doing good in the community, Hull House maintained religious credibility in the Progressive Era. As far as these liberal and progressive thinkers were concerned, it demonstrated the next stage in the evolutionary development of religion. Addams agreed that Hull House was a part of "a distinct turning" occurring with respect to religion that was at once a "renaissance of the early Christian humanitarianism" and a new stage of human life in which Christianity could—and should—be found "not in a sect, but in society itself."[21]

The home Hull House residents built belonged—literally and figuratively—at an imperial intersection, reorienting the power and place of white women reformers in American public life. The domestic and social work they performed at the settlement acculturated immigrant and working-class neighbors to progressive national interests while also providing a platform for cultural exchange, introducing white residents to "foreign" languages, customs, goods, and festivals.²² Navigating this cultural crossroads served their personal and professional interests even though they did not often articulate this reality in these terms publicly. "The function of the settlement," settlement vanguard Robert Woods wrote, served "as a connecting link between the two great sections of society."²³ As a private home open to the public, settlement houses appeared to bridge the divide between differing ends of society—those imagined as the "lowest" segment of society and nationals at its highest stage of development—yet centered white middle-class experiences with poverty as evidence of their good works. Settlement workers at Hull House and elsewhere healed the pain they felt for society by creating space for their own power in improving the productivity of the nation. In this way, white settlement workers understood themselves as serving a mediatory role between nation and community. They identified needs, but also determined how those needs would be met. As Addams put it, the most valuable function of a settlement house was its ability to "discern and bring to local consciousness neighborhood needs which are common needs, and can give vigorous help to the municipal measures through which such needs shall be met."²⁴ Identifying what needs existed in the "neighborhood" (meaning, the needs of those *not* living in Hull House but in the surrounding community), and especially discerning proper needs (those shared across race, class, nationality, and religious identity rather than sectarian, partisan, or class-based needs), was the calling of a settlement worker. So too was assisting city, state, and federal officials and institutions in crafting secular, civic solutions. Existing political structures and processes were assumed to be the means through which progressive solutions would be executed, and the expectation was that such means would lead to satisfactory ends for all parties involved. Elevating the neighborhood, then, also required settlement workers to connect their working-class and immigrant neighbors to the state.

Social Surveillance as Moral Geography

At once a humanitarian mission, scientific endeavor, and nation-building exercise, the social survey fell neatly into the purview of Hull House's "civic enterprises," occupying what Addams identified as "that borderland between charitable effort and legislation." In the late nineteenth century, the "social survey" emerged as a new method of gathering information about a community, a new surveillance technology, and a social, religious, political trend in the emergent social sciences. According to the *Encyclopedia of the Social Sciences*, which was published at the height of social survey work in the 1930s, a social survey is "a first hand investigation, analysis and coordination of economic, sociological and other related aspects of a selected community or group. Such a survey may be undertaken primarily in order to provide material scientifically gathered upon which social theorists may base their conclusions; or its chief purpose may be to formulate a programme of amelioration of the conditions of life and work of a particular group or community."[25]

Social surveyors distinguished themselves from government officials who conducted the census by building and maintaining trust with the local community. Collecting data directly through in-person field work was essential, but social surveys tended to utilize investigators located *within* the community under investigation, even if only temporarily during the period of study. Ideally, social surveyors would live within or near their subjects prior to the start of the survey in order to begin with existing familiarity with the people and place they would investigate. An effective survey would provide comprehensive information about the community, counting and categorizing individual bodies, but also account for existing relationships, like distinct racialized or classed neighborhoods. Quantifiable observations of material goods or resources, like windows per house or plumbing facilities, contributed to the knowledge of the particular community and its place in American life more generally.[26] Investigators and their supporting institutions expected these identifiable and isolated "facts" to reveal existing social conditions and trends across a community, which would point to obvious public policy reforms to improve life in the neighborhood, city, or state. Once social problems became visible, the thinking went, the state could solve those problems and improve society through public policy.

The most ambitious and successful of these projects was *Hull House Maps and Papers* (1895), the first and most comprehensive social survey conducted through Hull House. Comprised of ten chapters providing synthetic essays on significant topics relevant to the neighborhood, *Hull House Maps and Papers* presented Chicago's Nineteenth Ward in ways distanced observers had not seen before. It supplied meticulously collected quantitative data about neighborhood residents along with qualitative analysis on key progressive issues, like sweatshops and child labor, as well as on specific racialized groups like "Bohemians," Italians, and Jews. What distinguished *Hull House Maps and Papers* from previous surveys, including the federal census, was its brilliantly colored maps visually depicting the data. Drawing upon a similar feature in Charles Booth's *Life and Labor of the People of London* (1889), *Hull House Maps and Papers* color-coded the presence and distribution of wages earned and differing nationalities but did so on the basis of building lots, or "households," rather than city blocks. Some buildings, such as tenements, were presented as multicolored to illustrate how people of different nationalities or incomes lived within the same location. Drawing viewers' attention to the plurality of nationalities in Chicago's Nineteenth Ward, the *Map of Nationalities*, for example, marks the presence of different nationalities with different colors ranging from white for "English-speaking (Excluding Irish)" residents to red for Russian residents to orange for Chinese residents to black for "Colored" residents. The colors, obviously reflecting a racist social imaginary, draw attention to the variety of nationalities present but also, in their own way, make the neighborhood attractive.

Hull House Maps and Papers was a biopolitical nation-building exercise, producing new ways of thinking and feeling about US empire in order to inform and administer a politics of life. The *Map of Nationalities*, in particular, informs viewers of the diversity of persons living in close quarters, depicting their proximity to one another as visually appealing through vibrant colors on the page. In this image of the city, monochromatic blocks appear abnormal and resistant to progress while multicolored buildings and blocks illustrated the future and mission of Hull House. This visualization of nationality data affirmed yet inverted the interpretation Josiah Strong had provided ten years earlier in his famous book *Our Country: Its Possible Future and Its Present Crisis* (1885): the United States had been invaded by immigrants. Instead of ruining the nation, as Strong argued, the *Map of Nationalities* implied that it made the neighborhood, and through it the nation, more beautiful. The *Map of Wages* similarly elicited strong emotive reactions, but in contrast draws viewers' attention to the stark differences in wages earned.

As Agnes Holbrook notes in her "Comments on the Wage-Map," income varied widely, depending on the season, number of wage earners in a family (which typically included women and children as laborers), and industry. Holbrook noted that brothels in particular appeared to have the widest margin in earnings for one location, ranging from five to fifty dollars a week (though data collection was limited in this instance). More shockingly, when the two maps were viewed together, observers could see that these brothels were "invariably occupied by American girls."[27] This disturbing fact, included among other tangible and quantifiable details, confirmed not only the need for greater reform efforts but also the necessity of continued scientific studies of "slum" life. In this way, *Hull House Maps and Papers* depicted the prevalence and intimacy of social difference less as a peril to American neighborhoods and more as a promise of future progress through further commitments to study, survey, and map local communities.

Maps and demographic data helped settlement workers, like missionaries before them, "organize and prioritize their mission efforts" and "shape the ways that other Americans who stayed at home saw the world."[28] Even though the women of Hull House would have understood their actions as distinct, especially in their science and secularism, their survey and mapping efforts contributed to "imperial connections" just as eighteenth-century missionaries did. Their effort to observe and catalogue the world occurred on similar terms, noting the attire and appearance, literacy and education levels, sexual modesty and promiscuity, work ethic and labor activities of those in their neighborhood.[29] Unlike the eighteenth-century missionaries before them, they did not utilize existing imperial relationships but rather introduced new methods and modes of feeling structuring imperial connections within US empire. In particular, *Hull House Maps and Papers* departed from what historian Emily Conroy-Krutz referred to as a "hierarchy of heathenism," an approach to missionary map making in which cultures and nationalities were ranked according to their civilizational progress and priority for evangelism.[30] Hull House surveyors were not interested in ranking the cultures, ethnicities, or nationalities represented in their neighborhood. *Hull House Maps and Papers* represented diverse nationalities and ethnicities not as outsiders or threats to American life but as equal participants within a shared neighborhood because Hull House embraced plurality, especially distinct ethnic, national, and religious groups residing in the same neighborhood. They projected a kind of enlightened cosmopolitanism, embracing difference as a sign and method of human progress. Such a position placed the women of Hull House in contrast to racist ideologies encouraging segregation in general and the protection of white women in particular from racially mixed public spaces and neighborhoods. The science, sentimentalism, and humanitarianism informing Hull House women encouraged close contact with neighbors and fellow residents who were not identified as white. Such close contact, while imagined as reducing social difference, increased Hull House women's social power, especially their credibility and legitimacy as social scientists and experts. While their collaboration with immigrant neighbors provides an important distinction to previous missionary efforts, their collaborations similarly strengthened imperial endeavors and relationships rather than resisting or challenging them.

Even though *Hull House Maps and Papers* insisted upon the objectivity of the facts depicted—as a marker of the professional credibility of its women authors and its legitimacy as a product in the developing field of social science—it was an interpretative tool revealing, as Religious Studies scholar Amy DeRogatis has argued, "the hopes and desires of the culture that produced the maps."[31] Through their effective research and analysis, Hull House residents mediated the changing urban landscape by offering a new "moral geography" embracing cosmopolitanism and nonsectarianism and encouraging white, middle-class Americans to collaborate with immigrant and working-class neighbors by settling in *their* communities.[32] Despite their varied audience, including government agencies, wealthy philanthropic societies, scholars, and Nineteenth Ward residents, Hull House researchers received widespread praise for their study.[33] Samuel McCune Lindsay, professor of sociology at the University of Pennsylvania, declared it "equal in excellence" to Charles Booth's maps.[34] Frederic Sanders of Columbia University commended the women of Hull House on their achievement, noting how their work made a persuasive case for specific policy reform. Praising the study for providing "a faithful picture of what is, and of what unquestionably is evil," he asserted that "this work should certainly help students of social science, statesmen, and economists to find the way to something better."[35] *Hull House Maps and Papers* provided a blueprint for teaching the state how to better understand, manage, regulate, and govern society. In presenting such an intentional image of the neighborhood, the investigators placed themselves at the cutting edge of social science and its social survey methodologies. Yet, as Jane Addams made clear in her preface, "sociological investigation" was not their goal; this was a "constructive work." Hull House surveyors were not distanced observers, but active participants.

The Power of Friendship

Although *Hull House Maps and Papers* takes an omniscient view of the neighborhood, the perspectives within were crafted through intimate and personal relationships. Key to their success was women researchers' ability to effectively move between the roles of "friend," "scientist," and "investigator" as persons who, regardless of their official title, cared about the community. For example, under the direction of Florence Kelley, a team of four investigators gathered evidence by going door to door interviewing individual Nineteenth Ward residents using a sixty-four-question "schedule."[36] Kelley joined Hull House in 1891; there she not only observed and studied local laborers as an emerging scholar of labor but also helped to organize labor unions as a Socialist. Living at Hull House and leading its Bureau of Labor, Kelley wrote to Friedrich Engels that she was "learning more in a week of the actual conditions of the proletarian life in America than any previous year" of her education. In May 1892, Kelley became a special agent of the Illinois Bureau of Labor Statistics appointed to investigate child labor in sweatshops. As a special agent, Kelley collected data as piecework, earning fifty cents for every completed "schedule," or data-collection card. She was expected to oversee one thousand schedules. Thrilled to be able to engage her intellect and draw upon the skills she had learned in college, Kelley found that her residence at Hull House contributed to her work. It made her more attractive as a state employee and made data collection easier. Her work, and her promotion of her work at the American Social Science Association, gained the attention of Carroll Wright, who was the head of the United States Bureau of Labor Statistics.[37] Wright personally invited Kelley to manage the Chicago-area study of a larger, federal investigation of "slums" in major cities.[38] Kelley applied this experience to her work for *Hull House Maps and Papers*, using data collected for the state and federal government and improving upon the techniques she learned by creating its maps with fellow Hull House resident Agnes Holbrook.

Hull House residents' unique social-cultural location as women, as nonsectarian social workers, and as emergent social scientists placed them adjacent to but distinct from other reformers, such as Christian missionaries, philanthropists, state officials, and university professors. Living in this social, cultural, and political borderland afforded Hull House women—especially those also possessing the privileges of whiteness—greater authority, legitimacy, and credibility in their neighborhood and outside of it. As fellow settlement house founder Robert Woods explained in *The Neighborhood in Nation-Building*, the friendships settlement workers formed in their neighborhoods allowed them to gather more local data, and better-quality data, than their colleagues employed at universities or with local, state, and federal government. Avoiding the "mechanical and inquisitive methods of the census-taker," settlement workers interacted with neighbors enough to be "on easy and familiar terms with them."[39] Establishing a relationship not just with individuals but with entire families and kinship networks allowed the "neighborly caller" to learn "what life means in the particular street or court where his new-found friends live," including "delicate" details like "cleanliness and sanitation outside the houses; the plumbing, the drainage, light and ventilation within" as well as "the inner nature of the people."[40] They uniquely *cared* about the neighborhood and home, which set their work apart from that of their institutional peers even as they collaborated with them.

Biopolitical feelings for the neighborhood and its residents afforded greater flexibility to work with a variety of state and nonstate institutions. Just as Florence Kelley moved among multiple positions—as Hull House resident, as Chicago factory inspector, and as federal labor investigator—other Hull House residents followed suit. For example, fellow Hull House resident Grace Abbott served as the superintendent of the Immigrant's Protective League, simultaneously representing Chicago immigrants and Hull House before Congress. In these roles, she and other Hull House residents "cooperate whenever [there is] an investigation of the immigrant colonies" while also "secur[ing] justice and opportunity for immigrants" through the league.[41] The knowledge and expertise gained by living among immigrants, settlement workers insisted, contributed to the credibility of the reporting they could do in their capacity as representatives of a reform organization. Such claims, however, also strengthened Hull House's ties to federal and state agencies. Partnership was a matter not only of ideological or strategic benefit but also of convenience, maximizing the productivity of reform work by connecting varied institutions. At this imperial intersection, Hull House bridged the divide among private charities, church missions, universities, and state governance by serving multiple institutions and constituencies simultaneously.

While Kelley, Holbrook, and Hull House residents received much-deserved credit for their anthropological and ethnographic work compiling and analyzing the data that would become *Hull House Maps and Papers*, their labor was not theirs alone. It was federal property. Their research was one piece of a larger series of case studies funded through a congressional joint resolution (S.R. 46) "providing for an investigation relative to the 'slums of the cities.'"[42] Hull House residents worked in dual roles as both friendly neighbors and federal investigators when they collected data door to door, replicated that data (typically by hand) to preserve it for the state and Hull House, and analyzed the data. Such a position allowed for Hull House residents to maintain the credibility and trust of a local "neighbor" in relation to their subjects of study, embody the legitimacy of a "social scientist," and hold the authority of a government official. Caring for the community, and other sentimental and sympathetic feelings motivating their work, obscured the asymmetrical power inherent in their various positions as investigators of their own community. The knowledge generated through this work could not have been acquired without intimate, domestic-level bonds; yet, these bonds reinforced the existing asymmetrical power relations between residents and neighbors. Hull House investigators, not the surrounding neighborhood, were empowered through their investigation. As with the experience of women missionaries, these Hull House residents "operated in conjunction with the U.S. government," receiving professional credentials and appointments through their friendly, scientific investigations and bolstering the "institutional apparatus of the colonial state."[43]

As historians of social surveys have pointed out, the leading women behind the Hull House settlement "each played a major role in reshaping the responsibility of American governments—state and federal—for human welfare. Each was a political force as well as a social reformer."[44] Part of the force they displayed was evident in their successful appointment to state and federal positions following publication. Julia Lathrop, for example, received an appointment to the Illinois State Board of Charities, which she held for three terms. President Taft would eventually appoint her as chief of the Children's Bureau in the Department of Commerce and Labor. Another part of the force these women researchers displayed was in popularizing local, state, and federal surveillance of urban areas deemed "slums" and strengthening the imperial biopolitical state. Investigative efforts to learn about the neighborhood were not permanent roles Hull House residents expected to serve, but temporary positions based on their familiarity with the community. As Addams envisioned it, Hull House endeavors would evolve into state and federal action. She explained, "Hull-House has always held its activities lightly, ready to hand them over to whosoever would carry them on properly."[45] Such an arrangement—in which Hull House residents served as agents of state or federal government when useful in such roles—aligned with Addams's vision for a settlement house. The caring relationships forged between Hull House residents and local neighbors, as she understood it, left residents "bound to see the needs of their neighborhood as a whole, to furnish data for legislation, and to use their influence to secure it."[46] Cultivating friendships while also remaining aware of how those relationships could be useful to the state shaped the contours of settlement workers' biopower, determining the health, vitality, and possibilities of life for the neighborhood and the nation.

Hull House was—and continues to be—imagined as an exceptional place in Gilded Age and Progressive Era America. In contrast to nativists and Americanists, Hull House embodied a secular, nonsectarian, progressive worldview in which immigrants were co-collaborators in the social-cultural life of their local neighborhood and, by extension, central to the creation of a more cosmopolitan America. Despite the heartwarming feelings this place and the ideologies supporting it inspired, its exceptional status—like other "spatial exceptions"—helped to sustain the logics and structure of empire.[47] Its existence seemed to provide evidence of the progressive direction of the United States as welcoming to immigrants, a refuge to the down and out, and a haven for nonsectarian and nonpartisan democratic participation. When placed in the context of the larger neighborhood and the Nineteenth Ward as a microcosm of nineteenth-century US empire, however, Hull House can also provide evidence of the overwhelming need of such ameliorative efforts in light of an imperial biopolitics encouraging life for certain populations and slow, painful deaths for others. Even settlement workers' efforts to know more about the surrounding "slum" they lived in points to evidence of an imperial logic to find, possess, and utilize information in order to better see and feel the city, state, and nation's way forward. Such endeavors were understood and explained as seeking to better "serve" the less fortunate, but the acquisition of data and decision making about local populations in practice sustained and advanced US empire. The possibility of liberating solutions and progressive civilizational evolutions were the discourses justifying social surveys, but were not necessarily the actual outcomes experienced.

Mapping Imperial Biopower at Home

Hull House Maps and Papers provides one example of the way local surveillance and neighborhood mapping became normalized as a legitimate method of research in the social sciences and a standard practice for city, state, and federal governance. Hull House women paved the way by serving as friends, scientists, and state agents in this work. With better social bonds engineered through both sentimentality and science, they believed, the nation could "optimize" bodies through material and spatial arrangements. These views were distinct from racialized discourses reiterating superior/inferior dynamics among different races and classes of persons, but nonetheless were important in establishing both a moral geography in Chicago and a biopolitical feeling among progressives. It is precisely because Hull House is often presented as an antidote to imperial logics that it is worth studying in relationship to empire. As Paul Kramer has noted, studies of empire tend to focus on "invasions and impositions," more direct, recognizable, and explicit exploitative political practices and processes. In light of such a state of the field, he contended that examples in which the "dynamics of legitimacy," "creation of buy-in," or other "explicitly non-coercive modes of imperial power" are present are in need of greater attention.[48] Hull House and its efforts to research its local neighborhood provide such an example. It did not ideologically support US empire, yet it functioned to support and sustain an imperial biopower, an asymmetrical management of bodies to uneven life-enhancing benefit.

Hull House and its reform projects, like *Hull House Maps and Papers*, was an imperial enterprise simultaneously bolstering a cosmopolitan nationalism and critiquing nativist "100-percent" Americanism. Hull House sought to nurture a new kind of nationalism, and in the process advanced imperial logics, even *as* it challenged dominant capitalist and nativist national ideologies and social systems. In this complicated position, Hull House women were "neither pawns of nor apologists for the state," to borrow a phrase from *Competing Kingdoms* and its landmark study of Christian women missionaries. Imperial formations are often cast in binary terms, with extreme focus on formal political structures, state actors, and direct linkages to imperial ideologies; however, scholars of Christian missionaries, and especially women missionaries, have demonstrated how complex the relationship between "nonstate actors" and state power has been. Hull House residents resembled women foreign missionaries whose experiences, as historian Jane Hunter asserted, "fed back into American culture and ideology in the interwar years and ultimately represented a source of *challenge* to the dominant nationalist culture."[49] Even though the women of Hull House were not missionaries, and intentionally distanced themselves from exclusively Christian circles, discourses, and networks, they too were a group who "reinvented the meanings of American nationalism and imperialism as they negotiated competing nationalisms and imperialisms in varying colonial settings."[50] Women reformers, like the US empire in which they lived, did not hold fixed identities or social-cultural locations. Settlement workers, like Christian missionaries and other agents of an imperial "sentimental politics of life," participated in the nexus of religion and US empire for complex and conflicting reasons, laboring at sites of contestation built and maintained with competing interests, motivations, and goals.[51]

Hull House disrupted imperial power because it successfully intervened in horrifying industrial and social conditions, like child labor, and its residents—most notably Jane Addams—opposed colonial and capitalist endeavors; however, once we begin to see US empire as administered and regulated not according to specific bodies, races, political affiliations, or religious positions but by asymmetrical power relations, then the asymmetrical power foundational to settlement projects like Hull House reveals its location in the development of religion and US empire. Addams intentionally immersed herself in the heart of Chicago's immigrant "colonies" and encouraged other white, middle-class women to do the same in order to fulfill their desires for usefulness. Their usefulness recalibrated the neighborhood so that different immigrant "colonies" intersected with Hull House in order to live more fully and have access to opportunities they would not have otherwise had. Immigrant neighbors utilized Hull House for its services and educational opportunities; yet, Hull House's services bolstered imperial structures and technologies, including greater federal surveillance of immigrants and laborers. Most notably, Hull House's "civic engagements" justified surveillance through its sentimentalization of the science behind social surveys.

Recognizing these connections forged through Hull House does not diminish the life-saving and life-improving legislation Hull House residents secured on behalf of the community. It may, however, change the moral geography upon which those actions are interpreted. "Excavating sentimental biopower," Schuller explained, "disrupts some of our most cherished scholarly and popular narratives."[52] Addams and Hull House women already disrupted many narratives, because of their unique location at an imperial intersection—a welcome center to newcomers and an outpost for civilizational-national development—and their intentional crafting of a professionalized domestic space owned, occupied, and administered by women. By recognizing Hull House as a place within the US empire and indicative of US empire, we can redraw our mental maps and conceptual apparatus to make US empire more visible. Hull House's complex relationship to empire illuminates how imperial formations are located not in pure "foreign" or "domestic" spaces but rather in active sites of social construction and, as Paul Kramer explained, in "the work of cartographers and border guards, the tremendous power of which can only be apprehended if they are discarded as terms of art."[53] Widespread perceptions of empire as located only on the border of the United States, and of conceptual binaries (domestic/foreign, political/cultural, state/nonstate actors) that limit our view of imperial operations, have kept many scholars from recognizing—let alone analyzing and understanding—social locations, like that of settlement workers or social surveyors, and institutions, like Hull House, as indicative of the power of US empire "at home." The interplay of religion and US empire is located within the "domestic" space of the continental United States and comfortably within a residential home. This dynamic is not external or "foreign" to American life, but internalized as the way many white Americans, especially white middle-class women, have perceived their place and power in the world.

NOTES

1 Jane Addams, *Twenty Years at Hull House* (Urbana: University of Illinois Press, 1990), 66–69.
2 Addams, *Twenty Years*, 88.
3 Schuller, *The Biopolitics of Feeling*, 2.
4 Schuller, *The Biopolitics of Feeling*, 11.
5 For productive suggestions on this and other complex approaches to histories of empire, see Kramer, "Power and Connection," 1348–91.
6 *Hull House Maps and Papers: A Presentation of Nationalities and Wages in a Congested District of Chicago, Together with Comments and Essays on Problems Growing out of the Social Conditions*, Crowells Library of Economics and Politics (New York: Crowell, 1895) (hereafter HHMP).
7 "Hull House: A Social Settlement," in HHMP, 207; Agnes Sinclair Holbrook, "Map Notes and Comments," in HHMP, 4.
8 See Woods, *The Neighborhood in Nation-Building*, 59.
9 Addams, *Twenty Years*, 92.
10 Addams, *Twenty Years*, 117; Jane Addams, "Subjective Necessity for Social Settlements," in *The Jane Addams Reader*, ed. Jean Bethke Elshtain (New York: Basic Books, 2002), 17.
11 For a description of this "university settlement" approach, see Woods, *Neighborhood and Nation-Building*.
12 Sklar, *Florence Kelley and the Nation's Work*, 176; Addams, *Twenty Years*, 84.
13 Addams, *Twenty Years*, 449–50.
14 Addams, *Twenty Years*, 57–58.
15 Hodges, "Religion and the Settlement," in *Proceedings of the National Conference of Charities and Correction*, ed. Isabel C. Barrows (Boston: Geo. H. Ellis, 1896), 150.
16 See, for example, Schultz, "Jane Addams, Apotheosis of Social Christianity," 207–19.
17 Caird, "The Possibility of a Science of Religion," in *Evolution of Religion*, vol. 1 (New York: Macmillan, 1893), 15, www.giffordlectures.org; Addams, *Twenty Years*, 39–42.
18 Caird, "The Possibility of a Science of Religion," 15.

19 Hodges, "Religion and the Settlement," 153.
20 Hodges, "Religion and the Settlement," 152.
21 Addams, *Twenty Years*, 125; also, Addams, "Subjective Necessity for Social Settlements," 24.
22 For more on this complex relationship and exchange, see Hoganson, *Consumers' Imperium*.
23 Woods, *Neighborhood in Nation-Building*, 59.
24 Addams, *Twenty Years*, 321.
25 As quoted in Bulmer, Bales, and Sklar, *The Social Survey in Historical Perspective*, 2.
26 Bulmer, Bales, and Sklar, *The Social Survey in Historical Perspective*, 3.
27 HHMP, 28.
28 Conroy-Krutz, "The Hierarchy of Heathenism," 59–60.
29 Conroy-Krutz, "The Hierarchy of Heathenism," 58–59.
30 Conroy-Krutz, "The Hierarchy of Heathenism," 55–71.
31 DeRogatis, *Moral Geography*, 24.
32 "Moral geography" is a phrase in Religious Studies scholar Amy DeRogatis's book of the same name.
33 For example, see Emily Greene Blach, [Review of *Hull House Maps and Papers*], *Publications of the American Statistical Association* 4, no. 30 (1895): 201–3; Samuel McCune Lindsay, [Review of *Hull House Maps and Papers*], *Annals of the American Academy of Political and Social Science* 8 (1896): 177–81; and Frederic Sanders, [Review of *Hull House Maps and Papers*], *Political Science Quarterly* 11, no. 2 (1896): 340–42.
34 Lindsay, [Review of *Hull House Maps and Papers*], 178.
35 Sanders, [Review of *Hull House Maps and Papers*], 341.
36 Sklar, *Florence Kelley and the Nation's Work*, 228.
37 Sklar, *Florence Kelley and the Nation's Work*, 160.
38 This federal study, which drew upon the work of local investigators like Kelley, was published under the direction of Carroll Wright in 1894 as *The Slums of Baltimore, Chicago, New York, and Philadelphia* (Washington, DC: Government Printing Office, 1894).
39 Woods, *Neighborhood in Nation-Building*, 36.
40 A much more exhaustive list of details can be found in Woods, *Neighborhood in Nation-Building*, 36–37.
41 Addams, *Twenty Years*, 223.
42 "Enrolled Bills Signed," *Congressional Record–Senate* 23, no. 1 (July 20, 1982): S6429, www.govinfo.gov.
43 Mary Renda explores the experience of women missionaries and their relationship to the colonial state in "Doing Everything: Religion, Race, and Empire in the U.S. Protestant Women's Missionary Enterprise, 1812–1960," in Reeves-Ellington, Sklar, and Shemo, eds., *Competing Kingdoms*, 367–90.
44 Bulmer, Bales, and Sklar, *Social Survey in Historical Perspective*, 36.
45 Addams, *Twenty Years*, 313.

46 Addams, *Twenty Years*, 127.
47 Kramer, "Power and Connection," 1356–57.
48 Kramer, "Power and Connection," 1381.
49 Jane Hunter, "Women's Mission in Historical Perspective: American Identity and Christian Internationalism," in Reeves-Ellington, Sklar, and Shemo, eds., *Competing Kingdoms*, 23.
50 Reeves-Ellington, Sklar, and Shemo, eds., *Competing Kingdoms*, 2.
51 Schuller, *The Biopolitics of Feeling*, 136.
52 Schuller, *The Biopolitics of Feeling*, 3.
53 Kramer, "Power and Connection," 1357.

6

"They Call It Ghost Dance... But It's Feather Dance"

Indigenous Histories in the Study of Religion and US Empire

JENNIFER GRABER

James Silverhorn, descendant of a leading Kiowa family, peyote practitioner, and medicine bundle keeper, sat down for an interview in 1969.[1] He was asked about changes in Kiowa life. James spoke of his father, Haungooah (Silver Horn), a prolific artist and respected ritual leader. He talked about the Ghost Dance, including the reservation agent's effort to stop it. "They call it Ghost Dance," he recalled. "But it's Feather Dance." The Kiowa name for the movement, "*amakogia*," mattered. "*Amah*," James said, means "feather." Feathers, and the birds they adorn, abound in Kiowa story, history, and ritual. "*Kogia*," he told the interviewer, means "dance," a practice with significant personal and communal implications for Kiowas. *Amakogia*, or Feather Dance, evokes the Kiowa world within which the dance emerged. In contrast, the agent's name for the movement suggested haunting and fear. They "give it a bad name," James observed. "Then they broke it up. Stop it."[2]

This chapter explores how Kiowas engaged the *amakogia* to care for one another, affirm their place on the land, and engage powerful forces capable of renewing their world.[3] Starting with the Kiowa language name, I attempt an Indigenous framing of what is widely known as the Ghost Dance. My approach differs from earlier studies, written over many decades by ethnologists, anthropologists, and historians, that consider the dance within an imperial frame, or primarily in relation to US domestic empire. A short review of the scholarship reveals the imperial frame's origins, variations, and contemporary manifestations.

We start with Smithsonian ethnologist James Mooney, who crisscrossed the country to document the Ghost Dance. In late 1891, he traveled to Nevada to meet Wovoka, the movement's Paiute founder. He also observed dances and interviewed participants on the southern Plains. He traveled north with hopes of meeting Lakota dancers.[4] Like other "salvage anthropologists" of the period, Mooney recorded evidence of what he considered a dying way of life. In his 1896 report, he situated the Ghost Dance as the latest in a series of Native responses to European colonialism and US expansion. He designated dancers as friendly or hostile in regard to relations with settlers, modern or primitive in their perspectives on assimilation, authentic or opportunistic in their stance on visionary experience, and pacifist or militant in their responses to US Indian policy.[5] Mooney, therefore, transferred Euro-American assessments of Native responses to empire into his scholarship, establishing an "imperial frame" for future Ghost Dance study.

Mooney's influential report, like the census reports described in Sarah Dees's chapter, provides an important example of the way Euro-Americans produced knowledge about colonized people. As historian Paul Kramer has noted, imperial societies engage in meaning making around forms of perceived difference.[6] They establish racial, ethnic, and religious classifications and attribute meaning to them. These categories typically distinguish settler from Native, most clearly in tropes about civilized Euro-Americans and savage Indians. But imperial logics classify and value in other ways. They posit oppositions *between* and *within* colonized groups, usually by assessing their Native responses to imperial power. Mooney and later Ghost Dance commentators employed this "imperial frame" as they parsed Native activity and, to some degree, rationalized Euro-American responses ranging from pity to spectacular violence.

To be sure, scholarly work on the dance has not been static. Recent studies focus more on Native actors, priorities, and agency, as well as condemn American violence against movement participants. For instance, Louis Warren focuses on Native leaders and argues that the movement was forward thinking in Wovoka's disavowal of fighting and embrace of wage labor.[7] Gregory Smoak examines the Shoshone-Bannock version of the dance as an example of Native efforts to reinforce and refashion ethnic identity.[8] But even in these otherwise laudable works, the imperial frame and its freighted oppositions remain. Warren decries old arguments about Native traditionalism and argues for the movement's modernity. As Tiffany Hale has observed, the result is a text that renders the Ghost Dance "nonthreatening" to Euro-Americans.[9] Smoak, who does much to show the cultural consistency of movements like the Ghost Dance, also plays defense against Mooney's accusations. The dance, he writes, was "functional, not delusional."[10]

As James Silverhorn's interview suggests, analysis relying on an imperial frame, even when writers embrace the ostensibly positive characteristic in any given opposition, leaves much of the "Ghost Dance" unexamined. This is not to say that the imperial frame has nothing to offer. Rather, additional approaches are needed if scholars of empire are to prioritize not just Native voices but Native epistemologies. This chapter, then, starts with the Kiowa-language name for the movement and considers the feather, in ritual, story, song, and material culture. As Kiowa scholar Jenny Tone-Pah-Hote has observed, expressive culture, including creations that depict birds and employ feathers, functions as an important venue in which Kiowas understand and represent their identity.[11] We then turn to dance as a cultural form. As scholar of dance Jacqueline Shea Murphy has argued, Native dance has distinctive "capacities to articulate in profound philosophical, spiritual, and political ways."[12] An Indigenous frame, focused on *Native languages, symbols*, and *forms*, is one strategy for considering Native religious life in a way that attends to, but is not limited by, the conditions and knowledges of empire.

Symbols: Feathers and the Birds They Adorn

Kiowas trace their origins to the Yellowstone River Valley in what is now Montana. They later migrated to the Black Hills. Their move coincided with several Native nations arriving on the Great Plains, where enormous bison herds fed on the landscape's rich grasses. Rivers provided shores and bottomlands suitable for dwelling and foraging. Trade networks stretching south to New Spain made horses and guns available. Mounted and armed, Kiowas and other Plains peoples hunted buffalo, which became their primary source of food, shelter, and clothing. To follow the herds, they constructed tipis and moved frequently, at least in warm months. The confluence of buffalo, horses, and guns on the sun-fueled grasslands proved transformative, affecting foodways, dress, housing, stories, and ritual practice.[13]

Figure 6.1. Kiowa artist Wohaw's drawing of a tanager and a yellowhammer. Note the figure with a human head and bird-like body at the bottom. (Drawing of Indians and Birds by Wo-haw, Missouri Historical Society, St. Louis)

Less recognized, however, is the impact of Native people's encounter with new bird populations.[14] The Plains boast North America's primary bird migration route, the Central Flyway.[15] It serves as home to eagles, meadowlarks, hawks, flickers, and waterfowl. Drawing on older patterns of engaging the natural world, Kiowas and others related to birds as agents or persons. As one team of ethnobiologists put it, they developed both "ecological and cosmological knowledge" about birds. For example, Kiowa dance participant Guy Quoetone recalled hunting birds, working with feathers, and the powers associated with particular birds. Kiowa artists filled sketchbooks not only with depictions of landscapes, buffalo, kin, and ceremony. They also drew birds.

Human-bird interactions on the Plains took a number of forms. Native people told stories of birds with spectacular powers and human beings transformed into birds.[16] They associated birds with the earth's creation and other ancient events. Some gave their children names referring to birds. Others tattooed bird images on their bodies. They used bird materials to create tools for hunting, fighting, and healing. They adorned themselves with feathers and used them to pray. Bird parts were

Figure 6.2. Typical representation of a thunderbird, holding a pipe and arrows, in Plains Indian ledger art. (Plains Indian Art from Fort Marion by Karen Daniels Petersen, University of Oklahoma Press)

among the most common contents in medicine bundles.[17] To produce these items, Plains peoples trapped birds and engaged in an intercontinental trade of bird materials.[18]

The Plains were also home to birds with great power, particularly the Thunderbird. Rock art throughout the region features Thunderbird images.[19] Tribal stories abound with Thunderbird references.[20] Lakotas, who also lived on the northern Plains, considered Thunderbird one of the universe's sixteen most highly revered powers. They called it

"*Wakinyan*," a name containing the root word "*wakan*," or "that which is considered unknowable."²¹ Kiowas, on the other hand, connected Thunderbird to their origins. As Guy Quoetone noted, Thunderbird is a "bird of its own" and was present "in the beginning of time." Kiowas also associated Thunderbird with protection. "When people went to war," Quoetone said, they "want[ed] to carry that thunderbird emblem in their clothes."²²

Plains nations observed birds' habits and qualities to develop sophisticated taxonomies. Kiowas' Cheyenne neighbors regarded Thunderbird within a class of birds, including magpies and crows, that entire communities related to through ceremony.²³ They also attributed particular powers to certain birds. Kiowas, for instance, considered golden eagles to have power in regard to weather, war, and hunting. Yellowhammer tail feathers, they affirmed, could be used to cure illness.²⁴

Plains nations represented their varied bird engagements in their expressive culture. As noted above, bird parts appeared frequently in medicine bundles. Creators used bird images and materials to depict visionary experiences in which birds had spoken to individuals, giving commands or making promises. Some vision recipients painted these birds on tipis or adorned them with parts of these birds.²⁵ Others decorated shields, signaling the promise of protective power. Still others wore bird parts into battle as a sign of their invulnerability, as the oft-told story about a Kiowa fighter who wore a stuffed magpie on his headdress demonstrates.²⁶ Even the most mundane uses of feathers, such as their role in arrow construction, were connected to stories in which powerful beings taught their ancestors how to use bird parts to help them.²⁷

Like other Plains nations, Kiowas used feathers more than any other bird material. They told stories about learning to wear feathers from Lakota neighbors.²⁸ They adorned their hair with them and attached them to horses' manes. Feathers appeared on lances and other weapons. Some shield designs received in visions required feathers.²⁹ The most illustrious fighters signaled their accomplishments with feathers mounted in elaborate headdresses.³⁰ Members of Kiowas' most prestigious men's sodality, the Koitsenko, wore elaborate owl-feather headdresses painted with red clay.³¹

Feathers also appeared in Kiowas' largest communal ritual, the *Kado*, their version of the Plains Indian Sun Dance.³² Once again, Kiowas received a form of feather use from another nation, the Crow. In the Crow version of the dance, participants built a ritual structure resembling an eagle's nest. Eagles, according to the Crow, carried messages between the people and the Sun.[33] The Crow offered their ceremony to visiting Kiowas. They also provided a special object, the *Taime*.[34] A carved, human-like figure adorned with feathers, the *Taime* occupied the center of Kiowas' *Kado* structure. The ritual's leader used bird materials in additional ways, such as for feather fans for smoking, and thereby purifying, ritual objects. He blew an eagle bone whistle adorned with feathers at the ritual's high point. Feathers also featured among those who participated in and observed Sun Dance activities. Dancers engaged at the ceremony's high point wore feathers.[35] Kiowas of all ages brought feathers and other offerings to the *Taime* as they prayed for their families' health and protection.

Feathers played a conspicuous role in large-scale rites like the *Kado*, as well as smaller-scale healing rituals performed by specialists such as the Buffalo doctors. As in many Kiowa stories, more-than-human powers gifted Buffalo power to Kiowas at a perilous moment. In this case, a Kiowa woman was lost in a snowstorm after escaping her captors. A voice led her to a buffalo carcass, in which she sheltered for the night. Nestled inside, she received a vision in which Buffalo offered her healing powers requiring particular ceremonies, special objects, and proper bodily adornment. Feathers featured prominently as the woman shared her new powers with her brothers. The doctors wore hide robes decorated with Cooper's hawk feathers.[36] They treated sick patients using a buffalo tail painted red and trimmed with feathers. They created shields adorned with eagle wing feathers and designs providing protection from bullets.[37] Marshaling these tools, the doctors sang special songs and were thought to be able to cure any illness.

While feathers were central to many Kiowa rites of flourishing and protection, the eventual *amakogia*, or Feather Dance, drew upon other traditions with less conspicuous use of feathers. These included efforts to restore the buffalo and communicate with deceased kin, activities that occupied most Euro-American imaginings of the movement. They did not know that Kiowas, like other Plains nations, had long engaged in rites with similar aims. And even these, upon close inspection, involved frequent reference to birds and their feathers.

Figure 6.3. Silver Horn's calendar entries for summer 1881 and winter 1881–1882, including feathers at the top of the Sun Dance pole and Patepte's pitched red blanket with feathers at the top corners. (Detail from Silverhorn calendar, Sam Noble Oklahoma Museum of Natural History, the University of Oklahoma)

In the 1880s, the decade leading up to the *amakogia*, two Kiowa visionaries tried to restore the buffalo. The scale of herds' destruction cannot be overstated. Euro-American hunters killed millions of buffalo, first on the northern Plains and later on the southern. This purposeful elimination ended a ten-thousand-year period of buffalo abundance in the region.[38] In winter 1881–1882, a Kiowa man named Patepte claimed he could call the missing buffalo to return from under the earth.[39] His followers surely connected his effort with an older story about Kiowas' cultural hero, Saynday, who also released buffalo trapped under the ground.[40] Patepte's effort was unsuccessful, but the long-held notion that powerful beings could summon threatened animals persisted.[41] In the summer of 1887, a man named Paingya took up Patepte's mantle. He boasted even more powers, including control over whirlwinds and fire. Paingya said he could blow away and burn up Euro-Americans, along with any Kiowas who copied their way of life.[42] Kiowa calendars, the tribe's visual form of history keeping, depict both movements. One recalls Patepte's efforts with a drawing of the red blanket he fixed to two poles, behind which he ritually called on the buffalo. The blanket's poles are adorned with feathers similar to those placed at the top of a *Kado* pole. Another calendar, whose drawings have been unfortunately lost, detailed Paingya's ceremonial dress, specifically noting its feathers.[43] Bird materials, then, played an important role in earlier efforts to restore the herds.

Birds also featured in earlier traditions to communicate with dead loved ones. While some Kiowas had long claimed to receive messages from ancestors, this power was associated especially with the Owl doctors. According to many Plains nations, Owls had opposing characteristics. They contributed to healing, but also operated in relation to death, if not evil.[44] Among Kiowas, Owl doctors spoke to owls and received messages from them, including details about future events and lost items.[45] During visionary experiences, the doctors were transported to the realm of the dead and communed with spirits.[46] In the 1870s, for instance, an Owl doctor named Mamanti reported conversations with deceased relatives who gave him special powers, including the ability to repel bullets and know battle outcomes.[47]

Owl doctors used bird materials as they cured the living and communed with the dead. Some of the earliest Owl doctors wore owl skins over their heads.[48] Others used owl-feather fans to drive out disease.[49] Guy Quoetone recalled an Owl doctor who pitched a large tipi with a smaller one inside it. From inside the larger, the healer called on Owl for help. Hearing the doctor's call, an Owl alighted on top of the tipi, shaking the structure, calling out the name of the deceased kin and asking what relatives wanted to know. The Owl then departed, returning later and entering the smaller tipi. Bystanders said they heard the sound of "wings," as if "a bird [was] inside."[50] The Owl then offered messages from the deceased.[51] In the Owl doctors' work, powerful birds and bird materials facilitated Kiowa interaction with those who had died.

In sum, birds and their feathers featured prominently in Kiowa efforts to heal, protect, and renew the community. Their central importance in the *amakogia* reflected and built on this long history of birds as relatives and feathers as potent cultural symbols. At the same time, Euro-Americans failed to register the universe of meaning behind birds and feathers in Plains culture, even as they criticized Native interactions with other objects and images. They were quick to call Native ritual objects "idols" and body paint "savage." They decried the buffalo's centrality to

Kiowa material prosperity and cosmology. Critics deemed this reliance primitive. Buffalo hides stretched across mobile tipis lacked permanence. Skins worn as clothes betrayed an absence of refinement. Gratitude offered to Buffalo signaled religious sentiments out of place. Other Euro-Americans capitalized on Native people's buffalo relations. They called for the herds' destruction, and thereby an end to the Plains way of life.[52] The elimination proved devastating for Kiowas and other Plains nations. Even so, the people continued to relate to birds and use feathers, deploying them in their effort to survive US domestic empire.

Form: Native Dance

The second part of the movement's name, "*kogia*" or "dance," also reveals a connection to Kiowa stories and social relations. As anthropologist Loretta Fowler has observed, Native communities construct dance and other cultural forms to protect tribal values, even as these forms are flexible enough to confront and adjust to dramatic change.[53] Dance also operates on the personal level. For individuals, dance promotes quality of life by cultivating social bonds.[54] Or as Eric Lassiter has observed, songs and the dances they accompany invoke "layers upon layers of meaningful relationships."[55] Along with social dances, Kiowas performed dances to engage more-than-human powers. These included the *Kado*, as noted above. Kiowas also hosted a number of sodalities, groups that had particular responsibilities on dance occasions and served to reinforce Kiowa identity and connection.

Many Plains nations regard particular dance forms as gifts from more-than-human powers. Lakotas, for instance, claim White Buffalo Calf Woman gave them several rituals, including their version of the Sun Dance.[56] Members of the Crow nation had visionary experiences with a figure called Old Woman, from whom they learned Sun Dance steps and received objects crucial to its performance.[57] Dance, then, serves as a format through which Native nations come to know and then enact their obligations to great powers. Dance symbolizes reciprocal relations, including powerful beings' ongoing concern for the people.

Across the Plains, dance also provides a setting for modeling proper behavior and transmitting cultural values. In Kiowa life, men's sodalities encourage particular virtues, such as ritual cooperation and martial courage. In the nineteenth century, they inculcated skills necessary for raiding and war, held dances before battles, and celebrated those who fought successfully.[58] According to anthropologist William Meadows, five of the ten men's sodalities had practical responsibilities for hosting dances, feasts, and giveaways before and during the Sun Dance. Kiowas also had two women's sodalities in this period. Members of the Calf Old Women Society prayed for the sick and for men's safety in battle. The Bear Old Women Society was best known for its members' ability to aid those in extreme danger.[59] Both groups, like the five men's sodalities, met during the Sun Dance and used their power for communal benefit.

Despite sodalities' wide-ranging responsibilities, federal officials usually viewed their dance activity as a prelude to attacks on Euro-Americans. As a result, the Bureau of Indian Affairs issued a series of dance bans starting in 1883.[60] Along with bans on sodality dances, officials forbade Sun Dances as they perpetuated "heathenish" customs.[61] The ban was hardly the first colonial challenge to dance among Kiowas and other Plains nations. Reservation officials had employed many tactics, including military surveillance and withholding food rations. For over a decade, Kiowas had adapted the *Kado* in light of this harassment, as well as declining buffalo herds and other environmental challenges.[62]

As conditions made the Sun Dance and its attendant sodality-led dances harder to celebrate, Kiowas also engaged new dance. Forms of the War Dance have pre-Columbian origins on the Plains. Native peoples typically performed this dance before and after martial engagements. Versions of the dance circulated in the 1860s and 1870s, including a Pawnee form that combined tribal healing practices with rituals from an Omaha men's society.[63] Lakotas learned the dance from Pawnees, adapted it, and shared it. Kiowas received it from their Cheyenne neighbors in 1883. Kiowa men who had long served in sodalities proved particularly receptive. Their War Dance adaptation, the *Ohoma*, quickly took root in Kiowa life.[64]

This trajectory confirms Daniel Gelo's argument that Plains Indian dance has a history of "constant circulation and reinvention" in response to changing circumstances.[65] Not surprisingly, Kiowas' process of adapting the War Dance involved bird materials. Mrs. Hokeah recalled Cheyenne dancers who wore single feathers on their heads. The visitors offered the dance to Kiowas by placing single feathers on their heads.[66]

The dance introduced a new object, the feather bustle, to Kiowa life. Worn by the *Ohoma* leader, the bustle featured the head of a golden eagle with antelope horns fixed to the sides. A fan of eagle feathers splayed out below. Cloth strips, adorned with still more feathers, trailed downward. Like the dance itself, the bustle was given by the Cheyennes. A dancer tied it around his waist, facing backward. Kiowas viewed the bustle as the dance's true leader. As Mac Whitehorse later recalled, participants knew to "follow that bustle. . . . There are prayers on that bustle."[67]

In the decades prior to the *amakogia*, then, Kiowas participated in larger Plains dance practices that referenced tribal origins and myths, reinforced community values, and provided a setting for borrowing and adaptation. Dance included a material culture that signaled relations with and powers from more-than-human beings. Through dance, and particularly as bird materials appeared in dance settings, Kiowas declared their values and aspirations, as well as sought healing and flourishing as the *Kado* became increasingly difficult to perform. Dance signaled continuities with the past, providing a baseline from which Native people could address changing circumstances.

Symbol and Form: Wovoka's Dance Movement

Wovoka's *nanigukwa* or "dance in a circle" began with a vision.[68] Swept into the sky during an illness, he encountered more-than-human powers and saw departed loved ones. In a series of visions, Wovoka received moral instruction, songs giving him power over the weather, and a dance to initiate the world's renewal.[69] His people, Northern Paiutes, adapted their Round Dance traditions to Wovoka's specifications. They held hands in large circles, shuffle-stepping and singing long into the night. Soon, Paiute participants experienced trances in which they received new songs to accompany the dance. Some songs invoked *wûbi'doma*, or whirlwind, along with fog, snow, lightning, and dust.[70] References to weather reflected Paiutes' concern about recent droughts that threatened their food supplies. They also had cosmic implications. According to Wovoka, dramatic weather events would accompany the world's renewal and their dead relatives' return.[71]

Wovoka's visions marked him as a person with "*bbooha*," the Paiute word for "sacred power." To demonstrate the powers he received during his vision, Wovoka employed objects, including eagle feathers. Paiute informants recall Wovoka wielding a feather to hold back forest fires exacerbated by drought and settler deforestation. He doctored the sick and injured by bringing feathers close to the body, drawing out harmful substances, such as blood, splintered bone, and shattered glass.[72] Wovoka's dance movement, then, operated within a larger renewal project in which feathers evidenced power and protected sick and threatened people.

As word of Wovoka's visions and dance spread, tribal delegations came from every direction. Wovoka provided them with moral instruction, songs, and dance steps, as well as magpie feathers.[73] Abundant in the Great Basin, magpies were thought to overhear human conversations and carry messages to more-than-human beings.[74] When Native delegates returned home, they shared the dance with kin, presided over local adaptations, and developed new magpie references. According to Mooney, some Lakota practitioners painted magpies on their bodies. Arapaho dancers sang of receiving gifts of headdresses made from magpie tail feathers. Even though many Plains Indian nations lacked Paiutes' extensive magpie traditions, Wovoka's movement initiated new bird associations and prompted a brisk trade in magpie feathers.[75]

Throughout 1889 and 1890, practitioners on the Plains adapted Wovoka's movement to their particular concerns. Like Paiutes focused on drought and deforestation, Lakotas and Arapahos identified threats to their environment, including buffalo slaughter, epidemic disease, and Euro-American efforts to take their land. They developed songs about disruptive natural calamities, including earthquakes. Other songs referred to the contrasting fates of Native dancers and Euro-Americans, the former of whom would receive gifts of fruit and progress to a renewed world, while the latter lost access to food and were left behind.[76]

Their emerging ritual repertoire of songs, images, and objects also referenced birds with whom they had long associations. During a dance-vision, one Arapaho practitioner received a song calling on "the young Thunderbirds, the young Thunderbirds." Lyrics in the Teton (Sioux) dialect referenced birds' ability to move between human and more-than-human worlds. "The whole world is coming. A nation is coming," participants sang. "The Eagle has brought the message to the tribe.... The Crow has brought the message to the tribe."[77] Songs also referenced

Native attention to birds that transformed dramatically during their life cycle, such as juvenile bald eagles with brown and white speckled plumage that matured into the adult's iconic, contrasting colors.[78] During a vision, one Arapaho practitioner saw a related change upon encountering his deceased father in a dance-vision. "I am looking at [my father]." He "is beginning to look like a bird."[79]

Clearly, visions experienced while dancing referenced traditions about birds as beings with great power and unique capacities. For practitioners, songs attested to the possibility of human, bird, and more-than-human powers' cooperation to secure them against myriad threats. The leading Arapaho dance leader promised that Euro-Americans would be pushed out by a wall of fire while Native dancers, "enabled by means of the sacred feathers," would "surmount the flames."[80] As object and form, birds and dance served as resources for imperiled Plains Indian nations.

Object and Form: *Amakogia*

Kiowas received Wovoka's dance movement in October 1890 as disease struck, communal land holding was under threat, and Euro-American hunters destroyed the region's remaining buffalo. Faced with hardship, Kiowas acted to affirm and protect communal life. They held *Ohoma* dances and tried to celebrate the Sun Dance. Buffalo doctors and other healers aided the sick. Birds and their feathers remained central to rituals, stories, and adornment. Wovoka's dance movement resonated with these traditions. Indeed, it came to them in the form of a feather.

Sitting Bull, from the nearby Arapaho nation, brought the feather to Kiowas.[81] In late 1889, he joined a pan-Indian delegation, met Wovoka, and participated in an intertribal dance. He returned to the Cheyenne and Arapaho reservation in September 1890. While a few Arapahos had tried to start dances earlier, Sitting Bull prompted hundreds to participate.[82] He then traveled to the Kiowa reservation and told listeners about meeting his dead uncle in a dance-vision. They had hunted together and killed a buffalo, which fell to the ground and resurrected before them. Kiowas listened eagerly to Sitting Bull's promise of healing and renewal. They began to hold dances under his direction.

Like Wovoka with his visitors, Sitting Bull provided Kiowa dancers with instruction, songs, steps, and powerful objects, including feathers.

When participants appeared on the verge of trance, he waved a feather in front of their faces. He brandished feather fans over dancers collapsed on the ground. Practitioners, upon waking, told of meeting relatives and receiving new songs. Jimmy Quitone, Guy's father, saw a "coming party of the dead" in a vision. Before leaving, Sitting Bull gave feathers to seven men and seven women to signal a transfer of leadership.[83] Kiowas continued dancing. As the movement grew, they referenced their own feather and dance traditions, calling it "*amakogia*," or "Feather Dance."

Soon, a single feather worn on the head became the movement's primary symbol. Some dancers also donned crow and magpie feathers.[84] Like Sitting Bull, Kiowa leaders used fans to interact with dancers. Some practitioners had bird-related visions, including feathers given to them as gifts and dancers transformed into birds.[85] These experiences resonated with Kiowas' historic encounters with birds who brought messages, affected the weather, connected with the dead, promised protection, and offered healing.

The *amakogia* shared some emphases with the Sun Dance, which was last attempted in summer 1890. Participants in both rites called on great powers to pity them and act on their behalf. In other ways, however, the *amakogia* differed. The *Kado*'s high point involved a small number of men dancing for four days without food or water. Women and children, along with other men, encouraged dancers from the sidelines. The *amakogia* also drew onlookers, but it boasted many more dancers. On some occasions, hundreds of men and women, young and old, held hands in a circle, shuffle-stepped, sought visions, and called for the world's transformation.

The *amakogia* also focused on a narrower set of concerns. The *Kado* had served as a site for making and fulfilling vows related to protection and flourishing. It also provided opportunities to make offerings related to family and health concerns. Kiowas asked great powers to act on their behalf and thanked them for past provision. The *amakogia* certainly concerned protection and kin, but in more specific ways. For instance, movement songs told of great powers using nature to disrupt colonial expansion. Participants sang of earthquakes, tornados, and whirlwinds.[86] Dancers affirmed they would be lifted up onto a new earth.[87]

They also prayed specifically for the buffalos' restoration. In the *Kado*, they had thanked Buffalo for life-sustaining gifts. In the wake of the herds' destruction, the *amakogia* projected their return. "He gets up again, he gets up again," dancers sang. Bianki, a movement leader, envisioned villages where buffalo meat cooked in pots and dried on racks. In another vision, he saw massive herds of ponies and buffalo. Kiowa dancers also encountered deceased loved ones. Songs recounted individual reunions experienced during trance and promised large-scale resurrection. One woman's dance-vision involved "travelers . . . coming on a march." Anticipating their arrival, she cooked fruit for her once-lost relatives.[88] Some *amakogia* songs combined all these elements. One dancer emerged from his vision. He sang, "The spirit host [of ancestors] is advancing. . . . They are coming with the buffalo . . . they are coming with the (new) earth." James Silverhorn recalled another song: "In the future you going to see something. Smoke gonna come down from heaven. You're going to see somebody."[89]

Despite reservation officials' efforts, the *amakogia* continued. But in February 1891, a leading Kiowa man, Ahpeahtone, returned from Nevada. He visited Wovoka with the hope of having his recently deceased child restored. Wovoka proved unable and Ahpeahtone encouraged Kiowas to abandon the movement.[90] Some did. Sitting Bull and others continued, but the disagreement stalled the dance's momentum. When spring came and went with no resurrection of herds or loved ones, the *amakogia* dissolved. The next few years brought hardship, including rising child mortality due to measles and malnutrition.[91] Federal officials opened new boarding schools, separating more children from their families. Reactions to the situation sometimes resulted in even greater pain. In winter 1891, for instance, three Kiowa boys ran away from school. Caught in a night blizzard, they froze to death.[92]

In summer 1893, some Kiowas turned again to the *amakogia*. By the next year, hundreds of Kiowas and their neighbors participated in the renewed, albeit changed movement. Practitioners still danced, sang, and wore feathers. But their visions and songs referred less to buffalo herds and natural cataclysm. The revived movement, which lasted until 1917, focused primarily on departed human kin.[93] Bert Geikomah recalled large *amakogia* gatherings where people flocked to dance leaders as they emerged from visions. They asked about their dead relatives.[94] Ella Brace attended Sunday *amakogia* gatherings and witnessed a dancer in trance: "He fell back, you know, and he don't breathe. Go about 2 or 3 hours, then he woke up. . . . He got to come up again . . . and then they got to tell the news to whoever he get news for, he tell them." Brace continued, describing those who experienced visions. "They'll tell you what's going on in heaven. They meet their folks. . . . We talk to them in person. Person to person spirit."[95]

Kiowa women featured prominently in the revived movement. They wielded feather fans, donned painted dresses, and wore the *amakogia*'s iconic single feather in their hair.[96] They sought connection to lost children and protection for those still living. Jack Hokeah, who later became a prominent artist, told of many women dancing.[97] Moses Poolaw remembered his grandmother dancing until she fell to the ground in trance.[98] Myrtle Ware accompanied her aunt to dances. She recalled leaders bringing messages to grieving mothers. "I saw your daughter and she sent you a song," one said. "That song I'll sing and you must keep always that song so that you will never forget her."

Hokeah recalled the ways Kiowa women integrated older traditions into the *amakogia*. He attended a dance where the tribal medicine bundles were present. Brought from Kiowas' original lands in the far north, the bundles contained powerful objects and received prayers and offerings from those seeking health and protection. Jack's grandmother brought him into a tipi pitched just beyond the *amakogia* circle. Holding an offering of cloth, she told Jack to kneel before the first bundle. Placing the cloth, her hands, and Jack's on the outer layer, she "talked" to the bundle. She prayed for Jack's "future." After finishing with the first bundle, she ushered Jack to the next, one by one, making offerings and reciting prayers to each.[99] Concern for Jack's future makes sense in light of his grandmothers' biographies. His maternal grandmother, Pau-quoot, had one child, Daisy, with her first husband. Between 1910 and 1914, during the *amakogia*'s final years, Pau-quoot lost her spouse, remarried, lost her second husband, and finally, Daisy.[100] O-tah-ty, Jack's paternal grandmother, also suffered during the *amakogia* years. The 1910 census reports that she birthed eleven babies. Only three, including Jack's father, lived to adulthood.[101]

The *amakogia*'s emphasis on family connection and preservation is also suggested by participants' kinship ties.[102] For example, Lily Rose Maunkee joined the dance with her father, "Kiowa Bill" Maunkee, and stepmother, Chatkehoodle. All three suffered losses during the *amakogia* years. Bill and Lily lost her mother and two siblings. Between 1900

Figure 6.4. Black Bear's calendar entry for summer 1890. The dancer holds a feather fan and wears a painted dress and feather. (Division of Anthropology, Catalog No: 50.1/ 6208 A31, American Museum of Natural History)

and 1915, Chatkehoodle lost her first husband, as well as six of her eight children. The grieving trio danced and sought visions for years, even when the reservation agent threatened to withhold their food rations.[103] Kinship ties also connected *amakogia* participants to earlier dance forms, healing rites, and ritual labor. For example, Little Joe (Hahtogo) joined the movement years after his father-in-law, Tchaka, served as a leader in Patepte's 1881 effort to revive the buffalo.[104] Several dancers had healing experience. At least four worked as Buffalo doctors.[105] Other participants had parents and grandparents who were Buffalo and Owl doctors.[106] Still other dancers, including James Silverhorn, also cared for medicine bundles.[107]

These kinship connections and concern for their own dead, I suggest, explain why the post-1893 *amokogia* included more particularly Kiowa elements than the 1890 version, which relied more on objects and songs received from neighboring Plains peoples. Accounts of the later movement reveal less focus on buffalo herds' return to the Plains or an entire world restored. As they focused on deceased kin, dancers integrated not only bundles but also several *Kado* features, including a central tree, eagle bone whistles, and the *Taime*.[108] The dance also featured altogether new elements that some Kiowas embraced as they sought power and connection. By the late 1890s, Christian missions dotted the reservation. Kiowas affiliated with them affirmed the Christian heaven as a site for reunion with the dead.[109] Some *amokogia* participants, as they sought the deceased in trance, encountered Jesus.[110] Others claimed that Jesus would return and bring the buffalo with him.[111]

With references to past practice and adaptations suited to contemporary concerns, the post-1893 *amakogia* exemplified Kiowa ritual creativity when faced with grave threat. Dance still served as a format for sustaining community and adjusting to change. Feathers remained potent symbols employed to connect, heal, and renew. Those who danced in the face of government persecution welcomed powers, old and new, to help them. The *amakogia* featured feathers and dance, as well as bundles, cedar, whistles, and Jesus.[112] Within a dance circle densely packed with symbols, practitioners prayed for their families and nation. They danced to restore their beloved world.

It is unclear how long Kiowas would have performed the *amakogia* if accorded the freedom to do so. In 1894, missionaries recommended that tribal police stop a dance planned for August.[113] In 1895, they called in a company of infantry.[114] In 1916, the agent threatened to withhold cash annuities, which were treaty-guaranteed and crucial for even a minimal standard of living. Kiowas sought legal counsel. They wrote the secretary of the interior. They consulted congressmen, but to no avail. In December, the agent withheld money from ninety dancers. He made release of the funds contingent on signing affidavits promising to quit. By summer 1917, more than half the dancers signed.[115] Bert Geikomah, a practitioner with five children to feed, held out. Decades

Figure 6.5. Silver Horn's calendar entry for summer 1915, showing Agent Stinchecum's effort to suppress the *amakogia*, symbolized by his words breaking a feather. (Detail from Silverhorn calendar, Sam Noble Oklahoma Museum of Natural History, the University of Oklahoma)

later, he recalled other pressures, including the agent's threat to jail dancers.[116] Eventually, the specter of starvation crushed the *amakogia*. James Silverhorn's father, a dancer and calendar keeper, memorialized the event. The agent's demands, represented by a wavy line, break the *amakogia* feather in half.

Conclusion

Despite every American effort to stop it, the *amakogia*, like other dance forms, nurtured new ways of being Kiowa under changing circumstances. Attention to its language, objects, and form reveals a Kiowa world in which birds, feathers, and dance connected them to more-than-human powers, origin stories, powerful objects, beneficent neighbors, healing, prosperity, and even the beloved dead. Employing this Indigenous frame need not undermine what is revealed through analysis of imperial knowledge production. Work such as Dees's investigation of methods and categories used in census counts helps us see how these culturally formed perceptions shaped formations of colonial power. The Indigenous frame, however, shines a light on the colonized. It explores the epistemologies within which Kiowas and other Native nations perceived and acted as disaster threatened. It draws attention to

Native agency and creativity. It helps us track change. And in the case of the *amakogia*, it shines a light on the visionaries and healers, the Native women and children, at the movement's center.

NOTES

1 Many thanks to Clyde Ellis for his feedback on this piece.
2 James Silverhorn, interview T-18, 30–31, Oklahoma Federation of Labor Collection (hereafter OFLC), M452, Box 5, Folder 2, Western History Collections, University of Oklahoma, Norman, Oklahoma. All OFLC materials have the same box and folder numbers.
3 While most scholarship uses the phrase "Ghost Dance," some offer Kiowa renderings. Candace Greene uses Dr. Gus Palmer Jr.'s rendering, "*á:mádècùngà*," for the Feather Dance. See Greene, *One Hundred Summers*, 198. James Mooney offered "*mânposo'ti guan*," meaning "dance with clasped hands." See Mooney, *The Ghost-Dance Religion and the Sioux Outbreak of 1890* (hereafter *GDR*), 791. There is no definitive form of written Kiowa. Along with Palmer's, which I use unless otherwise noted, scholars use Parker McKenzie's system.
4 Mooney did not witness the dance among Lakotas. See Moses, *The Indian Man*, 63.
5 For the contrast between peaceful and hostile, see Mooney, *GDR*, 777, 783. Other Euro-Americans, especially missionaries, typically framed Ghost Dance practitioners as Christian or traditionalist. Mooney was less interested in this opposition, although he noted that "Christian" Lakotas did not participate. See *GDR*, 852.
6 Kramer, "Power and Connection."
7 Warren, *God's Red Son*, 7–8.
8 Smoak, *Ghost Dances and Identity*, 3–6.
9 Warren, *God's Red Son*, 5–6, 9–10; Hale, "Aligning Disciplinary Ends," 462.
10 Smoak, *Ghost Dances and Identity*, 3.
11 Tone-Pah-Hote, *Crafting an Indigenous Nation*, 3. For her elaboration of a particularly Indigenous modernity, 89.
12 Murphy, *The People Have Never Stopped Dancing*, 29.
13 On the cultural impacts of migration to the Plains, see Hämäläinen, *Lakota America*.
14 J. H. Moore's consideration of Cheyenne migration is a useful example. See "The Ornithology of Cheyenne Religionists," 187–88, 190–91.
15 Johnsgard, *Wings over the Great Plains*.
16 Silverhorn, interview T-18, 20, OFLC.
17 Chandler, *The Winged*, 56, 59, 82–85.
18 Zedeño, Murray, and Chandler, "The Inalienable-Commodity Continuum," 100–125.
19 For one example, see Ripps and Keyser, "Spirits on the Wing," 73–88.
20 Lowie, *The Religion of the Crow Indians*, 202.

21 Hollabaugh, *The Spirit and the Sky*, 53, 164. Some tribes on the Missouri River shared this understanding of thunder and control of weather. Chandler, *The Winged*, 26, 31.
22 Guy Quoetone, interview T-100, 18, 22–23, OFLC.
23 J. H. Moore, "The Ornithology of Cheyenne Religionists," 178, 181.
24 Silverhorn, interview T-18, 24–25, OFLC.
25 Ewers, *Murals in the Round*, 27–28, 30–31, 33.
26 Jordan, "Reclaiming the Past," 80.
27 Scott and Iseeo, *Through Indian Sign Language*, 240.
28 Scott and Iseeo, *Through Indian Sign Language*, 184–85.
29 Chandler also details bird images on shields across Plains Indian nations. See *The Winged*, 59–61.
30 Scott and Iseeo, *Through Indian Sign Language*, 160, 173; Kracht, *Kiowa Belief and Ritual* (hereafter *KBR*), 117–18.
31 The sodalities are often called military societies, although they had many functions beyond warfare.
32 Greene, *One Hundred Summers*, 196.
33 Chandler, *The Winged*, 66–67, 90–92, 49.
34 Voget, *The Shoshoni-Crow Sun Dance*; Kracht, *KBR*, 152–60.
35 Scott and Iseeo, *Through Indian Sign Language*, 208.
36 The informant used a common nickname, "prairie swifthawk." Guy Quoetone, interview T-23, 6, OFLC
37 Scott and Iseeo, *Through Indian Sign Language*, 159–60.
38 Meredith, *Dancing on Common Ground*, 11.
39 Kracht, *Religious Revitalization among the Kiowas* (hereafter *RRK*), 82–84.
40 Marriott, *Saynday's People*, 12–23.
41 Mooney, *Calendar History of the Kiowa Indians*, 287–89.
42 Kracht, *RRK*, 84–85.
43 Greene, *One Hundred Summers*, 231. Mooney also noted Patepte's (or Datekan) feathered robe. See Mooney, *GDR*, 906.
44 Chandler, *The Winged*, 43–45, 53.
45 Kracht, *KBR*, 108–9. Owl Societies are common across Plains Indian nations. See Chandler, *The Winged*, 78.
46 Kracht, *KBR*, 108.
47 Nye, *Bad Medicine and Good*, 222–25. Mamanti was also a Buffalo doctor. See Ewers, *Murals in the Round*, 33.
48 Guy Quoetone, interview T-26, 18, OFLC.
49 Kracht, *KBR*, 108.
50 Quoetone, interview T-26, 1, OFLC.
51 Quoetone, T-26, 18, 34, OFLC; Kracht, *KBR*, 109–10. The "Shaking Tent" ritual appeared in other Plains and Woodlands practices of healing and mourning. See Chandler, *The Winged*, 45.
52 Hubbard, "Buffalo Genocide in Nineteenth-Century North America," 292–305.

53 Fowler, *Shared Symbols, Contested Meanings*, 10.
54 C. Ellis, *A Dancing People*, 8.
55 Lassiter, *The Power of Kiowa Song*, 199.
56 Walker, *Lakota Belief and Ritual*, 33.
57 Voget, *The Shoshoni-Crow Sun Dance*, 82–85.
58 Meadows, *Kiowa Military Societies*, 3; C. Ellis, *A Dancing People*, 40–42.
59 Meadows, *Kiowa Military Societies*, 7, 310–24.
60 Wenger, *We Have a Religion*; McNally, *Defend the Sacred*, 33–68.
61 C. Ellis, *A Dancing People*, 60.
62 Mooney, *Calendar History of the Kiowa Indians*, 359, 356. Kiowas sometimes held the dance in far-off locales with the hope of evading much notice. They periodically delayed the celebration when it took months to locate a buffalo for use in the central complex (347). They even substituted a cow one year (355).
63 Gelo, *Indians of the Great Plains*, 217–18; Meadows, *Kiowa Military Societies*, 254–55.
64 C. Ellis, *A Dancing People*, 19, 31, 34, 46–48, 51.
65 Gelo, *Indians of the Great Plains*, 217.
66 Meadows, *Kiowa Military Societies*, 262; Kracht, *KBR*, 118.
67 Meadows, *Kiowa Military Societies*, 263–69. Mac's father, Charley White Horse, participated in the Feather Dance. See Kracht, *RRK*, 137–38.
68 On the Paiute name, see Hittman, *Wovoka and the Ghost Dance*, 63. On the visions, see Mooney, *GDR*, 764–71.
69 On Wovoka's power to make rain, see Jay Miller, "Basin Religion and Theology," 78–79. On receiving songs from more-than-human powers, see Vander, "The Creative Power and Style of Ghost Dance Songs," 114, 118.
70 Hittman, *Wovoka and the Ghost Dance*, 93–94, 300–301.
71 Mooney, *GDR*, 1054–56.
72 Hittman, *Wovoka and the Ghost Dance*, 143–45, 186, 214–15. The Paiute word for sacred power is also written as *"puha."*
73 Mooney, *GDR*, 775, 901. On magpie feather distribution, see Hittman, *Wovoka and the Ghost Dance*, 92, 251–52, 257. On paint as an "animating power," see Chandler, *The Winged*, 56. On red as a color signifying joy in Great Basin cultures, see Jay Miller, "Basin Religion and Theology," 68.
74 Chandler, *The Winged*, 50.
75 Mooney, *GDR*, 998–99. Cheyennes, unlike some Plains tribes, had extensive magpie traditions. See J. H. Moore, "The Ornithology of Cheyenne Religionists," 181.
76 For natural-calamity references, see Mooney, *GDR*, 958, 970, 973, 976. For references to Euro-Americans, see Mooney, *GDR*, 961, 972, 978.
77 Mooney, *GDR*, 968, 1072.
78 J. H. Moore, "The Ornithology of Cheyenne Religionists," 184–85.
79 Mooney, *GDR*, 973.
80 Mooney, *GDR*, 786.
81 This Sitting Bull (Arapaho) is not the more famous Lakota Sitting Bull.

82 Kracht, *RRK*, 90–91.
83 Kracht, *RRK*, 90–99. Kracht writes that Patepte also named seven men and seven women in his earlier effort to revive the buffalo. Kracht, *RRK*, 82.
84 Kracht, *RRK*, 92.
85 Mooney, *GDR*, 1083–84.
86 Mooney, *GDR*, 1082; Daisey and Jack Hokeah, interview T-178, 7, OFLC
87 Mooney, *GDR*, 786. James Silverhorn recounted dancers predicting tornados. See Silverhorn, interview T-18, 32, OFLC.
88 Mooney does not provide the woman's name. See Mooney, *GDR*, 1087.
89 Silverhorn, interview T-18, 33, OFLC.
90 For a full account of this meeting, see Kracht, *RRK*, 101–3.
91 US Office of Indian Affairs, *Annual Report of the Commissioner of Indian Affairs, for the Year 1891* (Washington, DC: Government Printing Office, 1891), 351. Kiowa calendars keepers also memorialized the measles epidemic.
92 Mooney, *Calendar History of the Kiowa Indians*, 360.
93 Kracht, *RRK*, 103–5. Kiowa informants remember Setzepetoi (Afraid of Bears) claiming an earlier vision about a restorative dance, which he later took to be the Feather Dance. Boyd, *Kiowa Voices*, 91. Setzepetoi also had a record of openness to new forms of dance. He served as a whipman in the *Ohoma*. See Meadows, *Kiowa Military Societies*, 269.
94 Bert Geikomah, interview T-74, 13–14, OFLC.
95 (Lou) Ella Brace, interview T-173-2, 2–3, OFLC. Her name appears as Luella Brace on most public documents, although the 1903 Kiowa census lists her as Luella Aunkehau.
96 Kracht, *RRK*, 117.
97 Hokeah, interview T-178, 4, OFLC.
98 Mose (Moses) Poolaw, interview T-471, 3–4, OFLC.
99 Hokeah, interview T-178, 5, OFLC.
100 Her first husband, Waterman, is buried in Red Stone Cemetery. Daisy no longer appears in Kiowa census records after 1913. Year: 1913; Roll: M595_213; Page 57; Line 24; U.S., Indian Census Rolls, 1885–1940.
101 Year: 1910; Census Place: Mcmaster, Comanche, Oklahoma; Roll: T624_1248; Page: 14A; Enumeration District: 0056; FHL microfilm: 1375261, U.S., Indian Census Rolls, 1885–1940. Pau-quoot's husband, Hauvahte, was also involved in the Feather Dance. His calendar entries refer to it frequently; see Greene, *One Hundred Summers*, 233–35. Thanks to William Meadows for his help with Jack Hokeah's genealogy.
102 For another example, White Buffalo (Konad) helped revive the dance in 1893. White Buffalo had perhaps six children, three of whom were born during the revived *amakogia*. Even as the dance reinforced kinship ties, participants felt those connections threatened. His parents, Poor Buffalo, who also participated, and Sa-Poodle (Rain), died in 1901 and 1902, respectively. His oldest child, Bert, was separated from the family while attending a Roman Catholic boarding school.

See Student Enrollment ledger, pages 41–42, Archives of St. Gregory's Abbey, Shawnee, Oklahoma. Relatives say Bert died, in 1909, at age twenty. Kracht, *RRK*, 137.
103 Kracht, *RRK*, 137.
104 Kracht, *RRK*, 137; Scott and Iseeo, *Through Indian Sign Language*, 131.
105 Guy Quoetone mentioned Red Buffalo, Tenehadl, Conklin Hummingbird, and Poolaw. See Quoetone, interview T-23, 23–24, OFLC. Other informants concur. See Poolaw, T-471, 3, OFLC; Eugenia Mausape, interview T-37, 11, OFLC; Jenny and Cecil Horse, interview T-142, 25–27, OFLC.
106 Poolaw, interview T-47, 3, OFLC. His father was a Buffalo doctor. Cecil Horse's father, Hunting Horse, was an Owl doctor.
107 On Silverhorn, see Kracht, *KBR*, 27. On Frank Given and Setzepetoi (Afraid of Bears), see *KBR*, 151. On White Fox, see *KBR*, 30.
108 Several informants mentioned the tree or cross in the middle. See Silverhorn, interview T-18, 34, OFLC; Hokeah, interview T-178, 3, OFLC; Brace, interview T-173-2, 2, OFLC; Louise Saddleblanket, interview T-56-2, 9, OFLC. On whistles, see Hokeah, T-178, 3, OFLC. On the Taime, see Kracht, *RRK*, 114.
109 Graber, *The Gods of Indian Country*, 167–68, 179–81, 185–87.
110 Bianki drawing, James Mooney Notes and Papers, oversize box, National Anthropological Archives, Suitland, MD; Brace, interview T-173-2, 2, OFLC.
111 Setzepetoi went further. He told Crawford that Jesus would appear to the Kiowa at noon on July 15, 1904. Kracht, *RRK*, 105, 114, 116–17; Kracht, *KBR*, 151.
112 For cedar references, see Brace, interview T-173-2, 2, OFLC.
113 Name illegible to Nichols, August 23, 1895, "Celebrations and Dances," Roll 47, Kiowa Agency Files, Oklahoma Historical Society, Oklahoma City.
114 Barber to Baldwin, September 26, 1895, "Celebrations and Dances," Roll 47, Kiowa Agency Files, Oklahoma Historical Society, Oklahoma City.
115 Kracht, *RRK*, 136–38. The agent also targeted the *Ohoma* Dance, 120.
116 His in-laws are also listed as dancers whose annuities were withheld. See Kracht, *RRK*, 137.

PART III

Entanglements

*Global Networks, Christian Missions, and
the Racial Projects of US Empire*

Global networks have been integral to imperial power, and the United States embodied this pattern as it became increasingly ascendant on a global scale after the Spanish American War of 1898. In this period, the United States poured military resources into the project of conquering and controlling new nations and peoples in the Spanish-speaking Caribbean and across the Pacific. As we saw in part 2, government officials and idealistic reformers worked in the late-nineteenth and early-twentieth centuries to classify and control racialized populations within the borders of the United States. At the same time, US officials rationalized an unprecedented scale of overseas domination by expressing a paternalistic aspiration to civilize and modernize the "little Brown Brothers," a disparaging reference to colonized non-White populations.

The chapters in this section illuminate the global networks of religion and reform that facilitated US imperial expansions at the dawn of the twentieth century, despite (and, ironically, sometimes through) reformers' efforts to imagine the world otherwise. They help us see how Black and White American reformers' efforts to improve conditions both domestically and globally were, perhaps inevitably, entangled with the tactics and technologies of US empire. As the United States brought greater influence to bear on the Philippines—including the Islamicate polities of Mindanao and Sulu—missionary-inspired forms of industrial education adopted and adapted older forms of imperial domination. Boarding schools for Native Americans anticipated and shaped those in the Philippines for Muslim youths, an enterprise that exhibited powerful entanglements of religion with empire and race. Meanwhile, late-nineteenth- and early-twentieth-century activists such as Ida B. Wells leveraged religious advocacy and social reform networks to address racism within the context of transnational collaborations, while revealing the conflicting consequences of colonialism beyond US borders. In Latin America, White US Protestant missionaries blended their religion with the US foreign policy of pan-Americanism to form a logic for the evangelization of this predominantly Catholic region. By doing so, they created a veil of harmony while propagating a racialized spirituality that sought to impose a new social order along racial and religious lines. What roles did religion play in this era of US imperial expansion? How did new religious networks and identities form and operate in the interstices of empire? In short, how did the new imperial entanglements reshape and implicate American religions?

7

"The Same Blood as We in America"

Industrial Schooling and American Empire

KARINE WALTHER

In February of 1900, the *Southern Workman*, a journal published by the Virginia-based Hampton Normal and Agricultural Institute for Negroes and Indians, printed a letter by its former student, John Henry St. Clare Walker. Writing from Hawaii, where his military regiment was temporarily stationed on its way to fight in the Philippine-American War, Walker noted that native Hawaiians had welcomed him and other Black soldiers into their homes: "They are fond of the colored people and claim to have the same blood as we in America. . . . They talk very intelligently about the overthrow of their government by the Americans, and about the future of the Islands."[1] Walker's observations revealed the complicated ways Hawaiians identified with people of color across imperial boundaries, views they expressed alongside their critiques of American imperial rule.

Walker's letter also recognized that Hawaii was "sacred" to Hampton. Samuel Chapman Armstrong, who founded the industrial school in 1868 with funding from the American Missionary Association, was born in Hawaii in 1839. He became an advocate of industrial education due to his father, who helped establish the model there in the 1830s, first as a Protestant missionary and later as the minister of public education. Armstrong absorbed his father's belief that manual training and Christian instruction, rather than a traditional liberal education, were necessary for people of color and should ideally include separating students from their families through boarding schools.[2] Although Hampton initially focused on educating African Americans, in 1878 Armstrong accepted subsidies from the US government to extend the school's racial paternalism to Native American students.

Walker's travels from Hampton, Virginia, to Hawaii, the Philippines, and back to Virginia reflected the global circulation of ideas about race, religion, empire, labor, and industrial education in the nineteenth and early twentieth centuries. This chapter analyzes these trajectories by tracing the spread of industrial education across the varied racial and religious landscapes of American Empire. Drawing on scholarly theories of internal colonialism, which highlight practices adopted by both the US government and nonstate actors, it applies an expanded view of empire that incorporates African Americans as colonial subjects.[3] While African Americans' status under slavery differed from the experiences of imperial subjects, their political, racial, economic, and societal exclusion after the Civil War often mirrored those of imperial subjects in the United States and abroad.[4] Moreover, domestic goals justifying the "reform" of people of color at home were intricately tied to US imperial claims about the necessity of spreading Christianity, progress, and civilizational advancement abroad.[5]

Despite—or perhaps due to—centuries of African American slavery and decades of coercive labor practices inflicted on native and immigrant workers in Hawaii and in the domestic United States, many white Americans felt an ongoing duty to inculcate a respect for manual labor in people of color.[6] Industrial schooling for Hawaiians, African Americans, and Native Americans in the nineteenth century was initially driven by Protestant missionaries, often with the support of the US government.[7] By 1900, 307 industrial schools had opened across the United States alone, 54 of which were led by missionary, religious, or other private organizations under contract with the US government.[8] Indeed, Walker's letter referenced that members of his segregated infantry included "Tuskegee boys," referring to graduates of the Tuskegee Institute in Alabama. Tuskegee was founded on the Hampton model in 1881 and led by its most famous graduate, Booker T. Washington, who obtained his position due to Armstrong's support. After the 1898 Spanish-American War, colonial officials and missionaries quickly extended the model to newly annexed territories in the Philippines and the Spanish Caribbean.[9]

As Walker's own experience demonstrates, the white exploitation of Black bodies extended to enlisting African Americans in the service of imperial warfare. Just as some Hawaiians believed they shared the same blood as people of color in the United States, many African Americans recognized their shared experiences with Filipino imperial subjects. Despite their service, many African Americans were deeply cognizant that justifications for annexation claiming Filipinos' racial and civilizational inferiority mirrored domestic rationales relegating African Americans to second-class citizenship.[10] Black soldiers who regularly witnessed the racist behavior of white soldiers and colonial officials towards Filipinos led many to identify with the imperial subjects they were meant to be fighting.[11] Like the Black activists profiled in chapter 8 who fought for racial justice both at home and abroad, many African Americans actively resisted the racial hierarchies undergirding American Empire in the Philippines.

The fact that Walker's letter was addressed to Hampton's leadership made it difficult for him to overtly critique the racial stereotypes that undergirded both the industrial school model and American Empire, had he the desire to do so. Armstrong's beliefs about racial inferiority drove his decision to found Hampton and contributed to his support for American imperial expansion. Such views were regularly reaffirmed in the pages of the *Southern Workman* and in Armstrong's own writings. Armstrong believed people of color required white moral guidance no matter where they lived. As he argued in 1884, "The negro and the Polynesian have many striking similarities. Of both it is true that not mere ignorance, but deficiency of character is the chief difficulty, and that to build up character is the true object point in education. . . . Morality and industry generally go together. Especially in the weak tropical races, idleness, like ignorance, breeds vice."[12] In future publications, he incorporated Native Americans into the mix: "School training for the Hawaiians, the Africans, or the Indians should in the great majority of cases be elementary, industrial, earnestly and practically Christian . . . devoted to making self-reliant men and women of simple tastes, above their people yet of them and full of the spirit of missionary work for them."[13] He described Hampton's approach more crudely in a private letter, explaining that he applied "tender violence" to students and "boosted darkies a bit, and so to speak, lassoed wild Indians all to be cleaned and tamed by a simple process I have invented known as the 'Hampton method.'"[14] Walker was undoubtedly exposed to these views during his time at Hampton and addressed them in his letter: "There are a number

Figure 7.1. African American Students Attending a Cooking Class. Frances Benjamin Johnston, photographer. Hampton, Virginia, n.d. (between 1899 and 1900), Library of Congress, Washington, DC, www.loc.gov.

of Hampton students in our regiment, the Forty-ninth Infantry, and they are noted for their *strictness, promptness, and truthfulness*."[15] While his comments could be read as a subtle challenge to racial stereotypes, Armstrong, and perhaps Walker himself, would have attributed such qualities to Hampton's influence.

While Armstrong recognized that some people of color could successfully pursue "advanced studies," he believed the best approach was to educate them to contribute to society through their physical labor and Christian training.[16] While the merging of industrial schooling with Christian education originated with missionaries in private schools, many government-sponsored schools integrated religious courses in their curriculum as well and hired missionaries to both lead and teach in the schools. Many advocates of industrial schooling believed the relationship between Christianity and manual labor was mutually reinforcing. Christianity inculcated moral character and a respect for work—and a respect for work made students better Christians.[17]

At Hampton and other industrial schools, the curriculum sought to eliminate people of color's alleged moral vice and lack of work ethic through their curriculum, which included inculcating Anglo-Protestant gender roles and gendered divisions of labor. Male students learned to work the fields, take care of farm animals, and practice carpentry, leather work, and other appropriate trades, while female students learned laundering, sewing, cooking, and general housekeeping.[18] This "education" continued during the summer months, when schools leased students to work for white families, believing it would further aid their civilizational uplift.[19]

Of course, white advocates of industrial education were driven by more than just their concerns for reforming people of color's moral character or saving their spiritual souls. In this capacity, African Americans and imperial subjects shared another thing in common: economic elites depended on these populations to serve as obedient and productive workers. These efforts were grounded in a longer history of racial

Figure 7.2. African American and Native American Students Attending a Class in Hygiene. Frances Benjamin Johnston, photographer. Hampton, Virginia, n.d. (between 1899 and 1900), Library of Congress, Washington, DC, www.loc.gov.

Figure 7.3. Students Training in Blacksmithing. Frances Benjamin Johnston, photographer. Hampton, Virginia, n.d. (between 1899 and 1900), Library of Congress, Washington, DC, www.loc.gov.

capitalism and labor exploitation.[20] Before the Civil War, Southern slaveholders accrued massive profits from the institution and justified its continuation by arguing that they were inculcating "civilized" work habits and Christianity among their slaves.[21] After the war, white Southerners capitalized on the Thirteenth Amendment to the US Constitution to exploit the labor of African American prisoners.[22] After the war, Northern industrialists also began investing in the development of the Southern economy and donated money to industrial schools, eager to create a population of skilled and compliant labor.[23]

Both Armstrong and Richard Pratt, who founded the Carlisle Indian Industrial School in Pennsylvania in 1879, believed in the alleged "educative" benefits of slavery.[24] A report by the US Bureau of Education in 1901 drew on Armstrong's arguments to maintain that "two hundred and fifty years of slavery had indeed been in itself a great university, and the history of the world may be challenged to present a spectacle so remarkable as the growth of the pagan, often a bondman African of three centuries ago[,] into the American negro slave of 1860."[25] Slavery, the report further maintained, had taught the African "to work, and enabled him to obtain, even in a crude state, the language and the religion of the most progressive of northern nations."[26] Armstrong applied the same logic to native Hawaiians. Praising the work of the Hilo Boarding School in Hawaii, he noted that teachers had "trained native boys to be Christian, well-behaved, industrious and intelligent young men, who knew enough to do the work they had to do, yet were not stuffed with book-knowledge in a way to make them conceited or feel too far above their people and thus tempted to use them as their tools."[27]

The irony of Armstrong's statement was that many white advocates of industrial education saw it as a tool to facilitate the continued exploitation of people of color's labor. Their goal included teaching students to accept their inferior place under white rule and conform to

Figure 7.4. Students Learning to Lay Bricks. Frances Benjamin Johnston, photographer. Hampton, Virginia, n.d. (between 1899 and 1900), Library of Congress, Washington, DC, www.loc.gov.

racial hierarchies of power. Many white Southerners feared that if African Americans pursued a liberal education instead of one focused on manual labor, they would gain their own tools to further threaten white political, economic, and societal dominance.[28] Armstrong's industrial school model aligned with these views; Hampton was not intended to change the second-class status of African Americans, but instead instruct students to contribute economically to this unequal society.[29] More broadly, US government officials, who were facing simultaneous African American demands for political and economic equality alongside the rejection of imperial rule by many Filipinos, Hawaiians, and Native Americans believed industrial schools would prevent rebellious behavior by promising limited political and economic advancement in the future.[30] As an article in the *Southern Workman* argued in February of 1900 justifying the money the US government was investing in schools for Native Americans, it "is far wiser to pay school bills than army bills, to prevent outbreaks than to quell them."[31]

Hampton served as a model for schools across the United States and abroad, a fact the *Southern Workman* proudly noted in its issues. What contemporaries referred to as the "Hampton-Tuskegee Model" was replicated in schools across the country. Before opening Carlisle, Pratt had worked with Armstrong and the US government to bring Native American students to Hampton. The US government approved and funded Pratt's plan to open Carlisle on the basis of this experience.[32] Armstrong provided regular advice to industrial schools in Hawaii and helped found new schools there, sending Hampton graduates to serve as teachers in these institutions.[33]

In addition to manual training, industrial schools for Native Americans were designed to replace their culture with Anglo-American culture.[34] This entailed removing students from their families, replacing their native language with English, and converting them to Christianity.[35] Pratt relied on student labor to build a Christian chapel and assembly room at Carlisle, which became the school's most important building.[36] Hampton teacher Helen Ludlow proudly noted in 1881 that visitors hoping to see "real Indians" would be disappointed: "Aboriginal picturesqueness is certainly sacrificed to a great extent in civilization. One who is willing to relinquish the idea, however, of a menagerie of wild creatures kept for exhibition, will not regret to find instead a school

Figure 7.5. Native American Male Students in a Furniture-Building Class, Carlisle Indian School, 1901. Frances Benjamin Johnston, photographer. Carlisle, Pennsylvania, Library of Congress, Washington, DC, www.loc.gov.

of neatly dressed boys and girls, with bright eyes and clean faces, as full of fun and frolic as if they were the descendants of the Puritans."[37] The inculcation of Anglo-American values took other forms. Ludlow revealed that after her students learned to speak and read English, they could "take pleasure" in reading *Robinson Crusoe* and Christopher Columbus.[38] Ludlow's choice of texts that celebrated European imperial, civilizational, and religious expansion into indigenous lands was surely not coincidental. The school's location in the former Carlisle Barracks, where members of the US cavalry had previously trained to fight Native American nations, including those belonging to the school's future students, offered another potent symbol of the continuities of imperial rule.[39]

Just as Ludlow's chosen readings ignored the deadly impact of imperial expansion, her glowing depictions of cultural genocide overlooked the high rates of malnutrition, disease, and physical, emotional, and

Figure 7.6. Native American Male Students Training to Make Buckets and Tins, Carlisle Indian School, circa 1904. Frances Benjamin Johnston, photographer. Carlisle, Pennsylvania, Library of Congress, www.loc.gov.

sexual abuse experienced by many students in industrial schools.[40] The death rate was particularly high for Native American students. Hampton cemetery includes the graves of 38 Native American children, most of whom died in the decade Ludlow wrote her piece.[41] An additional 65 Hampton students died after being sent home due to illness.[42] By the time Carlisle closed in 1918, having run for 39 years, its cemetery contained the graves of 196 students.[43] Many more died during their summer work or, as at Hampton, after they fell ill at the school and were sent back home, a policy that lowered the school's death rates on paper.[44]

Although students were the primary victims of physical and sexual abuse at the hands of whites, Armstrong believed that they were the ones in need of moral surveillance and reform. He imposed a tight system of control over students' time and movement that replicated African Americans' experiences under slavery: "My boys are run up at 5 o'clock in the morning, called to military parade before breakfast, kept busy all day till 8 p.m., always under military discipline."[45] In addition to teaching obedience and discipline, this system, he believed, would prevent illicit sexual relations between students, which he euphemistically phrased as "the abuse of coeducation."[46] His efforts proved unsuccessful. Hampton ended its enrollment of Native Americans in 1923 in part due to the emergence of relationships between Native American and African American students, which scandalized the school's leadership and local community members who opposed racial miscegenation, including between people of color.[47]

While popular with white reformers, the Hampton-Tuskegee model faced critiques from African American intellectuals.[48] Criticizing the approach, W. E. B. Du Bois argued in 1903 that the model supported white Southern goals of keeping African Americans docile, obedient, and productive while maintaining their "silence as to civil and political rights."[49] He nonetheless cautioned Black intellectuals who believed

Figure 7.7. Native American Female Students in a Cooking Class, 1901. Frances Benjamin Johnston, photographer. Carlisle, Pennsylvania, Library of Congress, www.loc.gov.

that the only viable alternative was leaving the United States to seek refuge abroad, stating that this strategy overlooked the country's power to export the same practices abroad: "Nothing has more effectually made this programme seem hopeless than the recent course of the United States toward weaker and darker peoples in the West Indies, Hawaii, and the Philippines,—for where in the world may we go and be safe from lying and brute force?"[50] Du Bois was undoubtedly referring to the decades-old practice of African Americans migrating to nations such as Haiti and, later, the Dominican Republic, in search of "a black Promised Land."[51] His warnings about the pitfalls of expatriation merged with his stinging critique of American imperial rule. Resistance to industrial schooling also came from African Americans in the South who opened schools that offered Black students a traditional liberal arts education.[52]

When white Americans began spreading the Hampton-Tuskegee model to the Philippine Islands, they built on President William McKinley's justifications defending annexation. It was the country's duty, he had argued, "to educate the Filipinos, and uplift and civilize and Christianize them."[53] In 1901, the Bureau of Public Instruction, led by Fred Atkinson, hired six hundred Americans to teach in colonial schools and mandated that classes would be entirely in English.[54] As one bureau official argued, "The boy who in his school days has learned the language of a civilized nation, even if he has learned nothing else, has put himself en rapport with civilization.... It makes little difference whether he learns English, French, German, or Spanish, but it makes a great deal of difference whether he learns French or Tagalog, English or Bicol."[55] These views also echoed Armstrong's beliefs about Blacks and Hawaiians: "The acquirement of the English language by the negro is a wonderful help to his elevation. So the best Hawaiian families are those who have dropped the vernacular and speak English. Savage dialects are a part of a low, sensuous life, that must be forsaken together with its other belongings. English is a tonic for both mind and soul."[56]

School leaders at Hampton and in Hawaii expressed their support for imperial expansion and the extension of industrial education to the Philippines. The latter reprinted Rudyard Kipling's now infamous poem, "The White Man's Burden," in its school newspaper alongside the view that Filipinos should never be accepted as US citizens.[57] The *Southern Workman* highlighted the similarities between Hampton's goals and the education of imperial subjects abroad and published numerous recommendations on educational policy in the Philippines.[58] One article, which included strong praise for the benefits of industrial schooling, claimed that the Civil War, the Cuban War, and the Philippines War furnished "striking coincidences" for "in each case a serious consideration of the dark races forms a prominent feature," later specifying that the "uplifting of the darker races has been and is still one of the first things calling for consideration at the close of the three wars."[59] The author recommended that colonial officials consult American educators about industrial schooling and encouraged sending African American graduates to teach imperial subjects. The *Southern Workman* proudly noted that Atkinson had visited the school "for the purpose of observing its methods of dealing with backward races."[60] Atkinson's visit to Hampton and Tuskegee was made at the instruction of the first civil governor of the Philippines, William Howard Taft.[61] After his visits, Atkinson remarked that "the education of the masses here [in the Philippines] must be an agricultural and industrial one, after the pattern of our Tuskegee Institute at home."[62] Washington also supported industrial education in the Philippines, maintaining that it could solve the problems facing colonial officials, much as it was addressing those posed by newly freed African Americans in the South.[63] The transfer of the industrial educational model across imperial boundaries extended to European missionaries and imperial officers, who also toured these institutions and applied their methods in their own schools.[64]

Support for industrial schooling also came from the US Bureau of Education. Dismissing anti-imperialist critiques, a 1902 report noted that naysayers would quickly change their minds "if they could realize the prodigious significance of this great experiment at Hampton in the education of all races of men in their progress from pagan barbarism to a self-relying Christian civilization."[65] Annexation, the report maintained, was a divine duty that had come at an ideal time: "It is not so much fortunate as providential that the country has not been called to face this mighty responsibility of dealing with these new millions of the little children and wards of Christendom until, by a thirty years' experimenting at home, it had not only discovered but put in operation in every Southern State, by the agreement and cooperation of all sections, the Hampton methods of training the lower majority of this world on the lines of a Christian civilization."⁶⁶ God's providential global vision for the United States, it seemed, had brought about Hampton's existence as a stepping stone for the religious and civilizational upliftment of imperial subjects abroad.

Organizers of the "Model Indian School" exhibit at the 1904 St. Louis World's Fair also encouraged the application of their model to Filipinos: "One of the gravest tasks of any progressive nation is that of caring for alien wards, i.e., bearing 'the White Man's burden,' as told by Kipling."⁶⁷ Also adopting language undergirded with religious symbolism, they noted that "the school is designed not merely as a consummation, *but as a prophecy*; for now that other primitive peoples are passing under the beneficent influence and protection of the Stars and Stripes, it is needful to take stock of past progress as a guide to the future."⁶⁸ They suggested that the physical proximity of their exhibit to the Philippines exhibit served as a metaphor for these broader connections: "Over against the Indian on the grounds, just beyond Arrowhead Lake, stood the Filipino, even as over against the Red Man on the continent, just beyond the Pacific, stands the brown man of the nearer Orient; and it was the aim of the Model Indian School to extend an influence across both intervening waters which should be to the benefit of both races."⁶⁹ The exhibits were also designed to educate American schoolchildren. Physical molds of the Native Americans and Filipinos featured in the exhibits would be "distributed throughout the United States in schools and libraries as educational features," in the process reaffirming pseudoscientific ideas about race.⁷⁰

In the Philippines, colonial officials initially prioritized the opening of industrial schools for Christian Filipinos, whom they deemed superior to non-Christians. This decision was reinforced by Filipino Muslims' ongoing rebellions against American rule. This prioritization also conformed to colonial officials' categorizations of Filipinos as either "wild" or "civilized" based entirely on whether or not they were Christian.⁷¹ Officials distinguished between educating Filipinos "in letters, into letters, or entirely outside of letters," deeming the last option the most appropriate for most non-Christians.⁷² One official noted that for the Igorots, who belonged to the Lumad (animist) peoples, there was little hope of educating them "to the status of civilization."⁷³ Instead, they required schooling "to perform more efficiently the labor necessary for their rude state" through "a simple form of industrial training."⁷⁴ Reforming non-Christian Negritos, whom officials believed occupied the lowest racial and civilization status, was deemed "hopeless," and therefore education was completely unnecessary.⁷⁵ Despite categorizing Christian Filipinos as superior, colonial officials believed that as both Catholics and Filipinos, they too required religious and civilizational reform.⁷⁶ Taft noted that Catholic Filipinos were in "a state of Christian pupilage" that would presumably require decades of American Protestant rule to reform their alleged deficiencies.⁷⁷

Efforts to impose industrial education in the Philippines met with resistance from students who preferred to train for bureaucratic positions. Officials blamed their reaction on Spanish imperialists who had failed to inculcate in them a proper respect for manual labor. Colonial bureaucrats hoped that through American tutelage, Filipinos would eventually learn to embrace their proper place in the labor hierarchy.⁷⁸ The "delicate task" of quelling Filipinos' overambitious educational goals fell on American teachers.⁷⁹ To aid with this endeavor, in 1904 the Bureau of Education began publishing the *Philippine Teacher: A Periodical for Philippine Progress*, which offered guidance on industrial curriculum. This advice was crucial for the newly hired teachers, most of whom lacked experience in industrial education.⁸⁰ The journal repeatedly referred to the Hampton-Tuskegee model for inspiration.⁸¹ In 1912, the bureau launched a second journal, the *Philippine Craftsman*, "devoted to the advancement of industrial education," which included detailed lesson plans.⁸²

Meanwhile, the American military extended a different kind of education to Filipino Muslims.⁸³ One official explained that Muslims' opposition to colonial rule was so entrenched that the "education of the Moro must, therefore, follow his awakening to an appreciation of his feebleness as contrasted with the powers of a civilized nation."⁸⁴ Formal education could only proceed after Moros had learned their lesson on the field of battle. During the Moro Rebellion, which officially lasted from 1902 to 1913, the military carried out indiscriminate massacres of civilians, including children, torture, and the burning and razing of entire villages. One scholar estimates that fifteen to twenty thousand Moros died between 1903 and 1936, constituting over 5 percent of the total Filipino-Muslim population.⁸⁵ In 1933, one Moro leader who had collaborated with American colonial rulers maintained that this number was much higher and critiqued the futility of such a violent approach: "We haven't changed the Moro much although we have killed seventy thousand, six each day including Sundays and Holidays."[86] Official reports used euphemistic language to downplay this violence and justify the slow establishment of schooling: "The *misunderstandings* between the Americans and the Moros and the resulting *stress* . . . naturally militated against the success of educational work at that place."[87]

Despite this violence, colonial officials managed to open two industrial schools for Filipino Muslims in 1902 in Zamboanga and Jolo. Atkinson appointed Emerson Christie to head the industrial school in Zamboanga. Born in Turkey to missionary parents who passed onto their son their aversion for the Islamic faith, Christie noted that in accepting the position he was embarking on "the first chapter in the story of a modern crusade."[88] For Christie, industrial education went hand in hand with defeating the Islamic faith. Officials also opened a Moro Exchange in 1904 that they hoped would teach Filipino Muslims about the benefits of manual labor by allowing them to sell their items in local markets.

Meanwhile, American teachers attempted to teach Filipino Christian students to accept the benefits of American colonial rule and believe in their religious and racial superiority over non-Christians. Public schools assigned a textbook written by Prescott F. Jernegan, an American Baptist preacher who began teaching after his arrival in the Philippines in 1901. His textbook instructed students about the benevolence of American rule, Filipinos' rights and responsibilities as imperial subjects, and the proper trajectory they should follow for achieving full political citizenship. The textbook opened with the author's dedication "to the rising generation of Filipinos, whose intelligence, industry and patriotism shall make real the dream of their fathers—a self-governing Filipino state."[89] It went on to justify the "necessity" of categorizing Filipinos by race and religion with corresponding forms of governance: "The people of the various provinces differ greatly in race, religion, customs, education, and political training. There is no more important principle of lawmaking than that the government and laws of a people should be suited to the peculiar character and habits of that people."[90] These differences justified hierarchies of political rights: "The ideal form of government is a representative democracy, but not all peoples are fit and ready for that sort of rule. If the Moro were given complete self-government he would reestablish slavery; the Igorot, left to choose for himself, would honor and reward head-hunting; the Negrito would have no government beyond family government. Hence three different forms of provincial government have been established."[91] While his textbook sought to educate Filipinos in civic and moral responsibility, Jernegan himself had fled the United States in 1898 to avoid criminal prosecution, carrying with him over two hundred thousand dollars of stolen investor money gained from a fraudulent scheme promising that he could extract gold from seawater.[92]

Efforts to reform Filipinos through industrial education also came from Protestant missionary organizations. In 1899, New York philanthropist Horace B. Silliman donated ten thousand dollars to the Presbyterian Board of Missions to open a private religious and industrial school on Negros Island. The Silliman Institute opened two years later and replicated the Hampton model, to which Silliman had previously donated thousands of dollars.[93] David Hibbard, who was appointed to lead the institute, was instructed to tour Hampton before departing for the Philippines.[94] Taft visited the institute in 1903 and praised its efforts.[95] The *Southern Workman* later noted with pride that Silliman had become the "Presbyterian 'Hampton' in the Philippines."[96]

Another wealthy philanthropist, John D. Rockefeller, subsidized the opening of a Baptist industrial school in Jaro in 1905. The Jaro Industrial School based its model on the George Junior Republic, an industrial school in New York that sought to reform "delinquent" immigrant children by inculcating respect for discipline, manual labor, and good citizenship.[97] The school also explicitly compared itself to Hampton during its fundraising efforts.[98] The school in Jaro was led by former missionary to Burma William Valentine. Valentine left the school in 1913 to pursue graduate work, writing his thesis, "Moral and Religious Values of Industrial Education," which compared industrial schooling in the Philippines, Burma, and South Africa.[99] In 1915, he became the principal of the Manual Training and Industrial School for Colored Youth in New Jersey, referred to by contemporaries as the "Tuskegee of the North."[100] Valentine's trajectory further exemplifies how industrial schooling crossed the boundaries of empire. Meanwhile, the spread of industrial education from the United States to the Philippines was soon accompanied by the expansion of domestic practices exploiting the labor of prisoners.[101] Colonial administrators applied the George Junior Republic model to the Iwahig Penal Colony in 1904.[102]

While industrial schooling expanded for Christian Filipinos, efforts to establish schools in the Muslim-dominated southern provinces remained modest. The situation pushed Episcopalian missionary Charles Brent to open the Moro Industrial School in Jolo in 1916. Before his appointment as missionary bishop in the Philippines in 1901, Brent had ministered to poor African Americans and opened social service programs for poor immigrants in Boston, where he instituted a system requiring them to work in exchange for food and lodging.[103] He later noted in a speech at the Hampton Institute that he had the privilege of meeting Armstrong during this time.[104] After arriving in the Philippines, he began ministering to the American community in Baguio, opening a school for the children of white colonial officials in 1909. One of his motivations for opening the school was his belief that separating white children from their parents was morally detrimental to families, a view that stood in stark opposition to his later beliefs about separating Filipino Muslim children from their parents.[105]

Brent's project to open an industrial school for Moros began with a fundraising drive led by the National Committee for Upbuilding the Wards of the Nation. One of its pamphlets praised Brent's previous efforts convincing non-Christians to adopt capitalistic consumption and production: "Families who were dwelling in tree tops two years ago now have comfortable homes in decent villages and are cutting their grass with American lawnmowers. The telephone, telegraph, sewing machine, automobile, railroad, artesian well, farming tools, and other modern inventions are increasingly welcomed and used by natives, who are not devoid of intellectual capacity and have considerable manual dexterity."[106] The *Southern Workman* also praised Brent's efforts to help Moros "found real homes and maintain civilized communities until their savagery is fully outgrown," which could only be achieved by making "the Moros self-supporting and masters of several trades and occupations."[107] Brent's efforts to inculcate industrial and Christian values in Moros also received private support from high-level colonial officials.

Drawing on domestic industrial school practices, Brent maintained that Moro children needed to be separated from their parents. Writing about the Moro child, he argued, "Take him from the hovel where he lives; put him in a dormitory under the supervision of competent teachers; give him a minimum of literary and a maximum of industrial training."[108] He nonetheless conceded that many Moro children also required boarding schools because they were "orphans, made so by American rifles."[109] To sell his project, he noted that while "a wave of hopelessness sweeps over one when confronted by a mass of Moro or pagan adults," Moro children were "as impressionable, as appealing, as lovable as any children of color in the whole world."[110] While recognizing Moro children's lovability, he nonetheless felt compelled to qualify this trait in comparison to other "children of color," not children more generally.

Colonial officials at the highest levels continued to support the school after Brent's death in 1929. In 1939, on the twenty-fifth anniversary of the school's founding, supporters held a fundraiser at the Waldorf Astoria in New York City. The event was deemed important enough to receive coverage in the *New York Times*.[111] Attendees included former high-ranking colonial officials, members of Congress, and missionary and religious leaders, who delivered speeches praising Brent's legacy. General John J. Pershing, the former governor of the Moro Province, sent in his own praise, claiming that the school had done more to spread American "civilized ideals" to Moros than any other institution.[112] The range of attendees reaffirmed the ongoing links between religion and empire.

Domestic industrial schools also continued to receive support from the highest levels of the US government. In a 1908 speech at a Hampton fundraising event delivered shortly before his election to the presidency, Taft drew on his experiences to link industrial education at home and abroad, arguing that the "chief aspect" uniting efforts to reform African Americans and Filipinos was solving the "problem" of "bringing a Christian race, originally tropical and affected by its tropical origin, from a state of dense ignorance—general and political—and of industrial dependence to one of general and political intelligence and industrial independence."[113] To Taft, the solution was obvious: "No lessons of experience and actual trial have been more valuable to us in working out our problem in the Philippines than those of General William Armstrong and Booker Washington in the uplifting of the Negro race in the United States."[114] Echoing Armstrong, Taft also credited slavery for initiating the first stages of this educational process.[115]

Taft's support for industrial education continued after he won the presidency. In January of 1909, he delivered another speech to the African American congregation of the historic Big Bethel Church in Atlanta, Georgia, where he conceded that a handful of African Americans might benefit from a traditional education, notably to "teach the race the rules of hygiene."[116] He maintained, however, that the "great body of the race are those who are to be the workers, the manual workers, and what is needed for the great body of your race is primary and industrial education."[117] His speech outlined his own version of the "White Man's Burden" in the South, claiming, "Everyone of you knows in his heart, because everyone knows noble, earnest, sympathetic white men in the South, that your greatest aid and your greatest hope is in the sympathy and the help of these white men."[118] Revealing the ongoing religious undertones justifying racial paternalism, he thanked God for "the effort to uplift the race among the white men of the South, who feel themselves responsible for the whole of Southern civilization."[119]

Taft's depiction of white Southerners' alleged benevolence must have raised more than a few eyebrows among the members of his Black audience, who had witnessed the dire results of white beliefs about their "responsibility" towards African Americans. Less than three years earlier, a sensational news story alleging four assaults by Black men against white women in Atlanta prompted white mobs to lead a four-day riot that resulted in the killing of over twenty-five African Americans.[120] Only three months before Taft's speech, Georgia had also approved a literacy test deliberately designed to deny African American suffrage.[121] Extralegal violence against African Americans and racist voting laws were ubiquitous in Southern states during this time.[122] A few weeks later, Taft defended these laws in his presidential inaugural address, claiming they had nothing to do with race: "The right to vote will be withheld only from the ignorant and irresponsible of both races."[123] During his presidency, Taft balanced his professed support for African American political rights with his efforts to placate racist white Southerners by continuing his drumbeat in support of industrial education.

Although Americans expanded industrial education abroad in the following decades, African American demands gradually led to the transformation of industrial schools into fully fledged universities beginning in the 1920s.[124] After Walker returned from the Philippine American

War in 1901, his professional trajectory anticipated this domestic shift. He dedicated the rest of his life to educating African Americans in Virginia, but taught his students math and science instead of manual labor. In 1919, he accepted a teaching position at the Middlesex Training School in Virginia, taking over as principal the following year. While heading the school, Walker pursued the "advanced studies" Armstrong had previously discouraged for people of color, earning an MA in education from Virginia Normal and Collegiate Institute, the country's first public postsecondary institution for African Americans. He later obtained his school's accreditation with state authorities, only the second African American rural high school to gain this status in Virginia. Walker initially donated half his salary to hire new teachers and supplement the school's inadequate budget. The school was renamed in his honor in 1948.

Walker lived to see the 1954 US Supreme Court case declaring legalized segregation unconstitutional, a decision that further expanded educational pathways for African Americans. He worked for the school until June of 1959, passing away six months later at the age of seventy-six.[125] Despite the ruling, segregated industrial schools did not entirely disappear. In March of 1959, three months before Walker's death, the tragic story of the Arkansas Negro Boys Industrial School made the front page of national newspapers after a fire broke out in the school's dormitory. The dormitory's padlocked doors and windows trapped many of the students inside, resulting in the deaths of twenty-one boys.[126] The school purported to blend industrial education with juvenile detention, exploiting the labor of imprisoned students to run a twenty-six-hundred-acre "prison work farm" growing cotton and other crops, mirroring the coercive labor practices of adult prisons across the country. In reality, the work necessitated by the farm left little time for education.[127] One African American school worker informed journalists that most of the boys "were in for minor offenses, such as hubcap stealing, or because their parents had split and there was no place for them to go."[128]

While the emphasis on industrial schooling for children of color began to die out in the United States, the incarceration of African Americans and the exploitation of prison labor increased exponentially in the following decades, including in Arkansas.[129] In 2019, people of color constituted 46 percent of the total inmates in Arkansas's state prisons.[130] After the Arkansas Negro Boys Industrial School closed in 1968, the Arkansas Department of Corrections (ADC) took over the land, replacing the school with a state prison that relied on inmates to work the farm, a practice that continues until today.[131] In 2015, the ADC's statewide farming program extended over twenty-seven thousand acres of land and earned a net profit that year of almost $1.8 million.[132] The ADC's exploitation of Black bodies extended to making millions of dollars by selling their blood, a practice they were forced to end in 1994 after an international tainted-blood scandal, due in large part to prisons' shoddy medical practices.[133] Its broader prisoner labor schemes continued, however, and in 2019 alone provided the ADC over $16 million in profits.[134] This profit margin further benefited from an Arkansas state law prohibiting the paying of any wages for prison labor.[135]

The ADC, like industrial schools in the nineteenth and twentieth century and other prison labor schemes across the United States, justifies prison labor by claiming that it educates and reforms inmates. Indeed, the ADC's 2019 mission statement highlighted its effort to "strengthen the work ethic [of inmates] through teaching of good habits; and provide opportunities for staff and inmates to improve spiritually, mentally and physically."[136] The inclusion of spiritual reform was undoubtedly not coincidental. American Christian evangelicals were central players in policies and laws that fueled rising incarceration rates in the United States in the second half of the twentieth century, while simultaneously expanding their religious influence within prisons themselves.[137]

The high rates of physical, sexual, and mental abuse faced by inmates, often at the hands of prison guards, however, demonstrates the weaknesses of such claims and provide another somber echo to the past experiences of students of color in industrial schools.[138] These coercive labor practices build on a long history of racial capitalism that has permitted elites to reap economic benefits in the name of reform and uplift. In this capacity, the people of color imprisoned in the United States share "the same blood" as the African Americans, Hawaiians, Native Americans, and Filipinos who came before them.

NOTES

1 "Personal Notes," *Southern Workman*, February 1900, 112.
2 Samuel Chapman Armstrong, *Lessons from the Hawaiian Islands* (Hampton, VA: N.p., 1884), 213.

3 Gutiérrez, "Internal Colonialism," 281–95.
4 Pinderhughes, "Toward a New Theory of Internal Colonialism," 236.
5 See Ring, *The Problem South*.
6 See Beechert, *Working in Hawaii*; Jung, *Coolies and Cane*.
7 On the history of industrial education, see Beyer, "Manual and Industrial Education for Hawaiians," 2–5; and Barlow, *History of Industrial Education*.
8 US Office of Indian Affairs, *Report of the Commissioner of Indian Affairs, for the Year 1900*, part 1 (Washington, DC: Government Printing Office, 1900), 22.
9 Scholarly work examining the links between domestic and imperial industrial schooling includes Coloma, "'Destiny Has Thrown the Negro and the Filipino under the Tutelage of America'"; Steinbock-Pratt, *Educating the Empire*; Eittreim, *Teaching Empire*; Stratton, *Education for Empire*; Paulet, "To Change the World."
10 Gatewood Jr., *Black Americans and the White Man's Burden*; Marks, *The Black Press Views American Imperialism*; Russell, "'I Feel Sorry for These People.'"
11 Ngozi-Brown, "African-American Soldiers and Filipinos"; Gatewood, *"Smoked Yankees."*
12 Armstrong, *Lessons from the Hawaiian Islands*, 213.
13 Armstrong's letter cited in Hon. F. S. Lyman, "The Hilo Boys' Boarding School," *Friend*, December 1902, 25.
14 Cited in Lindsey, *Indians at Hampton Institute*, 112.
15 "Personal Notes," *Southern Workman*, February 1900, 112. Emphasis mine.
16 Hon. F. S. Lyman, "The Hilo Boys' Boarding School," *Friend*, December 1902, 25.
17 Armstrong, "From the Beginning," in Helen Ludlow, ed., *Twenty-Two Years' Work of Hampton Normal and Agricultural Institute* (Hampton, VA: Normal School Press, 1893), 1, 6; Beechert, *Working in Hawaii*, 21.
18 See for example Wm. L. Brown, "Some Problems in Indian Education," *Southern Workman*, April 1900, 212–18.
19 Mary C. Collins, "The Dependence of the Indian," *Southern Workman*, July 1900, 428; Helen Ludlow, "Indian Education at Hampton and Carlisle," *Harper's New Monthly Magazine*, April 1881, 666–67.
20 On racial capitalism, see E. Williams, *Capitalism and Slavery*; Robinson, *Black Marxism*; W. Johnson, *River of Dark Dreams*; Jenkins and LeRoy, *Histories of Racial Capitalism*. On racial capitalism and education, see Watkins, *The White Architects of Black Education*.
21 See Fox-Genovese and Genovese, *The Mind of the Master Class*.
22 See Blackmon, *Slavery by Another Name*.
23 J. D. Anderson, *The Education of Blacks in the South*, 87–92.
24 Armstrong, "From the Beginning," 3; "Slavery's Good to Negroes: Major Pratt Says It Was the Black's Bridge to Civilization," *New York Times*, December 20, 1900, 2.
25 The report also lauded the Hampton model. US Bureau of Education, *Report of the Commissioner of Education for the Year 1900–1901*, vol. 1 (Washington, DC: Government Printing Office, 1902), 414–15, 472–88. Quotation from 415.

26　US Bureau of Education, *Report of the Commissioner of Education*, 415.
27　Cited in Lyman, "The Hilo Boys' Boarding School," 25.
28　J. D. Anderson, *The Education of Blacks in the South*, 81.
29　Engs, *Educating the Disenfranchised*, 116.
30　Paulet, "To Change the World," 183.
31　Josephine E. Richards, "Indian Education: Does It Pay?" *Southern Workman*, February 1900, 82.
32　Ludlow, "Hampton's Twelve Years Work for Indians," in Ludlow, ed., *Twenty-Two Years' Work*, 315.
33　Beyer, "The Connection of Samuel Chapman Armstrong," 38–40.
34　On the history of Native American boarding schools, see Adams, *Education for Extinction*.
35　Ryan, "The Carlisle Indian Industrial School," 73.
36　Ryan, "The Carlisle Indian Industrial School," 73.
37　Ludlow, "Indian Education," 671.
38　Ludlow, "Indian Education," 663–64.
39　Fear-Segal and Rose, eds., *Carlisle Indian Industrial School*, 8.
40　Eittreim, *Teaching Empire*, 108–15; Bell, "Telling Stories out of School," 280, 287–88.
41　Buffalohead and Molin, "'A Nucleus of Civilization,'" 91 n.21.
42　Lindsey, *Indians at Hampton Institute*, 215.
43　Bell, "Telling Stories out of School," 387, 389. Bell calculated that at least 220 students died during Carlisle's existence.
44　Fear-Segal, *White Man's Club*, 332.
45　US Bureau of Education, *Report of the Commissioner of Education for the Year 1900–1901*, 476.
46　US Bureau of Education, *Report of the Commissioner of Education for the Year 1900–1901*, 476.
47　Lindsey, *Indians at Hampton Institute*, 261–62.
48　Du Bois, *The Souls of Black Folk: Essays and Sketches* (Chicago: A.C. McClurg, 1903), 33–44.
49　Du Bois, *The Souls of Black Folk*, 33, 39.
50　Du Bois, *The Souls of Black Folk*, 40.
51　See Christina Davidson, chapter 9 in this volume.
52　J. D. Anderson, *The Education of Blacks in the South*, 28–29.
53　James F. Rusling, "Interview with President McKinley," *Christian Advocate*, January 22, 1903, 810.
54　J. D. Anderson, *The Education of Blacks in the South*, 36.
55　US War Department, *Annual Reports of the War Department for the Fiscal Year Ended June 30, 1902*, vol. 10 (Washington, DC: Government Printing Office, 1903), 881.
56　Armstrong, *Lessons from the Hawaiian Islands*, 216.
57　"The White Man's Burden" and "What to Do with the Philippines," *Friend*, March 1899, 17.

58　Zackodnik, "Empire and Education in Hampton's *Southern Workman*," 156–76.
59　W. S. Scarborough, "Our New Possessions—An Open Door," *Southern Workman*, July 1900, 422–27.
60　"The Training of Teachers," *Southern Workman*, July 1900, 390.
61　Tarr, "The Education of the Thomasites," 157.
62　Cited in Brands, *Bound to Empire*, 68.
63　Booker T. Washington, "Relation of Industrial Education to National Progress," *Annals of the American Academy of Political and Social Science* 33, no. 1 (January 1909): 9.
64　Campbell, "Models and Metaphors," 90–134; Zimmerman, *Alabama in Africa*.
65　US Bureau of Education, *Report of the Commissioner of Education for the Year 1900–1901*, 484.
66　US Bureau of Education, *Report of the Commissioner of Education for the Year 1900–1901*, 484.
67　Marshall Everett, *The Book of the Fair: The Greatest Exposition the World Has Ever Seen* (Philadelphia: P.W. Ziegler, 1904), 272.
68　Everett, *The Book of the Fair*, 273. Emphasis mine.
69　Everett, *The Book of the Fair*, 273.
70　"Casts of Primitive Races," *New York Times*, July 26, 1904, 19.
71　Walther, *Sacred Interests*, 186–89.
72　US War Department, *Annual Reports of the War Department*, 774.
73　US War Department, *Annual Reports of the War Department*, 883.
74　US War Department, *Annual Reports of the War Department*, 883.
75　US War Department, *Annual Reports of the War Department*, 884; Baldoz, *The Third Asiatic Invasion*, 35–36.
76　Clymer, *Protestant Missionaries in the Philippines*, 196.
77　William H. Taft, *Census of the Philippine Islands: 1903*, vol. 1 (Washington, DC: United States Bureau of the Census, 1905), 530.
78　US War Department, *Annual Reports of the War Department*, 882.
79　US War Department, *Annual Reports of the War Department*, 882.
80　Tarr, "The Education of the Thomasites," 198.
81　See "Hampton Institute's Work for Negroes," *Philippine Education*, January 1914, 265, and "Education for Life," *Philippine Education*, April 1914, 389.
82　Bureau of Education, *Philippine Craftsman*, July 1912, 1.
83　The term "Moro" was initially applied to Filipino Muslims by Spanish colonial officials and later adopted by Americans. On the broader history of this term's usage see Charbonneau, *Civilizational Imperatives*, xv–xvi.
84　US War Department, *Annual Reports of the War Department*, 884.
85　Rodil, *The Minoritization of the Indigenous Communities*, 49.
86　Arolas Tulawie to American Chamber of Commerce (Manila), 1933, folder 31, box 28, Joseph Ralston Hayden Papers, 1899–1945, Bentley Historical Library, University of Michigan, Ann Arbor, Michigan.

87 Bureau of Insular Affairs, *Fourth Annual Report of the Philippine Commission, 1903*, part 3, (Washington, DC: Government Printing Office, 1904), 772. For a broader analysis of colonial schooling of Moros, see Charbonneau, *Civilizational Imperatives*, 73–93.
88 Tarr, "The Education of the Thomasites," 446; Emerson Christie, "The American Teachers in the Philippines," *Congregationalist and Christian World*, March 15, 1902, 11.
89 Prescott F. Jernegan, *The Philippine Citizen: A Textbook of Civics, Describing the Nature of Government, and the Rights and Duties of Citizens of the Philippine Islands*, 4th ed. (Manila: Philippine Education Company, 1912), iii.
90 Jernegan, *The Philippine Citizen*, 111.
91 Jernegan, *The Philippine Citizen*, 111.
92 See Persha, *The Great Gold Swindle*.
93 Carson, *Silliman University*, 73.
94 Carson, *Silliman University*, 25.
95 Carson, *Silliman University*, 22.
96 "A Hampton in the Philippines," *Southern Workman*, August 1920, 387.
97 "The Jaro Industrial School Republic," Folder 1, Box 51, International Ministries Pre–World War II Files, American Baptist Historical Society, Atlanta, Georgia; Salman, "'The Prison That Makes Men Free,'" 118.
98 "Jaro Industrial School," Folder 12, Box 50, American Baptist Historical Society.
99 Central Philippine University, "The Love Story behind Jaro Industrial School, Now CPU," February 15, 2019, https://cpu.edu.ph.
100 Goddard, "Bordentown," 51.
101 Mortimer L. Stewart, "Making Prisoners into Citizens," *Thirtieth Report of the Annual Lake Mohonk Conference on the Indian and Other Dependent Peoples* 30 (1912): 146.
102 Salman, "'The Prison That Makes Men Free,'" 118.
103 Norbeck, "The Legacy of Charles Henry Brent," 163.
104 Charles Henry Brent, "Self-Control and Stewardship," *Southern Workman*, July 1921, 300.
105 Zabriskie, *Bishop Brent*, 55–56.
106 "Upbuilding the Wards of the Nation," in "Missionary Work of Protestants," Box 170, Folder 1158, RG 350, National Archives, College Park, MD.
107 "Our Wards in the Philippines," *Southern Workman*, January 1914, 5–6.
108 Charles Brent, "Giving the Moro-Americans a Chance," *Independent*, April 26, 1915, 146.
109 Brent, "Giving the Moro-Americans a Chance," 146.
110 Brent, "Giving the Moro-Americans a Chance," 147.
111 "A Permanent Project," *New York Times*, December 19, 1939, 22.
112 "Proceedings of the Memorial Anniversary Dinner Held under the Auspices of the National Committee for the Moro School, Jolo," Bureau of Insular Affairs,

General Records, 1914–1945, Box 1277, Number 28011, Entry 5, RG 350, National Archives, College Park, MD.
113 Taft, "Address Delivered at Plymouth Church, Brooklyn, Monday March 16, 1908," in *Addresses Delivered by Hon. William Howard Taft before and after His Election to the Presidency of the United States, Touching the Negro Problem* (Nashville, TN: A.M.E. Sunday School Union, 1909), 7. Hereafter cited as *Addresses Delivered by Hon. William Howard Taft.*
114 Taft, "Address Delivered at Plymouth Church," in *Addresses Delivered by Hon. William Howard Taft*, 7.
115 Taft, "Address Delivered at Plymouth Church," in *Addresses Delivered by Hon. William Howard Taft*, 8.
116 "Address of Hon. Wm. H. Taft at Big Bethel Church, Atlanta, Ga.," January 16, 1909, in *Addresses Delivered by Hon. William Howard Taft*, 19.
117 "Address of Hon. Wm. H. Taft," in *Addresses Delivered by Hon. William Howard Taft*, 19.
118 "Address of Hon. Wm. H. Taft," in *Addresses Delivered by Hon. William Howard Taft*, 19.
119 "Address of Hon. Wm. H. Taft," in *Addresses Delivered by Hon. William Howard Taft*, 18.
120 Burns, *Rage in the Gate City*, 5.
121 McDonald, Binford, and Johnson, "Georgia," 69.
122 See Herron, *Framing the Solid South*.
123 "Extract from President Wm. H. Taft's Inaugural Address, Delivered at Washington, March 4, 1909," in *Addresses Delivered by Hon. William Howard Taft*, 38.
124 Gasman, *Envisioning Black Colleges*, 11–14.
125 Information in this paragraph taken from Walker's obituary, "Middlesex Negro Education, St. Clare Walker, 76, Dies," *Daily Press*, Virginia, January 27, 1960. See also the description of Walker's life on the St. Clare Walker Middle School website: http://scw.mcps.k12.va.us.
126 Stockley, *Black Boys Burning*, 55–57.
127 Stockley, *Ruled by Race*, 289.
128 "Fire Kills 21 Boys in Reform School," *New York Times*, March 6, 1959, 1.
129 See Alexander, *The New Jim Crow*.
130 ADC, "FY19 Statistical Information," April 20, 2020, The Official Website of the State of Arkansas, https://doc.arkansas.gov, accessed September 24, 2021.
131 ADC, *Board Report*, May 2019, The Official Website of the State of Arkansas, https://doc.arkansas.gov, accessed September 24, 2021, 12.
132 ADC, "Farm Operations Review 2014–2015," Prison Legal News, 2, 5, www.prisonlegalnews.org, accessed September 24, 2021.
133 Kovalcheck, "The Modern Plantation," 122.
134 ADC, "FY 19 Statistical Information."

135 Wendy Sawyer, "How Much Do Incarcerated People Earn in Each State?," April 10, 2017, Prison Policy Initiative, www.prisonpolicy.org/blog/2017/04/10/wages, accessed September 24, 2021.
136 Wendy Kelley, Director, Arkansas Department of Corrections, *2019–2020 Strategic Plan*, 3, Official Website of the State of Arkansas, https://doc.arkansas.gov, accessed September 24, 2021.
137 See Griffith, *God's Law and Order*.
138 Kovalcheck, "The Modern Plantation," 113–14.

8

Black Spiritual Protest in Global Imperial Contexts, 1893–1920

HEATHER D. CURTIS

On April 5, 1893, Georgia E. L. Patton boarded a steamship bound for the British Isles. From there, the twenty-eight-year-old African American physician sailed for Liberia to serve as a medical missionary. During the Atlantic crossing, Patton shared a cabin with another woman on a mission to alleviate affliction. Since the spring of 1892, when three of her friends had been murdered by a white mob in Memphis, Tennessee, Ida B. Wells had been vigorously protesting the violent and systemic oppression of black citizens in the United States. Now the thirty-one-year-old investigative journalist was taking her antilynching crusade abroad. After landing in Liverpool, Wells spent the next three months traveling across England and Scotland, speaking about "the many inhuman outrages" being inflicted on African Americans in her home country. By appealing to "the religious and moral sentiment" of the British public, Wells hoped to incite an international outcry against racial injustice.[1]

Once they parted ways, Patton and Wells would not cross paths again. Although their journeys diverged, these fellow travelers remained committed to a common project of redressing black suffering exacerbated by the rise of Jim Crow and the extension of American empire. While Wells's lifelong campaign for racial equality has been the subject of numerous studies, Patton's trailblazing career as one of the first African American missionary physicians has received far less attention from scholars. Taking their intersecting stories as a point of departure, this chapter examines how these pioneering women participated in wider movements of spiritual protest against white supremacy that spanned several continents and involved a diverse array of Christian actors who battled black oppression in a variety of imperial contexts. Bringing these global networks into view, I argue, reveals the critical role of theological ideas, religious institutions, and transnational communities in constructing and contesting the racial hierarchies that fueled the expansion of US empire and aggravated the distress of African-descended people across the world at the turn of the twentieth century.[2]

For both Patton and Wells, engagement with broader Christian efforts to combat racial injustice began during their formative years in the post-emancipation South. The chapter opens with an analysis of how, as students in schools founded by missionaries who advocated for African American rights, these young women were inspired by ideals of biblical egalitarianism to pursue higher education and professional training that put them in positions to aid others struggling to overcome adversity. Even as they embraced scriptural promises of human equality, however, Patton and Wells faced countervailing pressures to endorse programs of racial uplift rooted in theories of civilizational hierarchy and white supremacy put forward by proponents of American imperial expansion.

By following Patton and Wells abroad to Liberia, Britain, and back again, subsequent sections of this chapter examine their connections with Christian critics of empire who rejected these oppressive imperial logics on explicitly theological grounds. Through their collaborations with these visionary allies, I contend, Patton and Wells linked their attempts to relieve black affliction with broader campaigns to combat racial inequality on a global scale. Paying attention to the scriptural precepts that inspired these African American leaders in their fight against white supremacy at home and abroad, I conclude, illumines the centrality of spiritual protest in the formation of black liberation movements that have animated anticolonial, independence, and civil rights struggles from the turn of the twentieth century to the present.

Biblical Equality, Civilizational Hierarchy, and Black Education

Wells and Patton were both born into slavery during the Civil War. Wells was two months old when Abraham Lincoln issued the Emancipation Proclamation in September 1862. Patton was born a week after the Thirteenth Amendment to the United States Constitution passed the Senate in April 1864. Growing up during Reconstruction in Holly Springs, Mississippi, and Coffee County, Tennessee, respectively, Wells and Patton participated in the ongoing struggle of the nation's black citizens to secure political rights, economic independence, and social equality.

For both young women, as for many African Americans in the post-emancipation South, religious ideas and institutions offered resources for pursuing this goal. In schools founded and staffed by missionaries of the Methodist Episcopal Church (North), Wells and Patton learned to read from educators who "brought us the light of knowledge and their splendid example of Christian courage," Wells later recalled. As historian Kevin Gaines has argued, Wells's tribute confirms that "many of the white teachers who embraced the cause of freedmen's education" espoused "egalitarian racial attitudes" rooted in biblical passages such as Acts 17:26: "God hath made of one blood all nations of men to dwell on all the face of the earth." Abolitionists like Frederick Douglass and Angelina Grimké had deployed this scriptural text to demand immediate emancipation on the grounds that enslaved persons were human beings created in the divine image and therefore possessed "equal rights, irrespective of color or condition." Many of the Methodist educators who taught at Shaw University in Holly Springs, where Wells studied during her adolescent years, and at Central Tennessee College (CTC) in Nashville, where Patton enrolled in 1886, shared this conviction. As a result, the curriculum at these institutions offered what historian James Anderson has called a "classical liberal academic education" with the goal of developing "a black intelligentsia that would fight for political and civil equality."[3]

Over the course of her career as a pioneering journalist and tireless civil rights activist, Wells embodied this hope. Although she had to withdraw from Shaw in the early 1880s, Wells continued to pursue her studies independently while working as a school teacher to support her siblings. Orphaned at the age of sixteen when her parents died in a yellow fever epidemic, Wells moved with her younger sisters to Memphis in 1881 to be closer to extended family. After a conductor expelled her from a train when she refused to give up her first-class seat in 1883, Wells launched a legal challenge against racial discrimination in public transportation. When she lost the suit on appeal, Wells found an outlet for her frustration by writing in a black religious newspaper about the injustice she had experienced. Over the next several years, Wells established a national reputation as a correspondent for a number of prominent publications. As she embarked on this phase of her career, Wells expressed confidence that deploying her pen to expose injustice was part of a divine plan. "I do not fear; God is over all & He will, so long as I am in the right, fight my battles, and give me what is my right," she wrote. In 1889, she became the "only black woman of record to be an editor in chief and part owner of a major city newspaper," the *Memphis Free Speech & Headlight*.[4]

Like Wells, Patton overcame hardship and loss to pursue academic achievement and a profession that enabled her to ease the suffering of others. Also orphaned at age sixteen, Patton worked for six years in rural Tennessee before saving enough money to enroll at CTC. In 1886, she moved in with a brother who lived outside of Nashville so that she could walk two miles to classes each day. Despite ongoing financial difficulties, Patton completed the senior "normal course" for teachers in 1890 and then entered CTC's Meharry Medical Department to train as a physician. In February of 1893, she earned her degree. Not only was Patton one of the first black women to graduate from Meharry; she later became the first African American woman licensed as a physician and surgeon in Tennessee, and the first to practice medicine in Memphis.[5]

The Christian egalitarianism Wells and Patton encountered among teachers and fellow students during their studies inspired both women to break barriers of race, class, and gender in their efforts to help others. But the principle of biblical equality was not the only religious ideology animating educators in the Reconstruction-era South. In 1868, General Samuel Armstrong established the Hampton Normal and Industrial Institute in Virginia. As Karine Walther shows elsewhere in this volume, Armstrong's pedagogical philosophy was rooted in a theory of white supremacy that charged Anglo Americans with the task of "civilizing and Christianizing" dark-skinned "savages" around the globe through a regimen of manual labor. In contrast with programs of education premised on Christian egalitarianism, the "Hampton Idea" reflected and furthered Darwinian theories that ranked individuals, cultures, and nations along an ascending scale of civilization. Although proponents of this scheme indicated that "inferior races" could progress from their primitive state to higher levels of social development, they maintained that transformation was gradual and required oversight from the Anglo-Saxon Christians at the top of the hierarchy. As the rising influence of social Darwinism coincided with the expansion of imperialism across the United States and around the world, industrial education became a crucial means for exercising colonial rule.[6]

In the American South, Armstrong's model proved extraordinarily popular among conservative whites seeking to regain control over black citizens in the wake of emancipation. Industrial training, they hoped, would discipline formerly enslaved persons to accept their "proper place" within the economy as agricultural workers, mechanics, or domestic servants. Following the end of Reconstruction, African Americans experiencing the effects of escalating racism faced growing pressure to embrace the "ideology of uplift" put forward by supporters of industrial pedagogy. During this period, black citizens across the South struggled under oppressive sharecropping arrangements, decreasing access to education of any kind, and increasingly restrictive legislation that effectively excluded them from voting and almost all other forms of civic participation. Within this context, some African American leaders were willing to experiment with any strategy that might help alleviate black suffering. In 1884, for example, CTC opened an Industrial Department to prepare students for trades such as carpentry, blacksmithing, housework, and cooking. Although the school never abandoned its commitment to providing a liberal arts curriculum, the new emphasis on manual labor indicates that white-supremacist theories were shaping the curriculum even at institutions originally devoted to developing black political leaders, scholars, and professionals.[7]

The racialized rhetoric of "civilizing and Christianizing" also resonated with longstanding missionary concern for Africa among elite black Americans. As Sylvester Johnson demonstrates in chapter 3, black Christians participated actively in efforts to evangelize native Africans by sending missionaries and settlers to Liberia, founded by the American Colonization Society (ACS) in 1821. Although African Americans debated whether to endorse efforts to remove them from the United States through emigration, some found the prospect of playing a providential role in the Christianization of Africa and the possibility of achieving self-government apart from white domination compelling. With the demise of Reconstruction, an increasing number of black Americans embraced various "back to Africa" movements, including the expansion of missions to the "dark continent." For some, Kevin Gaines has argued, "the missionary enterprise, with its image of a 'pagan' Africa awaiting 'regeneration' by its elite progeny," offered a way "to demonstrate black progress in a racist society that barred most conventional routes to power and professional status." Reflecting this growing interest in Christian expansion, CTC opened an institute for African missions in 1888.[8]

By the time she completed her medical degree and embarked on her missionary journey in the spring of 1893, Patton had adopted the discourse of civilizational hierarchy that increasingly influenced black evangelistic enterprises during the post-Reconstruction era. "I go to Liberia for the good I want to do to others, to relieve the suffering, and to assist in radiating the light of Christianity and civilization to other parts of Africa," she explained. Similarly, in an 1891 speech before the American Association of Colored Educators, Wells showed that she also was not immune to the racialized ideology of missionary uplift. Lamenting the lack of "elevation and progress" among the majority of African Americans in the South, Wells called for educated race leaders who had absorbed "the civilizing and Christianizing influences thrown around them in these schools" to aid the "poverty stricken, ignorant and superstitious" masses who were "just learning the rudiments of self-government." Only when those who possessed "superior intelligence" succeeded in raising "the thousands who yet grope in darkness . . . to the required standard" would injustice abate. The barriers impeding racial progress, in this rendering, were not discriminatory laws that perpetuated political exclusion and economic inequality, but the moral failings of African Americans who refused to save money, exercise self-control, or educate themselves.[9]

By serving as agents of Christian mission who would help the unenlightened ascend the scale of civilization, Wells and Patton aimed to combat the disenfranchisement and bigotry they encountered in the American South. Their comments indicate the extent to which uplift ideology rooted in evolutionary theories of racial hierarchy had made inroads even among black leaders educated in institutions committed to the ethic of Christian egalitarianism. Despite the appeal of the developmental model of racial progress during desperate times, however, neither Patton nor Wells remained committed to this approach in the long run. Through their experiences overseas, both women became connected with Christian reformers who rejected white supremacy, questioned the superiority of Western civilization, and criticized racial injustice in the United States and imperial contexts across the globe by affirming the principle of biblical equality.

Patton's Mission to Liberia: Settler Colonialism, Civilization, and Holiness Missions

Patton traveled to Liberia during a tumultuous time in the nation's political history. From their arrival under the auspices of the ACS in 1821, black settlers had struggled to subdue the indigenous peoples whose lands they claimed for the purposes of establishing their own self-governing polity and "Christianizing" the African continent. Rather than evangelizing and incorporating native converts into their community, Sylvester Johnson has observed, "the Black missionary settlers directed most of their energies to military vigilance and warfare against sovereign Africans." By the time Liberia declared its independence as a democratic republic in 1847, the settlers had succeeded in displacing and disenfranchising indigenous peoples, denying them citizenship under the new constitution. But maintaining this system of minority rule required ongoing repression of native communities who continued to resist the authority of Americo-Liberians. During Patton's first summer in the country in 1893, for example, the government dispatched a military force to quell an uprising among the Grebo people—a group that consistently challenged their subjugation to the state.[10]

Although black settlers deployed the rhetoric of redemption as a rationale for their colonizing project, in practice Americo-Liberians segregated themselves from native Africans, lamenting their resistance to civilization and conversion. From the earliest days, most "missionaries" to Liberia, according to historian Walter Williams, were black clergymen more interested in ministering to settler congregations than evangelizing indigenous people. Few white missionaries chose Liberia for their foreign field, and most of those who did stayed only for short seasons due to illness or the difficult environment. One exception was Mary Sharp, a white Methodist who arrived in 1879 and remained until her death in 1915. Sharp's ministry to native Africans would eventually have a profound influence on Patton's efforts to relieve suffering in Liberia. Long before Patton boarded the steamship bound for Monrovia in

1893, Sharp was laying the groundwork that would make Patton's mission possible.[11]

Sharp's original assignment was as a teacher in Monrovia Seminary, an institution that catered to Americo-Liberians. Shortly after her arrival, however, she began to minister among the Kru people who lived in coastal villages just outside the capital city. Frustrated that native students were excluded from enrolling in school, Sharp invited her Kru pupils to come for instruction after hours and "expressed great dissatisfaction" with her Methodist sponsors for failing to support this work. In addition, she publicly accused Americo-Liberian settlers of "preaching to themselves" rather than evangelizing among indigenous Africans, whom they treated "far worse than they themselves had been treated as slaves." By 1883, Sharp's criticisms and activities had provoked so much controversy that Methodist authorities voted to recall her. Rather than return to the United States, Sharp severed her financial ties with the denomination and continued as an independent missionary for the next three decades.[12]

During these years, Sharp affiliated with the Holiness movement—a transnational and multiracial network of revivalists who stressed the power of the Holy Spirit to produce intense spiritual experiences, instantaneous conversion, and entire sanctification. Because they believed that all human beings—including those in "heathen darkness"—could be immediately transformed from sinners to saints, Holiness missionaries rejected theories of racial inferiority predicated on hierarchical models of civilization or evolutionary development. Leaders of the movement ordained indigenous ministers without any formal theological training no matter their "nationality, colour, or condition" and insisted that churches established by converts in colonial settings were equal to and independent from their counterparts in the metropole. They also counseled missionaries to avoid entanglements with denominational bureaucrats who might oppose their egalitarian message. Following the example of the apostle Paul, "faith missionaries" should trust God for their financial support—a strategy that would ensure their liberty to minister to indigenous communities without interference.[13]

Sharp's accomplishments in Liberia proved that maintaining autonomy from institutional structures bore fruit. Within six years of her arrival, she and her Kru converts had erected a church that could accommodate five hundred worshippers and double as a classroom space. Free to conduct her school without surveillance from the Methodist board, Sharp established an educational program based on her experience teaching in the South Carolina Sea Islands after the Civil War. Like the colleges that Patton and Wells attended, these institutions offered a classical curriculum designed to help formerly enslaved students achieve social and political equality. Sharp embraced similar goals for her Kru pupils. Her emphasis on preparing native Africans for professional careers set Sharp's pedagogy apart from the industrial education offered at another prominent training center for indigenous youth in Liberia. At the Lutheran Muhlenberg Mission, Daniel and Emma Day conscripted forty young Africans recaptured from a slave ship to build a coffee plantation. Residents at the compound learned to read and write (Day was a proponent of English-language instruction as a key component of the civilizing process), but the bulk of their education focused on agriculture and other modes of manual labor. By contrast, Sharp "trained scores of girls" as educators and "her boys have become preachers, teachers, government officials, merchants, and one . . . a leading physician." She also sent several African students to CTC, where they overlapped with Patton in the early 1890s.[14]

Sharp's protégés—Benjamin and Frank Payne, Harold Wood, and Gilbert Haven—arrived in the United States at a time when racist ideologies of civilizational hierarchy were threatening to eclipse the Christian egalitarianism that had animated struggles for black equality since abolition. As pupils in Sharp's school, these young men would have become familiar with the discourse of "African redemption" that drove the missionary enterprise. Even Sharp, in appeals for funds from supporters at home, occasionally contrasted the "moral and mental" darkness of "this *Lost Continent*" with the "civilized or Christian countries" that possessed a developed literature and "modern improvements." But Sharp's rhetoric of African uplift was premised on her foundational commitment to human equality. The white supremacy her students encountered in Tennessee was rooted in a "scientific" model of human evolution that insisted people of African descent belonged to a backward, inferior race best suited for submission to Anglo-Saxon rule. Given the dispossession, discrimination, and disenfranchisement these native boys and their communities had experienced at the hands of Americo-Liberians, this logic of imperial domination would not have been foreign to them, even if the particular racial dynamics of its implementation were different.[15]

Despite their familiarity with oppression by Americo-Liberian settlers, navigating Nashville's charged environment in the late 1890s proved difficult for these African students, especially as incidents of violence against black citizens escalated. In April of 1892, for example, two African American men accused of assaulting white women were brutally murdered in one of Tennessee's most notorious lynchings. After apprehending and hanging Henry Grizzard, a white mob stormed the jail where his brother Ephraim was being held for questioning. Although none of Sharp's pupils reported witnessing Ephraim's torture and execution, one of their classmates, a fellow African from the Cape Mount region of Liberia, recounted the event in vivid terms before an audience of white clergymen:

> I stood in a public square in the city of Nashville, and there I saw a black man torn out of prison. A rope was tied around his neck, he was dragged to the bridge, the other end of the rope was tied to the bridge, and they pushed him over. And I stood there and saw hundreds and hundreds of men and women of your race waving handkerchiefs and laughing at that man as he hung under the bridge. And his body was cut loose a few minutes afterwards and thrown away. I saw that with my own eyes.

For the African students at CTC, the lynching of Ephraim Grizzard exposed the barbarism at the heart of American Christian "civilization." Perhaps this assassination prompted Sharp's pupils to want to return home. When Patton left for Liberia twelve months after the murder, the youngest three went with her, cutting short their education by several years.[16]

During the Atlantic crossing, Patton shared with Wells that "she was early imbued with the desire to go to Africa as a medical missionary." No doubt this longstanding intention took more definite shape as Patton learned from her African classmates at CTC about the oppression indigenous people endured under Americo-Liberian rule. Through the Holiness-inspired Friends of Africa Society, founded by students at the college around 1890, Patton would also have been exposed to the "faith missions" model of fundraising. By heeding the call for independent workers, Patton ensured that she remained at liberty to minister among native Africans, free from the oversight of the Methodist board. During her time in Liberia, she focused on delivering medical care in a Krutown village. Although Patton did not leave behind a written account of her theological commitments, her status as a "faith missionary," her association with Mary Sharp, and her work with indigenous Africans make clear her sympathy for the egalitarian sensibilities of the Holiness movement. After illness forced her return to the United States in 1895, Patton opened a medical practice in Memphis. For the rest of her life (cut short by the tuberculosis she contracted in Liberia), she continued to support classical education for black students by donating ten dollars a month (a significant sum at that time) to the Freedmen's Aid Society.[17]

Even as she resorted to rhetoric that coupled Christianity and civilization in explaining her reasons for going to Africa, Patton's actions demonstrated a more durable commitment to racial equality grounded in a biblical theology of universal human rights. Like most Holiness missionaries, however, Patton remained focused on ministering to individual sufferers. Rarely did leaders in this movement explicitly apply the egalitarian implications of their theology to broader social or political injustices or engage in organized efforts to combat systemic racism in the United States and other imperial contexts. But some in Patton's orbit did draw on Christian ideals of human equality to protest physical and structural violence against black people in the American South and around the globe. One of these activists was Momolu Massaquoi, the African student at CTC who witnessed Ephraim Grizzard's lynching. Another was Patton's cabinmate en route to Liverpool: Ida B. Wells.[18]

Wells's Crusade for Justice: Black Affliction and Christian "Civilization" in Global Context

While Massaquoi was watching a white mob drag Grizzard from his jail cell in Nashville, Wells was mourning the brutal murder of three black friends in Memphis about eight weeks earlier. On March 9, 1892, Thomas Moss—a successful grocer—and two of his employees, William Stewart and Calvin McDowell, were abducted and shot dead by white vigilantes after a conflict with supporters of a business competitor.

This incident shattered Wells's confidence in the racial-uplift ideology she had lauded as a strategy for overcoming injustice just three months earlier. "The city of Memphis has demonstrated that neither character nor standing avails the Negro if he dares to protect himself against the white man or become his rival," Wells wrote in an editorial immediately following the lynching. The only option left to black citizens, she concluded, was to save their money by boycotting white businesses and "leave a town which will neither protect our lives and property, nor give us a fair trial in the courts, but takes us out and murders us in cold blood when accused by white persons."[19]

Over the next several weeks, Wells traveled to Oklahoma to investigate conditions for relocating to Indian lands recently opened for settlement. Until the Memphis murders, Wells remained equivocal about black emigration to the American West or to Africa. But once it became clear that white supremacists would continue to oppress black citizens, especially when they achieved success, Wells expressed her support for an African American exodus from the South. Her friend Thomas Moss's last words were, "Tell my people to go West—there is no justice for them here." Wells concurred and encouraged fellow Memphians to migrate. Several months later, she also publicly backed Bishop Henry McNeal Turner of the African Methodist Episcopal Church (AME) when he proposed a return to Africa as a "providential opportunity" for black citizens disillusioned by the possibility of achieving respect and due process in the United States. In an editorial entitled "Afro-Americans and Africa," Wells reiterated her own disenchantment with the developmental ideologies of race progress she had so recently espoused. Even in "the freest and most unprejudiced sections" of the United States, she lamented, "no matter how well dressed, courteous or intellectual," black citizens risked being "humiliated by this distinctively American prejudice." Why, she asked, should her people not "turn to Africa, the land of the forefathers, the most fertile of its kind, and the only one which the rapacious and ubiquitous Anglo-Saxon race has not entirely gobbled— where they would be welcomed by their race, and given opportunity to assist in the development of Africa?"[20]

Like many of her peers in this period, Wells saw imperial expansion as an opportunity for African Americans to "enjoy the full freedom of manhood and aspiration" apart from the increasingly virulent racism they faced in the South. Although the Memphis lynching had opened her eyes to the false promises of uplift ideology, she remained blind to the exploitative implications of settler colonialism for Native Americans being dispossessed of their lands as well as for indigenous Africans suffering under the repressive rule of Americo-Liberians. Instead, Wells extolled the "Romans who invaded Britain" and the Puritans who imposed "their indomitable will and energy" on "the bleak, barren, and inhospitable coast of Massachusetts" as models for "enterprising and intelligent Afro-Americans" who ought to view Liberia as "a threshold from whence" to "enter and possess the land."[21]

As an African native who had experienced the effects of American imperialism, Massaquoi offered a different perspective on dispossession, disenfranchisement, and the destruction of black lives. A "prince" of the Vai ethnic group, whose territory spanned the recently drawn border between the colonies of Liberia and Sierra Leone, Massaquoi had converted to Christianity from Islam against the wishes of his parents while studying at the St. John's Episcopal Mission in Cape Mount. With the help of American supporters, Massaquoi traveled to the United States in 1888 and enrolled at CTC, where he intended to study medicine at the Meharry Medical School. To help fund his education, Massaquoi toured the United States and Canada giving presentations about the history, culture, politics, religion, and prospects of the Vai people. In these lectures, Massaquoi called attention to the unjust treatment of native Africans by Americo-Liberian settlers, challenged racialized theories of civilizational hierarchy that positioned black "heathens" at the bottom of the development scale, questioned the Christian motives and deceitful practices of Western imperialists, and prophesied "future greatness" for an independent Africa free of colonial domination.[22]

In July of 1891, for example, Massaquoi addressed an audience of five thousand at a meeting of the National Education Association. Appearing in "native dress" to show "the love I have for my country," the nineteen-year-old spoke on the "outlook for Africa." Citing a passage that inspired black Christians throughout the African diaspora—"There shall come princes out of Egypt, and Ethiopia shall stretch forth her hands to God" (Psalm 68:31)—Massaquoi insisted that indigenous people were best qualified to lead their nations. In response to critics who argued that Africans were incapable of self-government and required the oversight of more "civilized" Western powers, Massaquoi referenced Haiti as an example of a country that had achieved political independence and stability under black leadership. He also disputed racist claims that black people did not possess the "intellectual capacities" to succeed in higher education and were better suited to industrial training. "This assertion has been proven false in your various colleges and universities to which the negro is admitted," Massaquoi declared. Although he commended missionaries for "leading many souls to the light of civilization and Christianity," Massaquoi condemned American and European merchants for fomenting political instability and immorality in African society by encouraging the consumption of alcohol. In fact, he questioned whether "civilization" had introduced more evils than it promised to eradicate. Certainly this was true in the case of Americo-Liberian settlers who had oppressed indigenous peoples: stealing their land "without paying for it," refusing to educate "native children in the public schools," and treating sovereign tribal leaders with contempt. "But through the grace of our loving Saviour," Massaquoi proclaimed, "the day is coming when discrimination shall be blotted out of our country, when Christian America and Europe will no more send that cursed water into our land, . . . and when Africa with her population shall stand on an equality with the most potential nations of the world."[23]

After witnessing the murder of Ephraim Grizzard, Massaquoi became even more forceful in his critiques of "the so-called . . . Christian nations" and the civilizational hierarchies that supposedly justified their imperial domination of "inferior races." "You speak about the savage in Africa," he complained to a group of white ministers in Boston. "But right here in this country I have seen more savagery than I have seen all my days in Africa." How could a nation that claimed to be "Christian" and "civilized" tolerate the torture and extrajudicial killing of human beings? he asked. "What does your lynching make you? What does it make your national song? It makes it false, for, my dear friends, I consider no country 'The home of the free, the land of the brave' where the weak are oppressed and where the heel of the strong is always upon the neck of the weak. And," he continued, "I believe in no flag that proclaims liberty abroad and that approves discrimination and ostracism within its borders." The United States, in Massaquoi's view, had no right to claim moral superiority on the world stage, and certainly was in no position to deny the God-given rights of Africans (or other allegedly "undeveloped races") to political, economic, and religious freedom.[24]

Although they lived in the same state for several years, Massaquoi seems not to have crossed paths with Wells before he was called home in the fall of 1892 to succeed his mother as leader of the Vai nation and eventually to become one of the first indigenous Africans to hold a post in the Liberian government. By the time Massaquoi returned to his native land, Wells had also left Tennessee. In May, a "committee of leading citizens" in Memphis had destroyed her newspaper office and threatened her life after she published an exposé challenging the claim that black men were lynched because they sexually assaulted white women. In fact, Wells wrote, the widespread murder of African Americans by white mobs was a response to the economic success and political engagement of the nation's black citizens: "an excuse to get rid of Negroes who were acquiring wealth and property and thus keep the race terrorized and 'the nigger down.'" When outrage over Wells's editorial erupted, she was far away from the conflagration that consumed her printing press, attending an AME conference in Philadelphia. Once it became clear that she could not return to Memphis, Wells relocated to Brooklyn and joined the staff of the *New York Age*, the nation's leading black newspaper. She also began to speak publicly about violence against African Americans.[25]

In September 1892, while attending a National Press Association convention in Philadelphia, Wells met English Quaker activist Catherine Impey, founder and editor of the journal *Anti-Caste*, which advocated "the brotherhood of mankind irrespective of colour or descent." The two women discussed their common struggle to combat racism and "agreed that there seemed nothing to do but keep plugging away at the evils both of us were fighting." Several months later, after returning to England, Impey received reports of the horrific lynching of Henry Smith, who was burned alive in Paris, Texas. "The fire lighted by this human torch flamed round the world," Wells later observed, moving Impey to urge Wells to bring her antilynching campaign to Britain and assist in forming a new international organization for fighting racial violence on a global scale. Wells received Impey's invitation on March 30, 1893, and set sail five days later.[26]

By the time Wells joined forces with Impey, the older activist had been working for several years to create a coalition of Christian reformers dedicated to dismantling "the entire system of race separation . . . not only in America" but around the world. Convinced that "all arbitrary distinctions based on differences of social rank are contrary to the mind of Christ," Impey implored followers of Jesus to repudiate unbiblical theories of scientific racism, white supremacy, and civilizational hierarchy that fueled imperial expansion and the oppression of people of color across the globe. "Religion teaches men that God is the Father of *all*," she wrote. Anyone who claimed that God "created separate races of men to dwell apart, . . . that a fair skin is always superior to a dark one, . . . that the strong should *compel* the submission of the weak, crushing . . . those who resist," was spreading the devil's lies. True Christianity required a rejection of segregation, settler colonialism, and social Darwinism in favor of a worldwide movement that would assume "the brotherhood of the entire human family" and advocate for equal rights for all God's children.[27]

Impey's expansive vision appealed to supporters such as Scottish evangelical Isabella Mayo, whose financial backing made possible the creation of a formal organization for the promotion of global equality. Like Impey, Mayo was an anti-imperialist who believed that "the best expression of vital Christianity" was "the brotherhood of all races of men." Together, the two activists recruited Caribbean-born evangelist Celestine Edwards, a well-known lecturer whose oratories earned him a reputation as "the Black Champion of Christianity," to serve as the association's first secretary and editor of its journal, *Fraternity*. When Wells arrived in the spring of 1893, eager to link her efforts to end lynching with a wider crusade, the group enlisted her as a spokesperson. Over the next several months, she traveled across Britain on behalf of the Society for the Recognition of the Brotherhood of Man (SRBM), establishing local branches and urging new members to engage in the struggle for justice.[28]

Through her affiliation with the SRBM, Wells developed a greater appreciation for the pervasiveness of racial oppression in colonial settings around the world. From the outset, her collaborators made clear that their enterprise must have a global scope. When Wells initially proposed that the organization be called the "Emancipation League" to signal its indebtedness to the abolitionists, for example, Impey and Mayo warned that this designation would narrow the movement's purview. "In India and other British colonies," they explained, "the dark races" were also "being unjustly treated." Therefore, "we must organize on the broad basis of brotherhood to all men" so that the association would be "free to work against all these evils wherever perpetuated." Edwards reiterated this point in his opening editorial for *Fraternity*. Even as the SRBM strove "to put an end to Negro lynching in America," he wrote, "we must not forget that the English in America, in Australia, the Cape of Good Hope, and South Africa, under our own British flag in India, inflict injustices upon native races that call for immediate amelioration. . . . We must never rest satisfied until *all* the sons of men have equal justice and equal opportunity."[29]

Edwards was especially influential in helping Wells locate her antilynching crusade within a wider frame. In 1894, he facilitated the reprinting of Wells's pamphlet *Southern Horrors: Lynch Law in All Its Phases* for an international audience. By retitling the work *United States Atrocities*, Edwards explicitly connected the lynching of African Americans with "outrages" committed by the Ottoman Empire in the brutal suppression of nationalist uprisings among Slavic minorities. "The object of the present pamphlet," Edwards explained, "is to create a strong public feeling against injustice . . . so that moral and religious influences will be brought to bear upon the American Government, as it was . . . upon the Turks." By comparing the "ruthless barbarity" against African Americans with "Bulgarian Horrors" of 1876, Edwards aimed not only to mobilize international sentiment against the United States but also to challenge the nation's claim to moral superiority.[30]

An incisive critic of imperialism, Edwards had begun to interrogate the United States' status as a Christian nation several years before encountering Wells. Although he lauded the "popular and democratic principles" the American government claimed to uphold, he was quick to point out its many failures to defend these ideals in practice. From European settlement to the present, Edwards argued, white Americans had enslaved, oppressed, and murdered black and indigenous peoples. Even as they pursued freedom for themselves, he noted, the Puritans sold Native Americans into slavery. "We do not forget what good these Puritans had done and suffered for liberty of speech, press, and conscience," Edwards wrote, "but we cannot help observing their brutality to a brave and capable people." Furthermore, "the cruel treatment" indigenous people experienced at the hands of colonial settlers was not relegated to the pages of history but was an enduring feature of American empire. "The work of extermination," Edwards observed, "is being carried on in the United States to this day." Ongoing violence against both Native and African Americans, Edwards concluded, exposed the hypocrisy at the heart of the "Christian imperialism" both in and beyond the United States. Calls to evangelize and civilize savage people around the globe only served to mask the real motives driving American and European expansion. "Murder, plot, greed, incautious ambition, cupidity, lies, and caprice were, and are the main factors in invading a country and turning loose upon an undisciplined horde the weapons of civilization," Edwards declared. For this reason, racialized programs of missionary uplift must be rejected in favor of a Christian egalitarianism that recognized the "God-given rights" of all human beings. "I do not ask for cant-ish sympathy for the Negro," Edwards insisted, "but justice—the common birthright of every man."[31]

During her time abroad, Wells began to echo many of Edwards's arguments in her own writings and speeches. When critics charged her with disloyalty for bringing complaints about racial injustice in the United States before an international audience, Wells retorted that lynching was part of a broader global problem that demanded the attention of "the world at large." Just as the British had decried the slaughter of Bulgarians fighting for freedom from imperial rule, so should they condemn the killing of black citizens striving for political rights, economic independence, and social equality. Like Edwards, Wells questioned the United States' standing as a Christian nation possessed of the power and responsibility to "elevate, refine, and ennoble" the world's supposedly inferior races. "It is the white man's civilization and the white man's government which are on trial," Wells proclaimed. How could a nation that was incapable of preventing the "inhuman slaughter" of its own citizens "write itself down a success at self government," let alone presume to impose its rule or preach its "system of morals . . . to the heathen"? By the time she traveled overseas, Wells had lost whatever faith she might have had in false prophets of missionary uplift who prescribed respectability and patient acceptance of white supremacy as the best way for African Americans to attain security in the United States. Black citizens should not have to earn rights that belonged to them as children of God and under the Constitution. Nor should they settle for "maudlin sympathy" or "palliation." "The Negro asks only justice and impartial consideration of these facts," Wells wrote.[32]

The Expansion of American Empire and the Ongoing Struggle for Black Equality

Through her interactions with visionary colleagues like Edwards and Impey, Wells learned to connect the plight of African Americans to broader global struggles against empire and white supremacy. Unfortunately, this transnational network was short-lived. A rift between Impey and Mayo that occurred soon after the establishment of the SRBM eventually resulted in the fracture and dissolution of the nascent organization. Although Edwards had hoped to carry the work forward despite the rupture among the founders, overwork and exhaustion took a toll on his health. After he died in July 1894, Wells refocused her energies on combating injustice within the United States rather than continuing the more expansive effort to secure equality for oppressed peoples around the world. Although she affirmed the importance of protesting "the evils of Caste" wherever they prevailed, Wells's resources for attending to the disenfranchisement of indigenous Africans by Americo-Liberian settlers, the burdens of native women in British India, or the afflictions of Pacific Islanders (Kanakas) on sugar and cotton plantations in Australia were severely limited by her circumstances. For a black woman experiencing firsthand the violence of systemic racism in the United States, sustaining concern for sufferers in distant colonial settings was extremely challenging without the ongoing support of well-funded international partners.[33]

When confronted with imperial oppression closer to home, Wells joined many African Americans in supporting freedom fighters in Cuba, a large percentage of whom were nonwhite. But unlike her SRBM allies, Wells never denounced the dispossession of Native Americans. Nor did she condemn unequivocally the United States' acquisition of colonial possessions in the wake of the Spanish American War. At a meeting of the National Afro-American Council in December 1899, Wells argued that "Negroes should oppose expansion until the government was able to protect the Negro at home." A number of Wells's colleagues took a much stronger stance against American imperialism. Bishop Alexander Walters of the AME Zion Church, for example, criticized the racialized ideology of civilizational hierarchy that President McKinley and others expressly employed to defend military occupation of the Philippines. "Had the Filipinos been white and fought as bravely as they have," Walters observed, "the war would have been ended and their independence granted a long time ago." Bishop Henry McNeal Turner, drawing on the principle of Christian egalitarianism, accused the United States of engaging in an "unholy war of conquest" against "a feeble band of sable patriots . . . maintaining a heroic but pitifully unequal struggle for their God-given rights." Although her own critiques of American expansionism were never as forceful, Wells's association with leaders like Walters and Turner drew her into a growing anti-imperialist movement among black activists at the turn of the twentieth century.[34]

In the coming years, Wells would continue to affiliate with black visionaries who opposed any expansion of American empire premised on the intersecting logics of white supremacy and civilizing missions. One of her most sustained collaborations was with fellow journalist William Monroe Trotter. From the start of their partnership, the two activists were united in opposition to ideologies of racial uplift through industrial education. They also shared a commitment to biblical egalitarianism that shaped their antiracist work as officers of the National Equal Rights League (NERL), which Trotter founded in 1908. When they met with President Woodrow Wilson to protest the segregation of federal offices under his administration in November 1913, for example, Trotter characterized racial discrimination as not only unjust and unconstitutional, but "un-Christian."[35]

Through Trotter and the NERL, Wells once again became connected with a community of transnational activists who linked the fight for African American equality with a worldwide struggle for black liberation. As racial violence in the United States continued to surge during World War I, the NERL joined forces with the Liberty League, founded by West Indian immigrant Hubert Harrison, to advocate for "the colored man's rights at home and abroad" by campaigning for federal antilynching legislation and planning a delegation to present "the colored world's demands" at the Paris Peace Conference of 1919. This coalition, according to Trotter's biographer, Kerri Greenidge, "insisted . . . that civil rights for colored Americans meant antiimperialist, anticolonial, and armed self-defense for dispossessed 'darker races' across the globe." Although Wells and Trotter were both elected to represent the group at Versailles, they were denied passports by a wary Wilson administration. Undaunted, Trotter disguised himself as a chef, obtained passage on a ship bound for France, and arrived in time to deliver the group's appeal to conference delegates. Although the peace treaty failed to include the Liberty League's demands in its provisions, Trotter urged supporters not to despair. "We should lose heart if we relied on man or men to win this fight, but," he wrote, "we turn from fainthearted leaders and cheer ourselves with the thought, 'The Lord God omnipotent reigneth.'"[36]

By placing his hope for justice in the promise of God's sovereign power, Trotter echoed a theme sounded by many black activists at a time when their efforts to alleviate affliction in imperial contexts across the globe were so often thwarted. When traditional missionary agencies declined to sponsor her ministry among indigenous people deprived of their rights under Americo-Liberian colonial rule, Georgia Patton trusted God to provide her financial support and worked alongside Holiness evangelist Mary Sharp to relieve the suffering she encountered in Krutown. As a young African student experiencing the exigencies of being black in the American South, Momolu Massaquoi looked forward to the day when Christ would blot out discrimination and elevate Africans to "take their stand among the free races of the earth." After a lifetime of laboring for the cause of universal Christian brotherhood to little avail, Celestine Edwards proclaimed that the "God of history" would exact retribution for "the crimes of Anglo-Saxonism . . . perpetuated against weaker peoples" in the United States and throughout the British Empire. From the earliest days of her struggle against white supremacy, Ida B. Wells sought divine assistance and guidance for her work. "Thou has always fought the battles of the weak & oppressed," she prayed when she learned that she had lost her first legal contest. "Come to my aid at this moment and teach me what to do, for I am sorely, bitterly disappointed." Throughout her life, Wells appealed to God for help as she challenged the structures of systemic racism in and beyond the United States.[37]

Motivated by their faith in divine justice and commitment to Christian egalitarianism, Wells and her fellow believers campaigned to dismantle the civilizational hierarchies that fueled imperial expansion and justified the subjugation of "the darker races" around the world at the turn of the twentieth century. Drawing on scriptural principles and theological precepts that had animated the movement to abolish slavery in the United States, these activists carried forward the crusade for racial equality into a new era and extended the scope of their concern for black suffering beyond national borders. Although their hopes for universal justice on a global scale remain unfulfilled, the tradition of spiritual protest Wells and her comrades embodied has continued to inspire antiracist struggles for liberation, decolonization, and human equality to the present day.

NOTES

1. Duster, *Crusade for Justice*, 87–89.
2. The only substantive scholarly analysis of Patton's work is Jenkins, "Missionary Photography."
3. Duster, *Crusade for Justice*, 22; Gaines, *Uplifting the Race*, 33; Angelina E. Grimké, *Letters to Catharine Beecher* (Boston: Isaac Knapp, 1838), 47; and J. D. Anderson, *The Education of Blacks in the South*, 66, 68.
4. Ida B. Wells, *The Memphis Diary of Ida B. Wells*, ed. Miriam DeCosta-Willis (Boston: Beacon Press, 1995), 50; Giddings, *Ida*, 155.
5. DeCosta-Willis, "Georgia E. L. Patton."
6. Anderson, *The Education of Blacks in the South*, 33–78; Bederman, "'Civilization,' the Decline of Middle-Class Manliness, and Ida B. Wells's Antilynching Campaign."
7. Anderson, *The Education of Blacks in the South*, 33–78; and Jay S. Stowell, *Methodist Adventures in Education* (New York: Methodist Book Concern, 1922), 169–71.
8. Redkey, *Black Exodus*; Kevin Gaines, "Black Americans' Racial Uplift Ideology as 'Civilizing Mission': Pauline E. Hopkins on Race and Imperialism," in Kaplan and Pease, eds., *Cultures of United States Imperialism*, 433–55; and Stowell, *Methodist Adventures in Education*, 169–71.
9. "Brief Autobiography of a Colored Woman Who Has Recently Emigrated to Liberia," *Liberia* 34 (November 1893): 78–79; Ida B. Wells, "The Requisites of True Leadership," in *The Light of Truth: Writings of an Anti-lynching Crusader*, ed. Mia Bay (New York: Penguin, 2014), 35–41.
10. S. A. Johnson, *African American Religions*, 201; and Jenkins, "Missionary Photography," 295.
11. W. L. Williams, *Black Americans and the Evangelization of Africa*.
12. Mary E. George, "Mary A. Sharp: Missionary to the Krus," *Missionary Review of the World* 35 (1912): 916–18; Frances J. Baker, *The Story of the Woman's Foreign*

Missionary Society of the Methodist Episcopal Church, 1869–1895, rev. ed. (New York: Eaton & Mains, 1898), 392–95; "Obituary: Miss Mary Sharp of Liberia," *Missionary Review of the World* 38 (1915): 78; and Israel, *Amanda Berry Smith*, 74, 83.

13 Case, *An Unpredictable Gospel*, 140.
14 George, "Mary A. Sharp," 916–18. On the Day Mission, see Jenkins, "Missionary Photography," 296.
15 W. L. Williams, "Ethnic Relations of African Students in the United States, with Black Americans"; Baker, *Story of the Woman's Foreign Missionary Society of the Methodist Episcopal Church, 1869–1895*, 393; Mary A. Sharp, "Monrovia, Africa," *Christian Standard and Home Journal* (December 2, 1862): 381; and Israel, *Amanda Berry Smith*, 75–76, 82.
16 "Address of Prince Momolu Massaquoi," *Our Day*, ed. Joseph Cook 8 (1894): 272–73; Duster, *Crusade for Justice*, 88–89; and *Catalogue of the Central Tennessee College, 1899–1900* (Nashville, TN: Marshall and Bruce, 1900).
17 Duster, *Crusade for Justice*, 88; Jenkins, "Missionary Photography," 293–314; and DeCosta-Willis, "Georgia E. L. Patton," 828–30.
18 On the Holiness movement's individualistic focus see Case, *An Unpredictable Gospel*, especially 122–26.
19 Duster, *Crusade for Justice*, 52.
20 Duster, *Crusade for Justice*, 51; and Wells, "Afro-Americans and Africa," in *The Light of Truth*, ed. Bay, 46–51.
21 Wells, "Afro-Americans and Africa," in *The Light of Truth*, ed. Bay, 46–51. For a summary of scholarship on Black-Native relations in this period, see Miles and Krauthamer, "Africans and Native Americans."
22 Smyke, *The First African Diplomat*; Smyke, "Massaquoi of Liberia"; Fatima Massaquoi, *Autobiography of an African Princess* (Basingstoke, UK: Palgrave Macmillan, 2013); and "An African Prince," *Nashville Banner*, September 5, 1892, 1.
23 Momolu Massaquoi, "In Search of an Education," *National Education Association Journal of Proceedings and Addresses*, January 1891, 239–43.
24 "Address of Prince Momolu Massaquoi," 272–73.
25 For Massaquoi's political career see Smyke, *The First African Diplomat*, and Massaquoi, *Autobiography of an African Princess*. Duster, *Crusade for Justice*, 58–67.
26 Bressey, *Empire, Race, and the Politics of Anti-Caste*, 19, 78–81; and Duster, *Crusade for Justice*, 82, 85.
27 Catherine Impey, "Editor's Annual Address," *Anti-Caste* (March 1895): 1–2; *Anti-Caste* Supplement (January 1891).
28 Isabella Mayo, *Recollections of Fifty Years* (London: John Murray, 1910), 170; Killingray, "Edwards, Samuel Julius Celestine"; and Bressey, *Empire, Race, and the Politics of Anti-Caste*, 86–92.
29 Emphasis added. Ida B. Wells, "The Society for the Recognition of the Brotherhood of Man," *Anti-Caste* (May–June 1893): 2–3; Celestine Edwards, "Fraternity," *Anti-Caste* (May–June 1893): 1–2.

30 Celestine Edwards, introduction to Ida B. Wells, *United States Atrocities* (London: Lux Publishing, n.d.), v–vii.
31 Celestine Edwards, *From Slavery to a Bishopric; or, The Life of Bishop Walter Hawkins of the British Methodist Episcopal Church* (London: John Kensit, 1891), 24, 106–8; Celestine Edwards, "This-world-ism," *Lux* (December 3, 1892), 273, quoted in Lorimer, "Legacies of Slavery for Race, Religion, and Empire," 731–55; and Edwards, introduction to Wells, *United States Atrocities*, vi.
32 Ida B. Wells-Barnett, *A Red Record*, in *The Light of Truth*, ed. Bay, 281, 308, 309; and Ida B. Wells-Barnett, *Mob Rule in New Orleans*, in *The Light of Truth*, ed. Bay 393.
33 Wells, *A Red Record*, 228. On the falling out between Impey and Mayo, see Duster, *Crusade for Justice*, 102–5.
34 Wells, quoted in *Cleveland Gazette*, January 7, 1899; Walters and Turner quoted in Gatewood Jr., "Black Americans and the Quest for Empire," 545–56. See also Mitchell, "'The Black Man's Burden,'" 77–99.
35 On Trotter, see Greenidge, *Black Radical*. "William Monroe Trotter's Address to the President," in Arthur S. Link, ed., *The Papers of Woodrow Wilson*, vol. 28 (Princeton, NJ: Princeton University Press, 1979), 495.
36 Greenidge, *Black Radical*, 256, 262, 233, 265.
37 Momolu Massaquoi, "Africa's Appeal to Christendom," *Century Illustrated Magazine* 69 (April 1905): 927–36; Celestine Edwards "Angel of History," *Fraternity* (November 1893): 7; and Wells, *The Memphis Diary of Ida B. Wells*, 141.

9

An Evangelical Occupation

The Racial and Imperial Politics of US Protestant Missions in the Dominican Republic

CHRISTINA C. DAVIDSON

In September 1911, US Protestant missionaries Philo W. Drury and Nathan H. Huffman surveyed the Dominican Republic on behalf of the Evangelical Union of Puerto Rico. Their report, "Occupancy of Santo Domingo by Evangelical Missions," characterized the Dominican Republic as an open Protestant missionary field, and neatly linked together US military intervention in Latin America and American missionization of the region.[1] In the report, Drury and Huffman ignored the long nineteenth-century history of Protestantism on the island and dismissed the faith and evangelical endeavors of Black lay preachers and missionaries.[2] Instead, they asserted that only an Anglo-US missionary effort would foster the "improvements and progress" that came with US empire: Western education, urban infrastructure, and full integration into an American-dominated capitalist system.[3] Their proposal also established an implicit racial hierarchy. Aware that Catholic Dominicans would view White US Protestant missionaries suspiciously, the surveyors advised US missionary boards to send Puerto Rican preachers, men who had trained under White Americans, to convert the island. Through the Puerto Rican connection, Dominicans would accept White Protestantism and reject Black Protestantism. In short, the occupation of Santo Domingo by Anglo-US evangelical forces reflected a White-supremacist religious worldview that placed Dominicans above "Negroes" (Haitians and Anglophone Blacks); Puerto Ricans above Dominicans; and Anglo-US Protestants, like God, above all others.

Considering Anglo-US Protestant evangelization of Latin America at the start of the twentieth century, this chapter examines the racial hierarchy that White US missionaries purposefully constructed and vigilantly guarded in the Dominican Republic. As the country that shares the island Hispaniola with Haiti, the Dominican Republic represented a racial borderland at the turn of the century, symbolically suspended between the Black republic and the United States (coded as White).[4] Anglo-US missionaries joined Europhile Dominican elites in a long campaign to disassociate the Dominican Republic from Haiti and racial Blackness and position the country as a non-Black, Latin nation. They did so because their beliefs in White Protestant supremacy mandated both spiritual and racial (i.e., cultural) conversion. Inspired by the United States' military intervention in Latin America, White US missionaries merged the US imperial project with their own. They fused the discourse of pan-Americanism with the contemporaneous Protestant ecumenical movement, and behind the veneer of Christian unity, they instilled racial hierarchy. This chapter argues that by constructing and imposing such racial hierarchy in the Dominican Republic, White US evangelicals engaged in a form of spiritual warfare diametrically opposed to Black Protestantism and the emerging anticolonial activism that Heather Curtis explored in chapter 8.

From Black State to Blank Slate

Despite the fact that Dominican historiography has characterized Protestantism as a foreign religion, Protestantism was arguably already fused into the local culture of Dominican port cities by the time of the country's independence from Haiti in 1844. Black emigrants from the United States established the first permanent Protestant congregations on eastern Hispaniola during the period of Haitian Unification (1822–1844) when thousands of African Americans settled in the Black republic between 1824 and 1826.[5] As with Canada and Liberia, US Blacks immigrated en masse to Haiti both to escape racial oppression in the United States and because they believed that God had ordained the island as a Black Promised Land.[6] Many African Americans who participated in the prominent Haitian emigration movement were affiliates of the African Methodist Episcopal (AME) Church, the first historical Black denomination in the United States. Once on the island, emigrants formed AME societies, but over time the congregations could not maintain communication with the denomination. US Black Methodists in Haiti then affiliated with the British Wesleyan church, which had sent missionaries to Port-au-Prince as early as 1816. Buoyed by the emigrant population, British missionary stations in the Haitian capital and the island's northern coast grew throughout the remainder of the century.[7] British Wesleyan missionaries catered to a predominantly Anglophone Black migrant population, but frequently conducted services in French and Spanish in order to minister to Catholic Haitians and Dominicans. Thus, by 1844, Protestantism had long existed on the island and had gained a few Haitian and Dominican converts. After Dominican independence, Black Protestants living on the northern coast and in the Dominican capital became Dominican citizens and joined in the new republic's struggle for national sovereignty.

The Dominican Republic's fight for sovereignty played out both on the island and in the international arena, and inevitably centered the question of race. Multiple battles between Haiti and the Dominican Republic ensued in the years after 1844 as Haiti attempted to regain its eastern territory and thereby protect the Black republic from White foreign invasion. Meanwhile, as it had with Haiti, the United States refused to officially recognize the Dominican Republic because of the country's large percentage of African descendants and the threat this free Black population posed to the US South. Europeans and some US lobbyists and filibusters who wished to colonize Dominican territory and reenslave Afro-Dominicans (and eventually Haitians), however, saw value in the island's division. They portrayed the island's conflict as a race war in which *White* Dominicans faced extermination from Black Haitians, despite the fact that the majority of Dominicans were of mixed Spanish and African descent.[8] This act of whitening the Dominican population vis-à-vis Haiti mirrored Europhile Dominican elites' own attempts to persuade the Western world that Dominicans were not Black like Haitians.[9] Whereas many Afro-descendant eastern-isle inhabitants had welcomed Unification in 1822 since the Haitian government had abolished slavery, Dominican elites—a class predominantly of European descent—despised the Black republic. Their prejudices against Haiti not only reflected deep-seated racist attitudes wrought in Atlantic-world slavery but also recognized the animosity that the United States and European governments directed towards eastern Hispaniola under the Haitian flag. Thus, in the decades after 1844, both Dominican elites and foreign opportunists characterized the Dominican population as a White nation.

The country's racial composition and proximity to Haiti remained a primary concern to both Dominicans and outsiders in the later part of the nineteenth century as the young republic struggled to maintain its independence. Facing Haitian invasion and distrusting the Dominican Republic's own Black masses, for example, some Dominican conservatives sought annexation to a more powerful Western nation. This group succeeded in 1861 when President Pedro Santana negotiated the Dominican Republic's annexation to Spain. The popular classes, however, feared that Spain would reinstitute slavery, and within two years the country rebelled against the Spanish crown and restored independence. The War of Restoration (1863–1865) ended the same year as the US Civil War (1861–1865). In the aftermath of the two wars, the United States finally granted diplomatic recognition to the Dominican Republic. But, shortly afterward, Dominican president Buenaventura Báez proposed annexing the Dominican Republic to the United States. US president Ulysses S. Grant favored this scheme since it aligned with his expansionist vision for the United States. For three years (1869–1871), the possibility that the Dominican Republic would join the union sat on the horizon. The plan ultimately failed because the majority of US politicians feared the incorporation of African-descendant Dominicans into the United States' body politic.[10]

Black Protestant communities on the northern coast and in the Dominican capital not only survived the turmoil of the nineteenth century but also adapted and became fixtures within the important port towns of Monte Cristi, Puerto Plata, Samaná, and Santo Domingo. Their survival partially depended upon the fact that, despite the Catholic Church's dominance across the island, Haitian and Dominican governments had protected Protestants' freedom of religion. Protestants also benefited from the British Wesleyans' missionary organization. Along with their counterparts in Port-au-Prince, Gonaives, and Cap-Haitien, Dominican Protestants participated in trade networks and Antillean anticolonial movements at century's end. Defending their freedom and new homeland, some Dominican Protestants even made a name for themselves during the War of Restoration. After the war, Protestant men continued to serve in the Dominican military, and a few even held government posts. In short, at the turn of the twentieth century, Black Protestants made up part of the Dominican nation despite the fact that not all Protestants identified as Dominican.

At the same time, Black Protestants living in Hispaniola represented a double-diasporic community as descendants of Africans and migrants from the United States and the greater Caribbean. This position tied them to broader Black networks than spanned the Protestant Atlantic world. In the last decades of the nineteenth century, these networks rekindled when the AME Church appointed missionaries to Port-au-Prince and Santo Domingo in 1878 and 1883, respectively. Since the AME Church's aims were to combat White Americans' racist stigma of the island and "uplift" Hispaniola's two Black republics, these renewed connections fostered conflict with local populations in ways similar to those Sylvester Johnson (chapter 3) has described in the case of Liberia.[11] Nevertheless, the forging of Black Protestant networks in Hispaniola at the turn of the century evidences the continuity between the Black rebellion against "epistemological warfare" identified by Katharine Gerbner (chapter 1) and the "spiritual protest" against global White supremacy that Heather Curtis has found among transnational Black activists (chapter 8). Through their religious networks, Black Protestants in Hispaniola engaged in the long freedom struggle for Black people, a battle waged both physically and spiritually. In other words, decades prior to Drury and Hoffman's visit in 1911, Protestantism had already made its mark on Hispaniola in the prayers, songs, and teachings of Afro-descendant migrants, Black lay preachers and teachers, and African American missionaries whose historical orientation towards Christianity and notions of spiritual freedom differed drastically from those of White US missionaries.

Nevertheless, when White Americans considered implementing Protestant missions in eastern Hispaniola in the first decades of the twentieth century, they claimed that the Dominican Republic represented a tabula rasa for Protestant missionary work, the place "where less evangelical work has been done than in almost any other of the [Latin American] countries."[12] What explanation accounts for this discrepancy? Anglo-US missionaries interested in evangelizing the Dominican nation asserted that British and African American missionaries had focused only on *foreign* migrant populations. They did not view African American emigrants' descendants and other Black Protestants as part of the Dominican Republic's body politic, and they rejected the notion that Black missionaries could effectively evangelize Spanish-Catholic Dominicans. These ideas depended upon White-supremacist ideology that racially divided Dominicans from "Negroes" and ranked the former above the latter for the purpose of imperial conquest. In this way, Anglo-US missionaries of the early twentieth century were no different from nineteenth-century US filibusters.

Early-twentieth-century Anglo-US missionary organization in the Dominican Republic represented a turning point in the history of Protestantism on the island. Whereas Black Protestant congregations linked the island to other places in the United States and the broader Caribbean, White US missionaries aimed to disassociate the Dominican Republic from the stigma of racial Blackness and the history of Black Protestant organization on the island. By doing so, they not only repeated a long nineteenth-century pattern of "whitening" as part of the imperial process but also tied this discursive practice to a fresh (albeit not unprecedented) show of US military force in the early-twentieth-century Americas.

In 1898, the United States' takeover of Cuba, Puerto Rico, and the Philippines during the Spanish American War marked the rapid intensification of US militaristic imperialism in the Americas. White US missionaries, like other US citizens, watched as multiple US interventions followed in quick succession. In 1903, the United States fomented Panama's split from Colombia, and quickly took control of the Canal Zone. Soon after, President Theodore Roosevelt's 1905 corollary to the Monroe Doctrine declared it the United States' duty to intervene in the affairs of any country where it deemed American lives and property at risk. The new doctrine was designed for the immediate US seizure of the Dominican Republic's custom houses (the primary source of the Dominican government's wealth) as well as for future application elsewhere.[13] US interventions in Honduras (1907, 1911, 1912) and Nicaragua (1912) soon followed. By the time the Panama Canal opened in October 1913, the United States had eagerly exercised its military muscle in the Caribbean and Central America. The US Marines' occupation of Haiti (1915) and the Dominican Republic (1916) would come next.

Witnessing these events, Anglo-US Protestant missionaries operating in Latin America felt that they should do more to evangelize the region. The US government had sent armies abroad to "civilize" the non-White races of the world, but Anglo-US missionaries believed that they had done little to combat the "idolatry" and "paganism" rampant in Catholic Latin America. The Bible, they asserted, would be more effective than guns in inculcating Anglo-Saxon mores. Thus, missionaries joined US troops in the colonial project. This union was not new. For centuries, Protestant missionaries had followed both troops and settler colonists westward across North America to convert Native American tribes to Christianity. Post-1898, this union was exported to the Caribbean. As scholar Mayra Rivera has argued regarding Puerto Rico, "The object of conquest was also made an object of mission."[14] Anglo-US missionaries merged the language of conquest with the notion of divine sanction. This discourse made "the *religion of the liberators* and the *other elements of their civilization* almost indistinguishable from each other."[15] In short, within this viewpoint, God had ordained White US Protestants for the conquest of non-White others; this was the White man's burden.

For White US Protestants interested in the Dominican Republic, the time to expand US missions in Latin America seemed at hand. Not only had the US government forged a path, but a year before Drury and Huffman visited Santo Domingo, Protestant leaders from the United States and Europe had met at the 1910 World Missionary Conference in Edinburgh, Scotland. Scholars have since recognized the 1910 conference as a defining event in the history of world missions due to the newfound sense of cooperation that it inspired among the various Protestant denominations represented.[16] The conference's lack of attention to the Protestant evangelization of Latin America, however, troubled a small group of White US missionaries working in the traditionally Catholic region.[17] This group believed it their duty to evangelize Latin America, and they initiated a hemispheric ecumenical movement to obtain this goal. The White US missionary enterprise in the Dominican Republic originated in this ecumenical movement, a campaign that was unequivocally imperialistic and racist in nature if not always explicit in evangelical discourse.

US Imperial Discourse and Christian Cooperation in Latin America

Anglo-US missionaries—like the US troops overrunning the region—aimed to reform Latin America in their Protestant White-supremacist image of the United States. To justify this imperial project, missionary leaders employed a religious discourse of pan-Americanism. US policy experts developed the concept of pan-Americanism in the 1880s as an economic strategy designed to advance US capital in Latin America. On the surface, pan-Americanist discourse emphasized hemispheric brotherhood, economic cooperation, and feelings of common destiny among the American nations.[18] Yet, beneath the façade of mutual cooperation, pan-Americanism served to establish US paternalistic dominance over Latin American trade relations, and acted as a euphemism for US empire.[19] In the 1910s, US missionaries tapped into the foreign policy discourse of pan-Americanism since the emphasis on hemispheric "brotherhood" and "friendship" dovetailed well with US Protestants' newfound passion for Christian union sparked by the Edinburgh conference. In the minds of US evangelicals, pan-Americanism became a religious discourse of hemispheric ecumenicism, or "Christian cooperation." This positive framing of US missions shielded Anglo-US Protestants from the imperial and racial violence intrinsic to their evangelical enterprise and buttressed the belief that God had sanctioned their work at a time when US military interventions snowballed across the Caribbean and Central America.

Missionaries' use of pan-Americanism as a religious discourse corresponded with specific actions. At Edinburgh, US Protestants brought the issue of Latin American evangelization before the Foreign Missionary Conference of North America, a regional branch of the World Missionary Conference. The members subsequently appointed a committee, the Committee on Cooperation in Latin America (CCLA), to review and discuss the matter. Three years later in 1913, the CCLA hosted its first conference in New York. The New York conference forced many interdenominational issues to the fore. Representatives of the major White denominations disagreed over the CCLA's attitude toward the Catholic Church, the prioritization of doctrinal allegiance versus Christian social work, and the extent to which the committee should consider

Congreso de la Obra Cristiana en la América Latina, Panamá, Febrero 10-20, 1916.

Figure 9.1. Photograph of Panama Congress participants printed in *Puerto Rico Evangélico* 4 (June 1916), 2. Archivo Histórico del Protestantismo en Puerto Rico, Biblioteca Juan Valdés, Seminario Evangélico de Puerto Rico, San Juan, P.R.

Latin Americans' aversion to "ecclesiastical Pan-Americanism."[20] CCLA leaders, however, dismissed any notion of potential Latin American opposition to their evangelical plans. Instead, they made arrangements for a second, larger ecumenical CCLA conference. The next meeting would take place in Latin America and would bring together all White North American, European, and Latin American Protestant missionaries currently operating in the region. The "Panama Congress" occurred February 10–20, 1916, and was purposefully staged around the 370th anniversary of Martin Luther's death (February 18, 1546).[21] Stationed in the Canal Zone, the CCLA hoped that this conference would "ground [pan-American] friendship in Jesus Christ" and establish an infrastructure for the expansion of US Protestant forces in Latin America (figure 9.1).[22]

US missionary leaders meant the CCLA to be a top-down homogenizing force. Besides the spirit of cooperation, this ethos projected the conceit of White Protestant supremacy. For example, during the Panama Congress, the CCLA declared itself "thoroughly representative of all Christian forces of Europe and North America serving Latin America."[23] The term "Christian," in their minds, referred exclusively to White Protestants. According to CCLA affiliates, Latin America, a region once colonized by the Spanish crown and Catholic priests, had never truly received the Christian gospel. Drury and Huffman had propagated this viewpoint when they wrote in 1911 that Dominican Catholicism was "wholly inadequate to lead men to a saving knowledge of Jesus Christ."[24] Like the union between missionaries and troops, this belief was not new. In the mid-nineteenth century and after the US Civil War (1861–1865), anti-Catholic prejudice surged as thousands of Catholic Irish and Italian people immigrated to the United States. In typical fashion, US missionaries of the early twentieth century characterized the Catholic Church as despotic, materialistic, and arrogant.[25] They accused Catholic priests of purposefully keeping Latin American populations in ignorance in order to control the masses. Moreover, they believed Latin Americans to be worse off still because they had suffered from Spanish colonialism. According to this black legend, Spain had acted more cruelly than other colonial powers, and racial mixing under Spanish rule had created a degenerate, lazy race, arresting the region's social and economic development. As the influential CCLA secretary and US foreign policy expert Samuel Guy Inman warned circa 1916, millions of working-class people were leaving the Catholic Church and "drifting into extreme socialism."[26] In short, the region needed Anglo-US deliverance. Only Anglo-US Protestantism could save Latin America from its avaricious Catholic *latifundia* past, guard it from an anarchist present, and launch it into a productive capitalist future.

CCLA planning documents reinforced this White-Protestant-supremacist logic and its link to capitalist enterprise. In preparation for the Panama Congress, for example, the CCLA's executive office collected data from American and European missionary boards operating in Latin America, including field reports, correspondence files, and survey responses.[27] The data provided intel on local populations and their societies, and mirrored the process of intelligence gathering conducted by US Marines and other colonial forces in Latin America, Asia, and Africa. Racial undertones pervaded the questionnaire sent out by the Commission on Survey and Occupation, whose very name underscored the intended White Protestant subjugation of the region. The survey placed missionaries in the role of caretakers of Latin American countries, and asked them to (1) name the "special significance" of "the country under your view to the life of other parts of the world"; (2) list the achievements and defects of the population; and (3) "place them in the foremost ranks of progressive civilization."[28] With these questions and others, the commission fixed Anglo-Saxon Protestants as the pinnacle of world civilization, and asked US and British missionaries to judge non-White peoples on a scale of humanity in which rank not only denoted a population's proximity to Whiteness but also its adoption of free markets and capitalist modes of production.

The CCLA's penchant for racial ordering appeared in other planning documents too, demonstrating the link among race, capitalism, and morality in the minds of Anglo-US missionaries. A hand-drawn ethnographical map of the Americas filed among other CCLA reports racially divided and categorized the hemisphere.[29] A "Survey of Moral and Religious Conditions in the Canal Zone" by Inman separated Panama City and Colón by racial and ethnic makeup in order to compare the "moral" conditions of each.[30] And, a report on Jamaica designated "the negro" as a "problem" for Anglo-US Protestant expansion in the Caribbean. "Primitive in their life, these islanders have in most cases become devotees to the more emotional type of religion, either Protestant or Catholic, seeking sensation rather than spiritual guidance," the author explained.[31] He drew the conclusion that Black people in the Caribbean needed White religious leadership to teach them the "dignity of labor."[32] In this case, White missionaries' racist judgments about Latin America and the Caribbean served not only to unite Anglo-Protestant Christian forces in the region but also to impose US racial hierarchy upon Latin American societies in order to perpetuate a racialized proletariat class for the sake of Western capitalism. Non-White peoples who did not embrace free markets or capitalist values were lazy, backward, and immoral, according to this logic.

US missionaries, of course, did not perceive themselves as acting in service of the United States' racist capitalist empire. Hypocritically, they characterized US military invasion of Latin American nations as overly materialistic (i.e., a sign of government greed), despite their own efforts—both in discourse and in praxis—to tie indigenous and Black peasants across the region to a capitalist world economy. Missionaries understood their work instead as part of the US Social Gospel, a progressive Christian movement that sought to provide Christian solutions to social problems. Social Gospel leaders adhered to a nonradical, middle-class creed that sustained prevailing racial and class hierarchies, but their blending of faith and social action was forward-thinking when compared to the ideology of conservative Christians who mandated a strict divide between the physical and spiritual worlds and condemned any form of social work.[33] Indeed, some conservative denominations refused to participate in the CCLA and its evangelical mission due to its social-assistance agenda in Latin America.[34] Such work included the founding of schools, newspapers, hospitals, Protestant seminaries, and libraries. In 1919 alone, for example, the CCLA suggested that evangelicals should establish thirteen schools across the region, including medical and law schools in Brazil; normal schools in Cuba and Brazil; training schools for women in Mexico, Puerto Rico, and Argentina; theological seminaries in Bolivia and Cuba; a junior college in Chile; and agricultural schools and a university in Mexico.[35] CCLA Protestant missionaries viewed such work as fundamental to their faith and the most effective path toward the region's evangelization and civilization. Social work to alleviate poverty, sickness, and illiteracy would bring potential converts to the doors of hospitals, schools, and churches. They believed that placing Bibles in the hands of individuals—instead of Catholic doctrine—would also empower Latin Americans to read the Bible for themselves while still under the guidance of local CCLA-backed missionaries.

To propagate their work, CCLA leaders formed regional subcommittees, subsidiaries of the CCLA, which established their own national organizations. White missionaries and Euro–Latin Americans who had already converted to Protestantism cooperated in the leadership of these groups.[36] Like their US counterparts, Latin American leaders were educated, middle-class, and of majority European descent. In general, they too viewed their local populations as backwards and the Catholic Church as inadequate in providing spiritual guidance and engendering needed social reform. Anglo-US CCLA leaders believed that this class of Protestant Euro–Latin Americans (and their would-be converted Catholic compatriots) played an essential role in the region's social and spiritual reform. The presence of Protestant Latin Americans made local reception to the CCLA's organization possible. Often such leaders were respected in their communities and knew how to navigate local politics. They also produced much of the local evangelical literature for CCLA-affiliated publications and served as the primary recruiters for new converts. Thus, not only did Latin American participation in the CCLA seem to counter any notion of the organization's inherent imperialism, but over the years it also proved the organization's success. As Spanish-language evangelical print literature proliferated, the Protestant population in Latin America grew incrementally.[37] This modest achievement was reflected at subsequent CCLA conferences. Whereas only 12 percent of the 481 participants in the CCLA Panama Congress were Latin American Protestants, that number grew to 28 percent at the Bolivia Congress in 1925 and 51 percent at the Cuba Congress in 1929.[38] The use of Spanish at CCLA conferences increased as well.

The history of Protestantism in Cuba and Puerto Rico demonstrates the CCLA's subsidiary national-level formation and provides relevant background for understanding subsequent events in the Dominican Republic. Protestant churches had existed in Cuba and Puerto Rico decades before the 1916 Panama Conference. White Americans and Cuban émigrés to the United States established the first Protestant missionary congregations in Cuba during the Ten Years' War (1868–1878), and Spain's liberal revolution of 1868 led to the public organization and legalization of congregations in Puerto Rico.[39] In 1898, this early Protestant activity received a boost with the United States' invasion of the islands during the Spanish American War. Within days of the United States' bombardment of San Juan on May 12, seven US missionary boards met in New York to divide Cuba and Puerto Rico between themselves. Each denomination would evangelize a preassigned territory in order to eliminate competition between the various evangelical forces. After the Spanish American War, US Protestant missionaries flocked to the islands, and church membership increased drastically. For example, by 1903, all major US missionary boards sponsored work in Cuba, and Protestant church membership reached nearly 3,000 people.[40] This number increased to 10,000 by 1910.[41] Statistics for Puerto Rico mirrored Cuba, with eighty-five Protestant church members in 1900, 7,893 in 1905, and 13,255 by 1910.[42] These numbers still made up a minuscule percentage of the islands' overall populations, but the growth rate seemed promising to various Protestant leaders who realized that by banding together they could present a united front against the Catholic Church. Accordingly, in 1905, Philo W. Drury proposed a summit of all Protestant missionaries operating in Puerto Rico. The meeting took place a year later when twenty-three US missionaries and one Puerto Rican formed the Federación de Iglesias Evangélicas de Puerto Rico. After the 1916 Panama Congress, this group became known as the Evangelical Union of Puerto Rico (EUPR).[43] Inspired by the CCLA's first meeting, missionaries in Cuba also moved towards cooperation, and hosted their first ecumenical conference in Havana in February 1917.[44]

For Drury, the leading US Presbyterian missionary in San Juan and the secretary of the CCLA's subcommittee on Puerto Rico, it made sense for US Protestant churches to work with the EUPR in their "occupation" of the Dominican Republic. He and other Anglo-US missionaries believed that Dominicans, like Puerto Ricans and Cubans, were Spanish-speaking *Latins*, whose culture and race originated from their White Spanish colonizers rather than from enslaved Africans and Haitian revolutionists. Thus, he advocated for Puerto Ricans to evangelize the mixed-race, mulatto republic. This vision of missionary work established a sliding racial scale of evangelization in which Anglo-US missionaries would instruct White-presenting Puerto Ricans who, in turn, would evangelize the racially ambiguous Dominican nation once "dominated" by Black Haiti. The sliding scale, in their minds, would restore a proper racial order that had been inverted when Haitians had "invaded" the Spanish eastern side of the island in 1822. The irony, of course, lay in the United States' own impending invasion of Hispaniola.

The Occupancy of Santo Domingo by Evangelical Forces

The EUPR's designs for "occupancy" of the Dominican Republic had a slow start. Preliminary hopes shattered with the assassination of Dominican president Ramón Cáceres in 1911 and the outbreak of war. In the following years, a few Puerto Rican preachers established Protestant congregations in the Dominican southeast, but these small groups consisted of Puerto Rican migrants and attracted few Dominicans. Prospects for missionary work, however, shifted when the United States invaded the island a few years later. In July 1915, the US Marines overtook Haiti, initiating a devastating nineteen-year occupation that, among other atrocities, stripped Haitians of their sovereignty, seized control of the government's wealth, imposed a new constitution, and caused up to 11,500 Haitian deaths.[45] Less than a year later—and just three months after the CCLA's Panama Congress—US forces repeated these offenses on the eastern side of the island, establishing an eight-year occupation of the Dominican Republic that produced much of the same.[46] Once again, missionaries followed the troops. The same year as the US invasion of Santo Domingo, the EUPR's board of directors organized a committee with representatives of five denominations (Congregational, Disciples of Christ, Methodist Episcopal, United Brethren, Presbyterian) to advance Dominican missions and voted to seek funding from Protestant church boards in the United States.[47] Three years later, the CCLA's secretary, Samuel Guy Inman, toured the Dominican Republic and Haiti with the US Marines in order to assess the best course for the island's evangelization. The occupation of Santo Domingo by evangelical forces had begun.

Inman's report of his tour, *Through Santo Domingo and Haiti: A Cruise with the Marines* (1919), demonstrates how racial and imperial ideology merged in evangelical missionaries' thoughts and plans regarding the Dominican Republic. In the report, Inman recited Anglo-US racial division of the island and reinforced Dominican elites' anti-Haitianism. The island and its people continually reminded the Anglo-US traveler "of the heart of Africa," on the one hand, and "the arrested development arising from Spain's abuse of the oldest of her American colonies" on the other, he wrote.[48] Inman further explained that for Anglo-US missionaries to ingratiate themselves with Dominican elites and gain access to the country, "Santo Domingo and Haiti should not be confused nor classified together." Still, even as Inman elevated Santo Domingo to a racial status above that of Port-au-Prince, he maintained his own racial biases against Dominicans. For example, while describing Dominicans as polite, gracious, and hospitable, Inman also used descriptors that revealed his disdain for the people he wished to evangelize. Dominicans, in Inman's mind, were "a sturdy race" who followed the "*mañana* spirit of the tropics."[49] Their patriotism, moreover, was "the greatest drawback" because it inspired a "frequent unwillingness to subordinate self for the general good."[50] The "general good" served as a euphemism for the US

Marines' occupation of the island. In other words, Dominicans' downfall was their refusal to submit to US rule.

It was precisely because Inman and other Anglo-US missionaries classified Dominicans as non-Whites that Inman portrayed the violent trappings of US empire as a needed public service. Like the religious discourse of pan-Americanism, the racist paternalism of US empire prevalent in Inman's writings veiled the violence of US colonial conquest on Hispaniola. As wars broke out between the Marines and Haitian and Dominican freedom fighters on both sides of the island, Inman declared that US forces had established "order and security, greater than have prevailed in Santo Domingo since colonial days."[51] He praised both the military governor of Santo Domingo, US admiral Harry Shepard Knapp, and his successor, Thomas Snowden, as leaders who felt genuinely interested in helping Dominicans. Knapp and Snowden, according to Inman, were outstanding officers despite the fact that US soldiers under their command notoriously tortured and killed guerilla captives, indiscriminately shot civilians and burned down their homes, routinely raped Dominican women, imprisoned political dissidents, and censored the press. "Much complaint is heard about the injustice of military rule in the interior and the low moral standards of the men," Inman admitted in an essay regarding the occupation.[52] Yet, he summarily dismissed the allegations: "One cannot help feeling ... that whatever mistakes they make are of the head and not of the heart."[53] In Inman's opinion, US officers and soldiers had good intentions—"as fine a spirit as any missionary"— but were inexperienced and misguided in running a colonial empire. The crimes against humanity that Anglo-US agents committed were a necessary evil in the eyes of the CCLA's administrator. The fact that US journals such as the *Interchurch Bulletin* reprinted Inman's views not only indicates that White Christians accepted Inman's perspective but also suggests that the same racist beliefs that fueled the US empire energized US White Protestantism as well.[54]

Inman and other White US Protestants believed that where the US Marines failed to develop the apparatus for a fair and just government in the Dominican Republic, US missionaries would succeed. In other words, by converting Catholic Dominicans to Protestantism and erecting institutions like hospitals and schools, Anglo-US missionaries would fulfill their role in "civilizing" Dominicans and preparing them for future self-government. The Dominican Republic had not sent representatives to the 1916 Panama Congress, but if Inman had his way, the Catholic nation would soon fall under the CCLA's purview, instigating widespread Protestant conversion. This shift would transform the Dominican nation into a modern state in which self-government was possible.

In practice, Inman and other Anglo-US missionaries' understanding of their evangelistic project depended upon strict adherence to White-supremacist racial hierarchies. Consequently, they rejected other models of Protestant missionization on the island. Besides dismissing the work of African American missionaries, CCLA leaders considered other Anglo missionaries who had initiated Protestant missions in the Dominican Republic prior to 1916. These groups included three British denominations—the Wesleyans, the Anglicans, and the Moravians—as well as the American Free Methodists, who arrived in Santiago in 1889, two decades before the CCLA's creation.⁵⁵ Upon meeting these groups during his tour, Inman (like Drury and Hoffman in 1911) imagined a segregated Protestant movement in which the British would serve the Black Anglophone migrant population while the CCLA directed its agenda towards Dominican elites who would in turn train the dark masses. Yet, whereas some White missionaries (like the British Wesleyan Emerson Mears) agreed with this division of labor, at least one minister made another suggestion.⁵⁶ Bishop Charles B. Colmore of the Episcopal Church of Puerto Rico explained that in Cuba and Puerto Rico, the Episcopalian leadership viewed Black Protestant migrant communities "as centers for the dissemination of work among the natives."⁵⁷ Colmore proposed that the same could take place in the Dominican Republic, where the Black migrant population had expanded due to the burgeoning sugar industry. "Much more advantage should be taken of the opportunity to care for [British Caribbean migrants] and use them as an influence in the community," Colmore proffered.⁵⁸ This suggestion, however, did not align with CCLA leaders' understandings of race relations on the island. Inman and others believed that Dominicans would never submit to Black religious authority.⁵⁹ The strict racial and ethnic segregation that the CCLA espoused ignored the long history of Black Protestantism on the island, prevented any possible White-Black missionary cooperation in the present, and sought to limit non-White racial solidarity and Black spiritual power that inspired resistance.⁶⁰

Instead of building up Black leaders—whether of African American, British Caribbean, or Catholic-Dominican descent—to evangelize and educate the lowest classes of Dominicans, Inman, Drury, and Hoffman turned to Puerto Ricans who had already accepted Anglo-US Protestantism and had internalized its embedded capitalist logic. A short analysis of the essays printed in the EUPR's journal *Puerto Rico Evangélico* during its early missionary period (1916–1921) demonstrates that Puerto Rican clergy closely aligned themselves with US evangelical leaders when it came to the Protestant occupation of Santo Domingo. In September 1918, for example, the journal dedicated its bimonthly issue to the neighboring island. A photograph of the Plaza de Colón, where the Dominican government had erected a statue of Columbus, the quintessential symbol of European conquest, appeared on the front page (figure 9.2).[61] Other photographs of Dominican ports, government buildings, bridges, hospitals, and industrial plantations covered the next two pages under the titles "The Dominican Republic Progresses" and "Undoubtable Signs of Dominican Progress."[62] An article by Drury, "Dominican Republic on Its Way to Progress," followed.[63] More articles such as "The Cry of Quisqueya" and "Evangelization of Santo Domingo" and letters from early Puerto Rican missionaries in the Dominican field urged readers to heed the "Macedonian Dominican" cry and declared that Puerto Ricans were responsible for conquering the neighboring republic as "ambassadors of Christ."[64] The figure of Jesus Christ remade in the image of the colonial *conquistador* matched US missionaries' own discourse regarding Puerto Rico in 1898 and the Dominican Republic in 1916. The warring Christ figure now appeared in Puerto Rico evangelical discourse: "Santo Domingo will be conquered so that it will really be free, not for the Spanish crown, nor for the North American eagle, but for the church of Christ, the great conqueror and liberator of souls and nations."[65]

The harmony between Puerto Rican and US missionaries' thoughts united them in their Christian action. As early Puerto Rican missionaries formed ties with Puerto Rican and Dominican laborers in the Dominican southeast, the CCLA and EUPR worked together to organize a joint missionary venture in the Dominican Republic. After Inman's 1919 tour, the EUPR formed the Committee on the United Occupation of Santo Domingo on January 13, 1919, and approved a budget of $4,270.[66] Then, in October 1920, Drury, on behalf of the committee, returned to

Figure 9.2. Front cover of *Puerto Rico Evangélico* and photograph of the Columbus statue in Santo Domingo. Archivo Histórico del Protestantismo en Puerto Rico, Biblioteca Juan Valdés, Seminario Evangélico de Puerto Rico, San Juan, P.R.

the Dominican Republic, where he quietly assessed the situation on the ground. Wary of opposition from the Catholic Church and Dominican nationalists, Drury advised Inman that the CCLA and EUPR should proceed cautiously and change the subcommittee's name. As someone in Santo Domingo briefed Drury, "If the Committee is to go by that name, have your letterheads printed in Chinese."[67] Dominicans already under the US Marines' occupation would not respond well to an occupation of another kind. That this self-evident fact had not informed the CCLA's nomenclature from the start further evidences the CCLA and EUPR's imperialist mindset. A mere name change, however, would not absolve the joint US–Puerto Rican evangelical forces from their conquistador faith; the plans for occupation continued. As Drury secretly scouted potential missionary properties in the capital, Inman organized a board of trustees composed of US denominational representatives who would fund the project. Ultimately, only three missionary boards—the United Methodist, the Presbyterian Church, and the United Brethren—signed on. The secretaries of these boards met for the first time on December 17, 1920, in New York, where they authorized the purchase of a church property in Santo Domingo for fifty thousand dollars and appointed Drury as the temporary superintendent of the mission. At their next meeting on January 28, 1921, the trustees formally organized the Board for Christian Work in Santo Domingo (BCWSD), elected Mrs. Fred S. Bennet of the Presbyterian Women's Board of Home Missions as president, and set a budget of eighty thousand dollars for the next two years.[68]

With the formation of the BCWSD and its substantial financial backing, White US missionary leaders dared to dream big. In 1921, the board planned two city facilities at the capital, Santo Domingo, and the interior city Santiago de los Caballeros, and smaller centers at San Pedro de Macorís, Puerto Plata, San Francisco de Macorís, and Sánchez. At the churches erected in these places, the missionaries would host various activities beyond Sunday worship. In Santo Domingo, these included "lectures on moral, hygienic, educational and religious topics, courses in religious education, public forum, clubs of various kinds for old and young, kindergarten, night school clinic and dispensary."[69] Moreover, the BCWSD planned a bookstore, printing press, hospital, nurses' training school, and "an industrial school along Hampton Institute lines" for the capital.⁷⁰ These services reflected a broader colonial agenda whereby White governments sought to "civilize" people of color in Hawaii, the Philippines, South Africa, and elsewhere through education.⁷¹ Parallel to what Karine Walther has argued in chapter 7, the desire to implement the Hampton schooling model, in particular, demonstrates how White US missionaries, despite their categorization of Dominicans as Latins, still racialized Dominicans as non-Whites who needed the same sort of labor disciplining as African Americans in the US South. At the same time, Anglo-US missionaries meant to control both the flow of evangelical information and the production of theological knowledge in the Dominican Republic. Theology would flow from the top down, from the United States to Puerto Rico to Santo Domingo. Already-trained "Porto Rican workers will be used as largely as possible in this program," an early report reiterated, and any Dominican converts who wished to join the ministry would be sent to the EUPR's seminary in San Juan.⁷²

Missionary dreams soon turned into reality. Early in 1921, three Puerto Rican preachers—Rafael R. Rodríguez, Alberto Martínez, and José Espada Marerro—left San Juan for Santo Domingo.⁷³ At the same time, the BCWSD elected Nathan Huffman as the first resident missionary superintendent in the Dominican Republic. Huffman, who had toured the Dominican Republic with Drury a decade prior, arrived in Santo Domingo in June 1921. According to church historian Edward Odell, Huffman promptly organized three missionary congregations in Santo Domingo and the sugar-producing towns of San Pedro de Macorís and La Romana.⁷⁴ Yet, in reality, this work had already been accomplished by the Puerto Rican missionaries who had arrived earlier in the year. These churches, led by Rodríguez (Santo Domingo), Martínez (San Pedro), and Marerro (La Romana), formed the backbone of a new denomination, the Iglesia Evangélica Dominicana (IED), and represented the local workforce of the BCWSD's missionary hierarchy. Another missionary, Ramón Pratts, would join the group later that year to lead an IED congregation at San Cristóbal. On the evening of January 1, 1922, these new IED ministers, along with Huffman and four delegates—two of whom were Puerto Rican women—hosted a special worship service in which they formally organized the Iglesia Evangélia Dominicana.⁷⁵ The plan for "occupancy" of the Dominican Republic by joint Anglo-US and Puerto Rican evangelical forces had finally materialized.

Conclusion

The US occupation of the Dominican Republic ended in 1924, just two years after the IED's founding. By then, Anglo-US evangelicals had developed a strong distaste for military violence. US Methodist bishop Francis J. McConnell, who toured IED churches in Santo Domingo that year, concluded, "No matter what we think of it, our imperialism will never win the respect of the Dominicans."[76] Even Inman, who had formerly characterized the occupation as a necessary evil, warned that US imperialism "bodes more evil than any other tendency on the American continent to-day."[77] At a cursory glance, it seems that after only two years on Dominican soil, Anglo-US missionaries' ideas about US empire had changed. Historians of religion, race, and US empire, however, know better.

This chapter provides a countercase to recent scholarship that has emphasized US missionaries' anticolonial activism.[78] Anglo-US missionaries remained agents of US empire whether or not they critiqued US imperialism because colonialism, like White supremacy, was part and parcel of their conquistador faith. Thus, despite notions of unity conveyed through pan-American Christian discourse and later disavowals of US imperialism, the relationship between White US missionaries and their intended converts was never meant to be equal, let alone reciprocal.

US missionaries did not recognize the racial imperial project embedded in their missionary enterprise. Consequently, in the Dominican case, Anglo-US missionaries limited their critique of American imperialism to US military action. In the same breath that McConnell, Inman, and other missionaries condemned military violence, for example, they praised the occupation for its social achievements—the building of modern roads, the founding of schools and hospitals, the enforcement of sanitary codes, and the establishment of IED Protestant churches throughout the island. The latest accomplishment had been one of their own making: "The success is due to the fine spirit of the cooperating [US missionary] Boards and to the type of leaders we have secured both from Americans and Dominicans," exclaimed McConnell.[79] He said nothing of the Puerto Rican missionaries who led the first IED congregations, nor the long history of Black Protestantism on the island. His worldview prohibited such acknowledgments. Any alternative ideology that challenged the racial segregation and ranking of "Whites," "Latins," and "Negros" also challenged the very nature of conquistador Christianity. This was the preoccupation that drove the US evangelical occupation of the Dominican Republic, Latin America, and elsewhere.

NOTES

1. Philo W. Drury and Nathan H. Huffman, "Occupancy of Santo Domingo by Evangelical Missions," *Latin American General Records, 1911-1974* (hereafter *LAGR*), box 7, folder 11, The Burke Library at Union Theological Seminary, Columbia University, NY (hereafter The Burke Library).
2. C. Davidson, "Redeeming Santo Domingo," 95-98.
3. I use "Anglo-US" throughout this chapter in order to clarify distinctions between White US citizens and Latin Americans of European descent.
4. García-Peña, *The Borders of Dominicanidad*, 9-12; Candelario, *Black behind the Ears*, 36 and 44-57.
5. For the 1824-1826 Haitian Emigration Movement see Fanning, *Caribbean Crossing*.
6. Maffly-Kipp, *Setting Down the Sacred Past*, 111.
7. Griffiths, *A History of Methodism in Haiti*; Lockward, *El protestantismo en Dominicana*, 111-23.
8. Eller, *We Dream Together*, 62-64; Horne, *Confronting Black Jacobins*, 180-81.
9. Nelson, "U.S. Diplomatic Recognition of the Dominican Republic in 19th Century," 10-14; Candelario, *Black behind the Ears*, 35-82; Eller, "'Awful Pirates' and 'Hordes of Jackals,'" 87-94.
10. Guyatt, "America's Conservatory," 976-77.
11. For "uplift" see Byrd, *The Black Republic*, 7.
12. Samuel Guy Inman, "Santo Domingo, Old and New," *Pan-American Magazine* 32 (1920): 121, accessed in *LAGR*, Box 7, folder 12, The Burke Library.
13. Veeser, *A World Safe for Capitalism*, 2-5.
14. Rivera, "En-Gendered Territory," 82.
15. Rivera, "En-Gendered Territory," 82.
16. Stanley, ed., *The World Missionary Conference, Edinburgh 1910*; I. M. Ellis, *A Century of Missions and Unity*; Rodano, ed., *Celebrating a Century of Ecumenism*.
17. Samuel Guy Inman, *Christian Cooperation in Latin America: Report of a Visit to Mexico, Cuba, and South America* (New York: Committee on Cooperation in Latin America, 1917), 32.
18. Coates, "The Pan-American Lobbyist," 22-25.
19. Coates, "The Pan-American Lobbyist," 24.
20. Sinclair and Solano, "The Dawn of Ecumenism in Latin America," 5.
21. Sinclair and Solano, "The Dawn of Ecumenism in Latin America," 5.
22. "Latin American Missionary Conference," *Committee on Cooperation in Latin America and Congress on Christian Work in Latin America Records* (hereafter *CCLA and CWLA*), Series 1, Box 1, folder 10, The Burke Library.

23 Inman, *Christian Cooperation in Latin America*, 32.
24 Drury and Huffman, "Occupancy of Santo Domingo."
25 Josiah Strong (1847–1916) exemplified these ideas; Josiah Strong, *Our Country: Its Possible Future and Its Present Crisis* (New York: Baker & Taylor Co. for the American Home Missionary Society, 1885), 46–59. Similar stereotypes appear in CCLA correspondence. See J. Milton Greene to S. G. Inman, May 13, 1915, *CCLA and CWLA*, Series 1, Box 2, folder 10, The Burke Library.
26 Samuel Guy Inman, "Latin America," *CCLA and CWLA*, Series 1, Box 1, folder 13, The Burke Library.
27 "Latin American Missionary Conference," *CCLA and CWLA*, Series 1, Box 1, folder 10, The Burke Library.
28 "Commission I. Survey and Occupation. Questions for Corresponding Members of the Commission," *CCLA and CWLA*, Series 2, Box 2, folder 8, The Burke Library.
29 "Ethnographical Chart of America. Showing the Proportion of Caucasians in Each Country," *CCLA and CWLA*, Series 1, Box 1, folder 13, The Burke Library.
30 Samuel Guy Inman, "A Survey of Moral and Religious Conditions in the Canal Zone, Panama City, and Colon," April 1917, *Samuel Guy Inman Records*, Box 1, folder 1, The Burke Library.
31 "Jamaica, the Lesser Antilles, Bahamas, Barbados and Trinidad. 'The Isles Shall Praise Him,'" *CCLA and CWLA*, Series 1, Box 1, folder 13, The Burke Library.
32 "Jamaica, the Lesser Antilles, Bahamas, Barbados and Trinidad. 'The Isles Shall Praise Him,'" *CCLA and CWLA*, Series 1, Box 1, folder 13, The Burke Library.
33 Bruno-Jofre, "Social Gospel, the Committee on Cooperation in Latin America and the APRA," 77.
34 Sinclair and Piedra Solano, "The Dawn of Ecumenism in Latin America," 5.
35 "Various Programs for Service in Latin America Suggested during the Life of the Committee on Cooperation in Latin America," *CCLA and CWLA*, Series 1, Box 2, folder 4, The Burke Library.
36 For history of converts see Dove, "Historical Protestantism in Latin America," 286–303.
37 Even with modest growth, Protestants remained under 1 percent of the population until the 1940s and 1950s. Bastian, "Protestantism in Latin America," 328.
38 Rooy, "Latin American Council of Churches," 113.
39 Martínez-Fernández, *Protestantism and Political Conflict*, 78–79; Gotay, *Protestantismo y política en Puerto Rico*, 5–9.
40 Martínez-Fernández, *Protestantism and Political Conflict*, 166, 168.
41 Martínez-Fernández, *Protestantism and Political Conflict*, 168.
42 Gotay, *Protestantismo y política en Puerto Rico*, 183–84.
43 Martínez-Fernández, *Protestantism and Political Conflict*, 168.
44 Inman, *Christian Cooperation in Latin America*, 47.
45 Renda, *Taking Haiti*, 10.

46 The most comprehensive book on the occupation is Calder, *The Impact of Intervention*. See also Tillman, *Dollar Diplomacy by Force*. For Dominican literature, see *Clío* 191 (2016): 1–254.
47 Odell, *It Came to Pass*, 148.
48 Samuel Guy Inman, *Through Santo Domingo and Haiti: A Cruise with the Marines* (New York: Committee on Cooperation in Latin America, 1919), 4.
49 Inman, *Through Santo Domingo and Haiti*, 35.
50 Inman, *Through Santo Domingo and Haiti*, 35.
51 Inman, *Through Santo Domingo and Haiti*, 22.
52 Samuel Guy Inman, "American Occupation of Santo Domingo," *LAGR*, Box 7, folder 11c, The Burke Library.
53 Inman, "American Occupation of Santo Domingo."
54 "Sees Santa Domingo as Virgin Field for Missionary Effort," Interchurch Bulletin cutout, n.d., accessed in *LAGR*, Box 7, folder 10, The Burke Library.
55 They did not count a small group of Pentecostals who worshiped in San Pedro de Macorís and later incorporated into the IED. Inman, *Through Santo Domingo and Haiti*, 49–50.
56 C. Davidson, "Redeeming Santo Domingo," 84–89.
57 "Report to the Commission by the Right Reverend Charles B. Colmore," *CCLA and CWLA*, Series 2, Box 3, folder 10, The Burke Library.
58 "Report to the Commission by the Right Reverend Charles B. Colmore."
59 C. Davidson, "Redeeming Santo Domingo," 98–100.
60 Here, I refer specifically to Black spiritual resistance movements on the island, including the Liborismo movement and the intersection of African Methodism and Garveyism in San Pedro de Macorís. See Lundius and Lundahl, *Peasants and Religion*, 31–122; García-Peña, *The Borders of Dominicanidad*, 82–83; García Muñiz and Giovannetti, "Garveyismo y racismo en el Caribe," 139–211.
61 "Estatua Erigida en la Plaza de Colón de la Capital de la República Dominicana en Honor del Descubridor de América," *Puerto Rico Evangélico* 7 (September 1918): 1. All citations to *Puerto Rico Evangélico* come from the Archivo Histórico del Protestantismo en Puerto Rico, Biblioteca Juan Valdés, Seminario Evangélico de Puerto Rico, San Juan, P.R.
62 "La República Dominicana Progresa," *Puerto Rico Evangélico* 7 (September 1918): 2; "Señales Indubitables del Adelanto Dominicano," *Puerto Rico Evangélico* 7 (September 1918): 3.
63 "La República Dominicana en Vías de Progreso," *Puerto Rico Evangélico* 7 (September 1918): 4.
64 "El Grito de Quisqueya," *Puerto Rico Evangélico* 7 (September 1919): 3; Marcelino Hidalgo Méndez, "Evangelización de Santo Domingo," *Puerto Rico Evangélico* 8 (July 1919): 9.
65 "El Grito de Quisqueya," *Puerto Rico Evangélico* 7 (September 1919): 3.
66 Odell, *It Came to Pass*, 148.

67 Philo W. Drury to Samuel Guy Inman, November 4, 1920, *Records of the Foreign Missionary Society of the Church of the United Brethren in Christ* (hereafter *FMS-UB*), folder 2279-5-6:05, General Commission on Archives and History, United Methodist Church, Madison, NJ (hereafter GCAH).
68 "Outline of Cooperative Work in Porto Rico and Santo Domingo," *FMS-UB*, folder 2279-5-6:07, GCAH. This document notes that the American Baptist Church agreed to take over the evangelical work in Haiti.
69 "Outline of Cooperative Work in Porto Rico and Santo Domingo."
70 "Outline of Cooperative Work in Porto Rico and Santo Domingo."
71 Engel, "The Ecumenical Origins of Pan-Africanism," 222–23.
72 "Outline of Cooperative Work in Porto Rico and Santo Domingo."
73 "Actas de la Segunda Asamblea de la Iglesia Evangélica Dominicana, Celebrada en San Pedro de Macorís, Enero 10 y 11 de 1924," Archives of the Iglesia Evangélica Dominicana, Santo Domingo, Dominican Republic (hereafter IED).
74 Odell, *It Came to Pass*, 153–54.
75 "Acta de las Sesiones de la Primera Reunión de la Conferencia Anual de la Iglesia Evangélica Dominicana, Celebrada en Santo Domingo, R.D. Durante los Días 16 y 17 de Enero de 1923," IED; Roca, *Horizontes de Esperanza*, 1:93–94.
76 F. J. McConnell, "A Glimpse at Santo Domingo," *FMS-UB*, Folder 2279-5-5: 22, GCAH.
77 Samuel Guy Inman, "Imperialistic America" (1924), *LAGR*, Box 8, folder 2, The Burke Library.
78 See for example, Hollinger, *Protestants Abroad*.
79 McConnell, "A Glimpse at Santo Domingo."

PART IV

Dialectics

Wastelanding, Weaponry, and Capitalist Exclusions

The powerful pairings of inclusion and exclusion, expansion and contraction, cosmopolitanism and provincialism, and other binaries have long shaped the way empires operate. This has certainly been true for the US Empire. As US global power waxed and waned through the Cold War, the War on Terror, and the global ascendance of neoliberal capitalism, the capacity of religion to define the boundaries of "America" and the "American" seemed greater than ever. The chapters in this section think across both intimate and global scales to wrestle with the contradictions and impositions of religion in the late-twentieth- and early-twenty-first-century US Empire. What sorts of political theologies have operated to facilitate and sustain US imperial power in this era? How has American Christianity engaged with the technologies of warfare and with logics of imperial expansion that rendered some populations expendable? What are the religious logics of techno-capitalist expansion, and what might the new benevolence of philanthropic finance reveal about the fissures and contradictions of US empire in the contemporary world?

The structure of settler colonialism remains at the heart of US empire, and the American Christian institutions and political theologies that emerged with and in service to this empire have continued to sustain its exclusions. Lands of the Navajo and Apache nations, for instance, were assigned to an "Indian diocese" by a Catholic Church that aimed to provide special care but too often treated them as dumping grounds instead. In a pattern of terrifying embodiment, sexual abuse became a devastating phenomenon among Christian communities in the so-called borderlands that the US Empire created. In the twentieth century, which witnessed the creation of the atomic bomb, napalm, and other technologies of barely imaginable destruction, it should come as no surprise that imperial technologies of war had profound implications for religion.

American evangelicals, as chapter 11 demonstrates, have engaged with and enabled imperial militarism through political theologies that pair perfectly with weapons such as napalm and, more recently, the targeted precision of the drone.

Among the most impactful developments in the recent history of religion and US empire are the tactics and practices of engaging Muslims as a special population. Such practices, building on long histories of colonial contact and domination, were heightened by 9/11, and facilitated a dramatic expansion of the security state. In this context, American Muslims have wrestled with tactics of locating themselves as fully *American*, fulfilling the lofty promises of American democracy—and, in the process, have sometimes also redrawn the lines of settler-colonial exclusion. Equally important in this period is the expanding role of capital at the nexus of religion and US empire. Markets and mercantilism of past eras have given way to prolific digital technologies and product innovation with an unprecedented scale of individualization or customization for consumers. Moral strategies, in this context, seem to bear ineluctable connection to commodities. Imperial systems have intersected with a laissez-faire system of commercialism and articulated new hopes of global uplift through the benevolent promise of philanthropic finance. Even the most ardent critics of capitalism's exclusions, as we learn in chapter 13, can find themselves (ourselves) folded back into its logics of never-ending consumption. Today the dialectics of religion and US empire continue to structure American cultural logics of inclusion and exclusion, to frame the political discourse of White Christian nationalism, and to shape the voracious excesses of neoliberal capitalism around the world.

10

The Trouble of an Indian Diocese

Catholic Priests and Sexual Abuse in Colonized Places

KATHLEEN HOLSCHER

In June of 2007, Roman Catholic bishop Donald Pelotte spoke before the annual gathering of the Catholic Theological Society of America about the challenges of leading the only Native American diocese in the United States.[1] Pelotte was a theologian, and the first US bishop of Native descent.[2] For two decades he had presided over the Diocese of Gallup, an ecclesiastical district that extends fifty-five thousand square miles across Diné Bikéyah, the lands of the Diné, or Navajo, people and of other tribes. "My diocese is unique in many ways," the prelate told his audience. He described its unusual span across state lines, to include New Mexico and Arizona. "When the diocese was established," he explained, "Pope Pius XII didn't want the Navajo Nation divided into two dioceses. Accordingly, the Diocese of Gallup is one of the largest geographically."[3] Pelotte reflected on the immense distances and other difficulties of ministering to a Catholic population he estimated at more than half Native American. He touched upon the poverty of his diocese (Gallup was and is the poorest diocese in the United States) and its reliance on outside money. He discussed his goals of improving cultural sensitivity and lay leadership. He concluded on an upbeat note, sharing the diocesan vision of being "a people of many cultures, each distinctive in its heritage, coming together as one family in prayer and the Eucharist."[4]

Addressing his theologian peers that summer day, Pelotte declined to mention a crisis unfolding at home. Four years prior, the Diocese of Gallup had released names of six priests alleged to have sexually abused minors within its boundaries.[5] By 2005, Pelotte had publicly apologized for the behavior of priests there, met with victims, and called for a "search and rescue mission" to find others, especially within Native communities.[6] In 2013 the Diocese of Gallup would file for Chapter 11 bankruptcy.[7]

Today, the number of Catholic leaders publicly accused of sexually abusing minors in the Diocese of Gallup stands at thirty-seven.[8] Thirty-two of these men were priests, three were religious brothers, and the remaining two were a lay teacher and a former seminarian. In addition, at least thirteen priests who lived in the diocese accumulated abuse accusations elsewhere.[9] This number makes the historical rate of alleged predators in Gallup, relative to its Catholic population, several times higher than in places like the Archdiocese of Boston and the Diocese of Pittsburgh, which get attention as hotbeds of clerical abuse in the United States. It is typical, though, of dioceses that reach across Indian Country. Nearly all of US dioceses that *do* have rates comparable to Gallup's—including in Alaska, Montana, and South Dakota—are ecclesial units that contain and oversee the Catholic spiritual care of colonized peoples.[10]

This chapter treats clerical sexual abuse of Native children and young people as settler-colonial violence. It traces how this abuse grew, unintentionally but unmistakably, out of a coherently Catholic system for saving souls. In doing so, the chapter relates a recent episode in a long history of Catholic participation in empire, and it also makes a methodological argument for approaching the "internal workings" of the Catholic Church—mixed up though they have always been with co-constitutive logics of race, economy, and state—as machinery that feeds empires' processes and produces its dispossessions.

Catholic sex abuse in Gallup is part of a pattern of sexual and gender-based violence faced by colonized people across North America. Sarah Deer has cautioned against characterizing this violence as an "epidemic," which risks neutralizing its character. "Using the word *epidemic*," Deer writes, "fails to account for the crisis's roots in history and law. Using the word *epidemic* to talk about violence in Indian Country is to depoliticize rape."[11] Deer joins other scholars and activists committed to exposing the political dimension of sexual violence in Native and First Nations communities by locating it amid US and Canadian settler colonialism.[12] Their work demonstrates how settler economies create the precarity Native children and adults live in, which in turn sets the stage for sexual predation. They have shown how territorial, state, and federal law and its enforcement fail to proportionately protect Native people. Their work highlights historical parallels between contemporary sex trafficking and "tactics used by colonial ... governments to subjugate [Native] women and girls," and points to how sexualization of Native people—or their racialized casting as promiscuous in the white imagination—has supported paired settler projects of seizing land and erasing sovereignty.[13]

These observations cast light on Catholic sex abuse in the Southwest, and other spaces created by US empire: when priests assaulted youth there, their acts emerged out of, and reinforced, structures of dispossession in ways this work describes. But studying religion and empire demands more than recording instances when colonial violence happens at the hands of religious actors; it requires asking hard questions about religion itself relative to their proliferation. Here I engage Deer's call for accounts of abuse in Native America that dig deeper than "epidemic." I do so by locating them in a Catholic Church that conformed to colonial processes, while behaving as a coherently—even stubbornly—religious body, in ways that communicated truths about God, and about its priests as God's earthly emissaries. My purpose is to demonstrate how the Church's internal logics, as expressed via its theology and doctrine, produced imperial violence across the twentieth century.[14]

Today journalists, survivors, and attorneys describe places where predatory priests accumulated as "dumping grounds." To characterize the Diocese of Gallup like this—as a peripheral site, used by the Church to discard clerical refuse—invokes a modern dynamic, one wherein interlocking systems of capitalism, colonialism, and white supremacy render marginal populations expendable "waste," polluted and pollutable, and transforms places they live into wastelands.[15] In this light, predatory priests landed in the US Southwest because bishops wanted to dispose of them *and* because those leaders failed to transfer categories of value to Native and Latino communities sufficient to save them from becoming sites for disposal. In this light, the US Catholic hierarchy's treatment of people as valuable (or not) extended norms of whiteness, citizenship, and economic productivity.

I begin from a grim pair of premises: first, that Diné Bikéyah and other Native lands are rendered dumping grounds via racial, economic, and political structures that sustain settler colonialism; and second, that

Catholic leaders who are also settlers participate in that dynamic. Rather than approach Catholicism reductively, as a site where these structures replicate, however, I ask how religious logics had a correspondent effect. In other words, without discounting the sway that US systems of politics, economy, and race have on the Church and its actors, I approach Catholicism itself, in its bold determination to mediate the relationship between heaven and earth, or between humans and their God, as subject for critique. The Diocese of Gallup was the creation of an institution governed *not* by an impulse to dispose, but instead by certainty: both in its exclusive ability to deliver human souls to heaven, and in its priests as vital to that process. During the twentieth century, clergy worked from the confidence that they, as men endowed with power to administer sacraments, possessed a unique capability for *cura animarum*, or care of souls.[16] The Gallup diocese began so that Latino and especially Native people inhabiting territory claimed by the United States would live nearer to priests and a bishop, and might better access that care. Gallup's first bishop embodied this Catholic surety when he sought out clergy from across the United States to staff his new diocese.

This Catholic institutional world, ordered by a mission to deliver souls to heaven, and by surety about the place of the Church and its representatives in the schema of salvation, also produced the practice of transferring abusive priests to the US Southwest. By the rules of this Catholic world, priests who sinned—and sex with children *was* unquestionably a sin—required relocation. But relocating an abuser was not disposing of him. Rather, transfers mitigated scandals that jeopardized souls in the places priests came from, and created opportunity for souls in new locales. To move a priest kept his bad acts secret. To protect his secrets preserved his reputation, and that of the priesthood. Protecting reputations was something more than and different from saving face; only a priesthood esteemed by lay people could continue to guard them effectively from the mortal peril of straying from faith. In new environs, a priest guilty of old sins could continue to administer the sacraments. A scandal-free reputation ensured that people he met there would trust him to do so.

To move a priest also protected him; in theological terms it insulated him from the compounded sin of sex that metastasized into scandal. So priests traveled to Gallup for their own spiritual benefit too. When

Catholic bishops discussed transfers, they expressed a collective will to protect the Church's reputation, and they also spoke in ways that reinscribed the extraordinariness of the priesthood—as an office that transcended men inhabiting it, while also entitling them to ongoing care. Relocations manifest such care. Between the 1940s and the 1990s, dozens and probably hundreds of clerics who abused youth came to the Southwest to visit the Servants of the Paraclete, a religious order with a raison d'etre of assisting "fallen" clergy return to grace. While men traveled to the Servants' monastery and "renewal center" in the Jemez Mountains of northern New Mexico with many personal motives, including to evade criminal prosecution, the order's constitution dictated that the center's purpose was to help priests heal body and soul. Some of the Servants' guests passed through the center to the Diocese of Gallup, and several abused children there. In all these ways, then, a Catholic world ordered by confidence in the Church, and in the specialness of priests—including sinful ones—to the work of salvation, caused troubled clergy to gather in Diné Bikéyah.

A New "Indian Diocese"

"Whatever else religions do, they move across time and space," writes Thomas Tweed. "And they have effects. . . . They leave trails. Sometimes those trails are worth celebrating. . . . Sometimes trails are sites for mourning."[17] While Catholicism moves along all sorts of routes, via objects, rituals, and relationships, the institutional Church and its sacraments—those proprietary rites it mandates for the soul's salvation—have always traveled with the bodies of ordained men. Catholicism arrived to Diné Bikéyah and adjacent Native lands in this form in the seventeenth century, with Franciscan clerics who moved north with the expanding Spanish Empire.[18] Between the seventeenth and the early nineteenth centuries, and again beginning in 1898, Franciscans ran missions to Native people in the region.[19] In the mid-twentieth century, clerical Catholicism moved into Diné Bikéyah in a new way, with a wave of "secular" or diocesan priests. These men traveled from east to west, across territory now claimed by the United States. They answered a fresh call for clergy to give spiritual care to Latino and especially Native communities, this time amid the parish infrastructure of a new diocese.

The decision to create the Diocese of Gallup supposedly happened in an airplane. In 1936 Cardinal Eugenio Pacelli soared over Diné Bikéyah. Peering down over the mesas, the man who would soon become Pope Pius XII "wondered how the scattered Indians in the area would be adequately served."[20] Three years later, the new pope established the Gallup diocese for this ministry. Carved out of the Diocese of Tucson and the Archdiocese of Santa Fe, it originally stretched ninety thousand square miles across western New Mexico and northern Arizona. It included a Catholic population of approximately forty thousand that, according to one early Church survey, was 27 percent Native, 58 percent "Spanish American" (sometimes also called "Mexican" in Church records), and 15 percent Anglo.[21]

Although Native Catholics were a minority at its inception, the Diocese of Gallup was created as an "Indian diocese," and its boundaries were drawn with Native peoples and lands in mind. In addition to the nearly thirty-thousand-square-mile Navajo reservation, the diocese's original borders contained lands of the Hualapai, Havasupai, Yavapai, Hopi, Zuni, Acoma, Laguna, and Jicarilla Apache tribes. Unlike other territorial Catholic dioceses in the United States, which nearly all respect the state borders, the Diocese of Gallup crossed the New Mexico–Arizona border, and had (as it still does) an eastern edge that conformed to the edges of the Jicarilla Apache and To'Hajillee reservations.[22]

The official history of the Gallup diocese emphasizes this design, and recounts archbishop of Santa Fe Rudolph Gerken's efforts to plot its shape: "Night after night . . . behind locked doors, . . . Gerken would get out a map and try to figure out how a diocese could be formed that would carry out the Holy See's wishes that the Indians receive better spiritual care."[23] The 1939 apostolic bull that erected the Diocese of Gallup delineated this territory, down to its eastern edge along the 106° 52′ 41″ meridian line, and clarified the need for its creation: "In promoting the good of souls it is of . . . advantage that the limits of dioceses be . . . changed that first of all they may meet the needs of the faithful."[24]

The new "Indian diocese" was an experiment for a US Catholic hierarchy that struggled to divide its attention between caring for white Catholic settlers and caring for Catholic peoples incorporated into the United States via enslavement and imperial subjugation. In the United States, as elsewhere in the world, dioceses were and are the basic architecture for ensuring that adults and children who are Catholic live lives, from birth until death, in close and regular contact with clergy. The first US diocese was established for this work in Maryland in 1789, and US dioceses since then have multiplied along with the expanding US land base, as well as increases in the Catholic population. In short, the history of US diocese creation has paralleled the history of colonial settlement, with new dioceses mirroring settlement patterns of Catholic immigrants from Europe and their descendants.[25]

Dioceses established in territory annexed by the United States, and already home to people who are Catholic, however, are exceptions to this rule. In such cases, the universal diocesan imperative to improve lay access to clergy and the sacraments has paired with a second, extradoctrinal motivation: to improve those people through oversight by religious leaders who are Euro-American or white. These dual imperatives drove the formation of dioceses in territory claimed by the United States as its new Southwest, beginning in the mid-nineteenth century, and it drove the movement of clergy to them from elsewhere in the United States and Europe. The establishments of the Diocese of Santa Fe in 1853 and of the Diocese of Tucson fifty years later are cases in point; the extension of the US diocesan structure across the former territory of Mexico turned upon the recognitions that the Mexican Catholic population incorporated into the United States needed clergy *and* that the best men for that work came from other places.[26]

When the Vatican carved the Diocese of Gallup from those dioceses in 1939, it extended this model to Native Catholics as well. The Gallup diocese "represents a foreign mission field in our country," Archbishop Gerken remarked at its creation. "[It] was primarily established . . . that a bishop might live in the midst of the largest and most populous Indian territory in the United States."[27] Though Gerken chose to describe Gallup as a mission field, the very creation of an "Indian diocese" indicated a transition *away* from missions for Native peoples. This transition made sense in a settler nation that still treated Native Americans as distinct under law but that also, as the twentieth century wore on, anticipated their sure assimilation into US society. Presided over by a resident prelate, and tied securely to a US episcopal hierarchy, the Diocese of Gallup—like southwestern dioceses before it—was the creation of leaders preoccupied with people they sought as full members of a

US Church, but whom they continued to distinguish as needy of special oversight and care. In line with a diocesan formula for care, Native Catholics would benefit from the proliferation of parishes, each staffed by its own pastor. In line with US Catholic practice, those clergy would be white transplants, rather than native to communities they served.

With the erection of the Diocese of Gallup, the coal-and-railroad-fueled border town of Gallup—population seven thousand—was bestowed with the "honor and dignity of an Episcopal City." The following October, Bernard Espelage was installed as bishop at the new Sacred Heart Cathedral, which occupied the second floor of a parochial school there.[28] Espelage, who was a Franciscan with prior experience in the Southwest, traveled to the installation from his province's home in Ohio. During the ceremonies, he expressed his gratitude in Spanish and English to the people who gathered in Gallup to meet him. Later, priests of the diocese "filed into the sanctuary and knelt before their new Bishop to kiss his ring and pledge their fidelity and cooperation in all the work that lies ahead."[29]

After the installation, Espelage surveyed his new see. Most of the priests at work in the region were Franciscans; at first the Gallup diocese contained approximately three dozen religious clergy, but only between six and nine of its own priests. Together these religious and diocesan priests shared responsibility for its existing secular parishes, which numbered between fourteen and twenty-five. The Franciscans also maintained a hundred or so mission churches in its jurisdiction.[30] Tasked with the job of creating more parishes, Espelage bent immediately to the work of raising money to erect churches and finding additional priests to staff them. During his thirty years as prelate, Espelage acquired the title of "Begging Bishop" for his frequent fundraising trips across the country.[31]

His efforts bore results. By the time Espelage submitted his resignation to Pope Paul VI in 1969, he had more than doubled the parishes in the diocese.[32] A decade later, in 1979, the Diocese of Gallup—despite an interim Vatican decision to reduce its territory—included fifty-eight parishes, nearly two dozen of which sat on reservations. By that time, it claimed fifty-two religious priests and forty-nine of its own priests, as well as five secular clergy from other dioceses working within its jurisdiction.[33] Like most US clergy during the twentieth century, the priests in Gallup were nearly all Anglo or white. Of the ninety-six men from this group identifiable by name, eighty had Anglo (i.e., non-Hispanic and not recognizably Native) surnames. Of forty-eight diocesan priests identifiable by name, three-quarters had Anglo surnames.[34] Although it is difficult to determine exactly how many of these men came to Gallup from elsewhere, the tiny local population of Anglo Catholics, along with institutional correspondence from the period, suggests that nearly all of them did.[35] Most would have come from places with large white Catholic communities in the eastern and midwestern United States.

Colonialism and Waste

Settler colonization is "a structure not an event," writes Patrick Wolfe. It is ongoing and is, at all points in time, characterized by the elimination of Native societies and the erection and maintenance of colonial society on expropriated land.[36] Although the United States invaded and claimed Diné Bikéyah in the mid-nineteenth century, the early years of the Gallup diocese corresponded with continued colonization of the region. This midcentury chapter was marked by new forms of Native erasure as the United States' government, its settler population, and its economic system—driven by wealth seeking, and built upon industries of resource extraction and weaponry—made new forays into those lands. The Diocese of Gallup was a Catholic initiative, but it aligned with the colonial forms of its moment.

The twentieth-century colonization of Diné Bikéyah also intersected with US imperialism overseas. The nation's accumulation of global power and influence during the "American Century," between 1940 and 1965, correlated with a federal government more confident than ever in its prerogative to assimilate Native people to the body politic, and committed to a corresponding strategy of terminating tribes. In policy, this translated to weakening federal treaty and trust responsibilities and to the 1956 Indian Relocation Act, which put pressure on individuals to relocate from reservations to urban settings.[37] At the same time—and not coincidentally—as the United States grew its global footprint through brandishing nuclear weapons, public and private interest in uranium changed life on the Navajo reservation. The same year when Espelage became bishop of Gallup, the US government formed a National

Defense Research Committee on Uranium. Soon after, the Manhattan Project transformed the unstable metal into the "most sought-after ore of the twentieth century." This desire for uranium transformed Diné Bikéyah until it was pocked with a thousand mines.[38] Owned and operated by non-Native corporations, these mines used Native labor to operate. They operated in spite of knowledge that uranium extraction correlated with cancers. The toxic radon the mines released poisoned miners, their families, and Navajo people who lived near them.[39]

Writing about uranium mining in Diné Bikéyah, Traci Brynne Voyles demonstrates how places get marked amid colonialism as "marginal, desert, or deserted," and thus suited for resource extraction and attendant environmental degradation.[40] "Remaking Native land as settler home," Voyles explains, involves a "construction of land as either always already belonging to the settler . . . or as undesirable, unproductive, unappealing: in short, as wasteland."[41] Amid this logic, places like Diné Bikéyah became sites "from which resources are . . . extracted and where (often toxic) waste is . . . dumped."[42] This process of wastelanding is racialized and racializing; it depends upon constructing not only places but also humans who live in them as pollutable. Voyles shows how mining in Diné Bikéyah developed in tandem with stories, in Hollywood and elsewhere, that cast Navajo people as symbols of "Indianness" destined to cede way to an atomic future: "Atomic modernity, signifying not only the defense of U.S.-style consumptive capitalism but also, more broadly, a brave new world of technological futurity, emerged on and through stories of Navajos and Navajo country, even as the real material effects of atomic modernity were constituted . . . on Navajo bodies."[43] Voyles offers these circulating stories as parts in a process by which colonized peoples become "themselves wastelanded."[44]

When one looks at the Diocese of Gallup and the mining that developed alongside it, fallout across the projects is hard to ignore. Activists emphasize a correlation between extractive industries and sexual violence against Native people in places where those industries set up shop.[45] Writing about sexual and gender violence that is part of the crisis of missing and murdered Indigenous women, Sherene Razack talks about disposability as a category that spreads between places and people. "There is a cartography that emphasizes disposability," Razack writes. "Victims live and work in areas where there are few services, including lighting and proper transportation (already abandonment); if their bodies are found, they are ... arranged to emphasize that they are garbage to be disposed of."⁴⁶ Native survivors, attorneys, and journalists also invoke a cartography of disposability to explain predator priests among Native communities. In the early 2000s, for example, dozens of Alaska Natives filed lawsuits accusing the Society of Jesus of using Alaska as a "dumping ground" for problem priests.⁴⁷ More recently, a Montana journalist wrote about how "the Catholic Church [has] been accused of using Indian reservations as [its] 'dumping grounds' for the worst recidivist priests."⁴⁸

In the years following its creation, the Gallup diocese also came to resemble a dumping ground. Not all the men whom Espelage and his successors recruited were sexual predators, of course. And of the dozens who *were* later accused of abuse, some had clean (or apparently so) records until they came to the Southwest. A few were even local—born and raised in Latino communities in the region. But many priests did arrive in the Diocese of Gallup after being accused of abuse in other parts of the country. Something similar happened in the neighboring Archdiocese of Santa Fe. Did bishops treat Gallup as a marginal place, where they could deliver priests with little consequence? Certainly, sometimes they did. This was accompanied by a failure to see Latino and Native Catholics as valuable parties in relocation decisions. Attending to the religious logics that organized bishops' decisions, as I do in the next section, does not negate this piece of the story. Rather, it reveals how a Catholic institutional world, governed by an internal code that preserved truths about the Church, and about the specialness of its priests, dovetailed with colonialist estimations of life and land to bring pedophile priests to Diné Bikéyah. Digging into this world, we find a system that moved priests in order to save souls, and doubled down on a commitment to support priests through their own spiritual recoveries.

Scandal and Redemption—a Tale of Two Priests

The transit of "problem" priests to and through the US Southwest was a collective effort, on the part of bishops and clergy both, to avoid the sin of scandal. Preventing scandal—or public disclosure of a priest's sins, sexual or otherwise—protected the stature, credibility, and moral authority of the priesthood. By doing so, it protected laity who relied on priests for salvation, and it cut spiritual losses of priests themselves. A Catholic theology of scandal was first elaborated by Thomas Aquinas in the thirteenth century, and in the centuries following it came to define the spiritual threat posed by rifts between pastors and people in their care.[49] Scandal was offered as a reason for relocating priests guilty of "solicitation" of laity in *Crimen sollicitationis*, a set of instructions issued by the Vatican in 1922 and again in 1962.[50] Following scandal theology, a priest's bad acts became more sinful—additionally sinful—the moment faithful Catholics learned about them. At the moment of revelation, one priest's offense became a "stumbling block" or sin-causing obstacle to faith for an entire community. Simply put, scandal introduced more sin for everyone, priests and ordinary people alike. After a priest raped a child, a well-timed relocation to a distant place could avoid scandal, and in doing so it could save souls.

The stories of two priests who came to Gallup from other places illuminate how scandal—or more accurately, institutional efforts to avoid it—set them on courses through the US Southwest:

Clement Hageman

In 1940, Father Clement Hageman arrived at Smith Lake Indian Mission on the checkerboard of tribal and allotted lands that make up the eastern edge of the Navajo reservation. The thirty-six-year-old priest came originally from Ohio, but he had been ordained into the East Texas Diocese of Corpus Christi. While assistant pastor there during the 1930s, Hageman had abused multiple boys.[51] Hageman was expelled from his home diocese as a result, and he drifted first to Connecticut. Maybe he committed abuse there too; during his time in New Haven, a local pastor wrote to Corpus Christi bishop Emmanuel Ledvina. "It is imperative that something be done for [Hageman]," the priest wrote. "It gives serious scandal . . . to have him living as he is."

This priest urged Ledvina to again relocate his wayward cleric, away from Connecticut, and to find him "some place of refuge."[52] He imagined a site where Hageman might be sheltered from his own reputation. "I am aware," he wrote in a follow-up letter, "that protection often works well with punishment, especially in the case of one whose mental as well as moral condition may easily render him a menace."[53] Ledvina too worried about "possible scandal" Hageman might create. He lamented that Hageman stubbornly refused his advice to apply to the Holy See for laicization.[54]

Three months later, Hageman landed in Smith Lake, prompting Bishop Espelage to contact his counterpart in Corpus Christi. The new bishop of Gallup wanted Hageman for his diocese, but he had heard that Hageman was "guilty of playing with boys." He sought clarification.[55] Ledvina replied by telegram, "BELIEVE MAN MIGHT BE GIVEN A CHANCE WOULD BE IMPOSSIBLE AROUND HERE CASE TOO WELL KNOWN AROUND HERE TRY HIM OUT MAYBE MIGHT PROVE TRUSTWORTHY AT LAST."[56] Thus began Clement Hageman's career in the US Southwest. That career would span four decades, and during it the priest allegedly abused dozens of minors. His mainly Latino victims would later claim he was "dumped" in their "impoverished nonwhite communities by church officials to avoid scandal."[57]

During his decades in the Southwest, Hageman became known as "the Route 66 priest" for his travel along that east-west thoroughfare.[58] Within the Diocese of Gallup, Hageman continued to move, from parish to parish, pushed by the same force that had driven him from Corpus Christi and Connecticut. In 1952, for example, Espelage moved Hageman from Holbrook to Kingman, Arizona, following reports of abuse. "It is not you who is to be considered," the bishop wrote the priest ahead of that move, "but all the Church as a whole. We cannot afford to have any kind of scandal whatever take place.... Should that happen all the good that you have done in Holbrook would be wiped away entirely."[59] A decade later Espelage moved Hageman out of Kingman, again "to prevent any further scandal." This time the bishop acted on reports of Hageman's public intoxication, including one episode in which the priest passed out drunk in especially scandalous fashion, "in front of the Rectory—broad daylight—subject to the stares of passers-by."[60] Hageman went briefly to Utah, but he soon returned to the Gallup diocese, where he remained until his death in 1975.

John Sullivan

John Sullivan arrived in the Diocese of Gallup twenty years after Hageman. Sullivan was ordained in the Diocese of Manchester, New

Hampshire, where his behavior with girls—including impregnating one, then encouraging an abortion—caused scandal. The bishop of Manchester, Matthew Francis Brady, suspended Sullivan from ministry in 1956, in hopes the penalty would make Sullivan "realize your course of constant serious scandal and divert you from it."[61] A year later, Bishop Brady contacted the Servants of the Paraclete. The bishop wrote the order's founder, a priest named Gerald Fitzgerald, and appealed to him to accept Sullivan at the Servants' Via Coeli monastery, tucked in the Jemez Mountains east of Gallup. "I have in the diocese, what is an old story to you, a problem priest for whom I am at a loss to find a place to serve," Brady explained to Fitzgerald. "His problem is not drink, but a series of scandal-causing escapades with young girls.... At times I have considered him insane, diabolically cunning, and again, as at present, sincerely remorseful.... There is no section of the [Manchester] diocese in which he is not known," Brady affirmed.

The bishop hoped Sullivan might minister somewhere else—sheltered, like Hageman before him, from a scandalous reputation. "The solution of [Sullivan's] problem," Brady surmised, "seems to be a fresh start in some diocese where he is not known."[62] Fitzgerald disagreed. The Servants' founder had opened Via Coeli a decade earlier, envisioning a place where troubled priests of all sorts might come—to avoid scandal, yes, but more importantly to devote their days to the penance and spiritual exercise that would restore them from sin to grace. And so Fitzgerald initially refused to receive Sullivan, unless the priest promised to remain in the monastery's confines for life. "A new diocese means only green pastures," Fitzgerald cautioned in his reply to Brady. "I have my own soul to save, and I do not dare recommend such men for the cura animarum."[63]

For five years, Sullivan refused Fitzgerald's precondition. During that time the priest tried, unsuccessfully, to find his own green pastures: seventeen dioceses denied Sullivan's request for a reassignment.[64] He also continued to abuse minors. In 1961, however, Sullivan relented and agreed to go to New Mexico—and by the time he relocated, things at Via Coeli had also changed. Within months Sullivan was permitted to move from the facility into Gallup to substitute for a sick pastor on an "emergency" basis. Despite Fitzgerald's recommendation that Sullivan return promptly to monastic life, Espelage decided to retain him. The

Gallup bishop "hoped to keep [Sullivan]," Fitzgerald now reported, "as he was . . . very much liked by the poor Mexican people among who he was working."[65] The new bishop of Manchester, Ernest Primeau, wrote hurriedly to Espelage, "I am very much concerned about [Sullivan] and the scandal which he has caused and may cause. I cannot assume responsibility for any which may result from your assignment of him to parish work in your diocese."[66] Nevertheless Sullivan remained in Arizona until the early 1980s, and he allegedly abused multiple victims there.

Sullivan's trajectory, from New Hampshire to Via Coeli, and onward to the Diocese of Gallup, shows how the Catholic Church's commitment to avoiding scandal coexisted with a related truth of that institution: that fallen priests remained special people, still able to do special things, and still worthy of extraordinary care. According to Catholic doctrine, priests guilty of sexual sins retained powers bestowed by ordination. And because Catholic sacraments functioned *ex opera operato*—by virtue of the ritual itself, rather than the moral state of the man administering it—even priests who had done despicable things could in theory effectively minister. This doctrine informed John Sullivan's optimism, as he looked for new work during the fifties. I am "constantly reminded of the serious and irreparable damage that I have inflicted upon the Church . . . caused by my many scandals," he wrote to Bishop Brady. "I know . . . that there are not too many Bishops who desire saddling their dioceses with problems such as my many weaknesses unfortunately tend to present." But some badly needed help, Sullivan rationalized, and so he petitioned his bishop to release him for ministry elsewhere. "I consulted the Catholic Directory, and . . . there are some Western Dioceses that are in need of priests," he wrote. "This decision . . . will first of all please God, and at the same time enable me to piece together my broken priesthood."[67] In this Sullivan read his cards right; ultimately the same logic informed Espelage's acceptance of the priest, despite his known risk, into the Gallup diocese.

The value of the priesthood, regardless of the acts of men inhabiting it, was expressed most perfectly in the Servants of the Paraclete mission, and in the spacious and irrigated grounds of Via Coeli. Fitzgerald created the Servants because he identified a need. A priest, he understood, carried the dignity of his office at all stages, and deserved to be treated thus. "The fallen priest is yet capable of resurrection, and . . . is treated in the Paraclete program as the sorrowful Mother treated the lifeless Body of her Son," he explained in a 1962 letter to the Vatican. "We aim to respect in the individual the priesthood which . . . he may not respect."[68] Via Coeli offered monastic seclusion; Fitzgerald created it to be a place where priests could devote their lives to prayer, along with physical healing, to achieve their souls' sanctification. "Returning a priest to grace, not necessarily returning him to the active ministry, was the essence of rehabilitation to Father Gerald," one former Servant explained. "A priest out of favor with the Church could not obtain salvation."[69] By the mid-sixties, however, the Servants' strategy—or what the order offered as the path to "fixing broken priesthoods"—shifted in a devastating way. Relying upon new psychological therapies, the Servants began to partner with bishops to reintroduce "guests" to ministry in nearby parishes, as part of a program of "graduated rehabilitation." "The men must be prudently tried on various social levels if their rehabilitation was to be complete," a staff psychologist for the Servants now explained. "The dignity and integrity of the human person demanded this."[70]

Of course, when the Servants reintroduced abusive priests to ministry, they did so at the expense of people in parishes where those men relocated. At least a half-dozen priests, and likely more, later accused of abuse within the Diocese of Gallup made their way into its churches via the Jemez Springs monastery. Within the Archdiocese of Santa Fe, which actually encompasses the Jemez region and Via Coeli itself, the number of former residents accused of abuse is higher still.

"New Mexico is in the middle of nowhere," explained one attorney representing abuse victims. "If you want to store nuclear waste, you do it here. If you want to set off nuclear bombs, you do it here. If you need a place to send pedophiles, well, there's always New Mexico."[71] In the US Southwest, the dumping-ground model moves easily across contexts, from environmental wastelanding to the depositing of clerical refuse. When it does, it speaks powerfully to the devastating effects of Catholic sexual abuse in this region, relative to other places; just as wastelanding produced extraordinary toxicities of air, soil, and water, so an extraordinary number of toxic priests lived and worked there, relative to a small Catholic population. At the same time, however, to suggest that the Catholic Church sought to discard priests in the US Southwest overlooks the religious logic that governed decisions bishops, superiors, and priests themselves made about relocations from east to west. By the rules of this institutional Catholic world, priests moved to Diné Bikéyah and adjacent lands during the twentieth century not because they were waste, but rather because they were—all of them, sinful and not—so very special. The exclusive part clergy played in the scheme of salvation, and the accompanying care lavished upon them by the Church and its actors, were orienting points in a coherently Catholic system that moved priests to the US Southwest. In this way, the Catholic character of the institution, and not simply its entanglements with US systems of politics, economy, and race, resulted in the proliferation of sexual violence among colonized people.

NOTES

1. Early material from this chapter appeared in a short essay for *The Revealer*. See Kathleen Holscher, "Priests That Moved: Catholicism, Colonized Peoples, and Sex Abuse in the U.S. Southwest," *The Revealer*, March 2, 2020, https://therevealer.org (accessed November 23, 2020).
2. Pelotte (Abenaki) was appointed coadjutor bishop of Gallup in 1986. Charles J. Chaput (Prairie Band Potawatomi) was appointed bishop of Rapid City in 1988, as the first Native ordinary bishop. Pelotte became bishop of Gallup in 1990.
3. Donald E. Pelotte, "The Call to Be a Bishop in a Native American Diocese," *Proceedings of the Catholic Theological Society of America* 62, 170, https://ejournals.bc.edu.
4. Pelotte, "The Call to Be a Bishop in a Native American Diocese," 171.
5. Elizabeth Hardin-Burrola, "Local Panel Names Sexually Abusive Priests," *Gallup Independent*, May 20, 2003, www.bishop-accountability.org (accessed November 18, 2020).
6. Elizabeth Hardin-Burrola, "Bishop Talks with Victims of Abuse, Outreach to Native Victims Is Discussed," *Gallup Independent*, May 9, 2005, www.bishop-accountability.org (accessed November 18, 2020). See also Elizabeth Hardin-Burrola, "Bishop Apologizes for Abuse," *Gallup Independent*, September 20, 2005, www.bishop-accountability.org (accessed November 18, 2020).
7. Elizabeth Hardin-Burrola, "Diocese of Gallup to File for Bankruptcy," *Gallup Independent*, September 3, 2013, www.bishop-accountability.org (accessed November 18, 2020).
8. Number is current as of November 2020, and is a sum of discrete names published by the diocese and BishopAccountability.Org. See "Credibly Accused List, Updated August 2, 2019," Diocese of Gallup, https://dioceseofgallup.org (accessed November 18, 2020); "Database of Publicly Accused Priests in the United States, Bishop-Accountability.Org, http://bishop-accountability.org (accessed November 18, 2020).
9. "Credibly Accused List."

10 Comparisons based upon number of publicly accused individuals in each diocese, to date, relative to the historical Catholic population of that diocese. Catholic population data taken from 1976, a year representing a near high point for reported incidents of abuse nationally. Publicly accused individuals collected from diocesan published lists and BishopAccountability.Org. Catholic population data taken from www.Catholic-Hierarchy.org. For national count of incidents by year of alleged occurrence, see *The Nature and Scope of Sexual Abuse of Minors by Catholic Priests and Deacons in the United States, 1950–2002*, Research Study Conducted by the John Jay College of Criminal Justice (Washington, DC: United States Conference of Catholic Bishops, 2004), 28. In Gallup and elsewhere, the high per capita rate of predators does *not* necessarily translate to more predators per resident priests; in fact—as this essay argues—a key part of the explanation for the high number of predators relative to Native populations is higher than "normal" numbers of priests imported to serve them.

11 Deer, *The Beginning and End of Rape*, x.

12 See A. Simpson, "The State Is a Man"; M. Goeman, "Ongoing Storms and Struggles"; A. Smith, *Conquest*. See also the August 2016 special issue in *Canadian Journal of Women and the Law* 28.2 (2016).

13 Deer, *The Beginning and End of Rape*, 61; A. Smith, *Conquest*, 293.

14 On the relationship of the Catholic Church to US imperialism, see Martinez, *Catholic Borderlands*; Moran, *The Imperial Church*. On resonances between Catholicism and secular imperialism, see Willie James Jennings, "Binding Landscapes: Secularism, Race, and the Spatial Modern," in Kahn and Lloyd, eds., *Race and Secularism in America*.

15 See Bauman, *Wasted Lives*; Voyles, *Wastelanding*.

16 See Rinere, "The Exercise of *Cura Animarum* through the Twentieth Century and Beyond." The Church's 1917 Code of Canon Law elaborated activities reserved for the priest, from solemn baptism to extreme unction for the dying. "In the broad sense," Renere explains, *cura animarum* was "understood as that care which a pastor of the Church ... gave to individuals in his charge which brought about the salvation of their souls" (33).

17 Tweed, *Crossing and Dwelling*, 62.

18 See Weber, *The Spanish Frontier in North America*. Franciscans focused on Pueblo peoples in the region, and did not establish permanent missions among the Diné until 1898.

19 For a summary of Franciscan missions to the Navajo at the turn of the twentieth century, see Vecsey, *On the Padres' Trail*, 209–14. See also Bodo, *Tales of an Enishodi*.

20 Elizabeth Kelly, *Diocese of Gallup Golden Jubilee, 1939–1989* (Albuquerque, NM: Starline Publishing, 1989), 9.

21 "Explanatory Breakdown of the Diocese of Gallup," Folder on Gallup Diocese 1940–1941; 1943; 1956–1957; 1962–1964; 1967–1971; 1973–1974; 1976, Archives of the Archdiocese of Santa Fe, Santa Fe, New Mexico.

22 The To'Hajillee reservation is a noncontiguous part of the Navajo Nation.
23 Kelly, *Diocese of Gallup*, 9.
24 "Translation of the Apostolic Bull 'Ad bonum animarum' for the erection of the Diocese of Gallup," Folder on Gallup Diocese, Archives of the Archdiocese of Santa Fe, Santa Fe, New Mexico.
25 The Roman Catholic Church in the United States is currently comprised of 177 territorial dioceses. US territories overseas are served by dioceses that are part of other (non-US) Catholic episcopal conferences, including those in Puerto Rico, American Samoa, and Guam.
26 The Diocese of Santa Fe was created in 1853, four years after the United States annexed Mexican territory via the Treaty of Guadalupe Hidalgo. The first bishop of Santa Fe, Jean-Baptiste Lamy, imported priests and religious from across the United States and Europe to build and staff parishes and schools for New Mexico's inhabitants. While Lamy saw himself as an institution builder in a region where Catholicism had collapsed, the reality is more complicated. Robert Wright has shown how Lamy's cadre of imported priests displaced New Mexican clergy who were increasing in number in years prior to the creation of the diocese. Wright, "How Many Are 'a Few'?"
27 Qtd. in "Indian Capital Becomes a Bishopric," *Indian Sentinel* 20.9 (November 1940): 141–42.
28 United States Department of Commerce, *Sixteenth Census of the United States: 1940, Population*, vol. 1, www2.census.gov (accessed March 4, 2020), 699.
29 "The Mission Travel Club: Installation Issue," *Travelling the Padres' Trail* (November 1940), Folder on the Diocese of Gallup, Archives of the Archdiocese of Santa Fe, Santa Fe, New Mexico.
30 "Explanatory Breakdown of the Diocese of Gallup." See also "Diocese of Gallup," *The Official Catholic Directory* (New York: P.J. Kenedy, 1940), 371–72. These numbers vary between sources; according to *The Official Catholic Directory* of 1940, the diocese had six secular priests and fourteen churches with resident priests.
31 Kelly, *Diocese of Gallup*, 11.
32 Kelly, *Diocese of Gallup*, 12.
33 *The Official Catholic Directory* (New York: P.J. Kenedy, 1979), 336. See also Vecsey, *On the Padres' Trail*, 213.
34 *The Official Catholic Directory* (New York: P.J. Kenedy, *1979*). Of the men accused of abuse, more than three-quarters had Anglo surnames, and more than half were secular priests.
35 Espelage's successor, Bishop Jerome Hastrich, was criticized by Archbishop Robert Sanchez of Santa Fe for importing unqualified men in an effort to grow diocesan priests during the seventies: "[Hastrich] presently is supporting seminarians around the country, as well as outside of America. Many of his clergy . . . question this policy of importing priests, as well as their qualifications to serve the Indian and Mexican-American." "Report on the Gallup Diocese," submitted by

Archbishop of Santa Fe Robert Sanchez to apostolic delegate Jean Jadot, January 5, 1976, Folder on the Diocese of Gallup, Archives of the Archdiocese of Santa Fe, Santa Fe, New Mexico.

36. Wolfe, "Settler Colonialism and the Elimination of the Native."
37. On termination-era policies, see Dunbar-Ortiz, *An Indigenous Peoples' History*, 170–74.
38. Voyles, *Wastelanding*, 2–3.
39. Brugge and Goble, "The History of Uranium Mining and the Navajo People."
40. Voyles, *Wastelanding*, 19.
41. Voyles, *Wastelanding*, 7.
42. Voyles, *Wastelanding*, 9.
43. Voyles, *Wastelanding*, 91.
44. Voyles, *Wastelanding*, 15.
45. See Nick Martin, "The Connection between Pipelines and Sexual Violence," *New Republic*, October 15, 2019, https://newrepublic.com (accessed November 7, 2020); "Man Camps Fact Sheet," Honor the Earth, www.honorearth.org (accessed November 7, 2020).
46. Razack, "Gendering Disposability," 297.
47. See, e.g., Scott Michels, "Lawsuit: Alaska Villages 'Dumping Ground' for Abusive Priests," *ABCNews*, January 21, 2009, https://abcnews.go.com (accessed November 3, 2020).
48. Seaborn Larson, "Montana Reservations Reportedly 'Dumping Grounds' for Predatory Priests," *Great Falls Tribune*, August 16, 2017, www.greatfallstribune.com (accessed November 3, 2020).
49. See Senander, *Scandal*; Carter, *Scandal in the Parish*. In his *Summa Theologica*, Aquinas defined scandal as "something less rightly done or said, that occasions another's spiritual downfall." See *Summa Theologica*, 2nd ed., translated by Laurence Shapcote of the Fathers of the English Dominican Province (Chicago: Encyclopaedia Britannica, 1990): II-II, Q.43.
50. "Instruction on the Manner of Proceeding in Cases Involving the Crime of Solicitation," The Vatican, www.vatican.va (accessed October 20, 2021). See also John L. Allen Jr., "1962 Document Orders Secrecy in Sex Cases," *National Catholic Reporter*, August 7, 2003, www.natcath.org (accessed October 20, 2021); John F. Wirenius, "'Command and Coercion': Clerical Immunity, Scandal, and the Sex Abuse Crisis in the Roman Catholic Church," *Journal of Law and Religion* 27, no. 2 (2011–12): 423–94.
51. D. A. Laning to E. B. Ledvina, April 24, 1939, BA-Gallup-Hageman-133–134.pdf, BishopAccountability.Org, www.bishop-accountability.org/documents/ (accessed November 30, 2020). BishopAccountability.Org is also a physical archive, located in Waltham, Massachusetts. BishopAccountability.Org pdf documents listed in this note and hereafter can be accessed electronically by combining the document's pdf citation with the following prefix: www.bishop-accountability.org/documents/.

52 M. Ernest Wilson to E. B. Ledvina, September 14, 1940, BA-Gallup-Hageman-126–127.pdf, BishopAccountability.Org (accessed November 30, 2020).
53 M. Ernest Wilson to E. B. Ledvina, September 21, 1940, BA-Gallup-Hageman-124.pdf, BishopAccountability.Org (accessed November 30, 2020).
54 E. B. Ledvina to D. A. Laning, April 25, 1939, BA-Gallup-Hageman-132.pdf, BishopAccountability.Org (accessed November 30, 2020); E. B. Ledvina to Maurice Francis McAuliffe, September 23, 1940, BA-Gallup-Hageman-121–122.pdf (accessed November 30, 2020).
55 Bernard Espelage to E. B. Ledvina, December 16, 1940, BA-Gallup-Hageman-120.pdf, BishopAccountability.Org (accessed November 30, 2020).
56 E. B. Ledvina to Bernard Espelage, December 21, 1940, BA-Gallup-Hageman-119.pdf, BishopAccountability.Org (accessed November 30, 2020).
57 Dan Frosch, "Accusations of Abuse by Priest Dating to Early 1940s," *New York Times*, July 10, 2011, www.nytimes.com (accessed November 6, 2020).
58 Elizabeth Hardin-Burrola, "Route 66 Clergy Abuse: Gallup Diocese Still Battling Arizona Sex Case," *Gallup Independent*, July 30 2012, www.bishop-accountability.org (accessed November 7, 2012).
59 Bernard Espelage to Clement A. Hageman, October 28, 1952, BA-Gallup-Hageman-088.pdf, BishopAccountability.Org (accessed November 30, 2020).
60 Eugene J. McCarthy to Bernard Espelage, September 7, 1961, BA-Gallup-Hageman-056.pdf, BishopAccountability.Org (accessed November 30, 2020); Bernard Espelage to Clement A. Hageman, November 12, 1963, BA-Gallup-Hageman-050.pdf, BishopAccountability.Org (accessed November 30, 2020).
61 M. F. Brady to John T. Sullivan, July 11, 1956, BA-Machester-Discover-6–267.pdf, BishopAccountability.Org (accessed November 25, 2020).
62 M. F. Brady to Gerald Fitzgerald, BA-Manchester-Discover-6–280.pdf, BishopAccountability.Org (accessed November 25, 2020).
63 Gerald Fitzgerald to M. F. Brady, September 26, 1957, BA-Manchester-Discovery-6-278-279.pdf, BishopAccountability.Org (accessed November 25, 2020).
64 See, e.g., Hilary Baumann Hacker, Bishop of Bismark, to M. F. Brady, December 18, 1957, BA-Manchester-Discovery-6–307.pdf, BishopAccountability.Org (accessed November 25, 2020).
65 Gerald Fitzgerald to E. J. Primeau, September 13, 1961, BA-Manchester-Discovery-6–381.pdf, BishopAccountability.Org (accessed November 25, 2020).
66 E. J. Primeau to Berard Espelage, October 16, 1961, BA-Manchester-Discovery-6–382.pdf, BishopAccountability.Org (accessed November 25, 2020).
67 John T. Sullivan to M. F. Brady, September 14, 1957, BA-Manchester-Discovery-6-281-282.pdf, BishopAccountability.Org (accessed November 25, 2020).
68 Fr. Gerald Fitzgerald, S.P., "Oasi Eucaristica, Servi Dei S. Paraclito," BA-Servants-of-the-Paraclete-0012-0016.pdf, BishopAccountability.Org (accessed November 23, 2020).
69 "Affidavit of John Feit," BA-Servants-of-the-Paraclete-6156-6176.pdf, BishopAccountability.Org (accessed November 23, 2020).

70 Meeting minutes, February 20, 1967, Albuquerque, NM, BA-Servants-of-the-Paraclete-2502-2505.pdf, BishopAccountability.Org (accessed November 23, 2020).

71 Bruce Pasternak quoted in Rich Henson, "Sex-Abuse Suits Jolt N.M. Archdiocese," *Philadelphia Inquirer*, January 17, 1994, www.bishop-accountability.org (accessed January 5, 2021).

11

Fire from Heaven

Napalm, the Drone, and Evangelical Territoriality in the Age of Empire

JONATHAN EBEL

This chapter explores the relationship of White evangelical Christians to American empire through napalm and the drone. My argument is that each of these weapons reflects an imperial territoriality shared by White evangelicalism, and threatens and punishes in accordance with notions of judgment dear to White evangelicals of the twentieth and twenty-first centuries. Harmony between these weapons and White evangelical approaches to a world they often depict as fallen and hostile shaped the logic of acceptance around two exercises of American imperial power: the Vietnam War and the ongoing wars against terrorist networks. But as the drone has changed the way imperial violence is waged and perceived, it has also troubled evangelical understandings of the White male body at war. Put another way, the ascendancy of the armed drone and the related emphasis on the body as territory have fed evangelical nostalgia for more intimate, more symmetrical approaches to war.

Through transitions in military sensibilities and myriad exercises of American power, evangelical support for the military has remained strong. This pro-military posture is most often expressed as reverence for the American soldier. But it also, necessarily, involves affection for the weapons soldiers use. By focusing this discussion on weapons, and by treating weapons as instances of theological discourse, I hope to move discussions of religion and war beyond the overly comfortable topic of soldierly suffering and sacrifice. Weapons force us to consider how American soldiers kill, damage, injure, and do the work of empire that most White evangelicals—indeed most Protestants—do not often discuss. This is historically and morally important. The military-industrial, imperial-religious situation in which we Americans find ourselves was not a given. It came from somewhere and was moved and shaped by forces we sometimes struggle to see. If we are to understand its making and, perhaps, imagine its unmaking, we must think about how American faiths have been interwoven with the science, the industry, and the territorial aims of war.

My approach to napalm and the armed drone has been shaped by recent histories of each, Robert Neer's *Napalm: An American Biography* and Christopher Fuller's *See It/Shoot It: The Secret History of the CIA's Lethal Drone Program*; by the private papers and public writings of napalm's inventor, Louis Fieser; and by the blossoming scholarship on and journalistic coverage of drones and drone warfare. The works of Derek Gregory, Lisa Hajjar, Andrea Miller, Keith Feldman, and the legal scholar Gabriella Blum have been especially useful.[1] I will return many times to Blum's essay on "The Individualization of War," which illuminates a different side of shifting territorialities, and to Andrea Miller's argument regarding the criminalization of interior states and the "always already present" terrorist in the "racialized Muslim body." As a group, though, these scholars and others involved in critical security studies have not engaged religion as a category of analysis, or even as a relevant factor in their inquiries.[2] Additionally, with the exception of Gabriella Blum, who traces a cultural, legal, and affective shift in understandings of whom we are at war with, these scholars engage drones and drone warfare as if they are their own context. This essay argues that religion has mattered and will continue to matter in the shaping of imperial military norms, aspirations, and apologetics, and that an important aspect of the religious history of any weapon is its relationship to other weapons and to wider sensibilities regarding war and enmity.

I come to this project shaped by other conversations as well. For eleven years—four on active duty—I served as an intelligence officer in the US Navy. For two and a half years, I was attached to an electronic attack squadron, where I was often involved in strike planning. This is the process by which knowledge about the operational capabilities and patterns of an adversary, along with known and inferred vulnerabilities, become executable plans to disable and destroy targets. An important stage of this process was studying the area surrounding a potential target, both to give air crews a sense of visible landmarks and to help determine whether the target could be struck without taking innocent life or destroying protected structures. Everyone involved in this process understood that perfect precision was a tall order. But we tried to plan well, and the aircrews tried to train well, and we prayed (some of us literally) that if our plans became reality, our actions and our weapons would bring injury to as few people as possible.

I served on active duty from 1993 until 1997, twenty years after napalm became a pariah weapon, and well before armed drones became an operational reality. I served before, to borrow from Gabriella Blum, the possibility of extreme precision created expectations of extreme precision. But we were already practicing a form of war in which precision mattered, in which the call for *in bello* discrimination rang loudly in our ears. We were also already practicing war as performance. For reasons both tactical and strategic, footage of strikes was incredibly valuable. For intel personnel, it was our most reliable means of immediate bomb-damage assessment. For other consumers, footage was proof of American military potency. If we could send a bomb down a three-foot-by-three-foot air vent from five thousand feet, what couldn't we do?

What strike footage was not was individualized. That is, the subject of the footage was the subject of the strike: a building, a bunker, a communication station. Individualizing aerial bombardment would have been a technological impossibility for us, and, in any event, our plans were formulated against nations and governments, not against individuals. I worked within a culture that thought about nations as systems that might, at some future time, need to be shut down for a period of days or weeks in order to achieve an objective. What eyes could we blind? What communication nodes could we shut down? How could we achieve maximum disabling effect with minimum physical and long-term infrastructural harm?

I offer this as background to an essay that seeks to make religious sense of napalm and the armed drone; the former weapon antithetical to the mission I knew, the latter its very apotheosis. I offer this also because, in retrospect and with the help of Blum's analysis of international law, I see more clearly that we were working at the beginning of a transition period vis-à-vis American understandings of war. We were moving away from the idea of war being fought against a collective, and toward a more "cosmopolitan" model, in which war is fought against individuals. According to Blum, this transition, which is now all but complete, has made the waging of war into police work—the pursuit of suspect individuals—and has elevated the *in bello* profile of civilians and their *in bello*/postbellum rights, separating them further than just-war thinking already did from complicity in a collective war effort, and re-centering military missions and global assessments of success or failure around responsibility for and to civilian populations in zones of war. Blum writes, "Modern aversion to war strengthened . . . the individualized view of legitimate violence: if war was ever to be tolerated, it would have to be not only a last resort but also as narrowly tailored as possible to be directed only against those most deserving of it. When carried out, it must distinguish with the utmost precision between the innocent and those who must be 'neutralized,' 'frustrated,' and, only begrudgingly, 'killed.'"[3] It is historically and morally important to name this transition, to note that the waging of war on behalf of American empire today, while still very much war and still tragically costly in human terms, is orders of magnitude more attuned to the innocence or the culpability of individuals than it was thirty years ago. There are many things to lament and to criticize about drone warfare. The desire to be precise, to discriminate, to limit deadly violence, is not one of them.[4]

Territoriality, Empire, and Evangelicalism

Territoriality in this essay simply means the ways that we conceive of the possession and control of territory, the different ways that individuals, leaders, and collectives can be territorial. The relationship of territoriality to empire or nation-state is obvious, if not always simple.[5] If an empire is to be anything, it must be territorial. It must demarcate and control territory. It must also acknowledge, perhaps only tacitly, nonpossession of territories beyond its reach. Cyberscapes, crypto-currencies, and armies of Internet trolls challenge us to imagine territory, possession, and control more expansively, but in so doing they underscore a fundamental truth of empire: uncontrolled territory is threatening territory.

The relationship between territoriality and evangelicalism is more complicated. One could argue that the two terms are antithetical. Territoriality is earthly, limited, and often tribal. Evangelicalism—not to mention Christianity more broadly—aspires to transcend tribes, limits, and earth. American evangelicals have, in the past, preached the need to subordinate earthly realms and modes of power to heavenly ones. Sometimes they still do. Yet there is no denying that evangelicals exist in time and place, involve themselves in multiple collectivities, and are shaped by complex allegiances. It should be no surprise, then, that American evangelicals express American imperial territorialities and weave them into and around their faith. This interweaving has yielded at least two distinct evangelical territorialities in the United States: a territoriality of borders and a territoriality of bodies. Though its genealogy is complex, the territoriality of borders is most clearly connected to the chosen-nation strain in American mythology, to westward expansion, and to international politics in the twentieth century.[6] Read in an imperial register, an evangelical territoriality of borders imagines persistent, grave threats to the homeland, assumes the righteousness of American foreign action, construes global expansionism as national missionary work, and supports the development and deployment of a military capable of confronting and containing evil. The starkest examples of the territoriality of borders come from the middle decades of the twentieth century: World War II, the Korean War, the Vietnam War, and the long Cold War. These conflicts were characterized by the view that virtue and vice, salvation and perdition, had a great deal to do with the nation-state within whose borders one lived.

The territoriality of bodies connects most directly to the intensely individualized soteriology of evangelicalism and America's individualist traditions. A focus on the body as territory to possess and control reflects pietist traditions of introspection and self-critique, the Arminian emphasis on the role of the will and individual action in attaining God's grace, and the influence of holiness teachings regarding victory over sin.[7] But this territoriality—given life in missionary work, conversion narratives, and attempts to legislate morality—also interacts with empire. It provides supporting logic for the vengeful treatment of suspected terrorists, for the targeting of Muslim men suspected of supporting Islamist/jihadist movements, and for legally and morally dubious programs of individualized preemption. But a territoriality of the body can also—in theory, at least—break down generalizations and bring nuance to evangelical engagements with global communities.[8] Since the earliest days of global missions, White evangelical missionaries have taken seriously the possibility that a person, a body, can be saved, claimed, and controlled—not necessarily in that order—irrespective of where on earth she or he lives. For much of White evangelical history, the kingdom of God has had no borders.[9]

These territorialities under different names figure prominently in recent scholarship on American empire and, specifically, on drone warfare. They are not presented with the same scholarly analysis within evangelical discourse, but the similarities are clear. Moreover, the convergence of the two literatures is mutually illuminating, and shows that weapons have their own religious logics, which convince and appeal. If napalm can be said to have made real the fires of hell for the damned, the drone can be said to vivify fantasies of omniscience and to operationalize bespoke divine judgment. Framed biblically, napalm situates evangelicals alongside the Israelites in the worship of a God who calls for unrelenting collective punishment, while the drone places evangelicals alongside the Psalmist in praise of a God of whom it can be said,

> You have searched me and known me!
> You know when I sit down and when I rise up;
>   you discern my thoughts from afar.
> You search out my path and my lying down
>   and are acquainted with all my ways.
> Even before a word is on my tongue,
>   behold, O Lord, you know it altogether.[10]

Napalm, the Drone, and Imperial Discourse

If the strength of America's empire has been tested seriously since the middle of the twentieth century, it has been in the rice paddies, jungles, and cities of Vietnam, and in the mountain passes of the tribal regions of Afghanistan, the streets of Fallujah, and Africa's diverse topographies. The Vietnam War left the United States, in Robert Bellah's words, "bewildered and unnerved" because it demonstrated the limits of the nation's "terrible power" when it came to controlling territory.[11] In Vietnam, the US arsenal featured napalm, an incendiary jelly created by combining aluminum naphthenate and palmitic acid.[12] Throughout America's twenty-first-century wars, that arsenal has included armed drones, the most significant advancement in weaponry since the machine gun. The use of napalm in Vietnam was greatly facilitated by aerial superiority that was convincing though not complete. Armed American drones operate in the skies over every theater of conflict today, vulnerable to little other than malfunction.

Though separated by decades of technological advances, napalm and the armed drone participate in imperial discourses that are technological, vertical, punitive, and missionary. That is, these weapons make empire evident by using designs and systems more advanced than what enemy forces develop and deploy; they drive home this superiority with attacks that move from high spaces to low spaces, from the realm of the winged to that of the earthbound. From on high, they categorize, judge, and punish.[13] But they punish differently, on the basis of different notions of guilt. Napalm is inherently indiscriminate. Its judgment and its punishment are collective. The armed drone is designed to be intensely discriminate, to punish on the basis of an individualized judgment, based sometimes on exhaustively chronicled activities, sometimes on life patterns, sometimes on activities categorized as suspect.[14]

Punishing violence is not, however, the entirety of either weapon's message. Each operates also as part of an imperial missionary network. Each speaks to nations and people of the cost of stiff-necked resistance and urges those below to find salvation in surrender. The discourses of power carried in these weapons have obvious theological resonances. It is a small step from their expression of technological superiority, their verticality, and the spectacle of their punishments—fiery and engulfing, frighteningly precise—to thoughts of divinity.

Napalm and a Territoriality of Borders

Napalm is a weapon of collective judgment created for a world defined by a territoriality of borders and for wars conceived as intercollective enterprises. Napalm's operational life began in 1943 in the Pacific theater of World War II. It was developed and patented by Harvard chemist Louis Fieser in the early stages of American involvement in the war. It was easy to produce, it was safe to transport, and it burned ferociously. Fieser and his team also developed fusing and a means of delivery that maximized napalm's incendiary potential. And once the burning began, especially in the population centers of Japan where wood was a common construction material, it did not stop until nearly everything was ash. The fires started by napalm burned hot and indiscriminately. All living within Japan's borders were condemned by those borders, damned to burn in their unredeemed nation. The connection of this fiery vision of judgment to American evangelicalism requires no elaboration.

In the final year of the war in the Pacific, the United States dropped fourteen thousand tons of napalm on Japan, destroying sixty-four Japanese cities and killing close to one million Japanese civilians. Historian Robert Neer describes the inferno that consumed Tokyo on March 9, 1945: "No one was spared. Seizo Hashimoto was thirteen years old. He saw a woman, dressed in a red kimono with gold and silver threads . . . perhaps a geisha, seized by a firestorm, whipped and twisted in the air, and ignited: a human torch. . . . 'In the dense smoke, where the wind was so hot it seared the lungs, people struggled, then burst into flames where they stood. The fiery air was blown down toward the ground and it was often the refugees' feet that began burning first.'" A woman burned to death as she delivered a baby, "filthy and burned in the face but alive."[15]

While fire engulfed Tokyo below, "updrafts flipped some of the giant airplanes [above], and bounced others up a third of a mile in seconds." Pilot Robert Morgan recalled, "The updrafts brought with them a sickening odor, an odor that I will never be able to get completely out of my nostrils—the smell of roasting human flesh. I later learned that some pilots and crewmen gagged and vomited in reaction to this stench."[16] By the time the fires had burned themselves out in Tokyo, as many as 124,000 civilians were dead. US Army Air Corps pilots used napalm to create similar infernos in sixty-three more cities before Japan surrendered. Looking back on that bombing campaign and his role in planning it, former secretary of defense Robert McNamara commented, "We were behaving like war criminals."[17]

Napalm saw heavier action in the Korean conflict. This war of borders crossed, reestablished, and crossed again offered ample opportunity to rain terror on the damned. In the space of three years of combat, the United States used over thirty-two thousand tons of napalm on military and civilian targets across the peninsula. Witnesses described heat so intense that it incinerated people where they stood and left survivors, crisp flesh dangling from their bodies, begging to be shot. Napalm attacks burned Pyongyang so thoroughly that only two of its buildings survived intact. North Korean and Chinese troops allegedly attempted to surrender to the aircraft that delivered the hellish substance.[18]

The horrific burning brought to East Asia by napalm made theological sense as part of the "great Manichean confrontation of East and West, the confrontation of democracy and 'the false philosophy of Communism,'" as a critical Robert Bellah wrote. Napalm expressed midcentury ideas about virtue and vice being demarcated by borders, fences, and walls. It showed the cost of life on the other side, the suffering that awaited those who embraced the sinful godlessness of communism. Billy Graham put it bluntly: "Communism is a fanatical religion that has declared war on the Christian God.... The [communist] program of world conquest is moving ahead at a steady pace.... We are being gradually encircled."[19] Napalm brought hell to homogenized, dehumanized collectives whose goal, the story went, was to surge over old borders, swallow nations, defeat the Christian God, and enslave God's chosen people. Napalm marked in immediately recognizable ways the border between the righteous and the damned.

Perhaps the challenge of identifying and maintaining borders in Vietnam helps to explain the breathtaking use of napalm there. Between 1962 and 1973, the United States and South Vietnamese allies used "about 388,000 tons of napalm," roughly ten times the amount used in Korea and twenty times the amount used to burn Japan.[20] In the communist-aligned forces fighting in Vietnam, American soldiers faced devotees of "a fanatical religion," fighters against "the Christian God" who, though supplied from the North, moved with relative ease across borders and found succor among residents of the South. There were, no doubt, strategic and tactical rationales for using napalm so heavily, but a theological rationale sat just below the surface. Without discrete and stable borders within which to unleash the fires of napalm, napalm itself could create those borders and make distinctions that were otherwise difficult to maintain, between good and evil, chosen and unchosen, friend and enemy.

A territoriality of borders is, however, difficult to maintain in light of the humanizing power of the media-sphere and, sometimes too, in light of evangelical soteriology. There is no better example of this than the "napalm girl" photo taken in 1972 by Nick Ut. The girl, Kim Phuc, is one of five children in the frame fleeing a napalm attack on their village carried out by the South Vietnamese Air Force. The village in which they lived may have harbored Viet Cong. Someone may have deemed it strategically or tactically important to mark that village as damned. But it is hard to consider those children as part of an encircling force, threatening American empire, attacking the Christian God. This was one moment among many that problematized the category of "enemy civilian" and argued for an approach to war defined by Blum's "cosmopolitan individualism," concern for the rights and the well-being of civilians living in a war zone, and the related territoriality of the body.

Still, a territoriality of borders animated evangelical political engagements, domestic and international, beyond Vietnam and through the Cold War. Writing in *The Unfinished War*, Walter Capps recounted how evangelicals embraced a territoriality of borders in the post-Vietnam world. Napalm was no longer burning villages and jungles, but it was not difficult to see the dividing line between the blessed and the damned. "The beliefs and actions of Dr. Jerry Falwell blend a re-enumeration of conservative or fundamentalist religious themes with a strong appeal to patriotism, frequently expressed in highly militaristic terminology. Indeed, the context within which Falwell is calling Christians to show allegiance to the Gospel is one in which the forces of good and evil are competing against each other from diametrically opposite positions. When these forces are then identified with the 'free world' and its adversary, and further as America and Russia... it is evident that the issue behind the Vietnam War continues."[21] The default assumption of this territoriality was and remains that the United States approaches the world from a position of virtue, and that nations that stand against the United States are morally and/or religiously suspect.

Armed Drones and America's Territoriality of the Body

Jerry Falwell promoted the Cold War territoriality of borders as loudly as any White American evangelical. But in the aftermath of the 9/11 attacks, he signaled a different understanding of territoriality. Falwell's jeremiadic reading of those horrors stands as a significant statement of a territoriality of the body. In a moment of national trauma, he focused not on the discontents of Muslim extremists but on his religious and political enemies within the United States. Unregenerate American bodies were, to him, soldiers in an undeclared "war on the Christian God." His conversation with Pat Robertson on *The 700 Club* took place two days after the attacks.

> The ACLU's got to take a lot of blame for this.... And I know that I'll hear from them for this. But throwing God out successfully with the help of the federal court system, throwing God out of the public square.... The abortionists have got to bear some burden for this because God will not be mocked.... I really believe that the pagans, and the abortionists, and the feminists, and the gays and the lesbians who are actively trying to make that an alternative lifestyle, the ACLU, People for the American Way—all of them who have tried to secularize America—I point the finger in their face and say "you helped this happen."

According to Falwell, the actions of this fifth column, advancing religious and political agendas different from his, had caused God to permit a deadly breach of America's borders. "The Lord has protected us so wonderfully these 225 years," Falwell noted, "[and] what we saw on Tuesday, as terrible as it is, could be minuscule if . . . God continues to lift the curtain and allow the enemies of America to give us probably what we deserve."[22]

Falwell's words reflect a consciousness, deeply rooted in evangelical history, of the difference between controlling territory and controlling or converting souls. Additionally, he describes diversity within the borders of God's New Israel as a threat to the righteous and to their empire. There is, Falwell notes, unconquered territory within the already-conquered territory: the territory of the body: the secularist body, the queer body, the pro-choice body. Falwell makes no mention of the Muslim body, but there is no doubt that he found it threatening as well. Writing of law enforcement and the US military, Andrea Miller, Keith Feldman, and Lisa Hajjar underscore the biases, limits, and illogics of American perceptions of Muslim bodies and the injustices—questionable prosecutions, targeted killings—born of those perceptions.

The corollary of accusing bodies within the chosen nation of betraying God and the nation is accepting the possibility that faithful bodies might dwell within a "corrupt" nation. This dialectic captures the challenge faced by the United States in its war against terrorist networks abroad. The enemy, whose bodies are territory to be defeated, is a small subset of a people, whose hearts, minds, and bodies are territory to be won. This is a conundrum of imperial and evangelical territoriality to which the armed drone has been the primary answer.

The armed drone was born in the era of borders, conceived initially to counter terrorist threats present in the 1980s. Iraqi-born Israeli Jew, Abraham Karem, brought his aerospace engineering talents to California in the 1970s, where he and a team of three worked out of his garage and bested the aerospace establishment. While designers inside the military-industrial complex struggled to get unmanned aircraft to stay aloft for two hours, as early as 1981 Karem and his team could keep prototypes flying "for 56 hours at a time." By the mid-1990s, a drone designed by Karem was flying reconnaissance missions over the former Yugoslavia.[23] But implementation was slow. As late as 2002, historian Christopher Fuller reminds us, America's drone warfare architecture consisted of "a temporary base in a small fenced-off section of Ramstein Air Base in Germany, consisting of no more than a satellite antenna . . . a thirty-foot square tent . . . and a couple of porta-potties."[24] Fuller writes further, "By the end of [President Obama's] first term, the hastily improvised system . . . had burgeoned into a crisscrossing network of runways, hangars, and relay stations ranging from Turkey to the Philippines to Afghanistan to the Seychelles . . . aptly dubbed by Ian Shaw a 'Predator empire.'"[25] This empire at the imagined borders of American empire is the realm of inexhaustible watchmen and the world's most patient hunters.

And it is this hunting that I want to examine as an expression of evangelical territoriality. Not just the killing, but the approach to killing: from on high, sensed but not seen, intensely personal.[26] The drone and its aptly named Hellfire missiles create the opposite of a conversion experience. It is the hand of Jonathan Edwards's angry God letting fly the storied arrow into the sinner's heart. In contrast to the uncontrolled fires of napalm, the drone punishes a small subset of a community, a single soul, perhaps a carload of intimates, a houseful of family. The drone seeks out individuals whose relations, patterns of movement, and aspirations are either known or imagined to be characteristic of a terrorist. In some cases, the United States intelligence community has a file describing plans, motivations, and aspirations. In others, they make inferences.[27] In both types of cases and those in between, the individualization of war and the treatment of the body as territory evoke fantasies of omniscience and omnipotence in drone operators and in evangelical observers.

Perhaps the best way into the theology of the drone and its connection to imperial territoriality is through drone operators themselves. Memoirs by former drone pilots Mark McCurley and Matt Martin include descriptions that show drones as instruments of theological discourse. Matt Martin wrote of the privileged knowledge born of the drone's verticality: "Looking down on all this, seeing the foibles and courage and decency, and all the various behaviors, emotions, and ways of mankind at its best and at its worst, I truly felt like an omnipotent god with a god's seat above it all."[28] Martin contends that he saw not just bodies and actions but the interior states of those bodies and the motivations behind actions. And for him, the work of fighting—the choosing, the marking, and the killing—created similar feelings. His involvement in "virtually every facet of the War on Terror," from "tracking Osama bin Laden . . . [to] fighting along with the Marines" was, on his account, like "God hurling thunderbolts from afar."[29] Fellow drone pilot Mark McCurley found this feeling of near divinity in more tactical moments, such as "firing up the . . . pod's laser illuminator," which gives an inbound missile its target. "It would shine down like a finger from God pointing out a target."[30] Later, when reflecting on an actual kill, McCurley used the God analogy again. "Travis ended the threat with a Hellfire missile. . . . The [infrared] beam was invisible to the naked eye, but under night vision goggles it looked like the finger of God stabbing accusingly at the ground."[31] McCurley's drone is involved in each phase of the attack, watching for targets, launching a missile from above, illuminating enemy bodies below so that troops on the ground can see, track, and kill them. The beam to which he refers makes these bodies visible, but visible only to those with (night-vision) eyes to see. The privileged have sight and knowledge. The damned are blind and foolish, believing they can escape divine justice. The very finger of God directs righteous warriors to their hiding places.

In the pilots' few words we see much of the drone's theology of omniscience, and the territoriality of the body to which it is bound. With the privilege of "empire's verticality," digital profiles, and assumptions about the Muslim male body, emotions become visible, intentions become discernible, foibles and courage and decency can be recorded. What a person has done, what they are doing, what they will do, become knowable, and justice can come to them from on high. Andrea Miller has written compellingly of the logic of preemption that characterizes the approach that our military and our judicial system have taken to Muslim men in the post-9/11 era. "Operating under the guise of preventing violent terrorist acts before they have the chance to cohere, these measures . . . render criminal the terrains of desire, imagination, and inspiration for the racialized Muslim body."[32] True enough. What she and others have looked past is the evangelical divine being invoked by and through these systems. The bodies of Muslim men are only the most recent collection of bodies whose interior dispositions are known, whose sins/crimes are "always already present," and who stand before an incensed God. The logic is as old as Luther, as American as Edwards, as ubiquitous as a Chick tract. What is new is the airborne technology that releases an intensely personal hell on the guilty.

Martin and McCurley used theological language to describe their rare perspective on war and their power to wage it. And though their reflections connect most often with a territoriality of bodies, borders matter theologically as well. Martin in particular reads the Iraqi landscape through a scriptural lens. "While Israel was cited more times in the Bible than any other nation, Iraq followed in close second place." This was not just any land. It was a land significant for the good that came out of it and for the evil that followed.

> Satan made his first appearance in Iraq. The Tower of Babel was built in Iraq. . . . Abraham hailed from a city in Iraq, as did Isaac's wife. . . . The Book of Revelation warned against the resurrection of Babylon from which, according to Biblical prophecy, the Antichrist would rule. Saddam Hussein had undertaken the task of restoring the ancient city before he was deposed by the U.S.-led invasion. . . . Civilization, according to the Bible, began in Iraq and would likely end in Iraq. Blood would rise to the level of a horse's bridle during the Battle of Armageddon in the End times.

Seen through this lens, drone attacks look more like signs of the times than moves in a secular war. But Martin's walk through biblical references and his dabbling in apocalyptic prophecy end where they began: with the privilege of empire's verticality. "[If] the Battle of Armageddon began," he wrote, "I was going to have a bird's-eye view of it."[33]

Though they relate to the drone as observers and admirers rather than operators, the evangelical professional class has found similar theological principles in the weapon. The drone's territoriality of bodies is a mark of its virtue. The God-feeling it creates is, if not exhilarating, at least homiletically useful. In August of 2014, evangelical pastor Ed Young delivered a sermon series to his Texas congregation with a full-sized drone model behind him and a recreational drone flying around the sanctuary. For Young the drone was an epistemic analogy to God: omniscient, omnipotent, and omnipresent. He smiled as he preached, "The Bible says from cover to cover, that we serve an all-everywhere, up-in-our-face, there's no way you could hide or shake-and-bake Him, God." Young made no direct reference to attacks on Muslim bodies, but his audience surely imagined Muslim men trying to "shake and bake" America's drones and America's God. Young continued, "We serve a God who is omni-present. He's everywhere, He knows everything, and can do everything." God, like a drone, is all around, always knowing, always able to act. Those gathered to take in Young's message heard briefly of the role drones play in helping "us fight against the bad guys," but the force of the comparison between the divine and a drone was not to generate fear of judgment. It was, rather, to emphasize God's desire to be with believers. "He is the omni-God, because we matter so much to Him. It's because of His love. It's because of His compassion. It's because He cares about you, and cares about me."[34]

The deeply theological endeavor of American warcraft has had to reckon with the questions raised by drones as they have become more prominent in the US arsenal. What does it mean for America to fight using drones? What are the implications when someone other than a "bad guy" meets her or his end? Where does the theodicy made necessary by war end, and the art of imperial apologetics begin? For some on the evangelical Left, the death of innocents in drone strikes reveals the drone to be another tool of unjust imperial violence. In their eyes, drones are, if not completely indefensible, at least grossly oversold as agents of a territoriality of bodies. Writing in the pages of *Sojourners* in 2013, Steve Holt calls out the seemingly "omniscient and omnipotent" drone for its limited knowledge and indiscriminate violence. He draws forward the fact that drone strikes often kill the innocent. "U.S. covert drone strikes have killed more than 3,000 people since 2004," Holt wrote in 2013. "Of that number, nearly 1,000 were civilians—including an estimated 200 children." And while Pastor Young and other evangelical leaders encourage followers to use the drone as a way to imagine the Bible and God, Holt implores readers to use both to critique drone warfare: "Christians follow a savior who preached nonviolence. He told his disciples not to take revenge, to turn the other cheek, to love their enemies, and not to repay evil with evil. He refused to react violently when false accusations . . . were levied against him, and was willing to lay down his life for a broken world. When the kingdoms of this world choose to use violence . . . the church . . . stands in opposition. . . . Drone warfare," Holt argues, "demands a religious response."[35]

The religious response to drones often has one foot in the realm of evangelical theology and another in the civil religious spaces of the US military. For some, the advance of the drone has meant a troubling retreat from the leveling environment of the battlefield. Paul F. M. Zahl wrote in a 2011 *Christianity Today* forum on the ethics of drone warfare that "drones prevent war from being a fair fight. They emasculate the enemy." Zahl continues, "This method of fighting reduces people on the ground to a condition of absolute helplessness, because they cannot fight back against unmanned drones." In light of twenty years of armed resistance to American operations in Iraq and Afghanistan, and innovations in weaponry to which US forces have struggled to adapt, it is not entirely clear what Zahl means by fairness, emasculation, helplessness, and an inability to fight back. He seems, however, to long for a symmetrical approach to warfare—the "possibility of making eye contact and fully realizing the human cost of the attack"—in which one body is lined up against one body. In the same forum, Daniel M. Bell Jr. wrote that distancing American bodies from the battle "is frequently interpreted [by enemies] as a sign of cowardice . . . and so as a lack of honor." Bell's concern, though, is less for combat efficacy and more for the future of character and courage among American soldiers. With the strenuosity of combat reduced or relieved by technology—a trend of which drones are but a small part—the connection among courage, physical risk, and virtue is imperiled. "Perhaps," Bell writes, "we are at the dawn of an era when moral courage will surpass physical courage as the distinguishing mark of soldiers." Those who possess this courage "resist viewing shadowy blips on a computer screen as mere avatars or bug splat." Moral courage, then, consists in developing a gaze that previous generations of soldiers refined through unmediated encounters with the enemy, a gaze that saw the enemy as human. Again, the distancing of the White male body from combat is a problem to be overcome.[36]

Timothy Oostendaarp, writing in the Church of God's *Philadelphia Trumpet*, interpreted the turn to drones as part of a related problem of absence foretold in scripture. His 2012 article, "In Drones We Trust," expresses the common concern that overreliance on technology and the subsequent disappearance of the White male body from the battlefield were "leading to mistakes that America's enemies have exploited and will continue to exploit." Continuing down this path of "technological warfare," he warned, would eventually put the United States in a vulnerable position with too few soldiers to fight and a necessary reliance on technologies that, when hacked, become useless. Oostendarp cited Ezekiel 7:14: "None goeth to the battle; for my wrath is upon all the multitude thereof." Hyper-attentiveness to a territoriality of bodies, in other words, would bring catastrophe to the nation's borders.

However one wishes to craft a "religious response" to drone warfare—portraying it as always and everywhere sinful, emphasizing the dangers of the changes to soldiering wrought by drones—this response needs to reckon with the fact that the drone *is* a religious response. It responds to the evangelical and imperial problem of a shift to a territoriality of bodies. This "utterly theological" weapon, to use Sarah Sentilles's words, expresses a startlingly high theological anthropology, asserts near omniscience, and condemns sinners to sudden, recorded, and therefore cataloged, consumable deaths.[37] But like all weapons of war, the armed drone can neither live up to its promise nor avoid the laws of unintended consequences. It cannot fly above the religious problems of unjustified suffering, ruptured rituals, noetic breakdowns, and the fear of apocalypse. At the same time, the drone creates related problems within the military, where strenuous living, danger, and the romance of war are the foundation of religious authority. Drone pilots report facing derisive comments, marginalizing labels, and a pervasive sense that the nature of their work makes them inferior warriors. They report as well having substantial moral struggles with fighting as they fight and killing as they kill.[38]

Conclusion

On Friday, January 17, 2020, then-president Trump spoke to a gathering of supporters at his Palm Beach redoubt, Mar-a-Lago. The purpose of the dinner, according to reporter Kevin Liptak, was to raise money for the Republican Party. As part of the evening's program, Trump gave his perspective on the killing of Iranian general Qassem Soleimani, carried out two weeks prior. General Soleimani was the leader of the Quds Force, an elite branch of Iran's Revolutionary Guard. Shortly after his arrival at Baghdad International Airport on January 3, 2020, a US-operated MQ-9 Reaper drone, armed with Hellfire missiles, struck the two-vehicle caravan in which Soleimani and an entourage were riding. There were no survivors. Trump described watching footage taken by "cameras that are miles in the sky" and listening to real-time, bespoke narration. He recalled a disembodied voice saying, "They're together sir," referring to General Soleimani and Abu Mahdi al-Muhandis, a leader in an Iranian-aligned Iraqi paramilitary. What followed, according to Trump, was a countdown of sorts.

> *Sir, they have two minutes and 11 seconds.*
> No emotion.
> *2 minutes and 11 seconds to live, sir. They're in the car, they're in an armored vehicle. Sir, they have approximately one minute to live sir. 30 seconds; 10, 9, 8 . . .*
> Then all of a sudden, boom!
> *They're gone sir. Cutting off.*
> I said, where is this guy? That was the last I heard from him.[39]

Many nation-states condemned the killing. Iran promised retaliation and delivered on that promise with missile attacks on two US bases in Iraq. Predictably, American evangelicals supported President Trump and affirmed his decision to kill a man whose career and reputation had been made supporting militants in their efforts to destabilize the outer reaches of the American imperium.

The killing of Qassem Soleimani stands out from other targeted killings as different in degree rather than kind. Soleimani was a high-profile target, a member of a national government, but judgment came to him from on high just as it did for a low-level Taliban fighter in North Waziristan. The evangelical affinity for this kind of killing, though surfaced by Trump in the aftermath of the strike on Soleimani, was not of his making. As with so much else in White evangelical culture, Trump illuminated rather than created. Through his dramatic recreation of the Soleimani strike, he invited supporters to join him in playing the hidden, seeing, judging God—to taste something of the omniscience and the omnipotence of drone warfare, and to partake of war's pornography.

But this celebration of the conquest of an unregenerate body was incomplete, as indicated by the president asking theatrically, "Where is this guy?" The absence of "this guy"—that is, the person who narrated the attack—is a consequential absence for both evangelicals and Trump. Absence, understood as an inability to locate, troubles myths of soldiering, virtue, and the redemptive power of danger. Absence, understood as a lack of presence, names the empty space in the ritual where "this guy"—the soldier—ought to be, so that he can be seen, sized up, persuaded to tell a story. Without "this guy" as a mediating presence, without his flesh, his uniform, there is no body in which the power of the nation is made visible, nobody available for adoration, veneration, and cooptation.

President Trump made no secret of his love for the discourses of power carried out through military ceremony and military weaponry. He attempted, though he failed, to make a secret of his disdain for the women and men who carry those weapons and whose bodies figure centrally in those ceremonies. It is entirely in keeping with what we know of the man that he adores things that sparkle and gleam and dismisses those that sweat and bleed. It is also in keeping with what we know of White evangelical masculinity that evangelicals would prefer heroes who suffer for the nation on their way to saving it. The masculinity that President Trump prefers and himself performs—shiny, bloodless, statuesque—and the masculinity dear to White evangelicals—suffering, victorious, proven—diverge in their qualities, but converge on the need to instrumentalize the soldier. Held up to the light, the president's dismissal of the losses and sufferings of American soldiers and their families—"losers" and "suckers," he called them—is of a piece with White evangelical anxieties regarding American drone warfare. Death in war and killings from on high challenge the primacy of the mythologized American soldier and confront observers with the unsettling ways in which that ideal male body can be eclipsed. Both provoke longings for an older, simpler way of managing threats to the United States and geopolitical danger more generally.

Map is not territory. Weapons are not victory. Both exist in an instrumental relationship to a thing they hope to control, a goal to be achieved. Yet both are essential elements of empire. Maps express territoriality. Weapons are the means of achieving and maintaining it. From the war in Vietnam down to today, evangelical support of the military and its work has been nearly constant. We could attribute this support to a well-established cult of the soldier and a broader embrace of the military as a stronghold of American virtue. Some would argue that evangelicals supported the Vietnam War because they believed in the cause of free-market capitalism, and that they support our current wars as a defense of democracy against an expansionist, oppressive Islamism. I would add to these explanations the weapons most closely associated with those wars and their resonance with evangelical territorialities of borders and bodies. The public embrace of napalm's collective damnation has given way to celebrations of the drone's tailored judgment and the taste of divinity that comes from casting an enemy into the abyss. These pieces of imperial technology are works of imperial theology. The stories they tell and the God they make visible belong closer to the center of histories of American warfare, where the practice of American empire already places them.

NOTES

1. Lisa Parks and Caren Kaplan, "Introduction"; Derek Gregory, "Dirty Dancing: Drones and Death in the Borderlands"; Lisa Hajjar, "A Lawfare and Armed Conflicts: A Comparative Analysis of Israeli and U.S. Targeted Killing Policies and Legal Challenges against Them"; Andrea Miller, "[Im]material Terror: Incitement to Violence Discourse as Racializing Technology in the War on Terror," all in Parks and Kaplan, eds., *Life in the Age of Drone Warfare*; Gabriella Blum, "The Individualization of War: From War to Policing in the Regulation of Armed

Conflicts," in Sarat, Douglas, and Umphrey, eds., *Law and War*; and Feldman, "Empire's Verticality," 325–41.
2. A. Miller, "[Im]material Terror," and Feldman, "Empire's Verticality," engage Muslim identity as part of a racializing matrix, but not as a religious tradition. None of the authors cited here examine the place of religion in shaping American imperial practices.
3. Blum, "The Individualization of War," 57.
4. Blum, "The Individualization of War," 58.
5. Gregory, "Dirty Dancing," and Feldman, "Empire's Verticality," encourage a broader conceptualization of territoriality, using the concept of "borderlands" and "frontier"/"homeland," respectively, to think through US drone strikes in the FATA region and the disregard that the United States has shown elsewhere for sovereignty and national borders. As both acknowledge, this disregard is not only about an atrophying sense of sovereignty or a growing disrespect for borders; it is also connected to the idea that war is being waged not against Yemen or Pakistan but against a network of individuals living within or adjacent to their borders.
6. Blum, "The Individualization of War," 48. Blum's view of war as an "intercollective effort" governed by "a predominantly state-oriented set of obligations" aligns with this evangelical territoriality of borders. We can see it also in the midcentury evangelical commitment to/adulation of the United States as described in W. Martin, *With God on Our Side*, and Dowland, *Family Values and the Rise of the Christian Right*.
7. Marsden, *Fundamentalism and American Culture*; Bowler, *Blessed*.
8. A. Miller, "[Im]material Terror," 114–15; Blum, "The Individualization of War," 55–58. Citing Junaid Rana and Stephen Salaita, Miller described the application of logics of preemption to the Muslim male body in which "the potential for terrorism is viewed as inherent." Blum notes from a different perspective that the same process of individualizing war that Miller's analysis presupposes has, though imperfectly realized, dramatically enhanced the rights and protections of civilians in war.
9. McAlister, *The Kingdom of God Has No Borders*.
10. Psalm 139, ESV.
11. Bellah, "Civil Religion in America."
12. Louis M. Fieser, *The Scientific Method: A Personal Account of Unusual Projects in War and Peace* (New York: Reinhold, 1964), 27–30.
13. Parks and Kaplan, eds., *Life in the Age of Drone Warfare*, 4, 8; Gregory, "Dirty Dancing," 27; Miller, "[Im]material Terror," 114–17; and Feldman, "Empire's Verticality."
14. Hajjar, "A Lawfare and Armed Conflicts," 70–71; Miller, "[Im]material Terror," 123–25.
15. Neer, *Napalm*, 79, 81.
16. Neer, *Napalm*, 81.
17. Williams, "The Fog of War."

18 Neer, *Napalm*, 94–95.
19 Billy Graham, "Christianity vs. Communism" (Minneapolis, MN: Billy Graham Evangelistic Association, 1951).
20 Guillaume, "Napalm in US Bombing Doctrine and Practice," 6.
21 Capps, *The Unfinished War*, 9.
22 The transcript of Falwell's conversation with Pat Robertson can be found in "PFAW President, Ralph. G. Neas, Addresses Divisive Comments by Religious Right Leaders," People for the American Way, www.pfaw.org (accessed October 1, 2021).
23 Peter Finn, "Rise of the Drone," *Washington Post*, December 23, 2011. See also Frank Strickland, "The Early Evolution of the Predator Drone," *Studies in Intelligence*, March 2013, 1–6.
24 Fuller, *See It/Shoot It*, 248.
25 Fuller, *See It/Shoot It*, 248.
26 Feldman, "Empire's Verticality"; and Miller, "[Im]material Terror."
27 Miller, "[Im]material Terror," 113.
28 Matt J. Martin and Charles W. Sasser, *Predator: The Remote-Control Air War over Iraq and Afghanistan: A Pilot's Story* (Minneapolis, MN: Zenith Press, 2010), 121.
29 Martin and Sasser, *Predator*, 3.
30 T. Mark McCurley and Keven Maurer, *Hunter Killer: Inside America's Unmanned Drone War* (New York: Dutton, 2015), 60.
31 McCurley and Maurer, *Hunter Killer*, 100.
32 Miller, "[Im]material Terror," 120.
33 Martin and Sasser, *Predator*, 65–67.
34 Ed Young, "Drones: Where Is God—Part 1," August 5, 2014, www.youtube.com/watch?v=zVJVnsqF8F8&feature=emb_logo.
35 Steve Holt, "Hellfire from Above," *Sojourners* 42.7 (July 2013): 20–23.
36 "Is It Wrong for the U.S. to Use Unmanned Drones to Kill People by Remote Control?" *Christianity Today*, August 2013, 64–65.
37 Sarah Sentilles quoted in Holt, "Hellfire from Above," 21.
38 See Pratap Chatterjee, "Drone Pilots Are Quitting in Record Numbers," *Mother Jones*, March 5, 2015; Ed Pilkington, "Life as a Drone Operator: 'Ever step on ants and never give it another thought?'" *Guardian*, November 19, 2015; and Matthew Power, "Confessions of a Drone Warrior," *GQ*, October 23, 2013.
39 Kevin Liptak, "Trump Recounts Minute-by-Minute Details of Soleimani Strike to Donors at Mar-a-Lago," CNN, January 18, 2020, www.cnn.com (accessed June 14, 2021).

12

American Islam, Settler Colonialism, and Democratic Empires in the Work of Robert D. Crane

ZAREENA A. GREWAL AND BRENNAN MCDANIEL

Introduction

Between 1956 and 1963, the US State Department sponsored five jazz tours around the world, launched as a form of cultural diplomacy to rehabilitate the image of the United States abroad. In 1956, Dizzy Gillespie and his band went to Asia, the Middle East, and Turkey, and, following student demonstrations against the United States in Athens, they made a last-minute stop in Greece. This was followed in 1958 by Dave Brubeck, who traveled to Asia and Europe, Louis Armstrong's intense forty-five-day trip to fourteen countries in 1960–1961, Benny Goodman's tour in the Soviet Union in 1962, and Duke Ellington's tour to the Middle East and India in 1963. The jazz ambassadors, most of whom, as Black men, were marginalized and oppressed racial minorities in the United States, were implicated as cultural diplomats in the structures of US imperialism as the Middle East became a primary region of interest.¹ Yet many of them expressed deep reservations about US foreign policies and resentment over the ways the tours gave racial cover to the government, indexing the ideological gap between the state's interests and the investments of those called on to represent the state. The musicians' experiences abroad nurtured different politics and attachments, including religious attachments, beyond a simple reflection of the US government's will to power and domination.² Like hundreds of thousands of Black Americans in this period, a few of the jazz ambassadors were considering converting to Islam, and one bassist and oud player from Brooklyn, New York, Ahmed Abdul-Malik, converted before traveling to Morocco. He was the son of West Indian immigrants from Saint Vincent although he claimed to be Sudanese.³ Although there is significant archival evidence of invented ancestries in Black Muslim convert communities in this period, scholarly analyses are expanding beyond questions of authenticity to race making and maintenance. Judith Weisenfeld's *New World A-Coming: Black Religion and Racial Identity during the Great Migration* brilliantly tracks the co-constitution of race and religion in Islamic movements (among other movements) in the United States, which recast the understanding of the Black self and Black history by restoring and redefining Black peoplehood, often through speculative "religio-racial" genealogical claims.[4] In this chapter, we focus on the speculative religio-racial claims of another American Muslim figure implicated in US empire, Robert "Farooq Abdul Haq" Crane (1929–2021), who claims Cherokee lineage but also narrates an Islamic history of the Cherokee. After Crane's conversion, as the specter of Islam replaced communism in official discourses as an existential threat to US power, his trajectory moved in the opposite direction from that of the jazz ambassadors during the Cold War. In contrast to them, Crane traveled from the center of US political power and policymaking in the Middle East to the social margins of the United States, specifically into American mosques and transnational Muslim institutions.

Crane had a distinguished career as a US diplomat (briefly nominated to be a US ambassador to the United Arab Emirates in 1981) and a high-level policy advisor in the Republican administrations of Nixon and Reagan. His political career survived a public feud with Henry Kissinger, who fired him as deputy director of the National Security Council in 1968 after Crane took a principled stance against Kissinger's aggressive foreign policy vision for the United States in the Middle East (particularly in relation to US support for the settler colony of Israel). A middle-aged convert to Islam in 1980, Crane was secretive about his new religious identity for a few years until he began a second career as a Muslim activist and intellectual based in northern Virginia, where he lived until he relocated to Qatar in 2011 to work at a research tank on the democratic dignity revolutions throughout the Middle East.[5] An erudite, highly educated, accomplished man who spent two years mastering Arabic and studying Islamic law and theology in Cairo, Egypt, after leaving government service, Crane became a local religious leader connected to several mosques in the District of Columbia, Maryland, and Virginia in the 1980s, serving congregations with immigrant majorities as well as those with Black American majorities. He also established himself as a religious leader in several national American Muslim institutions.[6] Crane offered his Muslim audiences biting critiques of US empire beyond US borders, but his critique of white supremacy and US settler-colonialism at home was comparatively anemic. We read Crane's uneven critique of US empire and his speculative Islamic histories of the Cherokee in relation to his political theological investments in a teleological view of the United States. Rather than an exhaustive review of his oeuvre (he authored and coauthored a dozen books), we offer a close reading of Crane's representations of the United States as a democratic empire.[7] We argue that he often talked *around* US settler-colonialism even when critiquing US empire, such as in the biographical account by Steven Barboza, "Word at the White House," in *American Jihad: Islam after Malcolm X*; Crane's memoir-essays in the *American Muslim*, such as "By the Hand" and "Reviving the Classical Wisdom of Islam in the Cherokee Tradition"; and excerpts from his forthcoming book published in the journal *Armonia*.[8] Crane imagined an Islamic future for the United States in which Muslims could "complete the American revolution," realizing its lofty democratic and spiritual promise.[9]

Hidden Scripts, Speculative Histories

Although Crane lived his life as a white man, he identified as mixed-race, as a descendant of white settlers and the Cherokee Wolf Clan. Crane was not an enrolled citizen of any of the three federally recognized Cherokee tribes, which raises questions about his self-identification. Eva Marie Garroutte argues in *Real Indians: Identity and the Survival of Native America* that, with the serious risk of those "playing Indian" notwithstanding, such self-identifications may connect individuals "to those they understand as 'their people'; it allows them to express something central to their sense of self, even when [legal, cultural, and biological] definitions of Indian identity close them out."[10] Although we recognize that the authority to determine who *is* and *is not* Cherokee is an important distinguishing feature of Cherokee national sovereignty, we read Crane's claims in a broader context of transnational Islamic thought and speculative claims about Islam's "red roots" in the Americas in order to interpret his writings, views, and political work. For the purposes of this chapter, we have not deeply probed the veracity of Crane's claims to Cherokee ancestors but, aided by Cherokee Nation genealogist Marjorie Lowe, we did not find any evidence that his paternal great-grandmother, Rebecca Caroline Shoemaker Bever ("Beaver") (1846–1936), was ever enrolled in the Cherokee Nation, the Eastern Band of the Cherokee Nation, or the United Keetoowah Band of Cherokee Indians, the three federally recognized Cherokee tribes, or recorded in the census as an Indian.[11]

This is a familiar Appalachian story, as Darlene Wilson and Patricia Beaver demonstrate. "Native American or mixed-ancestry 'grandmothers'" are ubiquitous in the "hidden scripts" of Appalachian family lore, religious initiation, and folk tales, linking white Americans to a complex racial past in which their ancestors took extreme measures to disempower those classified as nonwhite.[12] There is a long list of white public figures such as Bill Clinton, Johnny Cash, Miley Cyrus, and, of course, Elizabeth Warren who have been exposed as "playing Indian," but, as Phil Deloria reveals, this is a settler tradition with an expansive and violent history.[13] According to recent census data, there seems to be a *growing* number of Americans who make claims about having Cherokee ancestry.[14] There are many theories as to what motivates "pretendian" claims, and the motivations may strike some as counterintuitive. For example, in his book *Native Southerners: Indigenous History from Origins to Removal*, Gregory Smithers argues along the same lines as Wilson and Beaver that, paradoxically, claiming Cherokee ancestors was a way to claim authentic *white* southern identity.[15] As a reaction to the longstanding multiracialism of the region, historian Michell Chresfield documents, scientific and popular writing emerged alongside state administrative efforts (namely, antimiscegenation laws and census enumeration) to solidify a firm racial boundary between white and nonwhite throughout nineteenth- and early-twentieth-century Appalachia.[16]

Crane's genealogical claims are racial and, if fabrications, these claims are not only racist but a form of settler-colonial violence.[17] Rather than dismissing Crane's genealogical claims as merely "pretendian" outright, in part because we have not found much evidence of Crane accruing material or social capital from these uncorroborated claims, we have adopted Garroutte's more neutral language of self-identification. Garroutte emphasizes the gap between tribal sovereignty and tribal identity, or the tribe as a sovereign entity and a social community, quoting one of her Cherokee subjects who states, "The *tribe* will recognize who an Indian *is*. I mean, not the government [aspect of the] tribe, but the individual members of the tribe."[18] While these positions are not conclusive proof of Cherokee ancestry by any means, Crane *did* establish the social relationships and the recognition of other Indians that led him to cofound and hold leadership roles in the American Indian National Bank and the Native American Economic Development Corporation, as well as act as an ombudsman in the US government's Bureau of Indian Affairs in the 1970s.[19] Furthermore, Crane claimed some of the credit for Nixon's relatively good record on Native American issues related to sovereignty and his acknowledgment of the legitimacy of some of the demands of the Red Power movement.[20]

American Muslims have generally not questioned whether Crane was *really* Cherokee just as Noble Drew Ali's followers in the Moorish Science Temple did not (and do not) question his claims to Cherokee and Moroccan ancestry.[21] While the invocations of Cherokee nobility in these two American Muslim cases are not exactly the same, there is a shared resonance in these speculative histories. Islam's Cherokee roots recuperate Muslims and Islam in dominant American discourses in which civilization, white supremacy, and Christianity render Islam as a "bad religion," whether as a "primitive, Negro cult" during the Great Migration, as a premodern relic, or as *anti*modern fundamentalism in the context of the War on Terror.[22] However, Islam's Cherokee roots also recuperate the United States as a space to forge an Islamic, just future. In comparison to his sharp condemnation of the United States' imperial presence in the Middle East (in Saudi Arabia and Iraq), Crane was considerably more restrained in his critical representations of imperial violence by the United States against Indigenous nations even as he wrote explicitly about the policies of "genocide" and "ethnic cleansing" of white settlers.[23] We examine Crane's relatively more muted critique of US empire and his recuperation of the United States in relation to his invocations of his Cherokee roots and family history, and his revisionist historical claims and desires to recover a lost Islamic-Cherokee history. Rather than focusing on the veracity of his claims, our aim is to situate Crane's work and politics in the broader spectrum of politics of the American Muslim counterpublics that have been reading and listening to his words for over forty years.

Outsider Convert

Throughout American history, religio-racial minorities have constructed narratives of their persecution and marginality, with their status as religious outsiders linked to alternative and often transnational formulations of community that compete with the nation-state's horizon of belonging. For a wide range of American Muslim communities in the twentieth century, those transnational formations included identifications with the *umma* (the global community of believers) and/or ethnic, racial, or national diasporas, and often this manifested as a seeming embrace of their exclusion and a strong identification as religio-racial outsiders.[24] While his overall historical narrative may be too neat and formulaic, historian R. Laurence Moore argues that such outsider narratives paradoxically "Americanize" religious minorities. In fact, he contends that outsiderhood has been a more powerful force in the process of inventing Americanness than other, more obvious American (we would add settler) tropes such as the frontier.[25] By embracing religious outsiderhood, American Muslims have for nearly a century developed transnational moral geographies as Islamic critiques of the contradiction between the universal promise of legal citizenship in the United States and the ways they have been systematically excluded from American social citizenship. Outsiderhood and empire are major themes in Crane's writing and speeches.

Although Crane wrote for policymakers and managed the *Middle East Affairs Journal* from 1996 to 2001, Crane's primary audience has been lay American Muslims. Crane's speeches and writings for American Muslims often combine political analysis, Islamic theological arguments, polemics, and memoir. For example, he often wove stories of his conversion to Islam into essays in which he was making a theological or political argument. While conversion narratives are often saturated with meaning that exceeds the circumstances of the convert, in American Muslim contexts conversion narratives are always stories about race, not just in the details of the telling but in the iterative sense. How and why converts are inspired, invited, and pressured to tell (perform) their conversion narratives is linked to the racialization of Islam. Drawing on Judith Butler's theorization of excitable speech, scholars Mahdi Tourage and Marcia Hermansen provide case studies of Muslim conferences in the United States and Canada, where such performances are often staged. They argue that these performances by converts produce something greater than the sum total of the speech act and the pious comportment of the body of the speaker; performances of conversion narratives discursively construct and performatively enact Islamic belief. In this context, the performance of belief does not merely refer to or name the belief in the principles of Islam; it is the producer of what can be known of Islamic belief. In other words, performativity has the power to effect, enact, and produce what is being performed, in this case, the interiority of correct belief. Tourage and Hermansen argue that when these (usually white) converts make public appearances (often accompanied by their non-Muslim mothers, who offer their own supplemental testimonial) their testimonials are the pivotal point in the racial structural function of these conferences: "Compensating for the absence of an empowered and ideal Muslim community [the] interiority of its belief system [is fetishized] through display of" the converts' knowledge and appearance, displacing the racial traumas of the audience. We are persuaded by this reading of the fetishization of whiteness and the displacement of racial trauma, but we want to extend this analysis to the displacement of the latent settler-colonial anxieties of American Muslims. In the context of the fetishization of white converts, Crane did not necessarily accrue more social capital among his Muslim audiences through his claims to Cherokee ancestry. Indeed, he reported that Muslims showed neither skepticism about nor any particular interest in his ancestry.[26] In our reading of his conversion narratives, Crane's condemnation of US empire abroad and simultaneous recuperation of the United States as an originally Islamic nation destined to return to its Islamic roots through democracy displaces American Muslims' settler-colonial guilt.

Crane's conversion stories appear in his speeches, interviews, and articles. In keeping with this public ritual of recounting one's "embrace of Islam," as it is often called, each retelling reaffirms Crane's Muslim belonging and conviction and collective Muslim belonging in the Americas. Insofar as his Muslim audiences are compelled by his testimony, it validates the fundamental goodness and truth of Islam for those Muslims living in societies in which they are inundated with pervasive, racist representations of Islam as barbaric, backwards, and pathologically antimodern. Interestingly, the narrative arc of Crane's conversion, as he told it to Black Muslim journalist Steven Barboza in Barboza's collection of American Muslim oral histories (more precisely, conversion narratives), *American Jihad: Islam after Malcolm X*, is not the story of growing disillusionment and dissatisfaction with the religion of his family (Christianity) but the story of the slow and then sudden removal of the blinders of Crane's own Orientalist race-thinking. As Nixon's primary foreign policy advisor from 1963 to 1968 and his "personal advisor on world religions," Crane prepared research-based reports on "world religions," including Islam, for the president, whom he characterized as a serious student of comparative religion who carefully separated the ideals of each "religion from [the behavior of] its adherents."[27] Both Crane and Nixon saw Islam as a source of unparalleled value to the US government insofar as it could stave off communism in regions of interest such as the Middle East and North Africa. Crane explained to Barboza, "I never took Islam seriously, because all I knew about Islam was that good Muslims should kill Christians and the Muslim heaven is a whore-house. I was so disgusted I never wanted to learn anything about this religion. It was just *primitive*. And I had advised Nixon on Islam as an ally against the Communists. I thought it was a *disgusting* religion, but at least it could be used against Communism."[28] In the 1970s, Crane relocated to the Persian Gulf and briefly held a position as an advisor to the government of Bahrain. He recounted getting lost with his wife in the bazaar in Muharraq on a swelteringly hot day in the summer of 1977.

> I was about ready to pass out [from the extreme heat].... This old man came walking by and he recognized I was in trouble, so he invited us into his home, which was just across the street. We spent the rest of the day there. We had one banquet course after the other. We talked about all kinds of things, and he said he was a Muslim. I was amazed because he was such a good person. We never talked about Islam. We talked about what is good in the world, what's bad in the world, and what's important in the world. And the role of God in the world, but not about Islam. I said, This is weird.... [*Laughs.*] I concluded I better start learning about Islam. Obviously I'd been brainwashed. I studied the religion, and realized that everything in Islam is exactly what I had always believed. But I didn't like the idea of bowing. That to me was revolting.[29]

Crane's encounter with the wise, generous old man in Bahrain is characterized by both surprise at the depth of his hospitality and care and a recognition that they both already shared in the knowledge of that which is good and true. Conversion narratives "are not structured by a simple, linear temporality in which we embrace a new framework and reject an old one. Rather, conversion narratives require seeing the old framework with new eyes, thus converting the future and the past together. They are built on the slow discovery of clues leading to the inevitable climax of conversion."[30] The fusion of the chance encounter with an anonymous old man in the Middle East, being startled by the depth of his hospitality and generosity, and the immediate recognition of a common philosophy (or natural religion, *din al-fitra*, as Crane characterized it) that could be intuited as true are common features in the conversion stories of many American Muslim religious leaders who traveled abroad. The drama of the narrative is in the speed of the conversion, the immediacy of the "click" of recognition, which did not require persuasive argument but rather warm hospitality and reflections on universal truths.

This encounter in Bahrain spurred Crane to study Islam more deeply but also foretold another encounter that would move him beyond his lingering, racial repulsion towards Muslim prostration in prayer, the last obstacle to his conversion. In 1980, the College of Holy Cross sponsored a conference in Durham, New Hampshire, titled "Resurgent Islam: Prospects and Implications," gathering many of the great Muslim intellectuals from around the world. Thrust into this extraordinary meeting of Muslim intelligentsia who were collectively grappling with the global implications of the Islamic revolution in Iran, Crane was awed by their spirited debates. Thrilled by the intellectual exchange, he was even more moved by the Friday congregational prayers led by a charismatic and liberal Sudanese theologian, Hassan al-Turabi (1932–2016). Combining a classical Islamic education and a legal education that included a PhD from the Sorbonne, al-Turabi's writings on Islam and democracy reflect deep engagements with the disciplines of Islamic law and theology and the Western liberal tradition. Crane recounted, "Hasan al-Turabi was the leading Muslim in the world at that time. . . . When he made the *sujud* [prostration], the thought suddenly struck me that he's bowing to Allah. That never really sank in. All I saw was bowing, but then I realized he's bowing to Allah, and if he can bow to

Allah—he's ten times the man I am, so I decided I have to make *sujud* too. . . . So that's when I became Muslim."³¹ At the time, not only was al-Turabi widely regarded as the foremost theologian of Sudan, where he led the Muslim Brotherhood to winning more parliamentary seats than they had anywhere else in the Middle East, but he was also among the most influential Muslim intellectuals in the world, including in the United States. At first glance, it might appear that al-Turabi fits the same familiar Orientalist trope of the wise old sage or the noble savage as the elderly Bahraini man in the bazaar, a common feature not only in the conversion narratives of Muslim American seekers but in American travel writing as a genre.³² However, Crane's decision to continue to identify al-Turabi as the source of his inspiration breaks with the Orientalist trope of the noble savage precisely because al-Turabi cannot be reduced to a harmless, anonymous sage outside of modernity, without history or politics. Despite al-Turabi's direct role in bringing the brutal dictator Omar Al-Bashir to power (once in power Al-Bashir often acquiesced to al-Turabi but also periodically jailed him), al-Turabi remained a lifelong champion of democracy and a fierce critic of US empire. Credited as the intellectual architect behind Sudan's 1989 military coup, al-Turabi was widely regarded as one of the most influential, powerful, and notorious leaders of the Muslim Brotherhood in the world. Crane never identified as part of the Muslim Brotherhood, as many of his contemporaries did (not only Muslim American religious leaders but also many of those reading him), nor did he share his friend and colleague Ismail al-Faruqi's enthusiasm for Wahhabi theology. He also never disavowed al-Turabi although he was deeply critical of Al-Bashir's authoritarianism. Crane continued to publish some of al-Turabi's older writing on Islamic feminism and Islamic democracy in the *American Muslim* as recently as 2004.

As a government servant in the 1960s and 1970s, Crane had been a cautious Cold Warrior but, as a Muslim, he became a radical critic of US imperial power in the Middle East, though as we will show below, his critique of US empire was strikingly uneven. Before turning to the contradictions and inconsistencies in Crane's thought, we might linger on *why* a figure riddled with so many contradictions as al-Turabi appealed to Crane and to so many American Muslims in this period. After all, the progressive, reform-minded theologian committed to direct democracy was not only a vocal critic of US empire; he offered Sudan as a safe haven to those militarily resisting the United States in the 1990s (including Osama bin Laden). Part of the answer lies in the way al-Turabi was read as the ultimate religious outsider by American Muslims, particularly upwardly mobile Arab American immigrants who were part of the global Islamic revival. On the one hand, al-Turabi was a Black Arab man who was not only fluent in English and French; he also waxed poetic about the liberal tradition and democratic values, identifying convergences between John Locke, Adam Smith, and Jean-Jacques Rousseau and various Quranic verses and Muslim theologians and jurists.[33] On the other hand, he drew on the moral authority of Islamic scripture, law, and theology to make fiery, impassioned, and deeply compelling condemnations of US imperial interventions in the Middle East and the accompanying forms of legitimation of what historian Ussama Makdisi terms "the privilege to act upon others" provided by regional actors such as the Saudi government.[34] Crane was in close proximity to other American Muslim leaders who were either quietist or essentially cheerleaders of US empire in the DC area. Although he valued the religious expertise and rationalist philosophy of Iranian expatriate Syed Hussein Nasr, politically, Crane had always been drawn to far more radical, reform-minded Muslim thinkers, such as Iranian leftist intellectual Ali Shariarti, who emphasized the egalitarian message of the Quran and opposed American imperialism without rejecting the virtues of democracy. Crane considered Sudanese intellectual Abdullahi An-Na'im to be among the most brilliant of American Muslim intellectuals and also someone who inherits philosophers Russell Kirk and Edmund Burke, but at the same time, Crane remained deeply skeptical about An-Na'im's full-throated endorsement of secularism and secular human rights. Crane's religious views and political views (he used the descriptor "traditionalist" for narratives of both Islamic spiritual and democratic progress) have always been eclectic. Traditionalist Islam, in Crane's view, takes an ecumenical view of all religions, influenced by the perennialist views (but not the quietist politics) of Nasr. Rather than trying to identify Crane's Islamic school of thought (or narrow his thinking to one) in order to explain the appeal of al-Turabi, we understand al-Turabi's appeal to Crane in terms of the racial dimensions (and limits) of his critique of US empire and its alignment with

Crane's investments in American progress. In other words, in Crane's work Black Arab intellectuals such as al-Turabi and An-Na'im stand in place of antiracist and anti-imperialist critiques made by Black American Muslim thinkers. In our view, this glaring omission of Black American Muslim thinkers such as Malcolm X or Warith Deen Muhammad (whom Crane is often compared to) in Crane's oeuvre is as revealing as the scholars he chooses to cite. Black American Muslim critique belies the promise in American democracy that so much of Crane's polemic pivots on.

The United States figures as a democratic empire in the teleologic American Muslim religious imaginary Crane shares with many of his Muslim readers. Crane's writings and lectures about the intersections of religion and politics have primarily circulated in Sunni Muslim networks in which Arab Americans and South Asian Americans form majorities but also in some Black American Muslim communities such as those led by Warith Deen Muhammad, particularly in the 1980s, 1990s, and early 2000s. The United States was the political and economic haven for the post-1965 "brain drain" of immigrant professionals in scientific and technological fields from the Middle East and Asia whom the US government identified as a resource in the Cold War, a place where these immigrants might achieve the "American Dream." As these immigrants made their lives in the United States, the US government made a series of imperial interventions in the Middle East, bolstering brutal rulers and suppressing democratic and leftist movements under the guise of promoting postcolonial sovereignty, independence, and democracy. The imperial machinations of the United States *within* its own borders as a white-supremacist settler-colonial regime, a critique powerfully made by Black American Muslim leaders then and now, was perhaps too threatening for Crane and the audiences he wrote for and spoke to precisely because Black American Muslim critique forced them to reckon with their own complicity in the American racial-imperial order and their own investments in American (Muslim) progress. The fiery, elegant rhetoric of al-Turabi offered American Muslims like Crane a register in which to make a partial, outward-focused critique of US empire that left their own class and racial privilege intact and undisturbed, and still left open the possibility of an Islamic redemption for the country.[35] These political theological investments are evident in the ways Crane narrated his family history.

Crane's Family History and the (Multiculturalist) Rehabilitation of a Democratic Empire

Crane discussed his family history in several essays and speeches, often drawing on the trope of the outsider and presenting his Cherokee ancestors as belonging to an ethnic group rather than a sovereign Indian nation, bolstering a multiculturalist, recuperative historical account of the United States. Historian Matthew Jacobson argues in *Roots Too* that after the civil rights movement there was a white ethnic revival, in which the pilgrims at Plymouth Rock lost their prominence in the national myth to the hard-working, industrious immigrants who came later through Ellis Island.[36] Crane recast the white settlers in both his paternal and maternal family lines as immigrants: "The Cranes came over in 1636 to New Haven, Connecticut and some of them went down to Elizabethtown (now Elizabeth), New Jersey. On my mother's side, there's European blood that came to America in 1608 aboard the second ship to go to Jamestown. It was full of prisoners. My mother's family originated from the debtors who were released from prison on condition that they work for seven years in the colonies. That was almost like a sentence of death."[37] In an oddly recuperative move, Crane stresses the precariousness of his white settler ancestors, as people criminalized for falling into debt who were banished to the colonies and who nearly died in transit, rather than as genocidal settlers. Crane's recuperation of the white settlers in his family is notably more subtle and tepid when compared to the idealization of white settlers by his colleague and intellectual partner for many years, Palestinian intellectual Ismail Al-Faruqi, who was arguably a much more influential religious leader than Crane. In his writing and speeches, al-Faruqi explicitly idealizes white settlers as a class of suffering religious minorities, persecuted in their home countries, who found new freedoms in the "New World" and whom he likens to American Muslim immigrants such as himself.[38] While not as extreme as al-Faruqi's racist analogies, Crane's recuperation of white American settlers is quite jolting given what he was writing about the total political illegitimacy of Zionism and Israeli settlers in the same period and his regular comparisons between the Holocaust and the genocidal nature of the *Nakba* (the catastrophe of more than seven hundred thousand Palestinians—half of prewar Palestine's Arab population—being dispossessed from their homes in 1948 with the creation of Israel).

In Jacobson's formulation, in our post-civil-rights hyphen-nation, white ethnics have become more quintessentially American than WASPs. Their ethnic self-distancing from white privilege, with claims that their grandparents never killed an Indian or owned a slave, reduced racism to a dark and distant chapter of American history, allowing them to gloss over the persistence of racial discrimination in housing and hiring from which they directly benefited.[39] As Crane moves to talk about his immediate family, he articulates a depoliticized critique of the way the generational wealth of WASPs corroded the character of his mother and maternal grandparents (his mother divorced his father when Crane was young). "My mother's family was very wealthy. My grandmother's father was one of the financial founders of Northwestern University. My mother called my father a *barbarian*."[40] Crane's mother's epithet against her husband, who Crane claimed was the son of a Cherokee woman, is marked as both racist and classist. Just as with his conversion narrative, Crane's mother's racist and classist language of barbarity has a particular resonance for Crane's Muslim audience, all too familiar with being considered poor, backwards, antimodern, barbaric. Like Crane's father, many of the Muslim immigrants reading Crane achieved professional degrees and found material success in the United States, but such achievements failed to insulate them from racism and classism. Although these immigrants are not up-from-their-bootstraps Ellis Island immigrants, in the 1970s, 1980s, and 1990s, middle-class, upwardly mobile Muslim immigrants from the Middle East and South Asia could easily imagine themselves realizing the American Dream alongside white ethnics without acquiescing to white supremacy. In the context of the white ethnic revival, Muslim and diasporic outsiderhood allowed this class of Muslim immigrants, particularly Arab American Muslims, to carve out a space for themselves at the margins of the American mainstream; they could invest in the American Dream and enjoy not-quite-white privilege, without embracing white guilt or white supremacy.

Crane dramatized class tensions through the story of his parents' troubled marriage, describing how even his father's position as a Harvard professor was never enough for his WASP mother. "They couldn't survive together: two totally different views of life. With one, the only thing that mattered was money, and with the other, the only thing that mattered was living a virtuous life and being satisfied with your lot in life."[41] Importantly, when talking about his paternal relatives, Crane credited his Cherokee grandmother with being the moral center of the family: "My father taught economics at Harvard for ten years. His father never went past the sixth grade. Actually, he was a hobo back in the [1880s and 1890s]. He left home after the sixth grade and rode the rails for twelve years. He married my grandmother, from the Indian side, and she decided that their children had to get an education. Two boys got doctorates, and the two girls got college degrees—the first generation up from riding the rails and dirt farming in south central Indiana."[42]

In Crane's narrative, his Cherokee grandmother is the intellectual and spiritual anchor of the family. She not only prevents her husband and their children from falling into financial ruin and poverty; she passes on lessons about spiritual contentment with one's lot in life. Crane identifies himself as a recipient of her lessons through his circuitous journey through elite institutions of higher education. He started at Harvard at sixteen but transferred to Northwestern. He had planned on taking over the family's hardware business but, like his father, he found the materialist definitions of success imposed by his monied maternal relatives oppressive. "I worked [at the hardware store] twenty hours a week learning everything from the ground up. And then the family wanted me to go to Harvard Law School . . . to get background to run the company. I went to learn about justice."[43] Describing his own interest in the big questions about justice, humanity, and the good life that Harvard Law School failed to engage, Crane offers a story of a transcendent experience, a kind of conversion before his conversion. This second conversion narrative can be read as another way he lays claim to this spiritual wisdom passed down in his family through his Cherokee kin. He describes becoming deathly ill during a summer trip to the Rocky Mountains during college after eating pork and developing trichinosis. "Perhaps I did die in the hospital. Only Allah knows. Certainly I was no longer in this world. This was when I experienced the only absolute certitude that any human being can ever know . . . the light of Allah. . . . Allah also showed me the entire world from an enormous height and showed me millions of people on earth as individuals in one community."[44]

"Heretical" History: Crane's Revisionist Islamic-Cherokee Claims

Crane's narrative about his Cherokee kin was also the basis for what he calls "another native history of the Cherokees."[45] As Michel-Rolph Trouillot has argued, to understand the relations of power in the *process* of historical production, we need to account not just for professional historians but also for "artisans of different kinds, unpaid or unrecognized field laborers who augment, deflect, or reorganize the works of professionals."[46] Crane is not alone in his conviction and pursuit of uncovering lost connections among Indigenous peoples in the Americas, Muslims, and Islam. That is, US-based scholars, Muslim theologians/practitioners, and amateur researchers alike have endeavored projects of historical recovery with the aim of archiving the presence of Muslims and Islamic practices. Historian Sam Haselby, for example, recently offered a dynamic portrait of lesser-known fifteenth- and sixteenth-century voyages to the Western hemisphere, suggesting the arrival of Islam and Muslims before the start of the Protestant Reformation in 1517. Haselby claims that some of the first verbal exchanges between Indigenous peoples and European newcomers, however one-sided or unsuccessful, took place in Arabic, Islam's liturgical language.[47] In the 1990s and early 2000s, there was a great deal of pulp religious literature that circulated among mosqued Muslim Americans about African and Arab Muslim encounters with Native populations of what would come to be known as the Americas and about the Moorish ancestors of Native "mixed-race" tribes such as the Melungeons. Crane cited these accounts at times, even when they depart from the chronology of his own speculative history. For example, he cited a July 1996 article in the *Message*, published by the Islamic Society of North America, about Stand Watie, who in this revisionist account is dubbed "Ramadhan ibn Wati, who lived from 1806 to 1871 and governed during the time of the great split between the Union Cherokee and the Confederate Cherokee in the American Civil War. Chief (Emir) Ramadhan was a Confederate brigadier general . . . and his young son, Saladin Watie, [was] named after the famous liberator of Jerusalem in 1187, Salah al Din."[48]

While the reception of Crane's intellectual work among American Muslims is beyond the scope of our analysis, we aim to think through the racial logics that animate Crane's revisionist history. We are not arguing that Crane's particular historical narrative was or is a widely accepted narrative among American Muslims, but we want to juxtapose it against other such revisionist histories that also circulate in American mosques and elsewhere, such as Ivan Van Sertima's *They Came before Columbus*.[49] It is important to note that in his prefatory remarks, Barboza acknowledged that Crane "spoke for hours about his Cherokee family tree, [and] his roots to seventeenth century England," but Barboza chose to leave these elements out of his account although there is a rich history of such revisionist histories among Black Muslims that center Black Muslim West Africans (and not only as enslaved populations) and about which Crane is strangely silent.[50] What does Crane's unruly Islamic Cherokee history do? One way to read Crane's striking silence about enslaved African Muslims in his account is as a sign that he is ultimately more invested in a theological (perennialist) argument than a historical one, and the polemical nature of his writing on this topic supports such a reading.

By situating Crane's account amongst competing histories that circulate in American Muslim counterpublics of deep Islamic roots in this part of the world, we offer one model for how scholars of Islam in the United States might analyze such claims, beyond simply debunking them (though that is often an important intervention as well). Crane's vernacular historical sensibility and critique of power in the process of historical production is evident in his revisionist religious history of the Cherokee nation, a history he claims is also (but not exclusively) Islamic. Crane wrote,

> The spiritual heritage of individual nations in the great Native American community can be preserved only by their members, because anthropologists, government bureaucrats, and even academics either consciously or unconsciously, have their own agendas. Even within each nation, individual clans and groups differ in their own favorite origin stories and prefer their own historical spin. This diversity must be preserved, because its wisdom is part of the visions of past, present, and future that native legends say will be passed on to enrich people from foreign lands. [In one tradition] the Cherokee religion came from a great fleet of ships that brought "The Book" out of the East. This has been rejected as a "heresy"

by some "authorities," both Anglo and Indian. What is the truth? No one can say for sure, but this origin story deserves original research in the vast amount of materials still waiting to be mined for details.[51]

Although Crane concedes that these claims are considered "heretical by Anglos and Indians" alike, we are struck by how he narrates that the Quran was passed from "Muslim settlers" to the Cherokee nation and that its Islamic message and Islamic ritual practices are survivals, preserved in part in Crane's own family.

> For the Cherokees, the Trail of Tears was the last of the great acts of ethnic cleansing that began with the American Revolution. . . . In 1839, despite the decision of the U.S. Supreme Court under Chief Justice John Marshal that Cherokee sovereignty was higher than that of the State of Georgia, the president of the United States ordered the U.S. Army to drive the Cherokees in the middle of winter all the way to Oklahoma. Although reportedly a third of them died en route while the federal troops watched, not all of this third actually died. Three groups broke off from the Trail of Tears, one going to Ohio and two to Indiana, because they feared extermination once they would arrive in Oklahoma.[52]

Importantly, Crane's revisionist history is also a family history; Crane claims he learned this suppressed history directly from his Cherokee kin. He specifies what the Islamic survivals include beyond the "Book of the East": the call to prayer, the circumambulation during hajj, the theology of *din al-fitra* or natural religion. Crane claims that his great-uncle Joseph Franklin Bever/Beaver "was one of the last formally trained Cherokee imams" and that he received formal Islamic training for two years near Hillsboro, Indiana, in 1903.

> [In 1905] the U.S. government abolished the Cherokee religion and imprisoned everyone who performed the *salah* publically [sic]. The Katoowa Society was formed to fight back, but they were crushed. My great uncle then spent two years trying to organize all the Native American tribes to fight for religious freedom, but despite some interest among the Navajo, Hopi, Crow, and Blackfeet, he failed miserably and so went back to Indiana where I knew him as a boy. I was impressed because he knew the

names of 269 plants. He called the *Athan* every morning, but when challenged he replied simply that he was calling the hogs. Like all Cherokees, he started every prayer with "Ya Allah." All the prophets, starting with Abraham, are honored in the tradition. Until 1895, the Cherokees held the hajj, with *tawaf*, on the land of Uncle Henry Bever (spelled Beaver among the Oklahoma Ani Waya) three miles southwest of Hillsboro, Indiana. Until the last hajj, Cherokees came all the way from Oklahoma to attend, but only those with native fluency in Cherokee were permitted to participate, including my great-grandmother. . . . She helped raise me. . . . My great grandmother, who spoke only Cherokee after she announced that it was time to die, had coal black hair down to her waist when she was in her nineties.[53]

Another way of reading Crane's revisionist history is through the conventions of a genre of settler writing that ethnohistorian Jean O'Brien calls "lasting." She defines "lasting" as "a narrative construct of Indian extinction through what I call the 'last of the [blank]' syndrome, whereby local historians occasionally tell stories about people they identify as the last Indian who lived in places they claim as their own."[54] While Crane would never erase the contemporary Cherokee nation, he explicitly names his great-uncle as "the last of the Cherokee imams," in other words, the last of the (authentically Muslim) Cherokee. O'Brien argues that these "vanishing" and "last of the [blank]" tropes allow for an aggrandizement "of individuals claimed to represent the end of Indian histories, while also facilitating the much larger ideological project of 'lasting.'"[55] She contends that "lasting" as a settler rhetorical strategy is in a dialectic with settler "firsting."

> In juxtaposition to the many claims about "first" that local texts assert are an intriguing set of "lasts." The practice of what I call "lasting" in local narratives importantly participated in the production of a narrative of progress and historical time for non-Indians, mixture and degeneracy for Indians, and might be seen as juxtaposed with the notion of indelible pollution for African Americans. In these ways the very practice of historical writing participates in the creation of these temporalities of race. . . . The practice of lasting bolstered non-Indians' claims about their own modernity even while they purport to purify the landscape of Indians.[56]

Crane did not make an argument that pivots on "firsting." He made it explicit when he defined the stakes of his historical revisionism, a project he hoped would be taken up by second-generation immigrants to "indigenize" Islam, to render it legible as an American religion rather than a foreign (reviled) import, a narrative that once again erases Black American Muslim history and arguments. Crane wrote, "The definitive history of the Cherokees, and especially analysis of the relation of Islam to the founding of America has yet to be written. This is the task of young American-born Muslims, because they know that other Americans fear what they do not know and that this history would show that Islam is not foreign to America."[57] The irony is that the invocations of neither Crane's settler ancestors nor his Cherokee kin are enough to insulate him from being smeared as a foreign agent, a fifth column, as essentially and irrevocably un-American.

Conclusion: Smeared as Foreign

In 2013, though Robert Crane had relocated to Qatar, his career and Muslim associations cast a shadow over the political career of his son, John Ruedel Crane, in the States. Over the course of his twenty-five-year career in the Department of Defense, John Crane rose in the ranks to the position of assistant inspector general and director of both the Department of Defense and NSA's whistleblower programs; in formal charges filed in 2013 with the Office of Special Counsel, John Crane alleged that these watchdog programs fail to protect vulnerable whistleblowers from retaliation. In February 2013, a few months before the Edward Snowden case broke in the *New York Times*, John Crane was quietly and suddenly placed on administrative leave from his position as assistant inspector general. As he fought to be reinstated, Crane became a consultant for the General Accountability Project (GAP), which provided legal counsel to Snowden, and Crane vigorously and publicly defended Snowden's decision to illegally remove secure documents out of fear of sanction in print. In candid media interviews, Crane described the allegations in the formal charges he filed, including that key officials in the watchdog offices retaliated against whistleblowers, creating a chilling effect, citing officials' 2010 retaliation against whistleblower Thomas Drake for exposing corruption and wasteful spending in the National Security Agency.

As a result of the wide coverage of Crane's case, "counter-jihad" bloggers, identified with the global Islamophobia industry, seized on his father's religion as self-evident "proof" that Crane represented a fifth column within the government and should never have had security clearance. Counter-jihad blogger Christine Brimm smeared Robert Crane as a man with longstanding sympathies to Islamic terrorists (she specifically names Hassan al-Turabi and links him to Osama bin Laden) and a committed member of the global Muslim Brotherhood movement.[58] (One of the counter-jihad movement's most important and immediate policy aims is to get the Muslim Brotherhood designated as a terrorist organization; this would be an efficient way to destroy a wide swath of American Muslim institutions and organizations since the "stain" of the Muslim Brotherhood is so diffuse. This smear tactic was a remarkably effective War on Terror policy that devastated American Muslim charities, including a few Crane was attached to, in the wake of September 11, 2001, and most of those charities never recovered.) The Islamophobic smear of Robert Crane as a terrorist is patently absurd and baseless and certainly does not warrant a scholarly refutation. Yet the questions Brimm raises in her caustic blog—Who is Robert Crane and what are the influences on his thinking and political commitments?—deepen our understanding of how American Muslims have grappled with the United States as a democratic empire. Up until his death in 2021 at the age of 92, Crane continued to work on a four-volume book about Islam in a comparative religions series, wrestling with what the United States has been and continues to be in the world. Yet in his writing he remained unable or unwilling to confront the ethical and political imperative, *as a Muslim*, of naming the US government's ongoing settler-colonial violence against Indigenous peoples for what it *still* is.

NOTES
1. Von Eschen, *Satchmo Blows Up the World*; Lubin, *Geographies of Liberation*.
2. Aidi, *Rebel Music*.
3. Kelley, *Nathan I. Huggins Lectures*.
4. Weisenfeld, *New World A-Coming*
5. Robert D. Crane, "Reviving the Classical Wisdom of Islam in the Cherokee Tradition," *Al-Huda*, 2019 (2001), www.al-huda.com.
6. A generally arbitrary "listicle," "The Muslim 500," produced by Jordan's Royal Islamic Strategic Studies Centre, claims to identify the most influential Muslim

leaders around the world and has included Robert Crane since its inception in 2009.

7   This essay is deeply informed by Zareena Grewal's participation in a roundtable at the 2021 Middle East Studies Association meeting on "Democratic Empires and the Limits of Expression" in conversation with Alejandro Paz, Amahl Bishara, Sultan Doughan and Firat Bozcali.
8   Barboza, "Word at the White House," in *American Jihad: Islam after Malcolm X*; Robert D. Crane, "Jurisprudence," *Armonia*, August 2, 2017, https://armoniajournal.com.
9   Robert D. Crane, "Completing the American Revolution: A Spiritual Challenge to Islam," *Muslim Magazine/al-Muslimun* 1/3 (1998): 53–55.
10 Garroutte, *Real Indians*.
11 Margarie Lowe, personal communication with Brennan McDaniel, December 9, 2020. Lowe identified Cranes living in Checotah, Oklahoma, as descendants of Cherokees who traveled the Trail of Tears, but we did not find a direct link to Robert Crane's family. Tallbear, *Native American DNA*.
12 Wilson and Beaver, "Transgressions in Race and Place," in B. Smith, ed., *Neither Separate nor Equal*.
13 Deloria, *Playing Indian*.
14 Sturm, *Becoming Indian*.
15 Despite decades of Cherokee intermarriage with white settlers dropping off, white southerners began claiming "Cherokee blood" in the 1840s. White claims to Cherokee heritage had the effect of legitimating the antiquity of their native-born status. In a crucial moment of swelling southern pride, the claim that one's family had been there long enough to intermarry with Cherokees was a method of staking a claim to southern *white* identity. Smithers, *Native Southerners*.
16 Chresfield, "Creoles of the Mountains."
17 Patrick Wolfe and Stephen Pearson identify tenuous claims rooted in family lore to "Cherokee blood" in Appalachia as "the last bastion of settler-colonialism." Pearson and Wolfe, "'The Last Bastion of Colonialism.'"
18 Garroutte, *Real Indians*, 95.
19 Crane, "Reviving the Classical Wisdom of Islam in the Cherokee Tradition."
20 Dunbar-Ortiz, *An Indigenous Peoples' History of the United States*.
21 Weisenfeld, *New World A-Coming*, 46.
22 Mamdani, *Good Muslim, Bad Muslim*.
23 Crane, "Reviving the Classical Wisdom of Islam in the Cherokee Tradition."
24 Z. Grewal, *Islam Is a Foreign Country*.
25 R. L. Moore, *Religious Outsiders and the Making of Americans*.
26 Personal communication with the authors, July 1, 2021.
27 Barboza, *American Jihad*, 287.
28 Barboza, *American Jihad*, 286, italics added.
29 Barboza, *American Jihad*, 286.
30 Z. Grewal, *Islam Is a Foreign Country*, 228.

31 Barboza, *American Jihad*, 287.
32 Schmidt, *Restless Souls*.
33 For a thoughtful reflection on the charisma of al-Turabi, see Waleed AlMusharaf's "Candy from the Sheikh," *Mada*, March 10, 2016, www.madamasr.com.
34 Makdisi, "The Privilege of Acting upon Others."
35 Corbett, *Making Moderate Islam*.
36 Jacobson, *Roots Too*.
37 Barboza, *American Jihad*, 282–83.
38 Z. Grewal, *Islam Is a Foreign Country*.
39 Jacobson, *Roots Too*.
40 Barboza, *American Jihad*, 283, emphasis added.
41 Barboza, *American Jihad*, 283, emphasis added
42 Barboza, *American Jihad*, 283.
43 Barboza, *American Jihad*, 283.
44 Crane, "Patterns of Da'wa in America: By the Hand," *American Muslim*, March 10, 2007, http://theamericanmuslim.org
45 Crane, "Reviving the Classical Wisdom of Islam in the Cherokee Tradition."
46 Trouillot, *Silencing the Past*, 25.
47 Haselby, "Muslims of Early America."
48 Crane, "Reviving the Classical Wisdom of Islam in the Cherokee Tradition."
49 Sertima, *They Came before Columbus*.
50 Barboza, *American Jihad*, 282.
51 Crane, "Reviving the Classical Wisdom of Islam in the Cherokee Tradition."
52 Crane, "Reviving the Classical Wisdom of Islam in the Cherokee Tradition."
53 Crane, "Reviving the Classical Wisdom of Islam in the Cherokee Tradition."
54 O'Brien, *Firsting and Lasting*, xxiv.
55 O'Brien, *Firsting and Lasting*, 110.
56 O'Brien, *Firsting and Lasting*, 107.
57 Crane, "Reviving the Classical Wisdom of Islam in the Cherokee Tradition."
58 Christine Brimm, "Should Family Affiliations with Foreign Islamist Movements Prevent a Security Clearance?" *Counterjihad*, October 5, 2016, available at the Investigative Project on Terrorism, investigativeproject.org (accessed October 1, 2021).

13

Decolonization™

LUCIA HULSETHER

If you want a picture of American empire clinging to its smoldering ruins, arguably you should look no further than the philanthropic finance industry. In the words of an industry veteran, this is a "sleep-walking sector" of "zombies spewing the money of dead white people in the name of charity." It is "colonialism in empire's newest clothes," which "reinforces the colonial division of Us vs. Them, Haves and Have Nots, and mostly white saviors and experts vs. *poor, needy, urban, disadvantaged, marginalized, at-risk people* (take your pick of euphemisms for people of color)." Practiced postures of redistributive benevolence notwithstanding, most philanthropic foundations could be more accurately described as glorified tax shelters for the ultrarich, or as conscience cleansers for the beneficiaries of slavery and genocide, or both. The executors of these organizations, having inherited generational wealth from their tycoon forebears, bestow only a tiny fraction of that wealth on the same racialized populations that capitalism continues to exploit and dispossess. Philanthropy thus does nothing to change the colonial and racist power structures through which it has ascended. Such is the bleak picture painted by a philanthropic fund manager, Edgar Villanueva, in his recent polemic on how his work has betrayed the universalist principles it avows.[1]

And yet, writes the author, "There's a silver lining in this cataclysm." Justice and healing are still possible; their key lies in the very communities who have borne the most devastating blows of imperial capitalist greed. Villanueva spells out his critique, his hope, and his step-by-step plan for repair in his new book, entitled *Decolonizing Wealth: Indigenous Wisdom to Restore Balance and Heal Divides*. "In my own Native American belief system," Villanueva announces at the outset, "we are all relatives, literally all related to one another. We are also all infected with what I call the 'colonizer virus' which urges us to divide, control, and exploit" (1). When relations are skewed, "the indigenous worldview" calls for "medicine"—which can be anything, so long as it is "filled with or granted a kind of mystical or spiritual power" (7). Hence comes the premise of his main claim: capitalism has acted as a colonial scourge, but this is the case only because its curative potential is yet untapped. Villanueva offers a program to "come back together as one human race, and to restore balance to the land." To accomplish this, he writes, "we need to decolonize wealth . . . using money as our medicine" (2). Launched in the wake of his book's commercial success, his Decolonizing Wealth Project (DWP) will do this by redirecting investment returns toward nonprofits that champion the ideals of the organization.[2]

How does a scholar of religion and empire understand this self-avowed decolonial financier? There are many tactics we could use to try to place him. We could see him as empire's critic, here to truth-tell about the racism and colonialism at the heart of global capitalism. He also may be an outsider to the techno-capitalist modernity installed by settler colonialism, here to reintroduce what he calls "the indigenous worldview" to a human community desperate for healing. On the other hand, there is a way that he comes across less as an outsider than as an insider who saw how the sausage is made and chose to explain it to the rest of us. Or maybe this is just another business gambit. Villanueva could be an entrepreneur who figured out how to turn a profit off the MBAs scrambling to recover the ethics of their profession and clamoring for a how-to guide. And this thought leads to the worst-case scenario: he could just be a flat agent of American capitalist conquest, making a disingenuous excoriation of capitalism in the service of a personal brand. This would be internally consistent, since Villanueva never relinquishes his conviction that a system of monetized value can promote human good. How should critics pinpoint who Villanueva is, where his project tends, what its consequences are? The problem is not a lack of interpretive possibilities. It is that this converted financier could be everything for the student of religion and empire, or he could be nothing at all.

Villanueva's ambiguity makes him a worthy case study for scholars who have situated ourselves at this interpretive intersection. His treatise on decolonizing wealth, and his invocation of a vaunted "indigenous" episteme with which to do so, offers a portal into discussions of methodological judgment and political commitment in the study of religion and empire. Situated within a history of globe-trotting capitalists who have mobilized rhetorics of anticolonialism and avowed their respect for indigenous knowledges, he is not an outlier in the arc of American empire. He reflects a tendency among colonial actors to engage in practices of reflexive self-critique and apology for past mistakes, while simultaneously participating in the economies that they are disavowing. For Villanueva and his historical forebears, these positions have always been overlaid. Their work shows how performances of self-recrimination are not antithetical to colonial and neocolonial projects, but constitutive of how they absorb and manage difference.

Let me restate the point in sharper terms: insofar as these characters and these histories contribute a chapter to our chronicle of religion and empire, this is the least interesting thing one could say about them. Their significance lies in how they bring a reckoning for scholars who are subject to the circuits of neoliberal capitalism that Villanueva both rejects and prizes—a category that includes any of us whose learning and teaching is conditioned by the late modern university. Regardless of whether a given academic worker designates "capitalism" and "empire" as primary professional keywords, our intellectual labors and intellectual products are all but guaranteed to be entangled with geopolitical processes that these terms seek to name. More than this: if my criticism of Villanueva is to be met with any measure of success, it will be measured by the extent to which it is condensed into and able to be recirculated through keywords like "capitalism," "consumerism," and "empire." Villanueva's conflict over how and whether one can advocate "decolonization" within the frameworks of the philanthropic finance industrial complex thus maps the outlines of a predicament for scholarship on (and necessarily *of* and *in*) US empire. This is the problem of what happens to the critical analysis of empire—how its stakes change, what demands it makes on its audience—when its terms are parasitic on and regenerative of the conditions of colonialism.

Villanueva's work throws into confusion any model of interpretation that relies on a binary between "resistance" and "domination," or any of its derivative correlates: agency and oppression, critique and complicity, sincerity and instrumentality.[3] To engage his text is to be thrown back on the questions, What is the value of isolating "empire" as an object of study when one's thinking and writing is already disciplined by the conditions of empire? How does one mount a critique of American empire when a major idiom of empire's latest manifestation is one of reflexive self-critique and the waffling ambivalence that such critique catalyzes? Villanueva's treatise is a useful portal into these questions, not only because it is an exhibit of how empire reproduces itself through (what passes for) decolonial analysis but also because he reflects back to scholars of empire the ways in which our conceptual tools have colluded with imperial projects.

The Colonizer Virus

As eyebrow-raising as Villanueva's "indigenous wisdom" looks when propped among corporate leadership guides of the slickest university presses, on the most basic level his work joins a larger trend toward capitalist social responsibility in financial-services sectors, investment firms, marketing agencies, and corporate corner offices. He is representative of what I have elsewhere termed "capitalist humanitarianism," or the conviction that privatized systems of exchange can facilitate antiracist, feminist, and decolonial action.[4] Acolytes of a more humane capitalism will condemn expropriation, dispossession, and settlement. They will use the words "neoliberalism" and "colonization" as pejoratives, and they will call their audiences into consumer and investor practices that resist these oppressions. It is tempting to debunk such speech acts as either instrumental cynicism or false consciousness—that is, to read polemical critique of capitalist violence as incommensurate with a call for more finance capitalism. But to jump to this conclusion would be to miss the key way that his discourse recurs across social and intellectual domains, in particular in its reification of a universal human who must be recovered from capitalist fallout zones. While many scholars of religion and empire would be quick to assert distance from Villanueva's program—because we know to reject normative enlightenment "Man" and would not be caught dead talking about any essentialized "indigenous worldview"—we do share with him a tendency to critique empire via practices of revealing "domination" and "resistance." This discourse will always return us to the ground of liberal humanism, regardless of whether or not we avow it explicitly.

Villanueva's recourse to a curative indigenous wisdom rests on his account of how philanthrocapitalism has failed communities of color. Villanueva blames market-driven wealth-inequality ravages on "the colonizer virus," defined as "what remains in society, culture, and institutions after the conquest phase of colonization is done" (199). This colonizer virus, like every virus, is an alien intruder in the body, which in this case is the human social body that precedes its arrival. Once the virus finds a way in—and it has plagued "society, culture, and institutions" since European settler empire—it hacks and supplants the body's normal functions. This specific virus implants practices of "division, control, and exploitation" in a human family that would otherwise be united. Members no longer recognize one another as the natural biological and social kin that they are. The spread is silent and stealthy, lying in wait within institutions that appear healthy and passing undetected across generations, sparing neither the victims nor the inheritors of conquest.

In mobilizing epidemiological metaphor to describe the reproduction of coloniality and white supremacy through capitalism, Villanueva gives himself a specific set of terms on which to develop his argument. Some of the implications are obvious: viruses are not only intruders from outside, but they also can reveal a universal sameness insofar as they ostensibly affect anyone. The idea of an outside *invader* as the source of daily oppression—where the invader is not an actual settler but something transmitted by everyone—makes it possible for Villanueva to appeal to "society" as something independent of conquest and slavery.[5] To resist and finally eliminate the "colonizer virus" is to discover again the equal and multicultural human society that has been there all along. But to do this, the historical and present impositions of empire must be exhumed, confessed, and resisted.

Villanueva published his account of colonialism as "a virus" fourteen months before the novel coronavirus epidemic, as well as the spectacularly failed public health responses to it, multiplied across the globe. He did so nine months before the entire world would witness, from lockdown, state officials murdering black people on American streets and brutalizing the crowds that converged in mass popular uprising against the white-supremacist police state. Meanwhile, perhaps in line with *Decolonizing Wealth*, the mainstream press shared its own revelation that the

United States was at war with not one, but two, viral threats: COVID-19 and racism.[6] At times this metaphor was used to highlight the relationship between public health failures and structural racism, including the criminally disproportionate impact of the virus on black communities and the racist attacks on East Asian communities scapegoated for the pandemic. But the comparison actively elided what scholars of black history and thought have long taken as a premise, which is that racism is not a virus attacking from the outside but the constitutive condition of society and what it means to be "human" within it.[7] To imagine racism as a virus is to suppose that the world as it can be thought and known exists prior to it. It is to disentangle the modern world from its founding premises in slavery and colonialism. It is to value and construct the social in terms of a utopian past that should be restored. *Decolonizing Wealth* participates in this longer ideological project and reinforces one of its major consequences: banishing from intelligible discourse the conviction, enacted by freedom-dreaming collectives across at least two centuries, that resistance to modern capitalism is fundamental to any decolonial struggle.

Still, Villanueva stretches to channel the virus metaphor on behalf of his emancipatory hopes. He begins with the most compromised context he can find. "Nowhere," he warns, "is the virus more present than in how we deal with wealth." He then elaborates. The problem is not just that philanthropic institutions have been historically dominated by white men who tend to make their donations to white organizations. The problem is also that current "equity" and "inclusion" initiatives, which claim to be correcting this demographic imbalance, lack the curative power that they claim. "Diversity talk allows people to ignore racism. . . . It lets people off the hook about their responsibility in maintaining a colonial white supremacist society," writes Villanueva, before he quotes a colleague's quip that "you could have Halliburton run by African-Americans; it's still not necessarily a racially just organization" (61). The key word is "necessarily." There is still room to imagine the oil-drilling multinational corporation as a virus-free zone, if people of color were not just represented in executive offices and boards but fully able to "speak in [their] own voice, to offer [their] own divergent ideas, to bring [their] full self to bear on the work" (57). Until this point, inclusion is merely token assimilation into spaces that have not thrown off their white-supremacist and colonizer architecture.

There are moments when reading Villanueva can feel like reading a redacted version of the most cutting-edge critiques of American empire to come out of critical race and ethnic studies, American studies, and cultural studies over the last two decades. Numerous scholars have shown how the post-1945 ascension of the United States as the top global power was accompanied and justified through a discourse of liberal multiculturalism. This discourse constructed the nation's economic, cultural, and military empire as the arrival of freedom for formerly colonized subjects around the world. This discourse bred outward-projected spectacles of diversity—from the Cold War CIA program to tour black jazz artists through Soviet territories to the founding of the interdisciplinary study of minoritized difference at US universities—even as communities of color continued to endure pulsating police terror, economic predation, and social-safety-net failures in their everyday lives. These "official" multiculturalisms have multiplied during the neoliberal era, when corporate actors affix Black Lives Matter flags to their walls and make land acknowledgments, while signing off on racist economic violence down their supply chains.[8]

To the extent that Villanueva is clear-eyed on the hypocrisy of such gestures, his words can be instructive for readers who need tools for understanding that neocolonial domination often traffics in appeals to multicultural inclusion. But the framing of the problem as a "virus" makes it impossible for him to carry through the critique. The silver lining about viruses is that immune systems can develop defenses against them. This is precisely what Villanueva thinks that the most burdened victims of "the colonial virus" can offer to the rest of the world: "The separation paradigm that locked us out and made us Others actually cultivated our resilience strategies. To survive the trauma of exploitation, we always had to believe that the dominant worldview was only one option, even when it seemed ubiquitous and inevitable. This has made us masters of alternative possibilities" (109).

The colonized subject finds in the metropole that the system of oppression could, in the right conditions and with the right reforms, be the seed from which new possibilities could emerge. The second half of *Decolonizing Wealth* digs into the archives of colonial domination and retrieves from them the "indigenous wisdom" that emerged in the context of illness but now can provide an inoculation. The tool of domination can also be a tool of resistance because—and this is the key—resistance comes into being through histories of imperial domination.

Decolonial Inoculation

"Evolution occurs both by holding on to the adaptations that keep us thriving, and also abandoning the elements that keep us from thriving," Villanueva writes (108). A virus can prompt evolution. Therefore, Villanueva looks not only to some retrieved wisdom of the colonized but also to the aspects of colonialism—namely, a monetized system of value—that he considers to promote human flourishing. He understands that this program could be a hard sell, given all the evidence that capitalism has upheld white-supremacist and colonial systems of "division, control, and exploitation." He acknowledges this difficulty at the outset: "Some will say that the colonial system of wealth consolidation based on white supremacy has caused so much damage and suffering and is so intrinsically rotten that anything related to it, including ostensibly altruistic worlds of philanthropy or aid, cannot be fixed, cannot be trusted, should not be saved. I empathize with that perspective, yet I believe there are parts of the system worth holding on to. The both/and stance is how Native Americans have survived colonization" (109).

There are a number of things to notice about this claim, among them the outright affirmation that parts of "the colonial system of wealth consolidation based on white supremacy" are "worth holding on to." But equally important is how Villanueva interfaces with the contrary "perspective" that this system should be destroyed: he *empathizes* with it. This empathy injects a measure of critical ambivalence into his ultimate conclusion that a "both/and" approach—committing to both finance capitalism and a project of decolonization—is preferable. Not only does the denunciation of philanthrocapitalism clear space for its continued reproduction, but this reproduction is further perfected through a sentiment-driven equivocation about understanding the harms of the past and concern that it will be repeated.

It is in this both/and ambivalence that Villanueva may be most instructive as a subject for scholars of religion and United States empire. In his project to eviscerate colonialism and to repair it through recourse to an "indigenous" subjectivity, Villanueva anticipates and embodies the internal contestations attendant to any imperial project. Scholars working at the nexus of religion and empire have highlighted such discursive struggles in contexts of US colonialism, but usually our paradigms have mapped them in terms of when they "dominate" and when they "resist." For example, scholars have noted that the American military occupied foreign nations in the name of "religious liberty," but we will also qualify that the subjects of the colonial administration countermobilized this language in a bid for a nationalist sovereignty.[9] Or, scholars will map how white missionaries perpetuated empire by exporting their brand of Christianity to the global south, but we follow up these stories with reassurances that the lessons they learned in the field informed their later support for civil rights, anti-apartheid struggles, and other decolonial movements.[10] The structure of these claims is to follow the exposure of imperial sojourns with a caveat, an *and yet*, to qualify the critique. The point is that white Christian missionaries and managerial policymakers were globetrotting colonizers, to be sure, but they also sowed the seed of resistance to the white supremacy and American global hegemony of which they were a part. This structure of argument belongs as much to Villanueva as it does to American religious historians. The question, then, is about the consequences of writing empire in these terms.

Villanueva writes colonialism as an alien invader that perpetuates "domination, control, exploitation" and outlines the corresponding decolonial remedies to these symptoms in a chart.

COLONIZED → DECOLONIZED
DIVIDE → CONNECT
CONTROL → RELATE
EXPLOIT → BELONG

But, again, Villanueva is ambivalent: he knows that a literal reading of "decolonization" would mean the return of "sovereignty not over the land and its resources but also over social structures and traditions" to "those from whom it was all stolen." He urges his readers to accept that since "there is no future that does not include the settlers occupying Indigenous lands," the best option is to pursue collective healing toward diagrammed goals that steer away from redistributive politics (34). At the center of decolonization is "healing" the ties between colonizer and colonized, and doing so via the expression of trauma and sentiment.

The outcome of historical rehearsal is affected confession and atonement. The second half of *Decolonizing Wealth* proceeds as a series of seven steps toward decolonization: Grieve, Apologize, Listen, Relate, Represent, Invest, Repair. The steps begin with grief; both "we who were colonized" and "those who have embodied and sustained the colonizer virus" are classified as grievers. "The fear, anxiety, and mistrust that characterizes [sic] being a member of the 1 percent is no joke," Villanueva preempts his skeptics (103). Then he reminds readers that "the Native principle of All My Relations" means that settlers and settled must "engage in healing together" in both their private lives and their workplaces (114).

Grief clears ground for the possible second and also affect-driven step, Apology. The book recommends a script written by a white manager of a family foundation,

> To my Indigenous Relatives and Relatives of Color: I apologize for my ignorance of the harm that came to you and the horrors you survived through many generations. I apologize for my unconscious racism and white supremacy, and for the pain they have caused you. I apologize for the silent ways I gave my own comfort priority over your existence as a sovereign human being. When I dishonored you, I dishonored my own humanity and the humanity of all our children. I am sorry. I love you. Please forgive me (125).

Both grief and apology chisel out an affective commons for oncedivided subjects to reunite into a transcendental category of the human, from which all had been alienated. That is, Villanueva imagines that colonization takes away the humanity of the colonizers, whereas contemporary decolonial and black-studies analyses of empire would likely claim the opposite: that colonization is precisely what *makes* the humanity of the colonizers, insofar as it makes the foil onto which the coherent form of the "human" can find her positive shape.[11] So convinced is Villanueva about the dehumanizing effects of colonialism on colonizers that he includes a proposed apology to white people who have suffered the divisive "trauma" of the colonizer virus: "*To my European-Descended*

Relatives: I apologize for all the times I have judged you instead of allowing myself to feel the grief of our collective spiritual impoverishment and cultural amnesia. I apologize for seeing you as a monster of oppression, instead of a Child of Creation. I apologize for disassociating from you and denying that we are related. When I judged you, I judged my own ancestors, my children, and myself. I am sorry. I love you. Please forgive me" (125; italics in original).

The secular majoritarian discourse of universal humanity, extant in both apologies, seeks to pull wayward children back into a community of more "natural" relations whose differences are just variations on the same human theme. The Christian secular valences of the apology script, as well as its momentum toward universal belonging in a community of "Creation," erect the outlines of this subject: he is a sovereign individual in empathetic relationship with a community of sovereign individuals whose cultural differences do not undermine their common sameness.[12] If colonialism is a virus—something that happens to people to divide them—the apology is an inoculation against it: in the form of the acceptance and celebration of positive (nonviral) variation across a shared human form. Healing involves recovering these differences and mobilizing them toward unity.

Already it is clear that the key ingredient in Villanueva's medicinal cocktail is sentiment. If the sin is that I have denied someone else's sovereignty and value as a "Child of Creation," the solution to this is emotions like repentance and love. In other words, his program of decolonization is premised on the assumption that love and other forms of empathetic affect are incommensurate with violence and control. Villanueva goes so far as to recommend that funders ask potential grantees questions from a thirty-six-question "Generation of Interpersonal Closeness" script, made famous in the *New York Times* "Modern Love" column, to help "strangers along the path of relationship, breaking down barriers gradually by revealing people's concerns, hopes, dreams, and secrets" (108).[13]

We should read these gestures to cultivate intimacy in terms of their concerted effort to create what Lauren Berlant has termed "intimate publics," where "citizenship as a condition of social membership [is] produced by personal acts and values" and where "public good [is recognized] only in a particularly constricted nation of simultaneously lived private worlds."[14] Where Berlant refers to norms of the US nation-state in the context of family-values politics, the point goes further than this, illuminating the kinds of global multicultural citizenship produced by and for capitalist global markets, where the corporation is rewritten as a surrogate "family."[15] To interface in this sphere—to become qualified for transactions necessary to survive—means valuing "strong, authentic, caring human connection . . . over and above investment returns" (135).[16] The catch is that this is not a displacement of investment by relationships; it is a move to make investment conditional on a particular performance of affected interiority and status-transcending intimacy.

But in what universe is intimate attachment incommensurate with abuse? On the contrary, numerous scholars of empire have underlined the central role of intimacy—defined as both the activities imagined to happen in private and, more importantly, an ontology that prizes individual interiority—in colonial projects. "The human ability to enter into, know, and feel the psyche of another is not incompatible with dominant power," Talal Asad writes.[17] On the contrary, "it renders the other more vulnerable to precise control" because it is often a "condition of insinuating oneself into and manipulating social and psychological structures to one's own advantage."[18] Without jumping on board Asad's implied emphasis on intentional ends-oriented manipulation—one does not need intent to prove the presence of violence—we might consider how the dual cultivation of self-critique and other-empathy becomes the tool through which Villanueva doubles down on finance capitalism as the tool of his very material plan for decolonial repair.

Indigenous (Archival) Wisdom

What is empire if not the absorption of historical difference into an expanding territory, a common narrative of progress, or a hegemonic episteme? Postcolonial analyses of the archive as a technology of state power have rightly highlighted how the classification and preservation of "difference" contribute to state-building projects. "There is no political power without control of the archive, if not memory," writes Jacques Derrida. "Effective democratization can always be measured by this essential criterion: the participation in and access to the archive, its constitution, and its interpretation."[19] Here archival power is power to organize difference into a majoritarian principle of unity and legibility.

Derrida's quip has inspired research on where and how state control of physical archives has shored up domination, as well as deep dives into the ways revolutionary groups have seized archives toward projects of counterhistory and liberation.[20] This latter move to find resistance amid domination can ironically recapitulate the forms of legibility that Derrida diagnoses as only ever possible in the context of established disciplinary systems.

Roderick Ferguson builds on Derrida's project when he takes "archive" as a descriptor for institutions that "place" dissonant knowledge formations into a unifying order. For Ferguson, the prototype of institutional archiving, and of archival institutions, is the post-1960s university and its initiatives for multicultural inclusion within the interdisciplinary humanities. The turn to diversity within universities, which happens at the same time as multicultural optics become central to the optics of free market corporations, developed in the context of midcentury antiracist and feminist student demands for a decolonized and democratized education system. The university answered them with the codification of black studies and women's studies into the archive of legitimate university departments. It responded to radical critiques of its racism and misogyny by framing its core mission as a version of this same intervention, if a warped one. The modern university would evolve from its self-image as sacred guardians of a European Enlightenment heritage, and grow into a vision of itself as an archive of multicultural difference.[21]

When Villanueva retrieves "indigenous wisdom" from the debris of colonial pillage, then rereads the afterlives of colonization through its lens, he carries out this kind of incorporative work. The both/and approach pursues assimilation on two fronts: he assimilates "indigenous wisdom" into financial logics even as he mounts an argument that financial logics can dovetail with the "indigenous worldview." Nowhere is this combinatory project more explicit than in Villanueva's discussion of the potential of money to be "medicine." Anticipating his readers' reactions that "money is dirty," he cuts them off at the pass. "We forget that humans made money up out of thin air, as a concept, a tool for a complex society, a placeholder for aspects of human relations," he chides. "Money is like water. Water can be a precious life-giving resource. But what happens when water is dammed, or even when a water cannon is fired on protesters in subzero temperatures? Money should be a tool of love, to facilitate relationships, to help us thrive, rather than to hurt and divide us. If it's used for sacred, life-giving, restorative purposes, it can be medicine" (9).

Villanueva believes he has reached into the archive of indigenous wisdom and found the historical truth necessary to turn colonial domination toward a resistance project: what he repeatedly terms "medicine money." It is possible to read such moments in terms of a straightforward capture. Managers capture racial- and gender-justice movements with a gesture to inclusion that does little to alter its basic logic.[22] A Great Books program that has added Toni Morrison to its syllabus is still a program invested in the exclusivity of "greatness." A university that adds a women's, gender, and sexuality studies department to its roster may still deny its largely feminized and person-of-color hourly workers a living wage. A finance bank that begins to describe its philanthropic investments as "medicine" and consult shamans before making donations is engaged in a cynical appropriation. The point of the capitalist humanitarian archive, in all of these cases, would be containment: place your opponents before they displace you.

Yet Ferguson would warn that we must understand the archival placement of difference not in terms of victory or defeat but as a mandate to interrogate the juncture between hermeneutic practices and practices of institution building. "Institutions are the outcome and the locations of imagined communities, with interpretive modes representing the brick and mortar of those imaginations," Ferguson explains.[23] To focus on the continuities of capture is useful insofar as it prompts reflection on the exhaustion of political critique—here its abstraction into a narrow politics of recognition—and underlines the need for self-critique in moments of apparent activist success. But reading only for capture can overlook how strategies of inclusion, even ones we can interpret cynically, will change the stakes of the politics that follow. The university's epistemological norms did and do shift in response to student protests. Philanthrocapitalist institutions probably would shift their understandings of "credit" and "responsibility" if they prioritized the voices of black and indigenous people. This would be true for any archive, broadly defined. The question should not be about resistance vs. domination so much as about what hermeneutic structures and institutional forms have emerged to iron conflicts into reconciled wholes.

One reply to the potential of archival projects to be mobilized toward dominative or liberating ends would be to classify various archival institutions, and the interpretive practices possible within them, according to the end that they serve. "Look," we could say, "here is an archive of an empire that sought air-tight taxonomic knowledge over its subjects. But there is an archive that speaks the contingency and anxiety of the empire's governing officials."[24] There is an archive of a tyrannical state, recording its every victim by name, address, family, and photo. But here are human-rights defenders, some of them professional historians, recovering these same documents to create a counterhistory."[25] There is an archive that interpolates its user into the racist violence it both represents and reinstates. Here is how nevertheless it reveals alternatives to it."[26] These arguments replicate at the level of form the binary paradigm that has structured many discourses on religion and empire. As our judgments swing between poles of domination and resistance—Does money dominate or resist? Does the *story* we told about money dominate or resist?—they index less final revelation than our current strategies for managing the afterlives of colonialism and slavery.

Many disciplines have exhibited vexed relationships with their archives, but perhaps none more than the academic study of religion. Scholars in this field know that a preponderance of data, not to mention the category of religion itself, has its provenance in taxonomies imposed by colonial officials and Christian missionaries. We know that religion framed Europeans' encounters with and organization of difference in the worlds they were colonizing. These articulations of religious difference not only mapped populations according to type, but they often did so by proposing the conversion of colonial populations into human (Christian) subjects.[27] "Religion," like "empire" and "archive," becomes a word that forges unity out of the multiplicity that it generates through its own economies of distinction. In other words, we could see the colonial invention of religion as a taxonomic device as simultaneously the invention of religion as an imperial archive—an archive that self-reproduces through its imperative to keep mapping the differences that are just outside of the scholar's control. Religion names the effort to transpose the incomprehensible into something that can be—must be—recognized, plotted, and ultimately included in the unity that is human history. Religion is not just what scholars find inside imperial archives but also the institutionalizing exercise that is the practice of archiving. If we were to find "religion" or "empire" in Villanueva's treatise, it would not only be in his strange returns to indigenous spirituality but also and more significantly in his attempts to place that knowledge form within the archive of finance capitalism.[28]

This means that manifestations of empire under neoliberal globalization are not so stark as we have come to think. They are less likely to look like spectacular power plays and more likely to take the form of assimilative exercises structured around affect, attachment, and humanization. When the social body is inoculated with critiques of colonialism and infused with sentimental testimonies, it is possible to take concrete steps to "eradicate the colonizer virus from society" and, in so doing, from empire's archive of historical difference (34).

Reparative Finance Capitalism

Villanueva is concrete about the material outcomes—the investment and repair—to which he hopes intimate relations and historical facts will lead. They begin with another historical rehearsal that has been the engine of the analysis: the momentum of capitalist humanitarian reproduction comes from the historical critiques that clear ground for expansion, renamed "reparation."

Sometimes I think it would be possible to construct the cultural history of US empire as a history of ambivalent equivocations and shaky solidarity claims: a train of actors with "good intentions" explaining how what others may call invasion, colonialism, occupation, theft, or genocide is relative progress over a worse, prior state of being. Missionaries, policymakers, colonial officials, corporate executives, and many others have tended to identify US hegemonic dominance as improvement over whatever geopolitical arrangements predated it. Scholars of religion in the Americas know these narratives well, given that their earliest and starkest plot points are in the theological anthropologies that animated European campaigns of settlement and enslavement. For more than two centuries, a shape-shifting discourse of exceptional hegemonic benevolence has framed US neocolonial cultural and political power as a positive improvement over old systems of colonial rule.[29] Those drones flying overhead? The Coca-Cola bottling plants? The brutal sanctions on nations suspected to be socialist sympathizers? Those reeducation projects? That is not empire. Or, if it is, it is also liberation, at least in a relative sense. So have argued people directing the jets, gaming out Coke's next strategy, ordering the tariffs, and writing the lessons. They know how to identify oppression and dismantle it toward their own solutions; the difference in how imperial power works in the context of late capitalism is that the past oppressors get an encore, because they are also the ministers of repair.

"Decolonizing wealth is, at its essence, about closing the racial wealth gap," Villanueva begins. "Poverty is the product of public policy and theft, facilitated by white supremacy" (161). He recites a litany, naming, among other historical crimes, the "near genocide of Native Americans," "the slave trade and slavery," "Jim Crow," "the exclusions built into the New Deal that disadvantaged people of color by not counting certain professions worthy of benefits (such as farmworkers and domestic workers)," "white boarding schools that ripped Native American families apart," "how the benefits of the GI Bill were racialized," "redlining practices, "the elite universities of this country being built with profits of slavery and the fact that people of color still don't feel included today," "images in the media that constantly criminalize people of color," "the lack of police accountability for the killing of unarmed Native and Black men and women," "the inequality in bank loans and venture capital that impact [sic] people of color" and, more than anything else, how all these things "have worked together to keep wealth and well-being disproportionately concentrated on white communities" (161).

And, I mean, he is not entirely wrong. As audience to what is ultimately a happily ended jeremiad, I will cop to my ambivalence about certain qualities of Villanueva's intervention. It is true: I actually do wish that even a handful of the historical contexts that Villanueva names would inform scholarship and teaching on religion, empire, and capitalism. Also, Villanueva is nothing if not bold. He follows up the ticker-tape parade of crimes with a proposal. He urges philanthropic foundations to "tithe" 10 percent of their overall assets toward a "trust fund to which Native Americans and African Americans could apply for grants for various asset-building projects" like home ownership, start-ups, and education. He further specifies that there be "no specifications around how that money is spent, no reporting. No strings attached"—and that this happen "right now" (162). Even though I recoil at his enthusiasm for a privatized social safety net and progress-through-entrepreneurship, even though I know that it is a murderous lie to write the afterlives of slavery and genocide in terms of a "racial wealth gap," maybe I should give him credit for how he asks philanthropic finance organizations to be, if not exactly better, then at least less worse than they were a generation ago. At least he knows some of the literature, so much so that he has made it discursively indispensable to his argument on behalf of finance-driven decolonization. At least he is trying and, besides that, so much better than the bogeyman alternatives. Right?

It is this feeling—the reticence to outright condemnation, this pang to not play hardball with actors who were less awful than their historical peers, of being hamstrung over how to talk about colonized elites and sympathetic colonizers—that merits reflection. When I railroad myself into equivocation over whether Villanueva deserves the heat I have directed toward his book—as if the man's individual character, not the precedents and implications of a text he authored, were at issue—I have begun to repeat a version of the script he performs with respect to the colonizing entity that is philanthropic finance. We both are speaking as ambivalent subjects of neocolonial modernity. We both are seeing ourselves in colonial dynamics and questioning where our solidarities rest. We both are preoccupied with the affective lives of colonizers as they move from sincere-but-misguided benevolence to guilty self-implication to renewed commitment. We both know the tried-and-true recipe for maverick intelligibility under the conditions of empire: critique, equivocate, nod toward another possible world, critique again, equivocate again.

My internal conflict mirrors Villanueva's because this response is embedded in the structure of his script. The critique of colonialism inoculates the reader against a "colonizer virus" and produces a manageable case of colonial ambivalence. The prescribed dose does not overthrow colonialism; it prepares its recipients to exist in the world colonialism continues to make. "Like any clever virus," Villanueva writes, "the colonizer mindset keeps mutating and adapting, so in order to heal fully, we will need to be vigilant and get booster shots." What are booster shots if not new ways of confessing and condemning colonialism—not so much to partake in decolonial struggle but to become better adjusted, more empathetic within the empire whose archives we build and training centers we staff? Is my confession of these doubts just drawing me deeper in?

* * *

The fastest way to reify empire's discourse about itself is to valorize acts of resistance that occur within its grid of intelligibility or suppose that hesitation in the face of colonial itineraries is a wrench in the machine. These are the stories that get told in preparation for another expansion.

Decolonizing Wealth leaves the reader not in the philanthropist's boardroom but on the literal frontier of militarized colonial takeover of Native grounds. The final paragraph drops us at the Standing Rock Sacred Stone Camp during the protests against the Keystone XL Pipeline. It describes a Water Protector on the morning after a violent scene of retaliation the previous night: "The day after she and her fellow Water Protectors had been gunned down by the militarized police and National Guard using fire hoses and mace and rubber bullets—the very next day—she trudged back to the armed forces with candy in her hands. The Water Protector walked right back up to the same guards and police, moving slowly, her open palms offering the sweets, the way you might approach a feral animal, and she said, '*It's not you, we know it's not your fault, we're not mad at you, we're praying for you*'" (181).

This woman, he writes, is modeling the "Native way" of "bring[ing] the oppressor into our circle of healing" and making the oppressor feel "acknowledged and affirmed [as] a human being of infinite worth" (180–81). The answer to investment-fueled planetary terror and social movements against its continuation is to find the person who is doing the most to return humanity to the colonizer. When you find her, as Villanueva has done, there is a clear next step.

Here is what that step is *not*. It is not to wonder what could be happening right outside the frame, what else could be going on in the girl's head besides forgiveness of and prayer for the person who brutalized her. Maybe the woman is gaming out this last-ditch effort to quell the threat, to make sure her loved ones are not brutalized that evening. Maybe she is defiant, breaking rank with comrades who are against these conciliatory tactics. Maybe the candy is laced with Visine, for some gastrointestinal payback. Or maybe it should not matter to the scholar what she is thinking, only that the transaction staged a photograph that a philanthrocapitalist would use to suggest that the best response to militarized policing is to give the cops candy and, it follows, their humanness.

Do not think those things. Just tell her she is doing the right thing. If you have funds to spare, float her some cash. If you have a platform, give her some spotlight. Say with sincerity that you know it is the "Native way." Resistance to colonialism is this transparent, this sweet. Suggest to other protestors that until they choose to embody a more valuable form of (human) difference, they will never stop the water cannons, they will never get money, they will never be part of the circle of healing, they will always be alien to the Native way, they will end up in the path of empire's newest iron snake, from which not even the dead can find their shelter.

NOTES

1 Edgar Villanueva, *Decolonizing Wealth: Indigenous Wisdom to Heal Divides and Restore Balance* (Oakland, CA: Berrett-Koehler, 2018), 1–4. Hereafter page numbers are cited in the text.
2 Decolonizing Wealth Project, https://decolonizingwealth.com/ (accessed June 10, 2021).
3 The resistance/domination binary is the opposite side of the coin to a sincerity/instrumentality binary. We see this especially in accounts of empire that refer to colonizers' own personal ambivalence or good intentions as somehow contrary to the violent effects of their occupation. Sincerity and empathy are not opposed to domination, but complementary to it. This chapter is unable to delve fully into this relationship, which should be a subject of further scholarly work. I am indebted to Timothy Byram for his thinking on this point and many others in the chapter that follows. Byram, "Techniques of Intimacy."
4 Hulsether, *Capitalist Humanitarianism*.
5 Strangely absent is the history of contagion and virality as the metaphor to describe immigrants to the United States. Villanueva takes the trope and reverses it: the invader is not foreigners, but an abstract colonizer virus that is not identifiable with any particular subject position. On virality and colonization, see Ahuja, *Bioinsecurities*.
6 There are too many examples to list. Two representative ones include "PUP Acquires Ruha Benjamin's *Viral Justice*"; and Weiss, "The Two Pandemics."
7 See for example Sharpe, *In the Wake*; Fanon, *Wretched of the Earth*; Wilderson, *Red, White, and Black*; McKittrick, *Sylvia Wynter*.
8 Von Eschen, *Satchmo Blows Up the World*; Von Eschen, *Race against Empire*; Melamed, *Represent and Destroy*; Ferguson, *Reorder of Things*.
9 Wenger, *We Have a Religion*; Wenger, *Religious Freedom*; J. Thomas, *Faking Liberties*.

10 McAlister, *The Kingdom of God Has No Borders*; Curtis, *Holy Humanitarians*; Hollinger, *Protestants Abroad*.
11 Rifkin, *Settler Common Sense*; Lowe, *The Intimacies of Four Continents*.
12 On Christian secularism as a majoritarian discourse, see Asad, *Formations of the Secular*; Jakobsen and Pellegrini, *Secularisms*; Mufti, *Enlightenment in the Colony*; Fessenden, *Culture and Redemption*.
13 See Daniel Jones, "The 36 Questions That Lead to Love," *New York Times*, January 9, 2015, www.nytimes.com (accessed January 10, 2021).
14 Berlant, *The Queen of America Goes to Washington City*, 5.
15 On the corporation as family see Lofton, *Consuming Religion*.
16 He continues, "It means that those with wealth are not reduced to cash machines and those seeking funding are not reduced to gold diggers. There are people hiding inside the business suits" (135).
17 Asad, "Reflections on Violence, Law, and Humanitarianism," 390–418.
18 Asad, "Reflections on Violence, Law, and Humanitarianism," 390–418.
19 Derrida, *Archive Fever*, 4.
20 For a comprehensive analysis, see Weld, *Paper Cadavers*.
21 Ferguson, *Reorder of Things*.
22 Ferguson, *Reorder of Things*.
23 Ferguson, *Reorder of Things*, 16.
24 Stoler, *Along the Archival Grain*.
25 Many works straddle both concepts of "state control" and the "vulnerable state" in order to underline the contingency of state narratives. Two recent and strong examples of this genre of argumentation are Weld, *Paper Cadavers*, and Azoulay, "The Imperial Condition of Photography in Palestine."
26 Recent work among scholars specializing in the black Atlantic and the history of slavery have embraced the paradox of the archive as, in Jennifer Morgan's words, "both the home of those who commanded and the tantalizing place from which that command might be subverted" such that "engagement with the archive is an opportunity to confront the exclusionary powers that position racialized subjects as outside the national project." Morgan makes this argument in a recent special issue of *Social Text* that takes up slavery's archive as a site for ongoing racial terror *and* counternarrative. The special issue was followed by another, in *History of the Present*, that elaborated the conversation. It is a live topic, and scholars engaged with it have been particularly interested in the archive as "critical fabulation" that writes "with and against the archive" toward a fuller picture of the lives of the enslaved—and, perhaps, toward different futures in slavery's afterlife. For essays that introduce the question of slavery's archive and its command-subversion paradox, see Helton et al., "The Question of Recovery," and Connolly and Fuentes, "Introduction: From Archives of Slavery to Liberated Futures?" For a canonical article on slavery's archive, which is the foundation for this recent work, see Hartman, "Venus in Two Acts." For an argument for the stakes of understanding the archive as a contested space for historical knowledge production, including

dynamic discussions on the status of the archive within the historiography of slavery, see Smallwood, "The Politics of the Archive"; and J. Morgan, "Archives and Histories of Racial Capitalism."

27 For example: Chidester, *Savage Systems*; Keane, *Christian Moderns*; J. Z. Smith, "Religion, Religions, Religious."

28 The idea of religion as archive making draws from works that historicize religion and religious studies—not just to rehearse the moments in which the field has fallen into imperial archiving of difference but also to show how the field's modes of historicization and analysis of myths can be useful for redescribing and understanding projects like the one outlined in *Decolonizing Wealth*.

29 Melani McAlister coins the term "benevolent supremacy" to refer to post-WWII formations of this dynamic. See McAlister, *Epic Encounters*.

ACKNOWLEDGMENTS

This book was first envisioned by Sylvester Johnson and Tracy Leavelle, who codirected the Religion and U.S. Empire Collaborative Project in 2013–2015 with funding from the Kripke Center at Creighton University. We are grateful to the Kripke Center, to Tracy Leavelle, and to all the members of the original RUSE project for their help thinking through the questions engaged in this book: Julius Bailey, Edward Blum, Cara Burnidge, Emily Conroy-Krutz, Heather Curtis, Sarah Dees, Jonathan Ebel, Keith Feldman, Jennifer Graber, Michael Hawkins, Charles Strauss, and Karine Walther.

Our deepest gratitude is due to the indomitable Jennifer Hammer and Veronica Knutson at NYU Press, to the anonymous readers whose comments significantly improved this book, and to series editors Tracy Fessenden, Laura Levitt, and David Harrington Watt for their unwavering faith in this project. We also wish to thank Dominique Francesca of the Virginia Tech Center for the Humanities, who helped organize an April 2020 contributors' workshop that had to be moved online at the last minute; and graduate assistants Muhammed Shah Shajahan and Trevor Samraj of Virginia Tech.

Tisa Wenger thanks her Yale colleagues Zareena Grewal, Kathryn Lofton, Melanie Ross, Nicole Myers Turner, Sally Promey, and Almeda Wright. Conversations with students and colleagues in a Yale graduate seminar on Religion and U.S. Empire, cotaught in fall 2020 with Zareena Grewal, further clarified her thinking on these topics. Above all she is grateful to Rod Groff for his steady and supportive presence, and for making sure that all the practical stuff gets done. Sylvester Johnson thanks his former colleagues and graduate students at Northwestern University in the Department of African American Studies and the Department of Religious Studies and his current colleagues in the Department of Religion and Culture at Virginia Tech who offered generous feedback on research and conceptions of race, religion, and empire throughout the life of this collaborative project. He is especially grateful to Heather Nicholson, who has remained a rigorous and encouraging conversation partner.

Most importantly, we are indebted to our twelve magnanimous coauthors who shared their brilliant work for this project, especially during the global pandemic, which introduced incredible challenges to an already demanding undertaking. It has been a privilege to work with each and every one of you.

BIBLIOGRAPHY

Adams, David Wallace. *Education for Extinction: American Indians and the Boarding School Experience, 1875–1928.* 2nd ed. Lawrence: University Press of Kansas, 2020.
Agrama, Hussein Ali. *Questioning Secularism: Islam, Sovereignty, and the Rule of Law in Modern Egypt.* Chicago: University of Chicago Press, 2012.
Ahuja, Neel. *Bioinsecurities: Disease Interventions, Empire, and the Government of Species.* Durham, NC: Duke University Press, 2016.
Aidi, Hisham. *Rebel Music: Race, Empire, and the New Muslim Youth Culture.* New York: Vintage, 2014.
Akee, Randall, Paul Ong, and Desi Rodriguez Longbear. "US Census Response Rates on American Indian Reservations in the 2020 Census and in the 2010 Census." *UCLA American Indian Studies Center Publications*, May 15, 2020. www.aisc.ucla.edu
Alderson, Jo Bartels, and Jim Michael Alderson. *The Man Mazzuchelli: Pioneer Priest.* Madison: Wisconsin House, 1974.
Alexander, Michelle. *The New Jim Crow: Mass Incarceration in the Age of Colorblindness.* New York: New Press, 2010.
Anderson, Benedict. *Imagined Communities: Reflections on the Origin and Spread of Nationalism.* Rev. ed. London: Verso, 2006.
Anderson, James D. *The Education of Blacks in the South, 1860–1935.* Chapel Hill: University of North Carolina Press, 1988.
Angel, Michael. *Preserving the Sacred: Historical Perspectives on the Ojibwa Midewiwin.* Winnipeg: University of Manitoba Press, 2002.
Arista, Noelani. *The Kingdom and the Republic: Sovereign Hawai'i and the Early United States.* America in the Nineteenth Century. Philadelphia: University of Pennsylvania Press, 2019.
Armitage, David. "John Locke, Carolina, and the 'Two Treatises of Government.'" *Political Theory* 32, no. 5 (2004): 602–27.
Arrighi, Giovanni. *The Long Twentieth Century: Money, Power, and the Origins of Our Times.* London: Verso, 1994.
Asad, Talal. *Formations of the Secular: Christianity, Islam, Modernity.* Stanford, CA: Stanford University Press, 2003.
———. *Genealogies of Religion: Discipline and Reasons of Power in Christianity and Islam.* Baltimore, MD: Johns Hopkins University Press, 1993.
———. "Reflections on Violence, Law, and Humanitarianism." *Critical Inquiry* 41, no. 2 (2015): 390–427.

Azoulay, Ariella. "The Imperial Condition of Photography in Palestine: Archives, Looting, and the Figure of the Infiltrator." *Visual Anthropology Review* 33, no. 1 (2017): 5–17.

Balagangadhara, S. N. *"The Heathen in His Blindness—": Asia, the West, and the Dynamic of Religion*. Leiden: Brill, 1994.

Baldoz, Rick. *The Third Asiatic Invasion: Empire and Migration in Filipino America, 1898–1946*. New York: NYU Press, 2011.

Bambino, Don, Geno Tai, Aditya Shah, Chyke A. Doubeni, Irene G. Sia, and Mark L. Wieland, "The Disproportionate Impact of COVID-19 on Racial and Ethnic Minorities in the United States." *Clinical Infectious Diseases* (2020): 1–4. https://doi.org/10.1093/cid/ciaa815

Banner, Stuart. *How the Indians Lost Their Land: Law and Power on the Frontier*. Cambridge, MA: Belknap Press of Harvard University Press, 2007.

Barboza, Steven. *American Jihad: Islam after Malcolm X*. New York: Doubleday, 1994.

Barker, Joanne, ed. *Sovereignty Matters: Locations of Contestation and Possibility in Indigenous Struggles for Self-Determination*. Contemporary Indigenous Issues. Lincoln: University of Nebraska Press, 2005.

Barlow, Melvin L. *History of Industrial Education in the United States*. Preoria, IL: C.A. Bennett, 1967.

Barnes, Linda, and Inés Tlamantez, eds. *Teaching Religion and Healing*. Oxford: Oxford University Press, 2006.

Bastian, Jenn-Pierre. "Protestantism in Latin America." In *The Church in Latin America, 1492–1992*, ed. Enrique Dussel, 313–50. Tunbridge Wells, Kent: Burns & Oats, 1992.

Bauman, Zygmunt. *Wasted Lives: Modernity and Its Outcasts*. Malden, MA: Polity Press, 2002.

Bederman, Gail. "'Civilization,' the Decline of Middle-Class Manliness, and Ida B. Wells's Antilynching Campaign (1892–94)." *Radical History Review* 52 (Winter 1992): 5–30.

Beechert, Edward D. *Working in Hawaii: A Labor History*. Honolulu: University of Hawaii Press, 1985.

Beliso-De Jesús, Aisha M. *Electric Santería: Racial and Sexual Assemblages of Transnational Religion*. Gender, Theory, and Religion. New York: Columbia University Press, 2015.

Bell, Genevieve. "Telling Stories out of School: Remembering the Carlisle Indian Industrial School, 1879–1918." PhD diss., Stanford University, 1998.

Bellah, Robert N. "Civil Religion in America." *Daedalus* 96, no. 1 (1967): 1–21, www.jstor.org/stable/20027022 (accessed February 16, 2021).

Benjamin, Thomas, ed. *Encyclopedia of Western Colonialism since 1450*. 3 vols. Farmington Hills, MI: Macmillan Reference USA, 2007.

Berkhofer, Robert F. *The White Man's Indian: Images of the American Indian from Columbus to the Present*. New York: Knopf, 1978.

Berlant, Lauren Gail. *The Queen of America Goes to Washington City: Essays on Sex and Citizenship*. Durham, NC: Duke University Press, 1997.

Beyan, Amos Jones. *African American Settlements in West Africa: John Brown Russwurm and the American Civilizing Efforts*. New York: Palgrave Macmillan, 2005.

Beyer, Carl Kalani. "The Connection of Samuel Chapman Armstrong as Both Borrower and Architect of Education in Hawai'i." *History of Education Quarterly* 47, no. 1 (Feb. 2007): 23–48.

———. "Manual and Industrial Education for Hawaiians during the 19th Century." *Hawaiian Journal of History* 38 (2004): 1–34.

Bhabha, Homi K. *The Location of Culture*. Routledge Classics. London: Routledge, 2004.

Bilgrami, Akeel. *Secularism, Identity, and Enchantment*. Convergences: Inventories of the Present. Cambridge, MA: Harvard University Press, 2014.

Biondi, Martha. *The Black Revolution on Campus*. Berkeley: University of California Press, 2012.

Blackmon, Douglas A. *Slavery by Another Name: The Re-Enslavement of Black Americans from the Civil War to World War II*. New York: Doubleday, 2008.

Blauner, Robert. "Internal Colonialism and Ghetto Revolt." *Social Problems* 16, no. 4 (April 1, 1969): 393–408.

Blum, Gabriella. "The Individualization of War: From War to Policing in the Regulation of Armed Conflicts." In *Law and War*, ed. Austin Sarat, Lawrence Douglas, and Martha Merrill Umphrey. Palo Alto, CA: Stanford University Press, 2014.

Bodo, Murray, OFM. *Tales of an Enishodi: Berard Haile and the Navajos, 1900–1961*. Albuquerque: University of New Mexico Press, 1998.

Bollettino, Maria Alessandra. "Slavery, War, and Britain's Atlantic Empire: Black Soldiers, Sailors, and Rebels in the Seven Years' War." PhD diss., University of Texas at Austin, 2009.

Bowes, John P. *Land Too Good for Indians: Northern Indian Removal*. Norman: University of Oklahoma Press, 2017.

Bowler, Kate. *Blessed: A History of the American Prosperity Gospel*. New York: Oxford University Press, 2013.

Boyd, Maurice. *Kiowa Voices: Ceremonial Dance, Ritual, and Song*. Vol. 1. Fort Worth: Texas Christian University Press, 1981.

Brands, H. W. *Bound to Empire: The United States and the Philippines*. New York: Oxford University Press, 1992.

Brazer, Marjorie Cahn. *Harps upon the Willows: The Johnston Family of the Old Northwest*. Ann Arbor: Historical Society of Michigan, 1993.

Bressey, Caroline. *Empire, Race, and the Politics of Anti-Caste*. London: Bloomsbury, 2013.

Brewer, Holly. "Slavery, Sovereignty, and 'Inheritable Blood': Reconsidering John Locke and the Origins of American Slavery." *American Historical Review* 122, no. 4 (October 1, 2017): 1038–78.

Brown, Vincent. *Tacky's Revolt: The Story of an Atlantic Slave War*. Cambridge, MA: Belknap Press of Harvard University Press, 2020.

Browner, Tara, ed. *Music of the First Nations: Tradition and Innovation in Native North America*. Champaign: University of Illinois Press, 2010.

Brugge, Doug, and Rob Goble. "The History of Uranium Mining and the Navajo People." *American Journal of Public Health* 92, no. 9 (September 2002): 1410–19.

Bruno-Jofre, Rosa del Carmen. "Social Gospel, the Committee on Cooperation in Latin America, and the APRA: The Case of the American Methodist Mission, 1920–1930." *Canadian Journal of Latin American and Caribbean Studies* 9, no. 18 (1984): 75–110.

Bryant, Sherwin K. *Rivers of Gold, Lives of Bondage: Governing through Slavery in Colonial Quito*. Chapel Hill: University of North Carolina Press, 2014.

Buffalohead, W. Roger, and Paulette Fairbanks Molin. "'A Nucleus of Civilization': American Indian Families at Hampton Institute in the Late Nineteenth Century." *Journal of American Indian Education* 35, no. 3 (Spring 1996): 59–94.

Bulmer, Martin, Kevin Bales, and Kathryn Kish Sklar. *The Social Survey in Historical Perspective, 1880–1940*. Cambridge: Cambridge University Press, 1991.

Burin, Eric. *Slavery and the Peculiar Solution: A History of the American Colonization Society*. Gainesville: University Press of Florida, 2005.

Burnard, Trevor G. *Jamaica in the Age of Revolution*. Philadelphia: University of Pennsylvania Press, 2020.

Burns, Rebecca. *Rage in the Gate City: The Story of the 1906 Atlanta Race Riot*. Athens: University of Georgia Press, 2009.

Butler, Judith. *Excitable Speech: A Politics of the Performative*. New York: Routledge, 1997.

Byram, Timothy. "Techniques of Intimacy: The Search for Good Religion in the Historiography of Transnational Protestantism." Unpublished manuscript.

Byrd, Brandon R. *The Black Republic: African Americans and the Fate of Haiti*. Philadelphia: University of Pennsylvania Press, 2019.

Byrd, Jodi A. *The Transit of Empire: Indigenous Critiques of Colonialism*. First Peoples: New Directions Indigenous. Minneapolis: University of Minnesota Press, 2011.

Cady, Linell, and Elizabeth Shakman Hurd, eds. *Comparative Secularisms in a Global Age*. New York: Palgrave MacMillan, 2010.

Calder, Bruce J. *The Impact of Intervention: The Dominican Republic during the U.S. Occupation of 1916–1924*. Princeton, NJ: Markus Wiener, 2006 [1984].

Calloway, Colin G. *The Shawnees and the War for America*. Penguin Library of American Indian History. New York: Viking, 2007.

Campbell, James. "Models and Metaphors: Industrial Education in the United States and South Africa." In *Comparative Perspectives on South Africa*, ed. Ran Greenstein, 90–134. New York: Macmillan, 1998.

Candelario, Ginetta E. B. *Black behind the Ears: Dominican Racial Identity from Museums to Beauty Shops*. Durham, NC: Duke University Press, 2007.

Capps, Walter. *The Unfinished War: Vietnam and the American Conscience*. Boston: Beacon Press, 1990.

Carson, Arthur. *Silliman University, 1901–1959*. New York: United Board for Christian Higher Education in Asia, 1965.
Carter, Karen E. *Scandal in the Parish: Priests and Parishioners Behaving Badly in Eighteenth-Century France*. Montreal: McGill-Queen's University Press, 2019.
Case, Jay Riley. *An Unpredictable Gospel: American Evangelicals and World Christianity, 1812–1920*. New York: Oxford University Press, 2012.
Catron, John W. "Evangelical Networks in the Greater Caribbean and the Origins of the Black Church." *Church History* 79, no. 1 (2010): 77–114.
Césaire, Aimé. *Discourse on Colonialism*. New York: Monthly Review Press, 1972.
Chandler, Kaitlyn, et al. *The Winged: An Upper Missouri River Ethno-Ornithology*. Tucson: University of Arizona Press, 2016.
Charbonneau, Oliver. *Civilizational Imperatives: Americans, Moros, and the Colonial World*. Ithaca, NY: Cornell University Press, 2020.
Chidester, David. *Empire of Religion: Imperialism and Comparative Religion*. Chicago: University of Chicago Press, 2014.
———. *Savage Systems: Colonialism and Comparative Religion in Southern Africa*. Studies in Religion and Culture. Charlottesville: University Press of Virginia, 1996.
Chresfield, Michell. "Creoles of the Mountains: Race, Regionalism, and Modernity in Progressive Era Appalachia." *Journal of the Gilded Age and Progressive Era*, September 2020, 1–21. https://doi.org/10.1017/S1537781420000250
Ciment, James. *Another America: The Story of Liberia and the Former Slaves Who Ruled It*. New York: Farrar, Straus & Giroux, 2013.
Clymer, Kenton J. *Protestant Missionaries in the Philippines, 1898–1916: An Inquiry into American Colonial Mentality*. Urbana: University of Illinois Press, 1986.
Coates, Benjamin A. "The Pan-American Lobbyist: William Eleroy Curtis and U.S. Empire, 1884–1899." *Diplomatic History* 38 (2014): 22–48.
Coker, Daniel. *Journal of Daniel Coker, a Descendant of Africa*. Baltimore, MD: John D. Toy Printer, 1820.
Collins, James P. "Native Americans in the Census, 1860–1890." *National Archives Genealogy Notes* 38, no. 2 (Summer 2006): 1–7.
Coloma, Roland Sintos. "'Destiny Has Thrown the Negro and the Filipino under the Tutelage of America': Race and Curriculum in the Age of Empire." *Curriculum Inquiry* 39 no. 4 (2009): 495–519.
Connolly, Brian, and Marisa Fuentes. "Introduction: From Archives of Slavery to Liberated Futures?" *History of the Present* 6, no. 2 (2016): 105–16.
Conroy-Krutz, Emily. *Christian Imperialism: Converting the World in the Early American Republic*. United States in the World. Ithaca, NY: Cornell University Press, 2015.
———. "The Hierarchy of Heathenism: Missionaries Map the Globe." *Diplomatic History* 42, no. 1 (2018): 55–71.
Corbett, Rosemary. *Making Moderate Islam: Sufism, Service, and the "Ground Zero Mosque" Controversy*. Stanford, CA: Stanford University Press, 2016.
Corse, Theron. *Protestants, Revolution, and the Cuba-US Bond*. Gainesville: University Press of Florida, 2007.

Coviello, Peter. *Make Yourselves Gods: Mormons and the Unfinished Business of American Secularism*. Chicago: University of Chicago Press, 2019.
Cuffe, Paul. *Captain Paul Cuffe's Logs and Letters, 1808–1817: A Black Quaker's "Voice from within the Veil."* Edited by Rosalind Cobb Wiggins. Washington, DC: Howard University Press, 1996.
Curtis, Heather D. *Holy Humanitarians: American Evangelicals and Global Aid*. Cambridge, MA: Harvard University Press, 2018.
Dattel, Gene. *Cotton and Race in the Making of America: The Human Costs of Economic Power*. Government Institutes, 2009.
David, John Seh. *The American Colonization Society and the Founding of the First African Republic*. Bloomington, IN: iUniverse, 2014.
Davidson, Basil. *The African Slave Trade*. Rev. ed. Boston: Back Bay Books, 1988.
Davidson, Christina. "Redeeming Santo Domingo: North Atlantic Missionaries and the Racial Conversion of a Nation." *Church History* 89, no. 1 (March 2020): 74–100. https://doi.org/10.1017/S0009640720000013
Davis, Angela Y. *Abolition Democracy: Beyond Empire, Prisons, and Torture*. Seven Stories Press 1st ed. New York: Seven Stories Press, 2005.
Davis, David Brion. *Inhuman Bondage: The Rise and Fall of Slavery in the New World*. Oxford: Oxford University Press, 2006.
DeCosta-Willis, Miriam. "Georgia E. L. Patton." In *Notable Black American Women*, ed. Jessie Carney Smith, 828–30. Farmington Hills, MI: Gale, 1991.
Deer, Sarah. *The Beginning and End of Rape: Confronting Sexual Violence in Native America*. Minneapolis: University of Minnesota Press, 2015.
Dees, Sarah. "An Equation of Language and Spirit: Comparative Philology and the Early Study of American Indian Religions." *Method & Theory in the Study of Religion* 27, no. 3 (2015): 195–219.
——. "Religion and U.S. Federal Indian Policy." In *A Companion to American Religious History*, ed. Benjamin Park. Oxford: Wiley Blackwell, 2021.
Deloria, Philip Joseph. *Playing Indian*. New Haven, CT: Yale University Press, 1998.
Deloria, Vine, and Raymond J. DeMallie, eds. *Documents of American Indian Diplomacy: Treaties, Agreements, and Conventions, 1775–1979*. Norman: University of Oklahoma Press, 1999.
Denetdale, Jennifer Nez. "Discontinuities, Remembrances, and Cultural Survival: History, Diné/Navajo Memory, and the Bosque Redondo Memorial." *New Mexico Historical Review* 82, no. 3 (2007): 295–316.
Denison, Brandi. *Ute Land Religion in the American West, 1879–2009*. Lincoln: University of Nebraska Press, 2017.
DeRogatis, Amy. *Moral Geography: Maps, Missionaries, and the American Frontier*. Religion and American Culture. New York: Columbia University Press, 2003.
Derrida, Jacques. *Archive Fever: A Freudian Impression*. Religion and Postmodernism. Translated by Eric Prenowitz. Chicago: University of Chicago Press, 1996.
Dove, Stephen C. "Historical Protestantism in Latin America." In *The Cambridge History of Religions in Latin America*, ed. Virginia Garrard-Burnett, Paul Freston, and

Stephen C. Dove, 286–303. Cambridge: Cambridge University Press, 2016. https://doi.org/10.1017/CHO9781139032698.019
Dowland, Seth. *Family Values and the Rise of the Christian Right*. Philadelphia: University of Pennsylvania Press, 2015.
Dressler, Markus, and Arvind-pal Singh Mandair, eds. *Secularism and Religion-Making*. Reflection and Theory in the Study of Religion Series. New York: Oxford University Press, 2011.
Du Bois, W. E. B. *The Souls of Black Folk*. Edited by Brent Hayes Edwards. New York: Oxford University Press, 2008 (1903).
Dunbar-Ortiz, Roxanne. *An Indigenous Peoples' History of the United States*. Boston, MA: Beacon Press, 2014.
Duster, Alfreda M., ed. *Crusade for Justice: The Autobiography of Ida B. Wells*. Chicago: University of Chicago Press, 1970.
Duthu, N. Bruce. *American Indians and the Law*. New York: Penguin, 2008.
DuVal, Kathleen. *Independence Lost: Lives on the Edge of the American Revolution*. New York: Random House Trade Paperbacks, 2016.
Egerton, Douglas R. "Forgetting Denmark Vesey; or, Oliver Stone Meets Richard Wade." *William and Mary Quarterly* 59, no. 1 (2002): 143–52.
———. *He Shall Go Out Free: The Lives of Denmark Vesey*. Lanham, MD: Rowman & Littlefield, 1999.
Egerton, Douglas R., and Robert L. Paquette, eds. *The Denmark Vesey Affair: A Documentary History*. Gainesville: University Press of Florida, 2017.
Eittreim, Elisabeth M. *Teaching Empire: Native Americans, Filipinos, and US Imperial Education, 1879–1918*. Lawrence: University Press of Kansas, 2019.
Eller, Anne. "'Awful Pirates' and 'Hordes of Jackals': Santo Domingo/The Dominican Republic in Nineteenth-Century Historiography." *Small Axe* 44 (2014): 87–94.
———. *We Dream Together: Dominican Independence, Haiti, and the Fight for Caribbean Freedom*. Durham, NC: Duke University Press, 2016.
Ellis, Clyde. *A Dancing People: Powwow Culture on the Southern Plains*. Lawrence: University Press of Kansas, 2003.
Ellis, Ian M. *A Century of Missions and Unity: A Century Perspective on the 1910 World Missionary Conference*. Blackrock, Dublin: Columba Press, 2010.
Eltis, David. *The Rise of African Slavery in the Americas*. Cambridge: Cambridge University Press, 2000.
Emigh, Rebecca Jean, Dylan Riley, and Patricia Ahmed. *Changes in Censuses from Imperialist to Welfare States: How Societies Count*. New York: Palgrave Macmillan, 2016.
Engel, Elisabeth. "The Ecumenical Origins of Pan-Africanism: Africa and the 'Southern Negro' in the International Missionary Council's Global Vision of Christian Indigenization in the 1920s." *Journal of Global History* 13 (2018).
Engs, Robert Francis. *Educating the Disenfranchised and Disinherited: Samuel Chapman Armstrong and Hampton Institute, 1839–1893*. Knoxville: University of Tennessee Press, 1999.

Estus, Joaqlin. "Census Count Is 'an Act of Rebellion.'" *Indian Country Today*, January 20, 2020. indiancountrytoday.com

Ewers, John C. *Murals in the Round: Painted Tipis of the Kiowa and Kiowa-Apache Indians*. Washington, DC: Smithsonian Institution Press, 1978.

Fanning, Sarah. *Caribbean Crossing: African Americans and the Haitian Emigration Movement*. New York: NYU Press, 2015.

Fanon, Frantz. *The Wretched of the Earth*. New York: Grove Press, 1963.

Farr, James. "Locke, Natural Law, and New World Slavery." *Political Theory* 36, no. 4 (2008): 495–522.

Fear-Segal, Jacqueline. *White Man's Club: Schools, Race, and the Struggle of Indian Acculturation*. Lincoln: University of Nebraska Press, 2009.

Fear-Segal, Jacqueline, and Susan D. Rose. Introduction to *Carlisle Indian Industrial School: Indigenous Histories, Memories, and Reclamations*, ed. Jacqueline Fear-Segal and Susan D. Rose, 1–34. Lincoln: University of Nebraska Press, 2016.

———, eds. *Carlisle Indian Industrial School: Indigenous Histories, Memories, and Reclamations*. Lincoln: University of Nebraska Press, 2016.

Feldman, Keith. "Empire's Verticality: The Af/Pak Frontier, Visual Culture, and Racialization from Above." *Comparative American Studies: An International Journal* 9, no. 4: 325–41. https://doi.org/10.1179/147757011X13045212814529

Ferguson, Roderick A. *The Reorder of Things: The University and Its Pedagogies of Minority Difference*. Minneapolis: University of Minnesota Press, 2011.

Fessenden, Tracy. *Culture and Redemption: Religion, the Secular, and American Literature*. Princeton, NJ: Princeton University Press, 2007.

Fett, Sharla M. *Recaptured Africans: Surviving Slave Ships, Detention, and Dislocation in the Final Years of the Slave Trade*. Chapel Hill: University of North Carolina Press, 2016.

Fieser, Louis M. *The Lott Carey Legacy of African American Missions*. Baltimore, MD: Gateway Press, 1994.

———. *The Scientific Method: A Personal Account of Unusual Projects in War and Peace*. New York: Reinhold, 1964.

Fitts, Leroy. *Lott Carey: First Black Missionary to Africa*. Valley Forge, PA: Judson Press, 1978.

———. *The Lott Carey Legacy of African American Missions*. Baltimore, MD: Gateway Press, 1994.

Fletcher, Matthew L. M. *The Eagle Returns: The Legal History of the Grand Traverse Band of Ottawa and Chippewa Indians*. East Lansing: Michigan State University Press, 2012.

Foucault, Michel. *"Society Must Be Defended": Lectures at the Collège de France, 1975–1976*. Translated by David Macey. New York: Picador, 2003.

Fowler, Loretta. *Shared Symbols, Contested Meanings: Gros Ventre Culture and History, 1778–1984*. Ithaca, NY: Cornell University Press, 2018.

Fox-Genovese, Elizabeth, and Eugene D. Genovese. *The Mind of the Master Class: History and Faith in the Southern Slaveholder's Worldview*. New York: Cambridge University Press, 2005.

Frey, Sylvia R., and Betty Wood. *Come Shouting to Zion: African American Protestantism in the American South and British Caribbean to 1830*. Chapel Hill: University of North Carolina Press, 1998.
Fuller, Christopher J. *See It/Shoot It: The Secret History of the CIA's Lethal Drone Program*. New Haven, CT: Yale University Press, 2017.
Gaines, Kevin K. *Uplifting the Race: Black Leadership, Politics, and Culture in the Twentieth Century*. Chapel Hill: University of North Carolina Press, 1996.
García Muñiz, Humberto, and Jorge L. Giovannetti, "Garveyismo y racismo en el Caribe: el caso de la población cocola en la República Dominicana." *Caribbean Studies* 31 (2003): 139–211.
García-Peña, Lorgia. *The Borders of Dominicanidad: Race, Nation, and Archives of Contradiction*. Durham, NC: Duke University Press, 2016.
Garroutte, Eva Marie. *Real Indians: Identity and the Survival of North America*. Berkeley: University of California Press, 2003.
Gasman, Marybeth. *Envisioning Black Colleges: A History of the United States Negro Fund*. Baltimore, MD: Johns Hopkins University Press, 2007.
Gatewood, Willard B., Jr. "Black Americans and the Quest for Empire, 1898–1903." *Journal of Southern History* 38, no. 4 (1972): 545–66.
———. *Black Americans and the White Man's Burden*. Urbana: University of Illinois Press, 1975.
———. *"Smoked Yankees" and the Struggle for Empire: Letters from Negro Soldiers, 1898–1902*. Fayetteville: University of Arkansas Press, 1987.
Gelo, Daniel J. *Indians of the Great Plains*. New York: Routledge, 2018.
Gerbner, Katharine. *Christian Slavery: Conversion and Race in the Protestant Atlantic World*. Philadelphia: University of Pennsylvania Press, 2018.
———. "'They Call Me Obea': German Moravian Missionaries and Afro-Caribbean Religion in Jamaica, 1754–1760." *Atlantic Studies: Global Currents* 12, no. 2 (2015): 160–78.
Giddings, Paula J. *Ida: A Sword among Lions*. New York: Amistad Harper Collins, 2008.
Gin Lum, Kathryn. *Damned Nation: Hell in America from the Revolution to Reconstruction*. New York: Oxford University Press, 2014.
———. "The Historyless Heathen and the Stagnating Pagan: History as Non-Native Category?" *Religion and American Culture: A Journal of Interpretation* 28, no. 1 (January 1, 2018): 52–91. https://doi.org/10.1525/rac.2018.28.1.52
Go, Julian. *Patterns of Empire: The British and American Empires, 1688 to the Present*. New York: Cambridge University Press, 2011.
Goddard, Connie. "Bordentown: Where Dewey's 'Learning to Earn' Met Du Boisian Educational Priorities." *Education and Culture* 35, no. 1 (2019): 49–70.
Goeman, Mishuana. "Ongoing Storms and Struggles: Gendered Violence and Resource Exploitation." In *Critically Sovereign: Indigenous Gender, Sexuality, and Feminist Studies*, ed. Joanne Barker. Durham, NC: Duke University Press, 2017.
Goetz, Rebecca Anne. *The Baptism of Early Virginia: How Christianity Created Race*. Baltimore, MD: Johns Hopkins University Press, 2012.

Goldstein, Alyosha, ed. *Formations of United States Colonialism*. Durham, NC: Duke University Press, 2014.

Good, Dorothy. "Questions on Religion in the United States Census." *Population Index* 25, no. 1 (1959): 3–16.

Gordon, Sarah Barringer. "The African Supplement: Religion, Race, and Corporate Law in Early National America." *William and Mary Quarterly* 72, no. 3 (July 1, 2015): 385–422.

Gotay, Samuel Silva. *Protestantismo y política en Puerto Rico, 1898–1930: Hacia una historia del protestantismo evangélico en Puerto Rico*. San Juan: La Editorial Universidad de Puerto Rico, 2005.

Graber, Jennifer. "Beyond Prophecy: Native Visionaries in American Religious Studies—Más Allá de La Profecía; Los Visionarios Nativos en Los Estudios de la Religión Americanos." *American Religion* 2, no. 1 (2020): 41–100. https://doi.org/10.2979/amerreli.2.1.09

———. *The Gods of Indian Country: Religion and the Struggle for the American West*. New York: Oxford University Press, 2018.

Grandin, Greg. *Empire's Workshop: Latin America, the United States, and the Making of an Imperial Republic*. New York: Picador, 2021.

Greene, Candace S. *One Hundred Summers: A Kiowa Calendar Record*. Lincoln: University of Nebraska Press, 2009.

Greenidge, Kerri K. *Black Radical: The Life and Times of William Monroe Trotter*. New York: Norton, 2019.

Greer, Allan. *Property and Dispossession: Natives, Empires, and Land in Early Modern North America*. Cambridge: Cambridge University Press, 2018.

Gregerson, Linda, and Susan Juster, eds. *Empires of God: Religious Encounters in the Early Modern Atlantic*. Philadelphia: University of Pennsylvania Press, 2011.

Grewal, Inderpal. *Transnational America: Feminisms, Diasporas, Neoliberalisms*. Next Wave. Durham, NC: Duke University Press, 2005.

Grewal, Zareena. *Islam Is a Foreign Country: American Muslims and the Global Crisis of Authority*. New York: NYU Press, 2013.

Griffith, Aaron. *God's Law and Order: The Politics of Punishment in Evangelical America*. Cambridge, MA: Harvard University Press, 2020.

Griffiths, Leslie. *A History of Methodism in Haiti*. Port-au-Prince: Imprimerie Méthodiste, 1991.

Guha, Ranajit, and Gayatri Chakravorty Spivak, eds. *Selected Subaltern Studies*. New York: Oxford University Press, 1988.

Guillaume, Marine. "Napalm in US Bombing Doctrine and Practice, 1942–1975." *Asia Pacific Journal* 14, no. 23 (2016).

Gutiérrez, Ramón A. "Internal Colonialism: An American Theory of Race." *Du Bois Review: Social Science Research on Race* 1, no. 2 (September 2004): 281–95.

Guyatt, Nicholas. "America's Conservatory: Race, Reconstruction, and the Santo Domingo Debate." *Journal of American History* 94 (March 2010): 974–1000.

———. *Providence and the Invention of the United States, 1607–1876*. Cambridge: Cambridge University Press, 2007.
Hale, Tiffany. "Aligning Disciplinary Ends: Social History, Religious Studies, and Race in America." *Religious Studies Review* 45, no. 4 (2019): 461–67. https://doi.org/10.1111/rsr.14272
———. *Fugitive Religion: The Ghost Dance and Native American Resistance after the US Civil War*. New Haven, CT: Yale University Press, forthcoming.
Hämäläinen, Pekka. *Lakota America: A New History of Indigenous Power*. New Haven, CT: Yale University Press, 2019.
Handler, Jerome S., and Kenneth M. Bilby. *Enacting Power: The Criminalization of Obeah in the Anglophone Caribbean, 1760–2011*. Mona, Jamaica: University of the West Indies Press, 2013.
———. "On the Early Use and Origin of the Term 'Obeah' in Barbados and the Anglophone Caribbean." *Slavery & Abolition* 22, no. 2 (August 2001): 87–100.
Hardt, Michael, and Antonio Negri. *Empire*. Cambridge, MA: Harvard University Press, 2000.
Harris, Susan K. *God's Arbiters: Americans and the Philippines, 1898–1902*. Imagining the Americas. New York: Oxford University Press, 2011.
Harrison, Peter. *"Religion" and the Religions in the English Enlightenment*. Cambridge: Cambridge University Press, 1990.
Hartman, Saidiya. "Venus in Two Acts." *Small Axe* 12, no. 2 (June 2008): 1–14.
Haselby, Sam. "Muslims of Early America." *Aeon*, May 20, 2019. https://aeon.co
———. *The Origins of American Religious Nationalism*. Religion in America. New York: Oxford University Press, 2015.
Hechter, Michael. *Internal Colonialism: The Celtic Fringe in British National Development*. New Brunswick, NJ: Transaction Publishers, 1999.
Helton, Laura, et al. "The Question of Recovery." *Social Text* 33, no. 4 (December 2015): 1–18. https://doi.org/10.1215/01642472-3315766
Hermansen, Marcia. "Muslims in the Performative Mode: A Reflection on Muslim-Christian Dialogue." *Muslim World* 94, no. 3 (2004): 387–96. https://doi.org/10.1111/j.1478-1913.2004.00062.x
Hernandez, Kelly Lytle. *City of Inmates: Conquest, Rebellion, and the Rise of Human Caging in Los Angeles, 1771–1965*. Chapel Hill: University of North Carolina Press, 2017.
Herron, Paul E. *Framing the Solid South: The State Constitutional Conventions of Secession, Reconstruction, and Redemption, 1860–1902*. Lawrence: University Press of Kansas, 2017.
Hickman, Christine B. "The Devil and the One Drop Rule: Racial Categories, African Americans, and the U.S. Census." *Michigan Law Review* 95, no. 5 (1997): 1161–1265.
Hinshelwood, Brad. "The Carolinian Context of John Locke's Theory of Slavery." *Political Theory* 41, no. 4 (2013): 562–90.
Hittman, Michael. *Wovoka and the Ghost Dance*. Lincoln: University of Nebraska Press, 1997.

Hoganson, Kristin L. *Consumer's Imperium: The Global Production of American Domesticity, 1865–1920*. Chapel Hill: University of North Carolina Press, 2010.

Hollabaugh, Mark. *The Spirit and the Sky: Lakota Visions of the Cosmos*. Lincoln: University of Nebraska Press, 2017.

Hollinger, David A. *Protestants Abroad: How Missionaries Tried to Change the World but Changed America*. Princeton, NJ: Princeton University Press, 2017.

Holm, Tom. *The Great Confusion in Indian Affairs*. Austin: University of Texas Press, 2005.

Holscher, Kathleen. "Priests That Moved: Catholicism, Colonized Peoples, and Sex Abuse in the U.S. Southwest." *Revealer*, March 2, 2020. The Center for Religion and Media at New York University. https://therevealer.org

Honor the Earth. "Man Camps Fact Sheet." 2012. Honor the Earth. www.honorearth.org (accessed January 1, 2021)

Horne, Gerald. *The Apocalypse of Settler Colonialism: The Roots of Slavery, White Supremacy, and Capitalism in Seventeenth-Century North America and the Caribbean*. New York: Monthly Review Press, 2018.

———. *Confronting Black Jacobins: The United States, the Haitian Revolution, and the Origins of the Dominican Republic*. New York: Monthly Review Press, 2015.

Hoxie, Frederick E. *A Final Promise: The Campaign to Assimilate the Indians, 1880–1920*. Cambridge: Cambridge University Press, 1989.

Hubbard, Tasha. "Buffalo Genocide in Nineteenth-Century North America: 'Kill, Skin, and Sell.'" In *Colonial Genocide in Indigenous North America*, ed. Andrew Woolford, Jeff Benvenuto, and Alexander Laban Hinton, 292–305. Durham, NC: Duke University Press, 2014.

Huffman, Alan. *Mississippi in Africa: The Saga of the Slaves of Prospect Hill Plantation and Their Legacy in Liberia Today*. Jackson: University Press of Mississippi, 2010.

Hulsether, Lucia. *Capitalist Humanitarianism*. Durham, NC: Duke University Press, forthcoming.

Hurd, Elizabeth Shakman. *Beyond Religious Freedom: The New Global Politics of Religion*. Princeton, NJ: Princeton University Press, 2015.

Immerman, Richard H. *Empire for Liberty: A History of American Imperialism from Benjamin Franklin to Paul Wolfowitz*. Princeton, NJ: Princeton University Press, 2010.

Immerwahr, Daniel. *How to Hide an Empire: A History of the Greater United States*. New York: Farrar, Straus, & Giroux, 2019.

Israel, Adrienne. *Amanda Berry Smith: From Washerwoman to Evangelist*. Lanham, MD: Scarecrow Press, 2003.

Jacobson, Matthew Frye. *Roots Too: White Ethnic Revival in Post–Civil Rights America*. Cambridge, MA: Harvard University Press, 2006.

Jakobsen, Janet R., and Ann Pellegrini. *Secularisms*. Durham, NC: Duke University Press, 2008.

Jenkins, Destin, and Justin LeRoy, eds. *Histories of Racial Capitalism*. New York: Columbia University Press, 2021.

Jenkins, Earnestine Lovelle. "Missionary Photography: The Liberian Archive of Doctor Georgia Patton." *Visual Resources* 34, nos. 3–4 (2018): 293–314.
Jobe, Margaret. "Native Americans and the U.S. Census: A Brief Historical Survey." *Journal of Government Information* 30 (2004): 66–80.
Johnsgard, Paul. *Wings over the Great Plains: Bird Migrations in the Central Flyway*. Lincoln, NE: Zea Books, 2012.
Johnson, Greg. "Varieties of Native Hawaiian Establishment: Recognized Voices, Routinized Charisma, and Church Desecration." In *Varieties of Religious Establishment*, ed. Winnifred Fallers Sullivan and Lori G. Beaman, 55–71. Farnham, England: Ashgate, 2013. https://doi.org/10.4324/9781315548401
Johnson, Michael P. "Denmark Vesey and His Co-Conspirators." *William and Mary Quarterly* 58, no. 4 (2001): 915–76.
———. "Telemaque's Pilgrimage? A Tale of Two Charleston Churches, Three Missionaries, and Four Ministers, 1783–1817." *South Carolina Historical Magazine* 118, no. 1 (2017): 4–36.
Johnson, Sylvester A. *African American Religions, 1500–2000*. New York: Cambridge University Press, 2015.
———. "Religion, Race, and American Empire." In *Oxford Handbook of Religion and Race in American History*, ed. Kathryn Gin Lum and Paul Harvey, 61–78. New York: Oxford University Press, 2007.
Johnson, Walter. "On Agency." *Journal of Social History* 37, no. 1 (2003): 113–24.
———. *River of Dark Dreams: Slavery and Empire in the Cotton Kingdom*. Cambridge, MA: Harvard University Press, 2013.
Jordan, Michael P. "Reclaiming the Past: Descendants' Organizations, Historical Consciousness, and Intellectual Property in Kiowa Society." PhD diss., University of Oklahoma, 2011.
Josephson-Storm, Jason Ānanda. "The Superstition, Secularism, and Religion Trinary: Or Re-Theorizing Secularism." *Method and Theory in the Study of Religion* 30, no. 1 (January 2, 2018): 1–20. https://doi.org/10.1163/15700682-12341409
Jung, Moon-Ho. *Coolies and Cane: Race, Labor, and Sugar in the Age of Emancipation*. Baltimore, MD: Johns Hopkins University Press, 2009.
Kahn, Jonathon S., and Vincent W. Lloyd, eds. *Race and Secularism in America*. New York: Columbia University Press, 2016.
Kaplan, Amy, and Donald E. Pease, eds. *Cultures of United States Imperialism*. Durham, NC: Duke University Press, 1993.
Kauanui, J. Kēhaulani. *Hawaiian Blood: Colonialism and the Politics of Sovereignty and Indigeneity*. Narrating Native Histories. Durham, NC: Duke University Press, 2008.
———. "'A Structure, Not an Event': Settler Colonialism and Enduring Indigeneity." *Lateral* (blog), June 1, 2016, https://csalateral.org/issue/5-1/forum-alt-humanities-settler-colonialism-enduring-indigeneity-kauanui/ (accessed June 23, 2021).
Keane, Webb. *Christian Moderns: Freedom and Fetish in the Mission Encounter*. Berkeley: University of California Press, 2007.

Kelley, Robin. *Nathan I. Huggins Lectures: Africa Speaks, America Answers: Modern Jazz in Revolutionary Times*. Cambridge, MA: Harvard University Press, 2012.

Kertzer, David, and Dominique Arel, eds. *Census and Identity: The Politics of Race, Ethnicity, and Language in National Censuses*. Cambridge: Cambridge University Press, 2009.

Killingray, David. "Edwards, Samuel Julius Celestine." In *Oxford Companion to Black British History*, 143–44. New York: Oxford University Press, 2007.

King, Richard. *Orientalism and Religion: Postcolonial Theory, India, and "The Mystic East."* London: Routledge, 1999.

Kinney, Brandon G. *The Mormon War: Zion and the Missouri Extermination Order of 1838*. Yardley, PA: Westholme, 2011.

Koll, Karla Ann. "Volcanic Revolution on the Home Mission Field: Response of the United Presbyterian Church in the United States of America to the Revolution in Cuba." *Journal of Presbyterian History* 82 (Fall 2004): 149–68.

Kovalcheck, Riley. "The Modern Plantation: The Continuities of Convict-Leasing and an Analysis of Arkansas Prison Systems." *CLA Journal* 7 (2019): 96–130.

Kracht, Benjamin R. *Kiowa Belief and Ritual*. Lincoln: University of Nebraska Press, 2017.

———. *Religious Revitalization among the Kiowas: The Ghost Dance, Peyote, and Christianity*. Lincoln: University of Nebraska Press, 2018.

Kramer, Paul. *The Blood of Government: Race, Empire, the United States, and the Philippines*. Chapel Hill: University of North Carolina Press, 2006.

———. "Power and Connection: Imperial Histories of the United States in the World." *American Historical Review* 116, no. 5 (December 2011): 1348–91.

Landers, Jane. "Gracia Real de Santa Teresa de Mose: A Free Black Town in Spanish Colonial Florida." *American Historical Review* 95, no. 1 (1990): 9–30.

Lassiter, Luke E. *The Power of Kiowa Song: A Collaborative Ethnography*. Tucson: University of Arizona Press, 1998.

Lee, Sharon M. "Racial Classifications in the US Census: 1890–1990." *Ethnic and Racial Studies* 16, no. 1 (1993): 75–94.

Leroux, Darryl. *Distorted Descent: White Claims to Indigenous Identity*. Winnipeg: University of Manitoba Press, 2019.

Lewis, Bonnie Sue. *Creating Christian Indians: Native Clergy in the Presbyterian Church*. Norman: University of Oklahoma Press, 2003.

Lindsey, Donal F. *Indians at Hampton Institute, 1877–1923*. Urbana: University of Illinois Press, 1995.

Lippy, Charles H. "Chastized by Scorpions: Christianity and Culture in Colonial South Carolina, 1669–1740." *Church History* 79, no. 2 (2010): 253–70.

Lockward, George A. *El protestantismo en Dominicana*. 2nd ed. Santo Domingo: Editora Educativa Dominicana, 1982.

Lofton, Kathryn. *Consuming Religion*. Chicago: University of Chicago Press, 2017.

Logan, Rayford Whittingham. *The Diplomatic Relations of the United States with Haiti, 1776–1891.* Chapel Hill: University of North Carolina Press, 1941.

Lorimer, Douglas A. "Legacies of Slavery for Race, Religion, and Empire: SJ Celestine Edwards and the Hard Truth (1894)." *Slavery & Abolition* 39, no. 4 (2018): 731–55.

Lowe, Lisa. *The Intimacies of Four Continents.* Durham, NC: Duke University Press, 2015.

Lowie, Robert Harry. *The Religion of the Crow Indians.* Vol. 25. New York: The Trustees, 1922.

Lubin, Alex. *Geographies of Liberation: The Making of an Afro-Arab Political Imaginary.* Chapel Hill: University of North Carolina Press, 2014.

Lujan, Carol. "American Indians and Alaska Natives Count: The US Census Bureau's Efforts to Enumerate the Native Population." *American Indian Quarterly* 38, no. 3 (2014): 319–41.

———. "As Simple as One, Two, Three: Census Underenumeration among the American Indians and Alaska Natives." *Undercount Behavioral Research Group Staff Working Paper #2.* US Census Bureau, 1990.

Lundius, Jan, and Mats Lundahl. *Peasants and Religion: A Socioeconomic Study of Dios Olivorio and the Palma Sola Movement in the Dominican Republic.* London: Routledge, 2000.

Maffly-Kipp, Laurie F. *Setting down the Sacred Past: African-American Race Histories.* Cambridge, MA: Belknap Press of Harvard University Press, 2010.

Mahmood, Saba. *Religious Difference in a Secular Age: A Minority Report.* Princeton, NJ: Princeton University Press, 2016.

Makdisi, Ussama. "The Privilege of Acting upon Others: The Middle Eastern Exception to Anti-exceptionalist Histories of the US and the World." In *Explaining the History of American Foreign Relations*, ed. F. Costigliola and M. Hogan, 203–16. Cambridge: Cambridge University Press, 2016. https://doi.org/10.1017/CBO9781107286207.013

Mamdani, Mahmood. *Good Muslim, Bad Muslim: America, the Cold War, and the Roots of Terror.* New York: Pantheon Books, 2004.

Mandair, Arvind-Pal S. *Religion and the Specter of the West: Sikhism, India, Postcoloniality, and the Politics of Translation.* New York: Columbia University Press, 2009.

Marks, George P. *The Black Press Views American Imperialism, 1898–1900.* New York: Arno Press, 1971.

Marriott, Alice Lee. *Saynday's People: The Kiowa Indians and the Stories They Told.* Lincoln: University of Nebraska Press, 1963.

Marsden, George M. *Fundamentalism and American Culture: The Shaping of Twentieth-Century Evangelicalism, 1870–1925.* New York: Oxford University Press, 1980.

Martin, Joel W., and Mark A. Nicholas, eds. *Native Americans, Christianity, and the Reshaping of the American Religious Landscape.* Chapel Hill: University of North Carolina Press, 2010.

Martin, William C. *With God on Our Side: The Rise of the Religious Right in America.* New York: Broadway Books, 1996.

Martinez, Anne. *Catholic Borderlands: Mapping Catholicism onto American Empire, 1905–1935*. Lincoln: University of Nebraska Press, 2014.

Martínez-Fernández, Luis. *Protestantism and Political Conflict in the Nineteenth-Century Hispanic Caribbean*. New Brunswick, NJ: Rutgers University Press, 2002.

Marty, Martin E. *Righteous Empire: The Protestant Experience in America*. New York: Dial Press, 1970.

Masuzawa, Tomoko. *The Invention of World Religions; or, How European Universalism Was Preserved in the Language of Pluralism*. Chicago: University of Chicago Press, 2005.

May, Nicholas. "Holy Rebellion: Religious Assembly Laws in Antebellum South Carolina and Virginia." *American Journal of Legal History* 49, no. 3 (2007): 238.

Mbembé, Achille. *On the Postcolony*. Berkeley: University of California Press, 2001.

McAlister, Melani. *Epic Encounters: Culture, Media, and U.S. Interests in the Middle East since 1945–2000*. Updated edition, with a post-9/11 chapter. Berkeley: University of California Press, 2005.

———. *The Kingdom of God Has No Borders: A Global History of American Evangelicals*. New York: Oxford University Press, 2018.

McClurken, James M. *Gah-Baeh-Jhagwah-Buk: The Way It Happened; A Visual Culture History of the Little Traverse Bay Bands of Odawa*. East Lansing: Michigan State University Museum, 1991.

McCullough, Matthew. *The Cross of War: Christian Nationalism and U.S. Expansion in the Spanish-American War*. Studies in American Thought and Culture. Madison: University of Wisconsin Press, 2014.

McDonald, Laughlin, Michael B. Binford, and Ken Johnson. "Georgia." In *Quiet Revolution in the South: The Impact of the Voting Rights Act, 1965–1990*, ed. Chandler Davidson and Bernard Grofman, 67–102. Princeton, NJ: Princeton University Press,

McDonnell, Michael A. *Masters of Empire: Great Lakes Indians and the Making of America*. New York: Hill and Wang, 2015.

McKittrick, Katherine. *Sylvia Wynter: On Being Human as Praxis*. Durham, NC: Duke University Press, 2015.

McNally, Michael D. *Defend the Sacred: Native American Religious Freedom beyond the First Amendment*. Princeton, NJ: Princeton University Press, 2020.

———. *Ojibwe Singers: Hymns, Grief, and a Native Culture in Motion*. Oxford: Oxford University Press, 2000.

Meadows, William C. *Kiowa Military Societies: Ethnohistory and Ritual*. Norman: University of Oklahoma Press, 2010.

Melamed, Jodi. *Represent and Destroy: Rationalizing Violence in the New Racial Capitalism*. Minneapolis: University of Minnesota Press, 2011.

Melton, Gordon J. *A Will to Choose: The Origins of African American Methodism*. Lanham, MD: Rowman & Littlefield, 2007.

Meredith, Howard L. *Dancing on Common Ground: Tribal Cultures and Alliances on the Southern Plains*. Lawrence: University of Kansas Press, 1995.

Miles, Tiya, and Barbara Krauthamer. "Africans and Native Americans." In *A Companion to African American History*, ed. Alton Hornsby Jr., 121–39. Oxford: Blackwell, 2005.

Miller, Jay. "Basin Religion and Theology: A Comparative Study of Power (Puha)." *Journal of California and Great Basin Anthropology* 5, no. 1/2 (1983): 66–86.

Miller, Robert J. *Discovering Indigenous Lands: The Doctrine of Discovery in the English Colonies*. New York: Oxford University Press, 2010.

———. *Native America, Discovered and Conquered: Thomas Jefferson, Lewis & Clark, and Manifest Destiny*. Native America. Westport, CT: Praeger, 2006.

Mills, Frederick V. "Allen, Richard (1760–1831), American Methodist Preacher and Founder of the African Methodist Episcopal Church." *American National Biography*, February 2000. www.anb.org

Mitchell, Michele. "'The Black Man's Burden': African Americans, Imperialism, and Notions of Racial Manhood, 1890–1910." *International Review of Social History* 44, no. S7 (1999): 77–99.

Mooney, James. *Calendar History of the Kiowa Indians*. Washington, DC: US Government Printing Office, 1898.

———. *The Ghost-Dance Religion and the Sioux Outbreak of 1890*. Lincoln: University of Nebraska Press, 1991.

Moore, John H. "The Ornithology of Cheyenne Religionists." *Plains Anthropologist* 31, no. 113 (1986): 177–92.

Moore, R. Laurence. *Religious Outsiders and the Making of Americans*. New York: Oxford University Press, 1986.

Moran, Katherine D. *The Imperial Church: Catholic Founding Fathers and United States Empire*. Ithaca, NY: Cornell University Press, 2020.

Moreton-Robinson, Aileen. *The White Possessive: Property, Power, and Indigenous Sovereignty*. Minneapolis: University of Minnesota Press, 2015.

Morgan, Jennifer L. "Archives and Histories of Racial Capitalism: An Afterword." *Social Text* 33 (December 2015): 153–61.

Morgensen, Scott Lauria. "The Biopolitics of Settler Colonialism: Right Here, Right Now." *Settler Colonial Studies* 1, no. 1 (2011): 52–76.

Morris, Aldon D. *The Scholar Denied: W. E. B. Du Bois and the Birth of Modern Sociology*. Oakland: University of California Press, 2015.

Moses, L. G. *The Indian Man: A Biography of James Mooney*. Lincoln: University of Nebraska Press, 2002.

Mufti, Aamir. *Enlightenment in the Colony: The Jewish Question and the Crisis of Postcolonial Culture*. Princeton, NJ: Princeton University Press, 2007.

Murphy, Jacqueline Shea. *The People Have Never Stopped Dancing: Native American Modern Dance Histories*. Minneapolis: University of Minnesota Press, 2007.

Neer, Robert M. *Napalm: An American Biography*. Cambridge, MA: Belknap Press of Harvard University Press, 2015.

Nelson, William Javier. "U.S. Diplomatic Recognition of the Dominican Republic in the 19th Century: A Study in Racism." *Afro-Hispanic Review* 10 (1991): 10–14.

Newcomb, Steven. *Pagans in the Promised Land: Decoding the Doctrine of Christian Discovery*. 3rd ed. Golden, CO: Fulcrum Publishing, 2008.

Ngozi-Brown, Scot. "African-American Soldiers and Filipinos: Racial Imperialism, Jim Crow and Social Relations." *Journal of Negro History* 82, no. 1 (Winter 1997): 42–53.

Norbeck, Mark D. "The Legacy of Charles Henry Brent." *International Bulletin of Missionary Research* 20, no. 4 (October 1996): 163–68.

Nye, Wilbur Sturtevant. *Bad Medicine and Good: Tales of the Kiowas*. Norman: University of Oklahoma Press, 1962.

O'Brien, Jean M. *Firsting and Lasting: Writing Indians out of Existence in New England*. Minneapolis: University of Minnesota Press, 2010.

Odell, Edward Albert. *It Came to Pass*. New York: Board of National Missions Presbyterian Church in the U.S.A., 1952.

Osorio, Jonathon Kay Kamakawiwoʻole. *Dismembering Lāhui: A History of the Hawaiian Nation to 1887*. Honolulu: University of Hawaiʻi Press, 2002.

Ostler, Jeffrey. *The Plains Sioux and U.S. Colonialism from Lewis and Clark to Wounded Knee*. Studies in North American Indian History. Cambridge: Cambridge University Press, 2004.

Paquette, Robert L. "Jacobins of the Lowcountry: The Vesey Plot on Trial." *William and Mary Quarterly* 59, no. 1 (2002): 185–92.

Paré, George. *The Catholic Church in Detroit, 1701–1888*. Detroit, MI: Gabriel Richard Press, 1951.

Park, Benjamin E. *Kingdom of Nauvoo: The Rise and Fall of a Religious Empire on the American Frontier*. New York: Liveright, 2020.

Parks, Lisa, and Caren Kaplan, eds. *Life in the Age of Drone Warfare*. Durham, NC: Duke University Press, 2017.

Paton, Diana. *The Cultural Politics of Obeah: Religion, Colonialism, and Modernity in the Caribbean World*. Cambridge: Cambridge University Press, 2015.

———. "Obeah Acts: Producing and Policing the Boundaries of Religion in the Caribbean." *Small Axe: A Caribbean Journal of Criticism*, no. 28 (March 2009): 1–18.

———. "The Trials of Inspector Thomas: Policing and Ethnography in Jamaica." In *Obeah and Other Powers: The Politics of Caribbean Religion and Healing*, ed. Diana Paton and Maarit Forde. Durham, NC: Duke University Press, 2012.

Paulet, Anne. "To Change the World: The Use of American Indian Education in the Philippines." *History of Education Quarterly* 47, no. 2 (May 2007): 173–202.

Pearson, Stephen, and Patrick Wolfe. "'The Last Bastion of Colonialism': Appalachian Settler Colonialism and Self-Indigenization." *American Indian Culture and Research Journal* 37, no. 2 (May 22, 2013): 165–84. https://doi.org/10.17953/aicr.37.2.g4522v766231r3xg

Pelotte, Bishop Donald E. "The Challenges of the Call to Be a Bishop in North America Today: The Call to Be a Bishop in a Native American Diocese." *Proceedings of the Catholic Theological Society of America* 62 (May 2013). https://ejournals.bc.edu

Penner, Robert. "The Ojibwe Renaissance: Transnational Evangelicalism and the Making of an Algonquian Intelligentsia, 1812–1867." *American Review of Canadian Studies* 45, no. 1 (March 2015): 71–92. https://doi.org/10.1080/02722011.2015.1013264

Perdue, Theda. *"Mixed Blood" Indians: Racial Construction in the Early South*. Athens: University of Georgia Press, 2003.

———. *Slavery and the Evolution of Cherokee Society, 1540–1866*. Knoxville: University of Tennessee Press, 1979.

Perdue, Theda, and Michael D. Green. *The Cherokee Nation and the Trail of Tears*. Penguin Library of American Indian History. New York: Viking, 2007.

Pérez, Louis A., Jr. "Protestant Missionaries in Cuba: Archival Records, Manuscript Collections, and Research Prospects." *Latin American Research Review* 27, no. 1 (1992): 105–20.

Persha, Ron. *The Great Gold Swindle of Lubec, Maine*. Charleston, SC: History Press, 2013.

Pesantubbee, Michelene E. *Choctaw Women in a Chaotic World: The Clash of Cultures in the Colonial Southeast*. Albuquerque: University of New Mexico Press, 2005.

Phillips, Clifton Jackson. *Protestant America and the Pagan World: The First Half-Century of the American Board of Commissioners for Foreign Missions, 1810-1860*. Cambridge, MA: Harvard University Press, 1969.

Pietz, William. "The Problem of the Fetish, I." *RES: Anthropology and Aesthetics*, no. 9 (1985): 5–17.

———. "The Problem of the Fetish, II: The Origin of the Fetish." *RES: Anthropology and Aesthetics*, no. 13 (1987): 23–45.

Pinderhughes, Charles. "Toward a New Theory of Internal Colonialism." *Socialism and Democracy* 25, no. 1 (March 2011): 235–56.

Porter, Bernard. *Empire and Superempire: Britain, America, and the World*. New Haven, CT: Yale University Press, 2006.

Power-Greene, Ousmane K. *Against Wind and Tide: The African American Struggle against the Colonization Movement*. New York: NYU Press, 2014.

Pratt, Mary Louise. *Imperial Eyes: Travel Writing and Transculturation*. London: Routledge, 2008.

Promey, Sally M. "Material Establishment and Public Display." *Mediation. In Conversations: An Online Journal of the Center for the Study of Material and Visual Cultures of Religion* (2016). https://mavcor.yale.edu

"PUP Acquires Ruha Benjamin's *Viral Justice: How We Grow the World We Want*." Princeton University Press, https://press.princeton.edu (accessed January 1, 2021).

Raboteau, Albert J. *Slave Religion: The "Invisible Institution" in the Antebellum South*. New York: Oxford University Press, 1978.

Ramsey, Kate. *The Spirits and the Law: Vodou and Power in Haiti*. Chicago: University of Chicago Press, 2011.

Razack, Sherene H. "Gendering Disposability." *Canadian Journal of Women and Law* 28, no. 2 (2016): 285–307.

Redkey, Edwin S. *Black Exodus: Black Nationalist and Back-to-Africa Movements, 1890–1910*. New Haven, CT: Yale University Press, 1969.
Reeves-Ellington, Barbara, Kathryn Kish Sklar, and Connie Anne Shemo, eds. *Competing Kingdoms: Women, Mission, Nation, and the American Protestant Empire, 1812–1960*. Durham, NC: Duke University Press, 2010.
Renda, Mary. *Taking Haiti: Military Occupation and the Culture of U.S. Imperialism, 1915–1940*. Chapel Hill: University of North Carolina Press, 2001.
Rifkin, Mark. *Settler Common Sense: Queerness and Everyday Colonialism in the American Renaissance*. Minneapolis: University of Minnesota Press, 2012.
Rinere, Elissa, C.P. "The Exercise of *Cura Animarum* through the Twentieth Century and Beyond." *Jurist* 65, nos. 1 and 2: 31–54.
Ring, Natalie J. *The Problem South: Region, Empire, and the New Liberal State, 1880–1930*. Athens: University of Georgia Press, 2012.
Ripps, Lisa, and James D. Keyser. "Spirits on the Wing: Bird Images at Bear Gulch." *American Indian Rock Art* 34 (2008): 73–88.
Rivera, Mayra Rivera. "En-Gendered Territory: U.S. Missionaries' Discourse in Puerto Rico (1898–1920)." In *New Horizons in Hispanic/ Latino(a) Theology*, ed. Benjamín Valentín. Cleveland, OH: Pilgrim Press, 2003.
Robinson, Cedric J. *Black Marxism: The Making of the Black Radical Tradition*. Chapel Hill: University of North Carolina Press, 1983.
Roca, Hernán González. *Horizontes de esperanza: Historia de la Iglesia Evangélica Dominicana*. Vol. 1. Santo Domingo: Editora Búho, 2006.
Rodano, John A., ed. *Celebrating a Century of Ecumenism: Exploring the Achievements of International Dialogue*. Grand Rapids, MI: Eerdmans, 2012.
Rodil, B. R. *The Minoritization of the Indigenous Communities of Mindanao and the Sulu Archipelago*. Davao City, Philippines: Alternate Forum for Research in Mindanao, 1994.
Rooy, Sidney H. "Latin American Council of Churches: An Historical Approach." *Mission Studies* 20 (2003): 113.
Rubin, Andrew. *Archives of Authority: Empire, Culture, and the Cold War*. Princeton, NJ: Princeton University Press, 2012.
Rubin, Julius H. *Perishing Heathens: Stories of Protestant Missionaries and Christian Indians in Antebellum America*. Lincoln: University of Nebraska Press, 2017.
Rucker, Walter. "Conjure, Magic, and Power: The Influence of Afro-Atlantic Religious Practices on Slave Resistance and Rebellion." *Journal of Black Studies* 32, no. 1 (2001): 84–103.
Rugemer, Edward B. *Slave Law and the Politics of Resistance in the Early Atlantic World*. Cambridge, MA: Harvard University Press, 2018.
Russell, Timothy. "'I Feel Sorry for These People': African American Soldiers in the Philippine-American War, 1899–1902." *Journal of African American History* 99, no. 3 (Summer 2014): 197–222.
Ryan, Carmelita. "The Carlisle Indian Industrial School." PhD diss., Georgetown University, 1962.

Said, Edward W. *Orientalism*. New York: Vintage, 1978.
Saler, Bethel. *The Settlers' Empire: Colonialism and State Formation in America's Old Northwest*. Early American Studies. Philadelphia: University of Pennsylvania Press, 2015.
Salman, Michael. "'The Prison That Makes Men Free': The Iwahig Penal Colony and the Simulacra of the American State in the Philippines." In *The Colonial Crucible: Empire in the Making of the Modern American State*, ed. Alfred McCoy and Francisco Scarano, 116–28. Madison: University of Wisconsin Press, 2009.
Sarat, Austin, Lawrence Douglas, and Martha Merrill Umphrey, eds. *Law and War*. Palo Alto, CA: Stanford University Press, 2014.
Saunt, Claudio. *Unworthy Republic: The Dispossession of Native Americans and the Road to Indian Territory*. New York: Norton, 2020.
Schermerhorn, Seth. *Walking to Magdalena: Personhood and Place in Tohono O'odham Songs, Sticks, and Stories*. Lincoln: University of Nebraska Press, 2019.
Schipper, Jeremy. "'Misconstruction of the Sacred Page': On Denmark Vesey's Biblical Interpretations." *Journal of Biblical Literature* 138, no. 1 (April 17, 2019).
———. "'On Such Texts Comment Is Unnecessary': Biblical Interpretation in the Trial of Denmark Vesey." *Journal of the American Academy of Religion* 85, no. 4 (December 30, 2017): 1032–49.
Schmidt, Leigh Eric. *Restless Souls: The Making of American Spirituality*. 1st ed. San Francisco: HarperSanFrancisco, 2005.
Schuller, Kyla. *The Biopolitics of Feeling: Race, Sex, and Science in the Nineteenth Century*. Durham, NC: Duke University Press, 2018.
Schultz, Rima Lunin. "Jane Addams, Apotheosis of Social Christianity." *Church History* 84, no. 1 (2015): 207–19.
Schumann, Christoph. "A Muslim 'Diaspora' in the United States?" *Muslim World* 97, no. 1 (2007): 11–32. https://doi.org/10.1111/j.1478-1913.2007.00157.x
Scott, David. "Colonial Governmentality." *Social Text* 43 (1995): 191–220.
Scott, Hugh Lenox, and Iseeo. *Through Indian Sign Language: The Fort Sill Ledgers of Hugh Lenox Scott and Iseeo, 1889–1897*. Edited by William C. Meadows. Norman: University of Oklahoma Press, 2015.
Sehat, David. "The Civilizing Mission of Booker T. Washington." *Journal of Southern History* 73, no. 2 (May 2007): 323–62.
Senander, Angela. *Scandal: The Catholic Church and Public Life*. Collegeville, MN: Liturgical Press, 2012.
Sensbach, Jon F. *Rebecca's Revival: Creating Black Christianity in the Atlantic World*. Cambridge, MA: Harvard University Press, 2006.
Sertima, Ivan Van. *They Came before Columbus: The African Presence in Ancient America*. New York: Random House Trade, 2003.
Sharp, Mary A. "Monrovia, Africa." *Christian Standard and Home Journal*, December 2, 1862, 381.
Sharpe, Christina Elizabeth. *In the Wake: On Blackness and Being*. Durham, NC: Duke University Press, 2016.

Simpson, Audra. *Mohawk Interruptus: Political Life across the Borders of Settler States.* Durham, NC: Duke University Press, 2014.

———. "The State Is a Man: Theresa Spence, Loretta Saunders, and the Gender of Settler Sovereignty." *Theory & Event* 19, no. 4 (2016).

Simpson, Leanne Betasamosake. *As We Have Always Done: Indigenous Freedom through Radical Resistance.* 3rd ed. Minneapolis: University of Minnesota Press, 2017.

Sinclair, John H., and Arturo Piedra Solano. "The Dawn of Ecumenism in Latin America: Robert E. Speer, Presbyterians, and the Panama Conference of 1916." *Journal of Presbyterian History* 77 (1999).

Sklar, Kathryn Kish. *Florence Kelley and the Nation's Work: The Rise of Women's Political Culture.* New Haven, CT: Yale University Press, 1995.

Sleeper-Smith, Susan. "'[A]n Unpleasant Transaction on This Frontier': Challenging Female Autonomy and Authority at Michilimackinac." *Journal of the Early Republic* 25, no. 3 (2005): 417–43.

Smallwood, Stephanie E. "The Politics of the Archive and History's Accountability to the Enslaved." *History of the Present* 6, no. 2 (2016): 117–34.

Smith, Andrea. *Conquest: Sexual Violence and American Indian Genocide.* Durham, NC: Duke University Press, 2015.

Smith, Barbara Ellen, ed. *Neither Separate nor Equal: Women, Race, and Class in the South.* Philadelphia: Temple University Press, 1999.

Smith, Jessie Carney, and Shirelle Phelps, eds. *Notable Black American Women.* Detroit, MI: Gale Research, 1992.

Smith, Jonathan Z. *Relating Religion: Essays in the Study of Religion.* Chicago: University of Chicago Press, 2004.

———. "Religion, Religions, Religious." In *Critical Terms for Religious Studies*, ed. Mark C. Taylor. Chicago: University of Chicago Press, 1998.

Smith, Linda Tuhiwai. *Decolonizing Methodologies: Research and Indigenous Peoples.* London: Zed Books, 1999.

Smith, Mark M. "Remembering Mary, Shaping Revolt: Reconsidering the Stono Rebellion." *Journal of Southern History* 67, no. 3 (2001): 513–34.

———. *Stono: Documenting and Interpreting a Southern Slave Revolt.* Columbia: University of South Carolina Press, 2005.

Smith, Matthew J. "Settler Colonialism and U.S. Home Missions." *Oxford Research Encyclopedia of Religion*, February 2018. https://doi.org/10.1093/acrefore/9780199340378.013.392

Smithers, Gregory D. *Native Southerners: Indigenous History from Origins to Removal.* Norman: University of Oklahoma Press, 2019.

Smoak, Gregory E. *Ghost Dances and Identity: Prophetic Religion and American Indian Ethnogenesis in the Nineteenth Century.* Berkeley: University of California Press, 2006.

Smyke, Raymond J. *The First African Diplomat: Momolu Massaquoi (1870–1938).* Bloomington, IN: Xlibris, 2004.

———. "Massaquoi of Liberia, 1870–1938." *Geneve-Afrique* 21, no. 1 (1983): 73–105.
Stanley, Brian, ed. *The World Missionary Conference, Edinburgh 1910*. Grand Rapids, MI: Eerdmans, 2009.
Steinbock-Pratt, Sarah. *Educating the Empire: American Teachers and Contested Colonization in the Philippines*. New York: Cambridge University Press, 2019.
Stern, Philip J. *The Company-State: Corporate Sovereignty and the Early Modern Foundations of the British Empire in India*. New York: Oxford University Press, 2011.
Stewart, Dianne M. *Three Eyes for the Journey: African Dimensions of the Jamaican Religious Experience*. Oxford: Oxford University Press, 2004.
Stockley, Grif. *Black Boys Burning: The 1959 Fire at the Arkansas Negro Boys Industrial School*. Jackson: University of Mississippi Press, 2017.
———. *Ruled by Race: Black/White Relations in Arkansas from Slavery to the Present*. Fayetteville: University of Arkansas Press, 2009.
Stoehr, Catherine Murton. "Nativism's Bastard: Neolin, Tenskwatawa, and the Anishinabeg Methodist Movement." In *Lines Drawn upon the Water: First Nations and the Great Lakes Borders and Borderlands*, ed. Karl S. Hele. Waterloo, Ontario: Wilfrid Laurier University Press, 2008.
Stoler, Ann Laura. *Along the Archival Grain: Epistemic Anxieties and Colonial Common Sense*. Princeton, NJ: Princeton University Press, 2009.
Stratton, Clif. *Education for Empire: American Schools, Race, and the Paths of Good Citizenship*. Berkeley: University of California Press, 2016.
Sturm, Circe. *Becoming Indian: The Struggle over Cherokee Identity in the Twenty-First Century*. Santa Fe, NM: School for Advanced Research Press, 2011.
Sullivan, Winnifred Fallers. *The Impossibility of Religious Freedom*. Princeton, NJ: Princeton University Press, 2005.
TallBear, Kimberly. *Native American DNA: Tribal Belonging and the False Promise of Genetic Science*. Minneapolis: University of Minnesota Press, 2013.
Tanner, Helen Hornbeck. "Mapping the Grand Traverse Indian Country: The Contributions of Peter Dougherty." *Michigan Historical Review* 31, no. 1 (2005): 44–91.
Tarango, Angela. *Choosing the Jesus Way: American Indian Pentecostals and the Fight for the Indigenous Principle*. Chapel Hill: University of North Carolina Press, 2014.
Tarr, Peter James. "The Education of the Thomasites: American School Teachers in Philippine Colonial Society, 1901–1913." PhD diss., Cornell University, 2006.
Thomas, Jolyon Baraka. *Faking Liberties: Religious Freedom in American-Occupied Japan*. Chicago: University of Chicago Press, 2019.
Thomas, Lamont D. *Paul Cuffe: Black Entrepreneur and Pan-Africanist*. Illini books. Blacks in the New World. Urbana: University of Illinois Press, 1988.
Thornton, John K. "African Dimensions of the Stono Rebellion." *American Historical Review* 96, no. 4 (1991): 1101–13.
Tillman, Ellen D. *Dollar Diplomacy by Force: Nation-Building and Resistance in the Dominican Republic*. Chapel Hill: University of North Carolina Press, 2016.
Tinker, George E. *Missionary Conquest: The Gospel and Native American Cultural Genocide*. Minneapolis, MN: Fortress Press, 1993.

Tomek, Beverly C., and Matthew J. Hetrick, eds. *New Directions in the Study of African American Recolonization*. Gainesville: University Press of Florida, 2017.

Tone-Pah-Hote, Jenny. *Crafting an Indigenous Nation: Kiowa Expressive Culture in the Progressive Era*. Chapel Hill: University of North Carolina Press, 2019.

Trouillot, Michel-Rolph. *Silencing the Past: Power and the Production of History*. Boston: Beacon Press, 1995.

Tuitt, Frank, Bianca C. Williams, and Dian Squire. *Plantation Politics and Campus Rebellions: Power, Diversity, and the Emancipatory Struggle in Higher Education*. Albany: State University of New York Press, 2021.

Tweed, Thomas A. *Crossing and Dwelling: A Theory of Religion*. Cambridge, MA: Harvard University Press, 2006.

Tyler-McGraw, Marie. *An African Republic: Black and White Virginians in the Making of Liberia*. The John Hope Franklin Series in African American History and Culture. Chapel Hill: University of North Carolina Press, 2007.

Tyrrell, Ian R. *Reforming the World: The Creation of America's Moral Empire*. Princeton, NJ: Princeton University Press, 2010.

United States Government. *Tables showing the Number of Emigrants and Recaptured Africans Sent to the Colony of Liberia by the Government of the United States*. Washington, DC: Government Printing Office, 1845.

Urlsperger, Samuel, et al. *Detailed Reports on the Salzburger Emigrants Who Settled in America*. Athens: University of Georgia Press, 1968.

Vander, Judith. "The Creative Power and Style of Ghost Dance Songs." In *Music of the First Nations: Tradition and Innovation in Native North America*, ed. Tara Browner. Urbana: University of Illinois Press, 2009. http://ebookcentral.proquest.com

Vecsey, Christopher. *On the Padres' Trail*. Notre Dame, IN: Notre Dame University Press, 1996.

———. *Traditional Ojibwa Religion and Its Historical Changes*. Philadelphia: American Philosophical Society, 1983.

Veeser, Cyrus. *A World Safe for Capitalism: Dollar Diplomacy and America's Rise to Global Power*. New York: Columbia University Press, 2002.

Voget, Fred W. *The Shoshoni-Crow Sun Dance*. Norman: University of Oklahoma Press, 1984.

Von Eschen, Penny M. *Race against Empire: Black Americans and Anticolonialism, 1937–1957*. Ithaca, NY: Cornell University Press, 1997.

———. *Satchmo Blows Up the World: Jazz Ambassadors Play the Cold War*. Cambridge, MA: Harvard University Press, 2004.

Voyles, Traci Brynne. *Wastelanding: Legacies of Uranium Mining in Navajo Country*. Minneapolis: University of Minnesota Press, 2015.

Walker, J. R. *Lakota Belief and Ritual*. Lincoln: University of Nebraska Press, 1980.

Walther, Karine. *Sacred Interests: The United States and the Islamic World, 1821–1921*. Chapel Hill: University of North Carolina Press, 2015.

Ware, Rudolph T., III. "Slavery in Islamic Africa, 1400–1800." In *The Cambridge World History of Slavery*, ed. David Eltis and Stanley L. Engerman, 3:47–81. New York: Cambridge University Press, 2011.

Warren, Louis S. *God's Red Son: The Ghost Dance Religion and the Making of Modern America*. New York: Basic Books, 2017.

Watkins, William H. *The White Architects of Black Education: Ideology and Power in America, 1865–1954*. New York: Teachers College Press, 2001.

Weber, David. *The Spanish Frontier in North America*. New Haven, CT: Yale University Press, 1994.

Weisenfeld, Judith. *New World A-Coming: Black Religion and Racial Identity during the Great Migration*. New York: NYU Press, 2017.

Weiss, Max. "The Two Pandemics." *Baltimore Magazine*, August 2020, www.baltimoremagazine.com (accessed January 2, 2021).

Weld, Kirsten. *Paper Cadavers: The Archives of Dictatorship in Guatemala; American Encounters/Global Interactions*. Durham, NC: Duke University Press, 2014.

Wenger, Tisa. *Religious Freedom: The Contested History of an American Ideal*. Chapel Hill: University of North Carolina Press, 2017.

———. "Sovereignty." In *Religion, Law, USA*, ed. Joshua Dubler and Isaac Weiner. New York: NYU Press, 2019.

———. *We Have a Religion: The 1920s Pueblo Indian Dance Controversy and American Religious Freedom*. Chapel Hill: University of North Carolina Press, 2009.

Wheeler, Rachel M. *To Live upon Hope: Mohicans and Missionaries in the Eighteenth-Century Northeast*. Ithaca, NY: Cornell University Press, 2008.

Whyte, Kyle Powys. "Indigeneity and US Settler Colonialism." *The Oxford Handbook of Philosophy and Race*, February 23, 2017. https://doi.org/10.1093/oxfordhb/9780190236953.013.51

Widder, Keith R. *Battle for the Soul: Métis Children Encounter Evangelical Protestants at Mackinaw Mission, 1823–1837*. East Lansing: Michigan State University Press, 1999.

Wilderson, Frank B. *Red, White, and Black: Cinema and the Structure of U.S. Antagonisms*. Durham, NC: Duke University Press, 2010.

Williams, Bianca C., Dian Squire, and Frank Tuitt, eds. *Plantation Politics and Campus Rebellions: Power, Diversity, and the Emancipatory Struggle in Higher Education*. SUNY Series, Critical Race Studies in Education. Albany: State University of New York Press, 2021.

Williams, Deane. "The Fog of War: Eleven Lessons from the Life of Robert S. McNamara." *Metro*, no. 141 (January 2004): 56–62. https://doi.org/10.3316/informit.953305168449667

Williams, Eric. *Capitalism and Slavery*. Chapel Hill: University of North Carolina Press, 1944.

Williams, Walter L. *Black Americans and the Evangelization of Africa, 1877–1900*. Madison: University of Wisconsin Press, 1982.

———. "Ethnic Relations of African Students in the United States, with Black Americans, 1870–1900." *Journal of Negro History* 65, no. 3 (Summer 1980): 228–49.

Wisecup, Kelly. "Knowing Obeah." *Atlantic Studies* 10, no. 3 (September 2013): 406–25.

Witgen, Michael J. *An Infinity of Nations: How the Native New World Shaped Early North America*. Early American Studies. Philadelphia: University of Pennsylvania Press, 2012.

Wolfe, Patrick. "Settler Colonialism and the Elimination of the Native." *Journal of Genocide Research* 8, no. 4 (2006): 387–409.

Wood, Peter H. *Black Majority: Negroes in Colonial South Carolina from 1670 through the Stono Rebellion*. New York: Norton, 1975.

Woods, Robert A. *The Neighborhood in Nation-Building: The Running Comment of Thirty Years at the South End*. Boston: Houghton Mifflin, 1923.

Woolford, Andrew, Jeff Benvenuto, and Alexander Laban Hinton, eds. *Colonial Genocide in Indigenous North America*. Durham, NC: Duke University Press, 2014.

Wright, Robert E., OMI. "How Many Are 'a Few'?: Catholic Clergy in Central and Northern New Mexico, 1780–1851." In *Seeds of Struggle, Harvest of Faith*, ed. Barbe Awalt, Paul Rhetts, and Thomas J. Steele, SJ. Albuquerque, NM: LPD Press, 1998.

Yarema, Allan E. "The American Colonization Society: An Avenue to Freedom?" MA thesis, East Texas State University, 2006.

Zabriskie, Alexander C. *Bishop Brent: Crusader for Christian Unity*. Philadelphia: Westminster Press, 1948.

Zackodnik, Teresa. "Empire and Education in Hampton's Southern Workman: The South Pacific, the Caribbean, and the Reconstruction South." In *South Seas Encounters: Nineteenth-Century Oceania, Britain, and America*, ed. Richard Fulton et al., 156–76. New York: Routledge, 2018.

Zedeño, Maria Nieves, Wendi Field Murray, and Kaitlyn Chandler. "The Inalienable-Commodity Continuum in the Circulation of Birds on the North American Plains." In *Relational Identities and Other-Than-Human Agency in Archaeology*, ed. Eleanor Harrison-Buck and Julia A. Hendon, 100–125. Boulder: University Press of Colorado, 2018. https://doi.org/10.5876/9781607327479.c005

Zimmerman, Andrew. *Alabama in Africa: Booker T. Washington, the German Empire, and the Globalization of the New South*. Princeton, NJ: Princeton University Press, 2010.

ABOUT THE EDITORS

SYLVESTER A. JOHNSON, Professor and Assistant Vice Provost for the Humanities at Virginia Tech, is founding director of the Virginia Tech Center for Humanities and specializes in the study of technology, race, religion, and national security. Johnson has authored *The Myth of Ham in Nineteenth-Century American Christianity*, a study of race and religious hatred that won the American Academy of Religion's Best First Book award; and *African American Religions, 1500–2000*, an award-winning interpretation of five centuries of democracy, colonialism, and freedom in the Atlantic world. Johnson has also coedited *The FBI and Religion: Faith and National Security before and after 9/11*. A founding coeditor of the *Journal of Africana Religions*, he has published more than seventy scholarly articles, essays, and reviews. Johnson is currently writing a book on human identity in the age of intelligent machines and human-machine symbiosis. He is also producing a digital scholarly edition of an early English history of global religions.

TISA WENGER is Professor of American Religious History at Yale Divinity School, with secondary appointments in Religious Studies and American Studies at Yale. Wenger is the author of *We Have a Religion: The 1920s Pueblo Indian Dance Controversy and American Religious Freedom* (2009) and *Religious Freedom: The Contested History of an American Ideal* (2017). She is the editor of a forthcoming special issue of *Pacific Historical Review* on Religion in the American West; and coeditor of the book series Studies in U.S. Religion, Politics, and Law. As a Guggenheim Fellow for 2021–2022, she is writing a new book titled *How Settler Colonialism Made American Religion*.

ABOUT THE CONTRIBUTORS

CARA LEA BURNIDGE (PhD, Florida State University) is Associate Professor of Religion at the University of Northern Iowa. She is a historian of religion in the United States, and her scholarship examines the intersections of religion and politics in the late nineteenth and early twentieth centuries, with particular attention to progressive reform, citizenship, and US foreign relations. Her teaching examines the legacy of these issues through critical service-learning courses in partnership with local refugee communities in Iowa. Her first book is titled *A Peaceful Conquest: Woodrow Wilson, Religion, and the New World Order* (2016), and she is currently working on a religious biography of Elizabeth Cady Stanton.

HEATHER D. CURTIS (ThD, Harvard University) is the Warren S. Woodbridge Professor of Comparative Religions at Tufts University, where she also holds appointments in the Department of Studies in Race, Colonialism, and Diaspora, and the Department of History. Curtis received her doctorate in the History of Christianity and American Religion from Harvard University. Her research explores how religion has shaped responses to racial injustice, humanitarian disasters, economic crises, and bodily illness from the late nineteenth century to the present. Her recent book, *Holy Humanitarians: American Evangelicals and Global Aid* (2018), examines the crucial role popular religious media played in the extension of US philanthropy at home and abroad from the late nineteenth century to the early twentieth. Her award-winning first book, *Faith in the Great Physician: Suffering and Divine Healing in American Culture, 1860–1900* (2007), illuminates the connections and tensions among Christian devotional practice, medical science, and the changing meanings of suffering and healing in American culture. Curtis has served as a Senior Editor for the *Oxford Encyclopedia of Religion in America*, and as cochair for the Religion and U.S. Empire Seminar of the

American Academy of Religion. She is currently at work on a religious biography of Ida B. Wells.

CHRISTINA C. DAVIDSON (PhD, Duke University) is an interdisciplinary historian with specializations in Latin American and Caribbean history, African American Studies, and Religious Studies. In 2022, she will join the History Department at the University of Southern California as an Assistant Professor. Davidson has held postdoctoral fellowships at the John C. Danforth Center for Religion and Politics at Washington University in St. Louis and the Charles Warren Center at Harvard University. Her research explores diplomatic and cultural relations between the Dominican Republic and the United States in the late nineteenth and early twentieth centuries.

SARAH DEES (PhD, Indiana University) is an Assistant Professor of Religious Studies at Iowa State University. She is a scholar of American and Indigenous religions with interests in race, politics, and museum studies. She previously taught at the University of Tennessee, Knoxville, and held the Luce Postdoctoral Fellowship in Religion, Politics, and Global Affairs at Northwestern University. Her first book, tentatively titled "The Materialization of Native American Religions: The Smithsonian Institution, Settler Colonialism, and the Study of Indigenous Lifeways," will be published as part of the Critical Studies in the History of Anthropology series.

JONATHAN EBEL (PhD, University of Chicago) is Professor and Head of the Department of Religion at the University of Illinois, Urbana-Champaign. Ebel's research program involves religion and war, religion and violence, and lay theologies of economic hardship, all within the American context. He is the author of *G.I. Messiahs: Soldiering, War, and American Civil Religion* (2015) and *Faith in the Fight: Religion and the American Soldier in the Great War* (2010), and the coeditor with Professor John Carlson of *From Jeremiad to Jihad: Religion, Violence, and America* (2012). He is currently finishing work on a religious history of the Great Depression in agricultural California. Ebel was a Guggenheim Fellow in 2017 and a candidate for the US House of Representatives in 2018.

KATHARINE GERBNER (PhD, Harvard University) is Associate Professor of History at the University of Minnesota, where she teaches courses on Atlantic History, History of Religions, Magic & Medicine, and the Early Modern Archive. Dr. Gerbner's research explores the religious dimensions of race, authority, and freedom in the early modern Atlantic world. Her first book is titled *Christian Slavery: Conversion and Race in the Protestant Atlantic World* (2018). She is interested in how Afro-Caribbean ideas about healing, prayer, and worship influenced the construction of European categories such as religion and medicine.

JENNIFER GRABER (PhD, Duke University) is Professor of Religious Studies and Shive, Lindsay, and Gray Professor in the History of Christianity at the University of Texas at Austin, where she also serves as Associate Director of the Native American and Indigenous Studies Program. Graber works on religion and violence and interreligious encounters in American prisons and on the American frontier. Her books are titled *The Furnace of Affliction: Prisons and Religion in Antebellum America* and *The Gods of Indian Country: Religion and the Struggle for the American West*. Professor Graber teaches graduate seminars on religion and violence, religion and empire, and approaches to the study of religion in the United States.

ZAREENA A. GREWAL (PhD, University of Michigan) is an Associate Professor of American Studies, Religious Studies, and Ethnicity, Race, and Migration at Yale University. Her research focuses on American Muslims, race, gender, and transnational religious networks. Her first book, *Islam Is a Foreign Country: American Muslims and the Global Crisis of Authority* (NYU Press, 2013), is a historical ethnography of American Muslim seekers in the postcolonial Middle East engaged in debates about religious reform. Her forthcoming book traces the place of the Quran in the American imagination, particularly in relation to the culture wars. She has received awards for her writing and research grants from the Fulbright, Wenner Gren, and Luce foundations.

KATHLEEN HOLSCHER (PhD, Princeton University) is Associate Professor of Religious Studies and American Studies at the University of New Mexico, where she holds the Endowed Chair in Roman Catholic Studies. Her research considers the historical relationship between Catholicism and US settler colonialism; she is especially interested in how that relationship developed via church-state conflict and collaboration. Her work also attends to clerical sexual abuse and other forms of Catholic violence endemic to mission institutions that furthered colonial ends. Her book, *Religious Lessons: Catholic Sisters, Public Education, and the Law in Mid-Century New Mexico*, was published in 2012.

LUCIA HULSETHER (PhD, Yale University) is Assistant Professor of Religion at Skidmore College. She is a scholar of religion with particular interests in the history of capitalism and labor; religion in the Americas; feminist, queer, and critical race theory; and theory and method in the study of religion. Hulsether's first book is *Capitalist Humanitarianism* (forthcoming).

BRENNAN MCDANIEL is a PhD student in the Department of American Studies at Yale University. His work concerns the cultural history of religion and secularism, especially in rural America.

KARINE WALTHER (PhD, Columbia University) is Associate Professor of History at Georgetown University in Qatar. She is currently working on her second, forthcoming book: *Spreading the Faith: American Missionaries, ARAMCO, and the Birth of the US-Saudi Special Relationship, 1890–1955*. Her first book, *Sacred Interests: The United States and the Islamic World, 1821–1921*, was published in 2015. Before joining the faculty at Georgetown, Karine served as a visiting professor at Middlebury College, a postdoctoral fellow at the Belfer Center for Science and International Affairs, and a visiting lecturer at the Harvard Kennedy School.

INDEX

Abbott, Grace, 115
Abduction, 17, 65–66, 69–71, 78, 189
Abdul-Malik, Ahmed, 275
Abolitionism, 31, 68–69, 77, 181, 187, 194
Acoma Pueblo, 236
Act for the Better Ordering and Governing (1712), 23, 33
Act to Remedy the Evils Arising from Irregular Assemblies of Slaves, 27
Addams, Jane: European voyage, 103–104; Hull House management, 105; and pluralism, 106–109; and social surveys, 109–110, 114
Africa (Africans): anticolonial movements, 9; Catholicism and, 22–24; Dominicans of African descent, 205–207, 216–217; and European trade, 2; Ida B. Wells and, 190–191; Indigenous, 64–70, 77–80, 185–186, 189, 191, 193, 197; and Islam, 69, 290–291; Massaquoi and, 189, 191–193, 199; North Africa, 282; US Marines in, 212; West Africa, 3, 29, 63–71, 77, 291; West Central, 22, 24, 69–70. *See also* African Church; Liberia; Mississippi in Africa; South Africa
African Americans: colored (racial category), 91, 151, 167, 184, 198–199; in Edgar Villanueva's writings, 303, 314; emigrants, 1, 190, 204; and global racial reform, 13, 179–180, 184–188, 193–198; in Haiti and Dominican Republic, 204–207; and industrial schools, 151, 153–163, 168–172; and knowledge production, 83; and Liberia, 66–67, 77–80, 185–189; missionaries to the Dominican Republic, 219–220, 223; religion, 18, 25; and violence against Indigenous Africans, 77–79, 191–193, 197
Africana religions, 17–18, 20–21, 24–25, 28, 34–35. *See also* Obeah
African Church (in South Carolina), 30–33
African Methodist Episcopal Church (AME), 31, 66, 190, 193, 204, 207
African Methodist Episcopal Zion Church, 198
Agnostics, 106
Ahgosa (Ojibwe), 51
Ahpeahtone (Kiowa), 139
Al-Bashir, Omar, 284
al Din, Salah, 290
al-Faruqi, Ismail, 284, 287
Algonquin, 88. *See also* Anishinaabe
Allen, Richard, 31, 66
al-Turabi, Hassan, 283–286, 295
American Board of Commissioners for Foreign Missions (ABCFM), 45–48, 71–75
American Colonization Society (ACS), 63, 65–68, 78–79, 183, 185
American exceptionalism, 4, 58, 117, 313
American Missionary Association, 151
Americanism, 119
Andowish (Odawa), 49
Anglican, 6, 26, 106, 219

Anglophone world: Anglo-American authorities, 61; and education, 158–159, 182, 203–204, 207–209; empire, 73, 75–76, 83; gender roles, 155; missionaries, 13, 74, 203–204, 217–220, 223–224; priests, 236, 239; and racial power, 71; and racial priorities, 213–216; and religious imperialism, 210–213; settlers, 72
Anglo-Saxons, 182, 187, 190, 199, 209, 213
Animist, 164
Anishinaabe, 13, 41, 43–44, 48, 50–54, 57, 94. *See also* Odawa; Ojibwe; Potawatomi
An-Na'im, Abdullahi, 285–286
Apartheid, 9, 306
Appalachia, 88, 278
Arabs, 279, 285–288, 290
Arapaho, 136–137
Archer, James, 56
Archival wisdom, 309–313, 316
Argentina, 214
Arkansas Department of Corrections (ADC), 172
Arkansas Negro Boys Industrial School, 171–172
Armstrong, Louis, 275
Armstrong, Samuel Chapman, 151–162, 168–169, 171, 182–183
Armstrong, William, 169
Ashanti, 66
Asia, 3, 71, 99, 212, 261, 275, 286, 288, 303
Assiginac (Odawa), 49
Assimilation, 125, 237, 239: Edgar Villanueva and, 303, 310, 333; and the Census, 86–92, 95–98
Astor, John Jacob, 47
Australia, 3, 195, 197

Badin, Stephen, 49
Báez, Buenaventura, 206
Bahrain, 282–284
Baptism, 30, 32, 52
Baptists, 47–48, 53, 67, 166–167

Barbados, 26, 29
Bell, Jr., Daniel M., 268–269
Bennet, Mrs. Fred S., 22
Bennett, James, 56
Bennett, Rolla, 32
Big Bethel Church, 170
bin Laden, Osama, 265, 285, 295
Bingham, Abel, 47, 49, 52–53
Biopolitics, 12–13, 83–84, 98, 104–105, 111, 115–118
Birds: eagles, 127, 129–130, 135–137, 142; magpies, 129, 136, 138; owls, 129, 132; as symbols, 126–133, 138, 143; and the Feather Dance, 124–126, 134–137; Thunderbird, 128–129, 136
Black Lives Matter movement, 99, 304
Blackbird, Andrew (Odawa), 48–49
Blood: humanity of one, 181; and racial classification, 90, 151, 153, 172, 287; in religious practice, 27–28, 136
Board for Christian Work in Santo Domingo (BCWSD), 222–223
Bodies, male: Muslim, 266; white, 253, 269, 272
Bohemians, 111
Bolivia, 214–215
Booth, Charles, 111–113
Boyd, George, 45, 50
Brady, Matthew Francis, 244–245
Brazil, 214
Brent, Charles, 168–169
Brimm, Christine, 295
Britain (British): and Africa, 64–65; and African American Protestants, 179–180, 191–199; Africana religions and imperial policy, 19–21, 25–27, 30, 32; empire, 3, 5, 17; and Indigenous peoples, 41, 45–46, 73, 87; and the American Revolution, 29, 75–76; in the Caribbean, 205–208, 213, 219–220; and the slave trade, 68–69
Broughton, Thomas, 6
Brown v. Board of Education (1954), 171

Buffalo: doctors, 130, 141; foodsource, 126; in Kiowa art, 127; restoration, 131–134, 138–139, 141–142; slaughter, 136; and the Feather Dance, 137–144; White Buffalo Calf Woman, 133
Bulgaria, 195–196
Burial, 25
Burke, Edmund, 285
Burma, 167
Byzantine, 5

Cáceres, Ramón, 216
Calhoun, John C., 72
Canada (Canadian), 3–4, 44–47, 51, 191, 204, 232, 281
Canaanites, 32
Capitalism: and British colonialism, 3; and education, 168; finance capitalism, 301–305; free market, 272; and Hull House, 104, 119; and humanitarianism, 14; and labor exploitation, 156; and missionaries, 203, 212–213, 220, 222; neoliberalism, 229–230; and philanthropy, 298–300, 302, 305, 309, 311, 313–317; racial, 172; and slavery, 76; and waste, 233, 240
Carceral state, 9–10, 168, 171–172, 218, 292
CARES Act, 99–100
Caribbean: anticolonial movements, 9; and British concepts of religion, 25–29; enslaved rebellions in, 12, 29–30; and slavery, 17–18, 21, 68, 71; Spanish, 14, 149, 152, 207–210, 213, 219–220; and US colonization, 1. *See also* Cuba; Dominican Republic; Haiti; Jamaica
Caries, Zacharias George, 26
Carlisle Indian Industrial School, 156–161
Cary, Lott, 67
Cass, Lewis, 43–45
Catholic Theological Society of America, 231
CCLA. See Committee on Cooperation in Latin America
Central Intelligence Agency (CIA), 254, 304

Census. *See* US Census
Central Tennessee College (CTC), 181–184, 187–191: Meharry Medical School, 182, 191
Césaire, Aimé, 10
Chatkehoodle, 140–141
Cherokee, 71, 73, 85, 93. *See also* Crane, Robert
Cheyenne, 129, 134–137
Chickasaw, 18, 71, 73, 85, 93
Children (Child): abuse of, 160, 231–235, 242–244; in Crane's narrative, 289; deaths of, 139–141; and Department of Commerce and Labor, 117; Filipino, 168–169; of God, 194–197; of Indigenous Africans, 67–68, 77, 187–188; immigrant, 167; and Indigenous American education, 46, 50–51, 163–164, 192; industrial schooling for children of color, 169–172; killed in Vietnam, 262, 268; Kiowa ritual observers, 138, 144; labor, 111–112, 114, 119; missions to Indigenous American, 73, 75; "of nature," 67, 96; settler massacres, 165; and slavery, 68–69; Strangites and, 58; in Villanueva's work, 307–308. *See also* Industrial schools
Choctaw, 18, 71, 73–75, 85, 93
Christie, Emerson, 166
Civilization (civilized): and African missionizing, 63, 68, 183–186, 189–192, 196; and Doctrine of Discovery, 41–42; and education, 75, 152–159; 162–169, 223; hierarchies of, 8, 180–189, 194, 198–199; and Indigenous religions, 71–75; and Mackinac Island settler conceptions, 43–49, 57; and modernization, 149; and narratives of Indigenous decline, 58, 97; and Odawa Catholicism, 49–51; and progress, 112, 118, 120, 125, 152–155, 162; and Protestants in Latin America, 209, 213–214, 218; and religion, 5–6; and slavery, 156; Southern, 170; and the Census, 91, 97; and United States empire, 1, 8, 209, 239

Civil rights, 180–181, 198, 287–288, 306
Civil War: Confederacy, 290; and education, 156, 180, 187; and imperialism, 83, 152, 163, 206; and Liberia, 63, and Mackinac Island, 58; and slavery 33
Civilization Fund, 46, 50
Coca-Cola (Coke), 313–314
Coker, Daniel, 66–68
Cold War, 229, 257, 262, 276, 284, 286, 304
Colonialism: anticolonialism, 9, 14, 180, 199, 204, 206, 224, 300; decolonialism, 299–309, 316; extractive, 2, 41, 239–240; internal, 36, 152; metropoles, 2, 3, 64, 106, 186, 304; peripheries, 2, 3, 233; postcolonialism, 10, 286, 309; salt-water fallacy, 3. *See also* Settler colonialism
Colonizer virus, 299, 301–303, 307–309, 315–316
Columbus, Christopher, 159, 220, 291
Commission on Survey and Occupation, 212–213
Committee on Cooperation in Latin America (CCLA): and mission intel, 212–213; mission organization, 214–216; and pan-Americanism, 210–212; white supremacist assumptions, 217–220, 222
Communism, 261, 276, 282
Congregationalism, 45, 217
Cosmopolitanism, 113, 117, 119, 229, 255, 262
COVID-19, 99–100, 303
Crane, John Ruedel, 294–295
Crane, Robert (Farooq Abdul Haq): and American Muslim counter publics, 14; family history, 287–289; Islamic-Cherokee claims, 290–294; Muslim writings, 280–284; proclaimed Cherokee heritage, 276–279; and Traditionalist Islam, 285; US diplomat, 276–77, 284
Creed, 95, 106, 108, 214

Creek, 71, 85, 93
Crow, 130, 133, 136, 292
Cuba: schools, 214; and the CCLA, 215–216, 219; US occupation, 2, 64, 208; war, 163, 197
Cuffe, Paul, 66

Dakota, 88
Darwinism, 182–183, 194
Davis, Angela, 10
Dawes Act, 86
Day, Daniel, 187
Day, Emma, 187
Day, William, 59
Dejean, Pierre, 50
Demographic data, 17, 83–84, 112, 303. *See also* Social surveys; US Census
Denmark Vesey conspiracy, 20–21, 28–33
Diné (Navajo), 85, 292; Diné Bikéyah, 229, 231, 233, 235–236, 239–242, 247
Diocese of Gallup: as dumping ground for priests, 233, 239–242, 246; Indian Diocese, 229, 236–239; sexual abuse as settler-colonial violence, 232–235; sexual abuse in, 14. *See also* Hageman, Clement; Sullivan, John
Disciples of Christ, 217
Disposability, 240–241
Dissenters, 106
Diversity: and biopolitics, 83; Edgar Villanueva on, 303–304, 310; and Hull House, 111–112; religious, 19, 106–107; as threat, 263
Doctrine of Discovery, 8, 17, 41, 58
Dominican Republic (Dominicans): Afro-Dominicans, 205–206; and Catholicism, 212; and Du Bois, 162; evangelical occupancy, 216–223; Protestants in, 204–209, 215; US missionaries racialized vision of, 14, 203–204, 224–225
Dougherty, Peter, 51
Douglass, Frederick, 181
Drake, Thomas, 294

Drones: and evangelicalism, 14, 230, 253–256, 272; in imperial discourse, 258–259, 270, 313; omniscience and omnipotence, 258, 265–271; origins, 264; theology of, 265–270
Drury, Philo W., 203, 207, 209, 212, 216, 219–223
Du Bois, W. E. B., 9–10, 161–162
Dutch East India Company, 3

East India Company, 3
Edwards, Celestine, 194–199
Edwards, Jonathan, 264, 266
Egypt, 36, 191, 272
Ellington, Duke, 275
Elliott, Benjamin, 32
Elliot mission, 73–75
Engels, Friedrich, 114
Enlightenment, the, 5–6, 8, 301, 310
Epistemology, 9, 13, 32, 34, 84, 126, 143, 207, 311
Espelage, Bernard, 238–241, 243–245
Europe (European): and Africa, 64, 70, 192; Arapaho prophecies of European expulsion, 136–137; and buffalo, 131–133; definitions of religion, 5–6, 20, 25–26; definitions of secularism, 10–11, 42; in Edgar Villanueva's arguments, 302, 307–308; and education, 163; empires, 1, 17; Euro-American knowledge production of Indigenous peoples, 86–87, 91–92, 96–97; Europhile, 204–205; Ghost Dance's Euro-American imperial frame, 125–126, 130, 134; immigrants from, 83, 237; Jane Addams travels to, 103; and jazz ambassadors, 275; and mission conferences, 210–214; in Robert Crane's narratives, 287; and slavery, 2; and United States expansion, 85, 159, 195–196, 220, 290, 310–313
Evangelicals: and Donald Trump, 270–272; expansion in early Republic, 30; and imperial resistance, 49; and judgment, 260–262; and language of occupation, 216–223; literature, 215; and the carceral state, 172; in the Dominican Republican, 203–204, 207–210; and territoriality, 256–258, 262–265, 269; and weapons, 14, 230, 253–256, 266–268. *See also* Committee on Cooperation in Latin America
Evangelical Union of Puerto Rico (EUPR), 216–217, 220–223
Extermination/mass killing, 3, 17, 54, 71, 73, 84, 92, 95, 196, 205, 292–293
Extraction, resource: 2, 41, 167, 239–240

Falwell, Jerry, 262–263
Feasts, 24–25, 134
Feather Dance (*amakogia*), definition, 124; feathers and, 130, 138; site of US surveillance, 13, 84. *See also*: Birds
Fenwick, Edward, 47, 50
Ferry, Amanda, 46
Ferry, William, 46–47, 52, 59
Finance: and Black spiritual protest, 181–184, 193, 196; and Caribbean missionaries, 212–214; and Catholic colonialism, 232–234, 239, 247; and Choctaw mission, 75; and COVID-19, 99–100; and critical ethnic studies, 9; and empire, 2, 312; Indigenous, 72–77, 89; and industrial schooling, 152, 155–158; and Mary Sharp, 186, 199; and pan-Americanism, 210; and racial capitalism, 172; and religion, 8; and Robert Crane, 279, 289; and slavery, 17, 68; and social surveys, 110, 113; and the Society for the Recognition of the Brotherhood of Man, 194, 222. *See also* Philanthropy; Villanueva, Edgar
Fieser, Louis, 254, 259
Fitzgerald, Gerald, 244–246
Five Civilized Tribes. *See* Cherokee; Chickasaw; Choctaw; Creek; Seminole

Foreign Missionary Conference of North America, 210
France (French): and Catholicism, 44, 51, 59; as empire, 17, 27, 29, 41, 87; language, 162, 205, 285
Franciscan Order, 235, 238
Fraternity (journal), 194–195
Freedmen's Aid Society, 189
Fundamental Constitutions of Carolina, 19, 34

Geikomah, Bert (Kiowa), 139, 142
General Accountability Project, 294
George III (king), 76
George Junior Republic, 167–168
Gerken, Rudolph, 236–237
German Pietism, 23
Ghost Dance, Euro-American imperial frame, 124–126, 130, 134. *See also* Feather Dance
Gillespie, Dizzy, 275
Goodman, Benny, 275
Gordon, Nathaniel, 69
Graham, Billy, 261
Great Depression, 83
Great Lakes, 17, 41, 44, 88
Grimké, Angelina, 181
Grizzard, Ephraim, 188–189, 192
Grizzard, Henry, 188
Guam, 1, 64

Hageman, Clement, 242–244
Haiti: Black American migration to, 162; and Protestant missionaries, 14, 203–208; Revolution, 29–30, 32, 192, 216; and US imperialism, 216–218
Hamlin, Jr., Augustin (Odawa), 51–51, 57
Hampton Normal and Agricultural Institute for Negroes and Indians, 151, 182
Haq, Farooq Abdul. *See* Crane, Robert
Harrison, Hubert, 198
Harvard University, 259, 288–289
Haungooah (Silver Horn) (Kiowa), 124

Havasupai, 236
Haven, Gilbert, 187
Hawaii: and education, 13, 151–153, 157–158, 162, 172, 223; and the Census, 100; and US colonization, 1
Healing: and Africana religions, 7, 26; and Catholic priests, 235, 246; Edward Villanueva and, 298–299, 302–303, 306–308, 315–317; and Indigenous American religions, 52; and the Feather Dance, 127, 130, 132, 134–135, 137–144
Hibbard, David, 167
Hilo Boarding School, 157
Hispaniola: 204–207, 216, 218. *See also* Dominican Republic; Haiti
Hokeah, Jack (Kiowa), 140
Holbrook, Agnes, 112, 115–116
Holiness movement, 185–189, 199, 257
Holt, Steve, 268
Honduras, 208
Hopi, 236, 292
Hualapai, 236
Huffman, Nathan H., 203, 209, 212, 223
Hull House: and friendship, 114–118; *Hull House Maps and Papers*, 105, 110–119; and imperialism, 105–109, 118–120; nonsectarian, 106–109, 117; and sentimental biopolitics, 104–105, 121; social surveillance, 109–114. *See also* Social surveys
Humanitarianism, 14, 301, 311, 107–109, 113
Human rights, 189, 285, 312

Idols, 6, 49, 132, 209
Iglesia Evangélica Dominicana (IED), 223–225
Igorot, 164, 167
Immigration: Catholic, 212, 237; colonies, 120; and education, 167–168; European, 83, 237; to Haiti, 204; and labor, 83, 120, 152; Muslim, 276–277, 285–288, 294; West Indian, 275; white, 83–84, 105–109, 111–117, 167–168, 237, 287

Immigration Act (1924), 83
Immigration Act (1965), 286
Imperial frame, 1, 9, 13, 15, 18, 84, 99, 105, 124–126
Impey, Catherine, 193–195, 197
India, 3, 194–195, 197, 275
Indian Appropriation Act (1846), 88
Indian Relocation Act (1956), 239
Indigenous peoples (Indigenous North Americans): anti-Indigenous violence, 3, 13, 71–75; and Christianity, 1; converts of Christianity, 49, 53–54, 74–75, 92, 158; declension narrative, 57–58, 86–87, 92, 95–98; epistemologies, 9, 13, 32, 34, 84, 126, 143, 207; frame, 13, 84, 124, 126, 143–144; Mississippi Indians, 71–76; Mormons define Lamanites as, 55–56; playing Indian, 277–278; practices and ritual, 1, 7, 18, 84, 92, 96, 98, 134–135; religions, 13, 48–50, 64, 66, 71, 83–87, 92, 96, 98; and reservations, 4, 8, 14, 50–52, 85–95, 124, 134, 137, 139–142, 236–242; and slavery, 195, 236; and taxation, 87, 89–91; and war, 44–45, 49, 58, 72–74, 88, 129; worldview, 299, 301, 310. *See also* Africa (Africans); Indigenous; Europe: Euro-American knowledge production of Indigenous peoples; Polynesian; Sovereignty
Industrial schools: through Christian networking, 13, 149, 151–157; in Hawaii, 152–153, 162; in Liberia, 187; sexual abuse in, 160; in the Dominican Republic, 222; in the Philippines, 152, 163–169; in the United States, 152–153, 158, 162, 169–172, 182–183, 192, 198. *See also* Hampton Normal and Agricultural Institute for Negroes and Indians
Inman, Samuel Guy, 212–213, 217–220, 222, 224
Ireland, 49, 111, 212
Iroquois, 88

Islam: African, 69; Black, 276; Cherokee, 14, 276–277; contesting power, 7; counter-jihad, 295; counter publics, 279; and empire, 5; Filipino, 149, 164–168; Islamism, 272; jihadist, 257; profiled as violent, 257, 263, 266; Quran, 285, 292; racialized bodies, 254, 266–267; September 11, 2001, attacks, 230; settler-colonial guilt, 281. *See also*: Crane, Robert
Islamic Society of North America, 290
Israel, 263–266, 276, 287–288
Israelites, 32, 258: Lost Tribes of Israel, 55
Italy, 111, 212
Iwahig Penal Colony, 168

Jackson, Andrew, 72, 76
Jamaica, 17–18, 21, 26–29, 213
Jaro Industrial School, 167
Jazz ambassadors, 275–276, 304
Jefferson, Thomas, 1, 42, 76, 87
Jernegan, Prescott F., 166–167
Jesuits (Society of Jesus), 44, 57, 59, 241
Jesus Christ, 108, 142, 194, 211–212, 220
Jim Crow, 179, 314
Johnston, Charlotte (Ogenebugoquay) (Ojibwe), 49
Judaism, 5, 7: Jews, 6, 106, 111, 264

Kanakas (Pacific Islanders), 197
Karem, Abraham, 264
Kelley, Florence, 114–116
Kingsbury, Cyrus, 72
Kiowa: and birds, 124–133; and buffalo, 126–127, 130–133, 138–139, 141; and Buffalo doctors, 130, 138, 141; calendars, 131–132, 143; decline of buffalos, 134–136, 142; feather bustle, 135; *Kado*, 129–135, 138, 142; medicine bundles, 124, 128–129, 140–141; *Ohoma* (War Dance), 134–135, 137; Sun Dance, 129–130, 133–134, 137–138; *Taime*, 130–142; Thunderbird, 128–129, 136; women in revival movement, 140. *See also* Birds; Feather Dance

Kipling, Rudyard, 162, 164
Kirk, Russell, 285
Knapp, Harry Shepard, 218
Kongo, 22, 24, 70
Korean War, 257, 260–261
Kru, 186–189, 199

Labor (laborers): African day, 67; camps, 74; child, 75, 111–112, 114, 117, 119; dignity of, 213; as discipline, 223; extraction of, 2; and immigrants, 83, 120, 152; indentured, 79; and industrial education, 152–158, 164–168, 171–172, 182–183, 187; intellectual, 300; and morality, 153–155, 160, 167–168; mining 240; ritual, 141; sexual, 10; and social surveys, 112, 114–115; in the Dominican Republic, 220; wage, 125. *See also* Board for Christian Work in Santo Domingo; Slavery
LaFramboise, Magdeleine (Odawa), 46
Laguna Pueblo, 236
Lakota (Sioux), 94, 125, 128–129, 133–136.
Land: acknowledgements, 304; Anishinaabe, 50–52; domestication of, 48; Haiti as Black Promised Land, 162, 204; pagan, 79; and the Census, 90, 95; virgin, 72; wastelands, 233, 240, 246. *See also* Dawes Act; Diné: Navajo; Diné Bikéyah
Latin (language), 51, 57, 64
Latins: in Diocese of Gallup, 233–235, 241, 243; Latinx, 4, 14, 99; supposed descendants of Spanish colonizers, 216, 223; and the Census, 99
Law (legal): and African religio-medical practice, 7, 20–25, 29–35; anti-miscegenation, 278; and *Brown v. Board of Education* (1954), 171; and citizenship, 280; and Edward Snowden, 294; and incarceration rate, 172; Islamic, 276, 283, 285; and Jim Crow, 170, 181, 184, 199; and Liberia, 74, 78–79; and napalm, 254–255; and

Native Americans, 142, 237, 277; and Native American religions, 1; and obeah, 26–28; property, 8; and Puerto Rican Protestants, 215; and settler land acquisition, 74; and settler secularism, 42–48, 51; and sexual abuse, 232–233, 241; Strang lawsuit, 56; and the Census, 90, 93; and United States colonial rule, 8, 166. *See also* Slavery: slave codes
Liberia (Liberians): and abolitionism, 68–70; and Black Christian colonization, 13–14, 63–64, 66–68, 70–71, 79–80, 207; Black settler colony, 18, 204; constitutions, 78–79, 185; Georgia Patton in, 179, 185–189, 199; and missionaries, 183–184; population growth, 77; and violence against Indigenous Africans, 77–79, 191–193, 197; students in the United States, 187–189, 191; and transoceanic empire, 64–66. *See also* Massaquoi
Liberty League, 198–199
Lindsay, Samuel McCune, 113
Literacy, 32, 74, 112, 170, 214
Little Joe (Hahtogo) (Kiowa), 141
Ledvina, Emmanuel, 242–243
Locke, John, 19, 34, 285
Long Walk (Diné), 85
Louisiana Purchase, 29, 85
Lowe, Marjorie, 278
Ludlow, Helen, 158–160
Lumad, 164
Luther, Martin, 211, 266
Lutheran Muhlenberg Mission, 187
Lynching: antilynching and Ida B. Wells, 179, 189–198; of the Gizzards, 188–189

Mackinac Island: Christian settlement of, 43–48; Mackinaw Mission School, 46–47, 50, 52; Ojibwe missions on, 49–51; settler colonial site, 13, 41–43, 58–59; Strangites and, 54–58

Macketebenessy, William (Odawa), 50
Malcolm X (el-Hajj Malik el-Shabazz), 286
Mamanti (Kiowa), 132
Maps: and colonialism, 92, 94, 120; and Diocese of Gallup, 236, 240–241; ethnographic map of Dominican Republic, 213; interpretive tool, 113; of Mackinac, 43, 51; and scholarship, 300, 306, 312; and territoriality, 272. *See also* Hull House: *Hull House Maps and Papers*
Marerro, José Espada, 223
Marquette, Jacques, 44, 59
Marshall Islands, 1
Martin, Matt, 265–267
Martínez, Alberto, 223
Masculinity, 190, 268, 271–272
Massaquoi, Momolu, 189, 191–193, 199
Maunkee, Kiowa Bill (Kiowa), 140
Maunkee, Lily Rose (Kiowa), 140
Mayhew mission, 73
Mayo, Isabella, 194–197
Mazzuchelli, Samuel, 47
McConnell, Francis J., 224
McCurley, Mark, 265–266
McDowell, Calvin, 189
McKinley, William, 162, 198
Mears, Emerson, 219
Medicine: and carceral state, 172; Central Tennessee College, 183–184; Kiowa bundles, 124, 128–129, 140–141; missionaries, 179, 188–189, 191; money as, 299, 308, 310–311; obeah and, 26; religio-medical, 21. *See also* Midewiwin: "Grand Medicine Society"
Melungeons, 290
Methodism, 30–31, 48–49, 52, 67, 185–189. *See also* African Methodist Episcopal Church; African Methodist Episcopal Zion Church; Methodist Episcopal Church
Methodist Episcopal Church, 181

Mexico, 4, 85, 88, 214, 236–237, 245
Michilimackinac. *See* Mackinac Island
Midewiwin, 43; "Grand Medicine Society," 52–54
Military: and American discourses of freedom, 304, 306; bases, 4; in the Caribbean, 149, 203–204, 208–210, 213, 218, 224; and displacement of American Indigenous peoples, 8, 18, 72–73, 75–76, 83, 316–317; Dominican, 207; European, 17; function with religious campaigns, 7, 230; and industrial schooling, 151, 161, 165–166, 198; Joseph Smith and, 54–55; and knowledge production, 87, 134; and Liberia, 63, 66, 185; and Stono Rebellion, 22, 24; and Sudan, 284–285. *See also* Drones; Napalm; US Marines
Missionaries: in Anglophone world, 13, 74, 203–204, 217–220, 223–224; and capitalism, 203, 212–213, 220, 222; Georgia Patton's mission to Liberia, 185–189; medical, 179, 188–189, 191; 1, 13, 23, 46–47, 51–52; Roman Catholic, 1, 13, 150
Mississippi in Africa, 70–71, 75–79
Mixed-race (individuals and groups), 216, 277, 290
Model Indian School, 164
Monroe, James, 45, 72, 208
Monrovia, 77, 185–186; Seminary, 186
Mooney, James, 124–126, 136
Moorish Science Temple, 279
Morality: and alcohol, 192; and barbarism, 45, 83, 187, 195–196; and Catholic credibility, 241–243, 245; Ida B. Wells and, 184; and industry, 153–155, 160, 167–168; and racial hierarchies, 213; and Robert Crane, 280, 285, 289; and social surveillance, 109, 113, 118, 120; and weapons, 253, 256–257; Wovoka and, 135–136
Moravian, 26, 29–30, 219
Mormon, 43, 54–58

Moro Rebellion, 165–169
Morocco, 275, 279
Morse, Jedidiah, 45–46
Moss, Thomas, 189–190
Mughal Empire, 5
Muhammad, Warith Deen, 286
Museums, 92
Muslim Brotherhood, 284, 295
Muslims. *See* Islam

Napalm: and evangelicals, 253–255, 258, 264, 272; and Japan, 260; and Korea, 260–261; napalm girl, 261–262; technologies of destruction, 14, 229–230, 259; and territoriality, 259–262
Nasr, Syed Hussein, 285
National Committee for Upbuilding the Wards of the Nation, 168
National Defense Research Committee on Uranium, 239–240
National Equal Rights League (NERL), 198–199
National Security Agency, 294
National Security Council, 276
Nation-states, 2–4, 10–11, 256–257, 270, 280, 308–309
Native Alaskan, 100
Native American. *See* Indigenous
Nativism, 117, 119
Natural religion, 283, 292
Navajo. *See* Diné
Netherlands, 3, 64
Nicaragua, 208
Nixon, Richard, 276, 279, 282
Noble Drew Ali, 279
Northern Missionary Society. *See* American Board of Commissioners for Foreign Missions (ABCFM)
Northwestern University, 288–289
Nuclear warfare, atom bomb, 229, 239–240, 246
Nzinga, 69

Obeah, 21, 26–28, 30, 33
Odawa (Ottawa), 41, 43, 46, 48–51
Ojibwe (Chippewa or Chippeway), 41, 43, 49, 51–53, 56–57; Midē, 52–53; Midewiwin, 43, 52–53
Omaha, 134
Oostendaarp, Timothy, 269
Orientalism, 164, 282, 284
O-tah-ty (Kiowa), 140
Ottoman empire, 5, 195
Owl, 132, 141

Pacelli, Eugenio, 236
Pagan, 6, 46, 79, 157, 163, 169, 184, 209, 263
Paingya (Kiowa), 131–132
Paiute, 124, 135–136: Northern Paiutes, 135. *See also* Wovoka
Palestine, 287–288
Panama, 213; Canal, 208; Conference, 215; Congress, 211–212, 215–217, 219
Pan-Americanism, 204, 210–211, 218, 224
Patepte (Kiowa), 131, 141
Patton, Georgia E. L., 13; early life, 179–182; travels to Liberia, 185–189, 199
Pau-quoot (Kiowa), 140
Pawnee, 134
Payne, Benjamin, 187
Payne, Frank, 187
Peace of Westphalia (1648), 10
Pelotte, Donald, 231
Persian Empire, 5
Philanthropy: and education; 167; and finance, 229–230; and Hull House, 113, 115; and Liberia, 64. *See also* Villanueva, Edgar
Philippines, the: Christian Filipinos, 164–168; and education, 13, 149, 151–153, 162–170; Muslim Filipinos, 164–168; and US colonization, 1, 64
Pierce, Franklin, 57
Plains Indians: and birds, 127–130, 132–133, 136–137; and dance, 133–135, 137, 142; James Mooney ethnography, 125;

Kiowa homelands, 126–127; and the Census, 94
Plymouth Company, 3
Polynesian, 153, 197; Kanakas, 197
Poolaw, Moses (Kiowa), 140
Porter, Robert P., 94–95
Portugal, 5, 22–23, 64, 69
Postcoloniality, 10, 286, 309
Potawatomi, 41, 85
Pratt, Richard, 156, 158
Pratts, Ramón, 223
Presbyterianism, 30, 46–48, 51, 216–217: Presbyterian Board of Missions, 167; Presbyterian Women's Board of Home Missions, 222
Priesthood, 50, 234–235, 242, 245–246
Priests, Roman Catholic: *crimen sollicitationis*, 242; and colonialism, 212; *cura animarum*, 14, 234, 244; Indigenous, 50–51; at Mackinac, 46–49; predatory priests, 14, 231–234, 241; rehabilitation, 246; sexual abuse as colonial violence, 232; transfer of, 233–235, 241–242, 246–247. *See also* Dominicans; Franciscans; Hageman, Clement; Jesuits; Roman Catholicism; Sullivan, John
Primeau, Ernest, 245
Primitivism, 11, 42, 46, 125, 133, 164, 182, 213, 279, 282
Pritchard, Gullah Jack, 33
Protestantism: anti-Catholicism, 6, 106, 210–212, 214–216, 219; colonization of the Philippines, 165; competition with Catholics, 42, 48, 150; and the Dominican Republic, 203–204; free Blacks and Vesey Affair, 21, 30–33; gender roles, 155; on Hispaniola, 204–209; and industrial education, 151–152, 167; and Latin American imperial discourse, 210–216; and Liberian settlement, 71; missionaries, 1, 13, 23, 46–47, 51–52; Ojibwe converts, 49, 53–54; Reformation, 290; as single true religion, 6, 45, 59; and weaponry, 253. *See also* Civilization; Committee on Cooperation in Latin America; Evangelicals
Provincialism, 229
Puerto Rico, 1, 4, 203, 208–209, 214–216, 219–224
Puritans, 159, 191, 195
Puthuff, William, 44–45

Qatar, 276, 294
Quakerism, 66, 193
Quitone, Jimmy (Kiowa), 138
Quoetone, Guy (Kiowa), 127, 129, 132

Racial hierarchies: African American contestation of, 180, 182, 184–187, 191–194, 198–199; and evangelizing of the Dominican Republic, 203–204, 213–214, 219; of heathenism, 112; and industrial schooling, 158, 165–166; in Liberia, 78, 191; and religion, 11; and secularism, 42; and the Philippines, 153, 165–166
Reconstruction, 180, 182–184
Religion: definitions, 4–10, 20, 25–29; "good" religion, 8, 42–47, 50, 54–59, 87; religio-racial identity, 276, 280
Religious liberty (religious freedom), 58, 193, 195, 292, 306
Résé, Frederick, 50
Resistance: to Americo-Liberians, 185; capitalism's inability to counteract colonialism, 14, 104–105, 113; Indigenous, 45, 52, 95, 97; to industrial schooling, 162, 165; and the Dominican Republic, 219; to US empire, 2, 12, 268, 285; and Edgar Villanueva's philosophies, 300–306, 310–312, 316–317; white, 30
Revolutionary War, 29, 65, 75, 292
Richard, Gabriel, 46–47
Richmond African Baptists Missionary Society, 67

366 | INDEX

Ritual: Catholic, 235, 245, 269; Islamic, 290, 292, Kiowa, 124, 126, 129–137, 141–142; oath, 20, 26; obeah, 26; public, 281; of violence, 271
Roberts, Joseph Jenkins, 70
Robertson, Pat, 263
Rockefeller, John D., 167
Rodríguez, Rafael R., 223
Roman Catholicism: competition with Protestants, 42, 48, 150; as corrupted religion, 6; and Dominicans, 203, 205–206, 208, 218–220; eucharist, 231; and Filipinos, 165; and good religion at Mackinac Island, 42–48; and Haitians, 205; at Hull House, 106; Diocese of Gallup, 239–242; and Indigenous religion, 48–54; missionaries, 1, 13, 150; and scandal, 14, 234, 241–245; sexual abuse crisis, 14, 232–235; and the CCLA, 209–216, 222; and the Stono Rebellion, 21–24, 30. *See also* Diocese of Gallup; Priests, Roman Catholic
Roman empire, 5, 191
Roosevelt, Theodore, 208
Ross, Isaac, 75–77
Rousseau, Jean-Jacques, 285
Royal African Company, 3

Sabbath, 23, 47. *See also* Stono Rebellion: Sunday
Sacred Heart Cathedral, 238
Sacred: land, 151; oaths, 26; objects, 52, 137; power, 135; space, 34; time, 24, 34–35
Sanders, Frederic, 113
Santo Domingo: 1910 World Missionary Conference, 209; occupancy of, 203, 216–224, port of, 206; Protestant missionaries in, 203, 207. *See also* Board for Christian Work in Santo Domingo
Schoolcraft, Henry Rowe, 43, 48, 51, 88
Secularism: business, 48; Christian apology script, 308; definitions, 10–11, 42; Diocesan priests, 235, 238; and Hull House, 109, 112, 117; and Liberia, 63, 65–66, 68; Robert Crane and, 285; secularism studies, 10–11, 42; settler secularism, 42–45, 50, 54–55, 59; war and, 263, 267. *See also* Roman Caholicism: and good religion
Segregation, 113, 152, 171, 185, 194, 198, 219, 225
Seminaries, 185–186, 214, 223. *See also* Monrovia: Seminary
Seminole, 71–73, 85, 93
Settler colonialism: and erasure, 14, 85, 87, 233, 239, 293–294; logic of elimination, 86, 239; and racism, 90, 151, 153, 172, 210–216, 240–241, 287; Servants of the Paraclete, 235, 244–245; sexual abuse as, 232; and slavery 2, 5, 17–18; structure (not event), 3, 86, 117, 229–230, 239; and war, 83, 152, 163, 197, 257, 260–261. *See also* American Colonization Society; Civilization: hierarchies of; Europe: Euro-American knowledge production of Indigenous peoples; Indigenous Peoples; Industrial schooling; Liberia; Racial hierarchies; Spanish-American War; War on Terror
Seven Years War, 26–27
Sexuality: abuse, 160–161, 172, 229; academic study of, 9–10, 311; assault of Black people, 69; Catholic sexual abuse, 14, 231–234, 240–241, 245–247; heteronormativity, 9; James Strang, 56; and lynching, 193; modesty, 112
Sharp, Mary, 185–189, 199. *See also*: Kru
Shaw University, 181
Shawnee, 45, 49, 87: Tenskwatawa, 45, 49
Shawundais (John Sunday) (Ojibwe), 49, 52
Sierra Leone, 64–66, 191
Silliman, Horace B., 167
Silverhorn, James (Kiowa), 124, 126, 139, 141, 143

Sitting Bull (Arapaho), 137–139
Sioux. *See* Lakota
Six Nations, 93
Slavery: and abolitionism, 68–71, 200; Black Liberian settlers, 66–68, 71–72, 76–80; and capitalism, 2–3; and Christian conversion, 19; and citizenship, 89; and civil war, 63; as colonizer's virus, 302–303; and Communism, 261; and education, 152, 169–170, 187; and emancipation, 83, 180–183; and empire, 2, 5, 17–18; enslavers, 12, 17–18, 20–23, 31, 65, 68–70, 76, 156; feared reinstitution in the Caribbean, 205–206; and Indigenous peoples, 195, 236; and Islam, 291; and labor, 156–157, 160–161, 183; in Liberia, 78–79, 186; and Liberia's settlement, 64–66; and philanthropy, 312–315; plantation, 22–24, 71–76, 83, 187, 197, 220; racial slavery, 17–18, 76; rebellions (see Denmark Vesey conspiracy; Stono Rebellion; Tacky's Revolt); religion of the enslaved, 7, 12–13, 18, 20–21, 24–28, 216; slave codes, 24–25, 31–32, 34; subject of study, 9–10; and the Philippines, 167; white distancing from, 288, 298. *See also*: Abolition; American Colonization Society (ACS)
Slavs, 195
Slum, 112, 114, 116–118
Smith Lake Indian Mission, 242–243
Smith, Adam, 285
Smith, Henry, 193
Smith, Joseph, Jr., 54–55
Smith, Richard, 58
Snowden, Edward, 294
Snowden, Thomas, 218
Social gospel, 13, 84, 214
Social surveys, 109–114, 116–118, 120–121
Society for the Recognition of the Brotherhood of Man (SRBM), 194–195, 197
Soleimani, Qassem, 270–271

South Africa, 3, 6, 167, 195, 223
Southern Workman, 151, 153, 158, 162–163, 167–168
Sovereignty: African Indigenous, 64, 185, 192, 199; Cherokee, 14, 277–278, 287, 292; colonial semblances, 2; and Doctrine of Discovery, 8, 41; Edgar Villanueva on, 306–308; and Haiti, 217; and Liberia, 70, 79; Native Americans, 4, 8–9, 13, 17, 50, 59, 71–75, 84, 89, 91, 233; postcolonial, 286; and the Dominican Republic, 205; and US empire, 10, 12
Spain (Spanish): Caribbean, 14, 149, 152, 205–208, 212; and Catholicism, 21–23, 29–30, 235–236; concept of religion, 5; and education, 162, 165; as empire, 17, 27, 72–75, 212, 215, 217, 220; language, 162, 215–216, 238; War of Restoration, 206. *See also* Spanish American War
Spanish American War, 13, 64, 79, 149, 152, 197, 208, 215, 236
St. John's Episcopal Mission, 191
Standing Rock Sacred Stone Camp, 316
Stevens, Jedidiah, 46
Stewart, William, 189
Stono Rebellion, 26–31, 34; significance of Sunday, 21–25
Strang, Jesse James, 43, 55–58
Strong, Josiah, 111
Stuart, Robert, 47
Subaltern, 12
Sudan, 275, 283–285
Sullivan, John, 243–245
Sumter, Thomas, 75
Sun Dance, 129–130, 133–134, 137–138

Tacky's Revolt, 20–21, 25–30, 33
Taft, William Howard, 117, 163, 165, 167, 169–170
Taliban, 271
Teague, Colin, 67
Technologies, of destruction. *See* Drone; Napalm

Ten Years' War, 215
Tenskwatawa (Shawnee), 45, 49
Terrorism, 20, 253–254, 257, 264–266, 295
Teton (Sioux), 136. *See also* Lakota
Theology: and imperial violence, 233–234, 272, 313; Islamic, 276, 280, 283–285, 290–292; knowledge production, 223; missionary, 67; and napalm, 261; pagan, 6; political, 229–230, 277, 286; and postcolonial studies, 10; proslavery, 32; of scandal, 242; seminaries, 214; and social justice, 13, 179–180, 189, 200; theologians, 231; training, 186; weapons as discourse, 253, 259, 265–269
Thirteenth Amendment, 156, 180
Toynbee Hall, 104, 106
Trail of Death (Potawatomi), 85
Trail of Tears (Cherokee), 85, 292
Treaty of Washington (1836), 50–51
Trotter, William Monroe, 198–199
Trump, Donald J., 270–271
Turkey, 166, 195, 264, 275
Turner, Henry McNeal, 190, 198
Tuskegee Institute, 152, 158, 161–167

United Arab Emirates, 276
United Brethren, 217, 222
United Methodist Church, 222
United States, as Christian nation, 192, 195–196, 230
Uranium, 239–240
US Census: 2020 Census, 98–100; and claims to Cherokee ancestry, 278; early Native counting, 87–88; and Hull House, 110–111, 115; and indigenous religions, 13, 92–98; and knowledge production, 13, 125, 143; Native Americans in, 88–92; and taxation, 87, 89–91
US Constitution, 8, 11, 42, 54, 89, 171, 180, 197–198. *See also*: Thirteenth Amendment
US government offices: Bureau of Education, 156, 163, 165; Bureau of Labor Statistics, 114; Department of Housing and Urban Development (HUD), 100; Department of War, 71–72; Office of Indian Affairs, 88; Office of Special Counsel, 294; State Department, 275;
US Marines, 57, 208, 212, 216–218, 222, 265
US Navy, 254
US Virgin Islands (Danish West Indies), 29
Ut, Nick, 261–262

Vai, 191, 193
Valentine, William, 167
Vesey, Denmark, 28–30, 32–33. *See also* Denmark Vesey conspiracy
Vietnam War, 14, 253, 257–259, 261–262, 272
Villanueva, Edgar: ambivalence, 301, 305–306, 313–315; decolonial remedies, 299, 302–309, 316; indigenous wisdom, 301–304, 310–311; medicine money, 310–311; privatized social safety net, 314–315; and sentiment, 305–308, 313
Virgin Mary, 24
Virginia Company, 3
Virginia Normal and Collegiate Institute, 171
Virus: colonialism as, 299, 301–308, 313, 315–316; COVID-19, 99, 303; and evolution, 305

Wager (Apongo), 27
Walduck, Thomas, 26
Walker, John Henry St. Clare, 151–154, 170–171
Walters, Alexander, 198
Wampanoag, 66
War Dance, 134. *See also* Kiowa: *Ohoma*
War on Terror, 14, 229, 265, 279, 295
Ware, Myrtle, 140
Washington, Booker T., 152, 163, 169
Water Protector, 316

Watie, Stand (Cherokee), 290
Watie, Saladin (Cherokee), 290
Watson, Wingfield, 58
Wells, Ida B.: Afro-American Council speech, 197–198; American Association of Colored Educators speech, 184–185; meets Catherine Impey, 193–194; *Southern Horrors*, 195
Wesleyans, 205–206, 219
White: ethnics, 287–288; immigrants, 83–84, 105–109, 111–117, 167–168, 237, 287; middle class, 105, 109, 113, 115, 120–121, 214; nonwhite, 105–106, 197, 243, 278; saviors, 298; settlers, 42, 45–48, 51, 54–55, 277, 279, 287; and the Census, 90, 96; whiteness, 11, 115, 233, 281; whitening, 205, 208
Wilson, Woodrow, 198–199

Wood, Harold, 187
Woods, Robert, 109, 115
World Missionary Conference (1910), 219–220
World's Fair (1904), 164
World War One, 83, 198
World War Two, 12, 257, 259
Wovoka (Paiute), 124–125, 135–139
Wright, Carroll, 114

Yavapai, 236
Young, Brigham, 55, 57–58
Young, Ed, 267–268

Zahl, Paul F.M., 268
Zionism, 287
Zoroastrianism, 5
Zuni Pueblo, 236

www.ingramcontent.com/pod-product-compliance
Lightning Source LLC
Chambersburg PA
CBHW020350080526
44584CB00014B/961